THE DEBATABASE BOOK

THE DEBATABASE BOOK
A Must-Have Guide for Successful Debate

FOURTH EDITION

THE EDITORS OF IDEA
Introduction by Robert Trapp

international debate education association
New York - Amsterdam - Brussels

Published by

international debate education association

400 West 59th Street / New York, NY 10019

The topics and arguments included in *The Debatabase Book* represent the work of an international group of contributors with diverse points of view. We would like to thank the following for their contributions: James Action (UK), Jonathan Bailey (UK), Heather Begg (UK), Kumar Bekbolotov (Kyrgyzstan), Patrick Blanchfield (US), Amy Brown (US), Matt But (UK), Alex Deane (UK), Joe Devanny (UK), Thomas Dixon (UK), William J. Driscoll (US), Alastair Endersby (UK), Peter English (UK), Tom Hamilton (UK), Alexis Hearndon (UK), Sebastian Isaac (UK), Maryia Lahutsina (Belarus), Dr. Kevin J. Minch (US), Richard Mott (UK), Vikram Nair (UK), Drew Patterson (US), Richard Penny (Finland), Anca Pusca (Romania), Jacqueline Rose (UK), Christopher Ruane (Ireland), Jacob Russell (US), Daniel Schut (Netherlands), Jonathan Simons (UK), Andrea Stone (US), Jason Stone (US), Richard Stupart (South Africa), Nicholas Tan (Singapore), Hayden Taylor (UK), Eleanora von Dehsen (US), Alaina von Horn (US), Bobby Webster (UK), Robert Weekes (UK), and Marc Whitmore (UK).

Library of Congress Cataloging-in-Publication Data

The debatabase book : a must have guide for successful debate / by the editors of IDEA ; introduction by Robert Trapp. -- 4th ed.
p. cm.
Includes index.
ISBN 978-1-932716-49-8
1. Debates and debating. I. International Debate Education Association.
PN4181.D3945 2009
808.5'3--dc22
2009001136

Printed in the USA

IDEBATE Press

Contents

INTRODUCTION

Debatabase is a starting point on the road to participating in debates. The volume provides a beginning for those debaters who would like to learn about important topics being argued in the public sphere. Debaters can use this volume as a method of discovering the basic issues relevant to some of the more important topics being discussed in various public forums. It will provide debaters a brief look at some of the claims that can be used to support or to oppose many of the issues argued about by persons in democratic societies; it will also provide some sketches of evidence that can be used to support these claims. This volume is, however, only a starting point. Debaters interested in becoming very good debaters or excellent debaters will need to go beyond this volume if they intend to be able to intelligently discuss these issues in depth.

This introduction is intended to provide a theoretical framework within which information about argumentation and debate can be viewed; no attempt has been made to provide a general theory of argumentation. I begin with some basic distinctions among the terms communication, rhetoric, argumentation, and debate, progress to a description of the elements of argument that are most central to debate, and then to a discussion of how these elements can be structured into claims to support debate propositions. Following the discussion of argument structures, I move to a more detailed discussion of claims and propositions and finally discuss the kinds of evidence needed to support claims and propositions.

A caveat is needed before proceeding to the theoretical portion of this introduction. This introduction does not intend to be a practical, how-to guide to the creation of arguments. It does intend to provide the conceptual groundwork needed for debaters to learn how to create arguments according to a variety of methods.

Communication, rhetoric, argumentation, and debate

Communication, rhetoric, argumentation, and debate are related concepts. Starting with communication and proceeding to debate, the concepts become progressively narrowed. By beginning with the broadest concept, communication, and ending at the narrowest, debate, I intend to show how all these terms are interrelated.

Communication may be defined as the process whereby signs are used to convey information. Following this definition, communication is a very broad concept ranging from human, symbolic processes to the means that animals use to relate to one another. Some of these means are a part of the complex biology of both human and nonhuman animals. For instance, the behaviors of certain species of birds when strangers approach a nest of their young are a part of the biology of those species. The reason we know these are biological traits is that all members of the species use the same signs to indicate intrusion. Although all of our communication abilities—including rhetorical communication—are somehow built into our species biologically, not all communication is rhetorical.

The feature that most clearly distinguishes rhetoric from other forms of communication is the symbol. Although the ability to use symbolic forms of communication is certainly a biological trait of human beings, our ability to use symbols also allows us to use culturally and individually specific types of symbols. The clearest evidence that different cultures developed different symbols is the presence of different languages among human beings separated geographically. Even though all humans are born with the ability to use language, some of us learn Russian, others French, and others English. The clearest example of symbolic communication is language. Language is an abstract method of using signs to refer to objects. The concept of a symbol differentiates rhetoric from other forms of communication. Symbols, hence rhetoric, are abstract methods of communication.

Still, not all rhetoric is argumentation. Rhetorical communication can be divided into various categories, two of which are narrative and metaphor.[1] Just to give a couple of examples, the narrative mode of rhetoric focuses on sequential time, the metaphoric mode of rhetoric focuses on comparing one thing to another, and the argumentative mode of rhetoric focuses on giving reasons. All of these modes of rhetoric are useful in debate, but the mode of rhetoric that is most central to debate is argumentation.

Argumentation is the process whereby humans use reason to communicate claims to one another. According to this definition, the focus on reason becomes the feature that distinguishes argumentation from other modes of rhetoric.[2] When people argue with one another, not only do they assert claims but they also assert reasons they believe the claims to be plausible or probable. Argumentation is a primary tool of debate, but it serves other activities as well. Argumentation is, for instance, an important tool in negotiation, conflict resolution, and persuasion. Debate is an activity that could hardly exist without argumentation.

Argumentation is useful in activities like negotiation and conflict resolution because it can be used to help people find ways to resolve their differences. But in some of these situations, differences cannot be resolved internally and an outside adjudicator must be called. These are the situations that we call debate. Thus, according to this view, debate is defined as the process of arguing about claims in situations where the outcome must be decided by an adjudicator. The focus of this introduction is on those elements of argumentation that are most often used in debate.

In some regards this focus is incomplete because some nonargumentative elements of communication and rhetoric often are used in debate even though they are not the most central features of debate. Some elements of rhetoric, namely metaphor and narrative, are very useful to debaters, but they are not included in this introduction because they are less central to debate than is argumentation. Beyond not including several rhetorical elements that sometimes are useful in debate, this introduction also excludes many elements of argumentation, choosing just the ones that are most central. Those central elements are evidence, reasoning, claims, and reservations. These elements are those that philosopher Stephen Toulmin introduced in 1958[3] and revised 30 years later.[4]

The Elements of Argument

Although in this introduction some of Toulmin's terminology has been modified, because of its popular usage the model will still be referred to as the Toulmin model. Because it is only a model, the Toulmin model is only a rough approximation of the elements and their relationships to one another. The model is not intended as a descriptive diagram of actual arguments for a variety of reasons. First, it describes only those elements of an argument related to reasoning. It does not describe other important elements such as expressions of feelings or emotions unless those expressions are directly related to reasoning. Second, the model describes only the linguistic elements of reasoning. To the extent that an argument includes significant nonverbal elements, they are not covered by the model.[5] Third, the model applies only to the simplest of arguments. If an argument is composed of a variety of warrants or a cluster of evidence related to the claim in different ways, the model may not apply well, if at all. Despite these shortcomings, this model has proven itself useful for describing some of the key elements of arguments and how they function together. The diagrams shown on the following pages illustrate the Toulmin model.

The basic Toulmin model identifies four basic elements of argument: claim, data (which we call evidence), warrant, and reservation. The model of argument is most easily explained by a travel analogy. The evidence is the argument's starting point. The claim is the arguer's des-

1. As far as I know, no one has successfully organized modes of rhetoric into a coherent taxonomy because the various modes overlap so much with one another. For instance, narratives and metaphors are used in arguments as metaphors and arguments are frequently found in narratives.
2. This is not to say that other forms of rhetoric do not involve the use of reason, just that the form of rhetoric where the focus on reason is most clearly in the foreground is argumentation.
3. *The Uses of Argument* (Cambridge: Cambridge University Press, 1958).
4. Albert R. Jonsen and Stephen Toulmin, *The Abuse of Casuistry: A History of Moral Reasoning* (Berkeley: University of California Press, 1988).
5. Charles Arthur Willard, "On the Utility of Descriptive Diagrams for the Analysis and Criticism of Arguments," *Communication Monographs* 43 (November, 1976), 308–319.

tination. The warrant is the means of travel, and the reservation involves questions or concerns the arguer may have about arrival at the destination. Toulmin's model can be used to diagram the structure of relatively simple arguments.

Structure of an Argument

A simple argument, for instance, consists of a single claim supported by a piece of evidence, a single warrant, and perhaps (but not always) a single reservation. The following diagram illustrates Toulmin's diagram of a simple argument:

Simple Argument

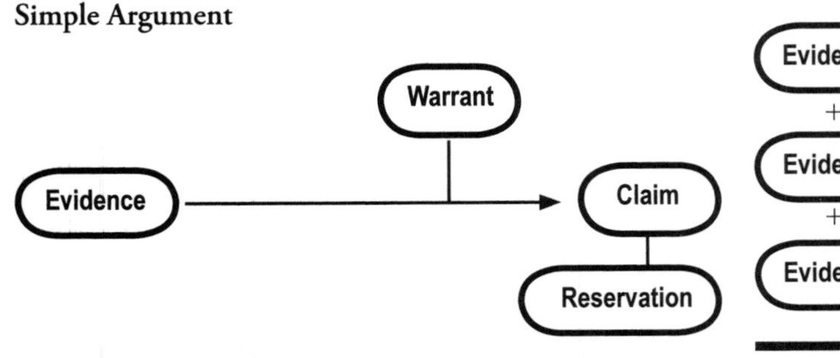

Toulmin illustrates this diagram using a simple argument claim that Harry is a British citizen because he was born in Bermuda. Here is how the structure of that argument was diagramed by Toulmin:

Simple Argument

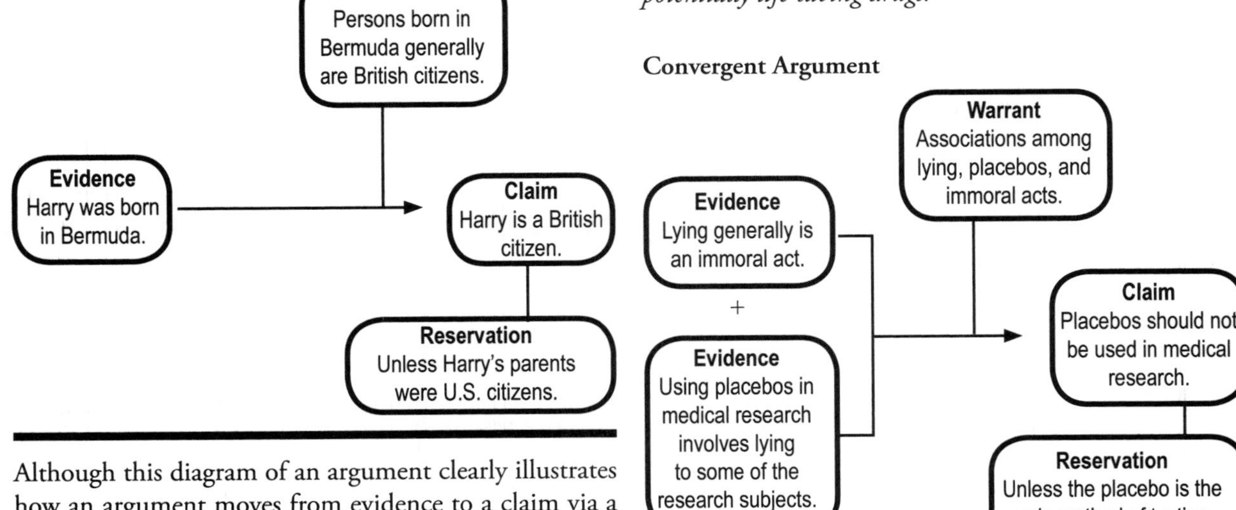

Although this diagram of an argument clearly illustrates how an argument moves from evidence to a claim via a warrant, very few arguments are ever quite as simple. For this reason, I have adapted Toulmin and Jonsen's model to illustrate a few different argument structures.

In addition to the simple argument suggested above, other argument structures include convergent and independent arguments. Although these do not even begin to exhaust all potential argument structures, they are some of the more common ones encountered in debate.

Convergent Arguments

A convergent argument is one wherein two or more bits of evidence converge with one another to support a claim. In other words, when a single piece of evidence is not sufficient, it must be combined with another piece of evidence in the effort to support the claim.

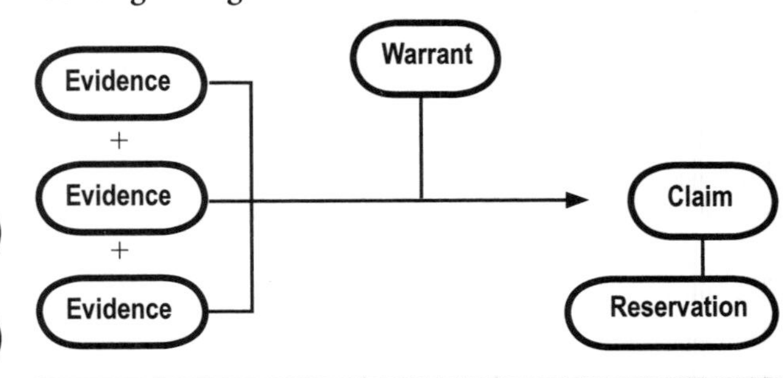

Consider as an illustration, the following convergent argument:

Lying is generally considered an immoral act. The use of placebos in drug testing research involves lying because some of the subjects are led falsely to believe they are being given real drugs. Therefore, placebos should not be used in drug testing unless they are the only method available to test potentially life-saving drugs.

Convergent Argument

This particular argument begins with two pieces of evidence. The first piece involves the value statement that "lying generally is considered an immoral act." This piece of evidence is a statement that is consistent with the audience's values regarding lying. The second piece of evidence is the factual statement that "the use of placebos in medical research involves a form of lying." The second piece of evidence involves the fact that when a researcher gives a placebo (e.g., a sugar pill) to a portion of the subjects in a study of a potentially life-saving drug, that researcher is lying to those subjects as they are led to believe that they are receiving a drug that may save their lives. The warrant then combines the evidence with a familiar pattern of reasoning—in this case, if an act in general is immoral then any particular instance of that act is likewise immoral. If lying is immoral in general, then using placebos in particular is also immoral.

The claim results from a convergence of the pieces of evidence and the warrant. In some instances, an arguer may not wish to hold to this claim in all circumstances. If the arguer wishes to define specific situations in which the claim does not hold, then the arguer adds a reservation to the argument. In this case, a reservation seems perfectly appropriate. Even though the arguer may generally object to lying and to the use of placebos, the arguer may wish to exempt situations where the use of a placebo is the "only method of testing a potentially life-saving drug."

The unique feature of the convergent structure of argument is that the arguer produces a collection of evidence that, if taken together, supports the claim. The structure of the argument is such that all of the evidence must be believed for the argument to be supported. If the audience does not accept any one piece of evidence, the entire argument structure falls. On the other hand, the independent argument structure is such that any single piece of evidence can provide sufficient support for the argument.

Independent Arguments

An arguer using an independent argument structure presents several pieces of evidence, any one of which provides sufficient support for the argument. In other words, a debater may present three pieces of evidence and claim that the members of the audience should accept the claim even if they are convinced only by a single piece of evidence. The following diagram illustrates the structure of an independent argument:

Independent Arguments

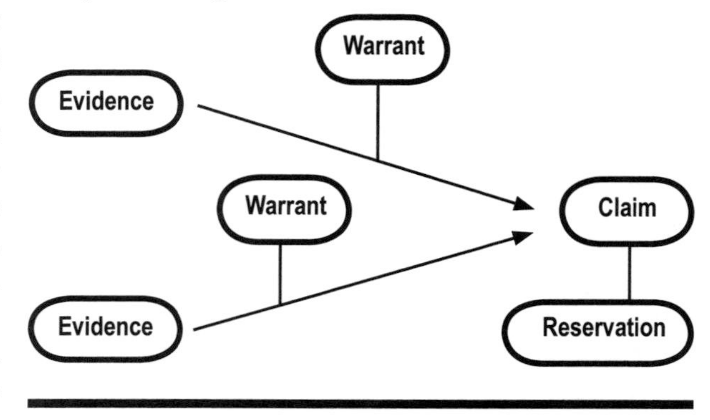

Take for instance the following argument against capital punishment:

On moral grounds, capital punishment ought to be abolished. If a society considers a murder immoral for taking a human life, how can that society then turn around and take the life of the murderer? Beyond moral grounds, capital punishment ought to be abolished because, unlike other punishments, it alone is irreversible. If evidence is discovered after the execution, there is no way to bring the unjustly executed person back to life.

This argument about capital punishment can be represented in the following diagram:

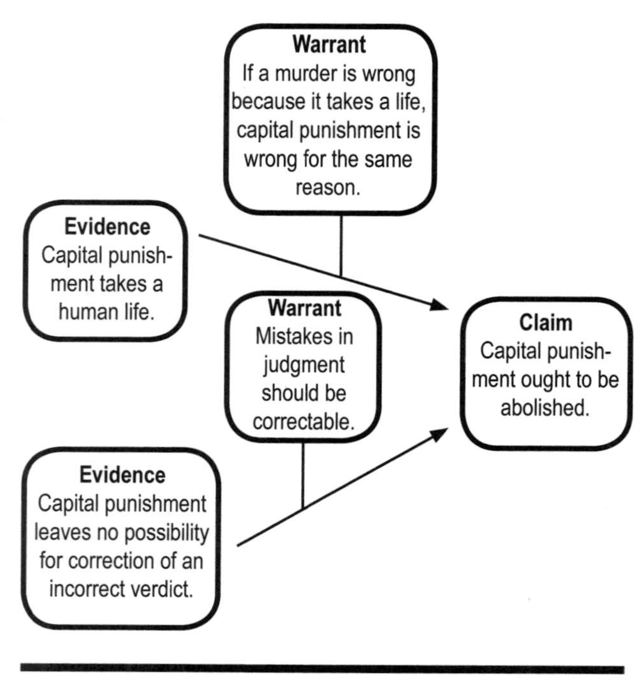

This example of an independent argument structure is based on two pieces of evidence, either of which is strong enough to support the claim that capital punishment ought to be abolished. The first piece of evidence involves the value of taking a human life, while the second involves the value of being able to correct a mistake. According to this argument, capital punishment ought to be abolished even if only one of the items of evidence is believed by the audience. The moral stricture against taking a life is, by itself, a sufficient reason to oppose capital punishment as is the danger of making an uncorrectable mistake. The strategic advantage of this form of argument structure is obvious. Whereas with convergent structures, the loss of one part of the argument endangers the entire argument, in the independent structure, the argument can prevail even if only a part of it survives.

The Toulmin diagram of an argument is useful because it illustrates the various parts of an argument and shows how they function together as a whole. The modifications with regard to argument structure make it even more useful. Still, the model has its shortcomings. One difficulty with the Toulmin diagram is that it does not provide any details regarding some of the elements. Some questions that the diagram leaves unanswered include:

- What are the different kinds of claims?
- How can different claims be combined to support various propositions?
- What are the different forms of evidence?
- What are the different kinds of argumentative warrants?
- What distinguishes good arguments from bad ones?

Claims and Propositions

Conceptually claims and propositions are the same kind of argumentative elements. Both are controversial statements that need reason for support. Both claims and propositions are created by a relationship between evidence and a warrant. Frequently, debaters combine several of these statements to support another statement. Each of the initial statements is a claim and the concluding statement is called a proposition.

Types of Claims and Propositions

Most authors divide claims and propositions into the traditional categories of fact, value, and policy. I have chosen not to use these traditional categories for two reasons. First, the traditional categories have no place for some important kinds of propositions that are not facts, or values, or policy. More specifically, the traditional categories have no place for propositions that seek to define concepts nor for propositions that seek to establish relationships between or among concepts. Second, the traditional categories separate evaluative and policy propositions while the system used here will consider propositions of policy as a specific kind of evaluative proposition. I use four main categories of propositions: definition, description, relationship, and evaluation. These categories, while they may not be exhaustive or mutually exclusive, provide a coherent system for the discussion of claims.

Definitions

Definitions answer the question, "Does it serve our purposes to say that Z is the proper definition of X?"[6] Arguing for a claim of definition involves two steps: positing the definition and making an argument for that definition. In carrying out the first step, one simply states that "X" is defined in this way. "Rhetoric is an action humans perform when they use symbols for the purpose of communicating with one another."[7] This sentence posits a definition of rhetoric.

Much of the time arguers perform the first step of positing a definition without constructing an argument to support it. They may do this because their audience does not require them to make an explicit argument in favor of the definition. The definition may, by itself, create a frame of mind in the audience that does not lead the audience to demand an argument in support of the definition. For instance, antiabortion forces in the United States succeeded in defining a procedure physicians called "intact dilation and extraction" as "partial-birth abortion."[8] Their definition was successful because it dominated the discourse on abortion and turned the controversy away from the issue of choice and toward a particular medical procedure that antiabortion forces could use more successfully. On the surface, the definition of "intact dilation and extraction" as "partial-birth

6. Perhaps a more accurate way of stating the question is "Does it best serve our purposes to say that Z is the proper definition of X?" This way of phrasing the question more clearly identifies the value dimensions of definitions—dimensions that will be discussed more fully later.
7. Sonja K. Foss, Karen A. Foss, and Robert Trapp, *Contemporary Perspectives on Rhetoric* (Prospect Heights, IL: Waveland, 1991), 14.
8. David Zarefsky, "Definitions" (keynote address, Tenth NCA/AFA Summer Argumentation Conference, Alta, Utah, August 1997).

abortion" may have seemed so sensible that no further argument was required.

An argument to support a claim of definition becomes necessary when the audience refuses to accept the definition that was posited without a supporting argument. An arguer's opponent will frequently encourage the audience to demand support for a definition. When antiabortion advocates defined their position as "pro-life," some in the "pro-choice" movement objected, claiming that "pro-choice" is also "pro-life." In cases like this one, the entire argument can turn on whether or not the arguer is able to successfully support a claim of definition.

In those instances when an arguer chooses to construct an argument to support a definition, the argument frequently revolves around the reasonableness of the scope and breadth of the definition. Is the definition so narrow that it excludes instances of the concept that ought to be included? Is the definition so broad that it fails to exclude instances that do not properly belong to the concept? Thus, in constructing an argument for a definition, an arguer might posit a definition, then argue that the definition is reasonable in terms of its scope and breadth. In fact, this is the criterion implicit in the objection to defining "antiabortion" as "pro-life." Choice advocates claimed that the definition of "pro-life" was so narrow in scope that it excluded pro-choice advocates. So, in some cases, the arguments supporting a claim of definition are important. In other cases, the definition becomes evidence (sometimes implicit) for further arguments about whether a claim of definition was actually made.

Definitions themselves frequently are important, but they are also important to subsequent argumentative moves. Definitions are important because they often do the work of argument without opening the arguer's position to as much controversy as would otherwise be expected. Definitions may avoid controversy in two ways: by implying descriptions and by implying values.

Definitions imply descriptions by including elements in the definition that properly require evidentiary support. For instance, an arguer might claim that affirmative action is unfair and might define affirmative action as "racial preference quotas." Whether affirmative action programs require racial preference quotas is a matter of much controversy. But if the definition is not contested by an audience member or by an adversary, the definition shortcuts the argumentative process by avoiding controversy.

Definitions imply values by including terms that are value laden. For instance, when antiabortion advocates define the medical procedure of intact dilation and extraction as "partial-birth abortion" or even as "partial-birth infanticide," the values associated with birth and with infanticide are likely to be transferred to the medical procedure as well. In this case, antiabortion forces succeeded in shortcutting the argumentative process by avoiding the value controversy that is inherent in their definition.

So claims of definition are important. Ironically, they probably are less important when they are actually completed with supporting evidence than when they are implicitly used as descriptive and value evidence for further arguments.

Descriptions

Descriptions may characterize some feature of an object, concept, or event or may describe the object, concept, or event itself. Examples of descriptive claims include:

- The rifle purported to have killed President Kennedy requires a minimum of 2.3 seconds between shots.
- Affirmative action programs must, by their nature, include hiring quotas.
- Jack Ruby was spotted in Parkland Hospital thirty minutes after President Kennedy was murdered.

Each of these statements is descriptive because they provide a verbal account or characterization of something. They are claims in the argumentative sense because they are controversial[9] and because they require reasons for support. Because some descriptions are not controversial, all descriptions are not descriptive arguments. Many or even most descriptions are not argumentative because they are not controversial. For instance, if a person simply describes observations of the colors of flowers—roses are red; violets blue—that person would not ordinarily give reasons to support these descriptions.

One kind of descriptive claim is a claim of historical fact. All statements about history are not historical claims. To be a historical claim a statement must be controversial and must require reason for its support. The statement, "O. J. Simpson won the Heisman Trophy,"

9. With regard to the first example, some people claim that this action requires closer to four seconds when one takes into account the fact that a shooter must reacquire the subject in the scope. Regarding the second example, some supporters of affirmative action argue that hiring quotas are required only for a company with a past record of discrimination. In the third example, the primary source of the claim regarding Jack Ruby was AP reporter Seth Kantor; the Warren Commission claimed that Kantor was mistaken in his report.

is not controversial and therefore not an argumentative claim. On the other hand, the statement, "O. J. Simpson killed Nicole Brown Simpson," not only is controversial, but also requires an arguer to present reasons supporting or denying it.

Another kind of description is a claim of scientific fact. Scientific facts are statements that command the belief of the scientific community: "The Earth is the third planet from the sun." A claim of scientific fact is a controversial scientific statement believed by a scientist or a group of scientists, but not yet accepted by the entire scientific community: "Cold fusion can be produced in the laboratory." Like other factual statements, all scientific statements are not claims of scientific fact either because they are not controversial or because they do not require reasons to be given in their support. To say, "The Earth is the third planet from the sun," is not a claim because it is not controversial and because a person making that statement would not be expected to give reasons to support it. But the statement, "Cold fusion can be produced in a laboratory," is a controversial statement, and the scientific community would challenge anyone making that statement to support it with reason and evidence.

Illustrating different examples of descriptive claims is important in and of itself because people frequently argue about descriptive claims with no goal other than to try to settle a controversy regarding an account of science or history. As just one example, several hundred books and articles have been written presenting many different accounts of the assassinations of John Kennedy, Robert Kennedy, and Martin Luther King. But beyond being important for their own sake, descriptive claims also are important because they are needed when arguing about subsequent kinds of claims as well.

Descriptive claims frequently are used as evidence in relational and evaluative arguments. A claim describing the nature of an object frequently is needed before arguing that one object is related to another object. People might need to argue, for instance, that hiring quotas are essential features of affirmative action (a descriptive claim) before they can argue that affirmative action leads to differential treatment of persons in hiring pools (relational claim). Similarly, people may need to describe an object or phenomenon prior to evaluating that object. In this example, they would need to describe affirmative action before they argue that it is either good or bad.

A scientific description can be the final product of an argument or can be used as evidence for the further development of another kind of argument. Whether the primary determinant of homosexuality is genetic or cultural is an interesting claim from a purely scientific perspective. People can argue the facts that support the genetic explanation or the cultural one. However, this claim frequently has been used in the debate about the morality of homosexuality.[10] So in the case of the determinants of homosexuality, the descriptive claim is both important for its own sake and for the sake of other potential claims as well.

Descriptive historical claims are interesting both because they make statements about whether or not an event occurred as asserted and because they can be used as evidence in making further arguments.

- Lee Harvey Oswald killed President John Kennedy.
- O. J. Simpson murdered Nicole Brown Simpson and Ronald Goldman.
- U.S. ships *Maddox* and *Turner Joy* were attacked by the North Vietnamese in the Gulf of Tonkin.

Each of these is an interesting and controversial claim of historical fact. These and other claims of historical fact also can be used as evidence for relational and evaluative arguments. For instance, the argument that the *Maddox* and *Turner Joy* were attacked by the North Vietnamese was used by President Johnson to persuade the Senate and the House of Representatives to pass the Gulf of Tonkin Resolution giving Johnson a blank check to pursue the war in Vietnam. Subsequently arguments that the attack was, at best, provoked and, at worse, faked were used by opponents of the Vietnam War to show that Johnson's actions were improper and even immoral.

Relationship Statements

Descriptive claims are about the nature of reality —what is the essence of X or Y. Claims of relationship depend on, but go beyond, the essence of X or Y to the relationship between X and Y. Claims of relationship assert a connection between two or more objects, events, or phenomena. Like descriptive claims, claims of relationship can be important in their own right or they can serve as evidence for the development of evaluative claims. Consider these claims:

- Secondhand smoke contributes significantly to health problems.
- The scandals of the Clinton administration are like those of the Nixon administration.
- Advertising has changed the role of women in the United States.

10. Some argue, for instance, that because the tendency for homosexuality is genetic, it is not a "choice" and therefore cannot be considered moral or immoral.

All of these are claims of relationship because they assert a relationship between two objects or concepts (secondhand smoke and health, Clinton and Nixon, advertising and women). The relationships asserted in these examples are of two kinds: of contingency and of similarity.

Contingency

Some claims of relationship assert a relationship of contingency. The secondhand smoking example and the advertising example are of this kind. In each case, these claims assert that one object or phenomenon is dependent on another in one way or another. Sign and cause are two ways objects can be dependent on one another via some form of contingency.

Relationships of sign are one way to show that one thing is dependent on another thing.

Consider these:

- The pain in your child's abdomen probably means she has appendicitis.
- The palm print on the Mannlicher-Carcano rifle proves that Oswald handled the rifle supposedly used to shoot President Kennedy.

Both of the previous statements are claims about relationships of sign. The pain in the abdomen as a sign of appendicitis is dependent on the belief that the child actually has abdominal pain and a belief in the relationship between that pain and her appendix. The belief that Oswald handled the rifle that supposedly was used to shoot President Kennedy is dependent on the belief that he actually left his palm print on the murder weapon.

Arguments of sign played a very important—perhaps crucial—role in the criminal trial of O. J. Simpson for the murders of Ron Goldman and Nicole Brown Simpson. The prosecution claimed that the presence of a bloody glove near Simpson's home was a sign that he was the murderer. In a dramatic turn of events, Simpson tried on the glove in the presence of the jury; it appeared to be too small to fit on his hand. This evidence allowed the defense to support its own claim in quite poetic language: "If the glove doesn't fit, you must acquit." According to the prosecution's claim, the glove was a sign of Simpson's guilt. According to the defense's claim, the glove signaled his innocence. This was a clear case where the argument centered around the relationship between the bloody glove and Simpson's guilt or innocence.

In the Simpson example, the claim of sign is important because if it were believed, the claim alone is sufficient to establish guilt (or innocence, depending on the nature of the argument). But like other claims, a claim of sign also can be used as evidence to establish a different claim. Say, for instance, that a person claims that "Photographs from the yacht, 'Monkey Business,' showed that presidential candidate Gary Hart was an adulterer." The photographs are not direct evidence of adultery, but given their nature, they are strong signs of infidelity. One could then use this claim of sign to support an evaluative argument: "Gary Hart is not worthy of being president since he is an adulterer." In this case, the claim of sign becomes evidence to support an evaluative claim.

Relationships of sign may or may not involve relationships of cause. The relationship between pain and appendicitis is one of both sign and cause. The pain is a sign of the appendicitis and the appendicitis is a cause of the pain. A causal relationship is not directly involved in the example of the double murder of Goldman and Brown Simpson or in the example about Oswald's palm print on the rifle. Although the palm print and the bloody glove were signs of murder, they were not causes of the murder.[11] Thus, relationships of sign are different from relationships of cause at least in terms of their focus.

Causal relationships are important in many forms of argument. The kind of causal claim varies from one instance to the next. A few examples include contributory causes, necessary and sufficient causes, blocking causes, and motive or responsibility.

Contributory causes are special kinds of causal statements. In many or most cases, a single event is not the cause of an effect. Certain conditions predispose certain effects; other conditions influence the occurrence of those effects. Finally, some condition precipitates that effect. For example, consider these three possible claims about the causes of heart attacks:

- Genetics are the cause of heart attacks.
- A high cholesterol diet can cause heart attack.
- Vigorous exercise causes heart attacks.

We know that some people are genetically more predisposed to heart attacks than others. If a person who already is predisposed to heart attacks regularly consumes a diet high in cholesterol, that diet contributes to the likelihood of heart attack. Suppose a person dies of a heart attack while on a morning jog. What was the

11. One can make a case for a causal relationship between the murder and the bloody glove in that the act of committing the murder caused blood to get on the glove. The causal relationship between the palm print and the Kennedy murder is less direct, although one could say that the act of murdering President Kennedy caused Oswald's palm print to be on the murder weapon. This last claim is a weak one since the palm print could have been on the rifle long before the assassination.

cause? Genetics? Diet? Exercise? The answer is that all three factors may have been contributory causes. No single cause may have caused the heart attack, but all three conditions in combination may have resulted in a heart attack.

Necessary and sufficient causes frequently deal with singular causes rather than contributory causes. "Money is essential to happiness" is an example of a claim of necessary causation. To say that money is a necessary cause of happiness is not to say that the presence of money automatically leads to happiness. The claim does, however, imply that without money happiness is impossible. If one wanted to make a claim of sufficient causation using the same example, one might claim that "money is the key to happiness." Depending on how one interpreted that claim, it might mean that money brings happiness regardless of other conditions. In that case, one would have made a claim about a sufficient cause.

Necessary and sufficient causes are useful when arguing about relationships between and among various phenomena. They are also useful as evidence from which to construct other kinds of claims, particularly claims that evaluate a course of action. When an arguer proposes a strategy to eliminate an undesirable effect, evidence derived from a claim about a necessary condition of that effect is useful. Having made a claim about a necessary cause, one can forward a proposal to eliminate that necessary cause and thus eliminate the effect. For instance, if people believe that overeating is a necessary condition of obesity, they could use this causal claim as evidence to convince others that they need to quit overeating. Thus, making a claim about a necessary cause is a good way to support a plan for eliminating an effect.

Similarly, evidence derived from a claim about a sufficient cause is a good way to support a plan for producing an effect. If one can present a proposal that adds a sufficient cause, one can then claim that the proposal will produce some good effect. For instance, some diet commercials claim that their products are sufficient to cause one to lose weight. This claim of a sufficient causal condition can then be used as evidence to convince buyers to try their diet programs. Implied in such a claim is that regardless of what else one does, following the proposed diet will lead to weight loss.

Statements about motive are causal claims about the effects of human agents. Many causal claims, like those already discussed, are related to physical or biological phenomena. The relationships among genetics, diet, exercise, and heart disease are biological relationships. Various elements in a biological system affect other elements in that same system. In a similar manner, motives are a kind of causal explanation when human choice is involved in creating effects. Why, for instance, do senators and representatives stall legislation for campaign finance reform? Why do corporations knowingly produce dangerous products? The answers to these questions involve causal claims, but causal claims of a different order from those discussed earlier.

In an earlier example, genetics, diet, and exercise did not "choose" to cause heart disease. But in human systems choice is frequently an important element in determining what actions lead to what effects. One might claim that "representatives' and senators' self-interest motivate them to stall campaign finance reform" or that the "profit motive induces corporations knowingly to produce dangerous products." The kinds of causal questions that deal with motives are very useful when arguing about the effects of human actions.

Like other causal claims, claims about motive are useful as evidence in the construction of evaluative claims. A claim based on a senator's motive for stalling campaign finance reform might, for instance, be used as evidence to construct a further claim relevant to the wisdom of reelecting that senator. A claim that a particular corporation's desire for profits led to the production of unsafe products might be used as further evidence to support a claim asking for a boycott of that corporation.

The claims of relationship that have been discussed so far have involved relationships of contingency. In relationships of contingency, one phenomenon depends on or affects another. These claims of relationships have generally been divided into the categories of signs and cause. However, claims of contingency are not the only kind of claims of relationship. Claims of similarity are equally important kinds of relational claims.

Similarity

In addition to relationships based on contingency, other statements of relationship assert a relationship of similarity. A claim of similarity asserts that two or more objects or concepts are similar in important ways. Claims of similarity are frequently found in what is called argument by analogy or argument by parallel case. Examples of claims of similarity include:

- Abortion is virtually the same as infanticide.
- The Clinton administration is like the Nixon administration.
- Capital punishment is state-sanctioned murder.

Each of these examples shares certain characteristics. First, each example includes two objects or concepts (Clinton and Nixon, abortion and infanticide, and capital punishment and murder). Second, each example states that the two concepts or objects are similar in important regards.

Claims of similarity are useful when an arguer wants to do nothing more than support the idea that two or more objects and concepts are similar. Although the claim focuses on the similarity between the objects, it frequently carries another implied claim of evaluation. The claim that capital punishment is state-sanctioned murder is not a value-neutral statement. When confronted with such a claim, most audiences begin with the assumption that murder is a negatively valued concept. An arguer who succeeds in supporting the claim of similarity also succeeds in transferring the negative value associated with murder to the concept of capital punishment. In all of the above examples of claims of similarity, the arguer has two different purposes: to show that the two concepts or objects have similar characteristics, or to show that the two concepts or objects are evaluated in similar ways.

In some cases, the audience may not have enough familiarity with either of the two objects to understand the values associated with them. In such a case, a claim of similarity is sometimes the first step toward proving a claim of evaluation. Consider a hypothetical claim that states "Senator X's medical care plan is similar to one instituted in Canada." If the audience knew nothing about either Senator X's plan or the Canadian one, the arguer might establish this claim to be used as evidence in a later evaluative claim that "Senator X's plan should be accepted (or rejected)." In this case the arguer might present an evaluative claim regarding the success of the Canadian plan and then combine the two claims—one of similarity and one regarding acceptance or rejection.

Thus, claims of relationship fall into three broad categories: sign, causation, and similarity. In some cases, claims of relationship are supported by evidence built on claims of fact. Likewise, relational claims can be used to establish evaluative claims.

Claims of Evaluation

Evaluative claims go beyond descriptive claims and claims of relationship to the evaluation of an object, event, or concept. Evaluative claims are more complex kinds of claims because they ordinarily require some combination of other definitions, descriptions, and relational statements.

Evaluative claims bear a family resemblance to one another because they attach a value to one or more objects or events. Still, evaluative claims are so vast in number and in characteristics that they can be more easily viewed in these three categories: those that evaluate a single object, those that compare two objects with respect to some value, and those that suggest an action with respect to some object.

Claims That Evaluate a Single Object

Some evaluative claims simply argue that an object is attached in some way (positively or negatively) with some value. These kinds of claims involve both an object of evaluation and some value judgment to be applied to the object:

- Capital punishment is immoral.
- Private property is the root of all evil.
- Capitalism is good.

These examples of claims that attach a value to a single object all contain some object to be evaluated (capital punishment, private property, capitalism) and some value judgment that is applied to the objects (immoral, evil, good).

Some claims, like those mentioned above, imply rather broad value judgments. Others may contain more specific ones:

- Capital punishment is unfair in its application to minorities.
- Private property has led to an uncontrolled and immoral ruling class.
- Capitalism provides incentive for individual enterprise.

These examples contain value judgments that are more specific than the broad ones cited earlier.

Claims That Compare Two Objects

Instead of evaluating a single object, some claims compare two objects with respect to some value to constitute a second category of evaluative claim. Unlike the previous category of evaluative claims, claims in this category include at least two objects of evaluation and at least one value judgment to be applied to those objects. Consider these claims:

- Lying is more proper than hurting someone's feelings.
- Reagan was a better president than Clinton.

Each of these examples contains two objects (lying and hurting someone's feelings; Reagan and Clinton) and one value judgment to be applied to each object (more proper and better president).

Claims of Action

Claims of action, sometimes called claims of policy, are yet another category of evaluative claim:

- Capital punishment should be abolished.
- The United States should adopt a policy of free trade with Cuba.

These claims evaluate a concept by suggesting that action be taken with respect to that concept. Because an action can be evaluated only by comparison or contrast to other possible actions, claims of action by necessity compare at least two objects. The claim that capital punishment should be abolished compares the presence of capital punishment with its absence. The claim regarding free trade with Cuba implies a comparison of a policy of free trade with the present policy of trade embargo. In this regard, claims of action are similar to claims that compare two objects.

In a different regard, claims of action are different from the other categories of evaluative claims in that they rarely state the value judgment used to compare the two objects. The reason the value judgment is not ordinarily stated in the claim is that an action claim is frequently supported by a variety of other claims of evaluation each of which may be relying on a different value judgment. The claim about the abolition of capital punishment, for example, might be supported by other evaluative claims like

- Capital punishment is immoral.
- Capital punishment contributes to the brutalization of society.
- Capital punishment is racist.

To complicate matters even more, evaluative claims of action inherently are comparative claims. To argue in favor of a particular action is possible only in comparison to other actions. For instance, the previous claims imply that capital punishment is less moral, more brutal, and more racist than the alternatives. Because action claims usually require multiple, comparative claims as evidence to support them, action claims generally are more complicated than the other categories of claims.

According to this category system, evaluative claims are generally divided into three types: claims that evaluate a single object, claims that evaluate two or more objects, and action claims. As indicated, one evaluative claim can sometimes be used as support for another evaluative claim, leading eventually to complicated claims built on a web of other claims.

In addition to the fact that evaluative claims are used both as the end product of an argument and as evidence for other evaluative claims, almost all evaluative claims are dependent on earlier descriptive claims and relational claims. Depending on whether or not the audience is familiar with and accepts the arguer's descriptive of the concept to be evaluated, the arguer making an evaluative claim may also want to explicitly make prior descriptive claims as well. In the previous examples, for instance, one can easily see how an arguer might need to describe certain features of capital punishment, private property, lying, Clinton, Reagan, free trade, or Cuba before launching into an evaluation of those concepts.

In many, but not all instances, an arguer also would need to use a claim of relationship as evidence to support the evaluative claim. To illustrate instances when a relational claim is and is not needed, consider the two examples of claims evaluating a single object. The claim that "capital punishment is immoral" can be supported by describing a feature of capital punishment (that it is the intentional taking of a human life) and evaluating that feature negatively (the intentional taking of a human life is an immoral act). A description and an evaluation are all that are necessary; relational evidence is not needed. The second claim that "private property is the root of all evil" is different. To make this claim, one first might describe the concept of private property, then argue that private property leads to greed and selfishness (a relational claim), then argue that greed and selfishness are evil. A significant difference exists between the first argument and the second one: The first requires relational evidence and the second does not. In the first instance, the argument is evaluating an inherent feature of capital punishment; in the second, the argument evaluates an effect of private property. When arguing an inherent feature of a concept, relational evidence is unnecessary because the evaluation is of the feature rather than of an effect of the feature. But many times, by the nature of the claim, an arguer is forced to evaluate an effect of a concept. In those instances, the arguer is required to establish the effect by means of relational evidence.

In summary, four categories of evidence and claims include definitions, descriptions, relational statements (of contingency and of similarity), and evaluations. Sometimes claims are the end products of arguments; at other times they are used as evidence for the construction of further claims. This introduction has presented a category system and begun to explain how various types of claims are related to one another when one is used as evidence for another. This introduction has done little or nothing toward explaining how one constructs arguments for these various types of claims. The methods and processes of constructing these claims are the topics of later chapters.

Theory and Practice

This essay has provided some theoretical background relevant to argumentation in debating. Specifically, it has provided a discussion of the Toulmin model of argument and a more detailed description of two of Toulmin's elements: claims and evidence. The reason for focusing on these two elements is that the remainder of this volume provides information that can be transformed into evidence and claims to support propositions. Claims and evidence are the foundational elements of supporting propositions. Warrants and reservations, which are more likely to be individual creations than foundations, did not receive the same detailed discussion.

When using this volume, debaters need to remember that it is only a starting point. Good debaters, much less excellent debaters, will need to go beyond this volume. They will need to engage in individual and perhaps collective research into the details of other claims and evidence.

Then, of course, comes the actual practice of debating where debaters will be required to combine the evidence provided in this volume and from their own research with warrants and reservations to support claims and to combine those claims into arguments supporting or refuting propositions.

Robert Trapp
Professor of Rhetoric
Willamette University
Salem, Oregon, U.S.A.

℘ DEBATE TOPICS

ABORTION ON DEMAND

Whether a woman has the right to terminate a pregnancy, and, if so, under what conditions, is one of the most contentious issues facing modern societies. For some, the question is even more fundamental: At what stage is the fetus to be regarded as a child? The battle lines are drawn between "pro-life" supporters, who argue that abortion is never permissible, and "pro-choice" adherents, who emphasize the mother's right to choose. In 1973 the US Supreme Court ruled that abortion was legal in its landmark decision Roe v. Wade. *Since then antiabortion groups have pressed to have the ruling overturned and have succeeded in having several states pass laws limiting the conditions under which abortion is permitted. Both antiabortion and pro-choice groups have made support of* Roe *the litmus test for political and judicial candidates wanting their backing.*

PROS

Women should have control over their own bodies—they have to carry the child during pregnancy and undergo childbirth. No one else carries the child for her; it will be her responsibility alone, and thus she should have the sole right to decide. If a woman does not want to go through the full nine months and subsequent birth, then she should have the right to choose not to do so. There are few—if any—other cases where something with such profound consequences is forced upon a human being against her or his will. To appeal to the child's right to life is just circular—whether a fetus has rights or not, or can really be called a "child," is exactly what is at issue. Everyone agrees that children have rights and shouldn't be killed. Not everyone agrees that fetuses of two, four, eight, or even twenty weeks are children.

Not only is banning abortion a problem in theory, offending against a woman's right to choose, it is also a practical problem. A ban would not stop abortion but would drive it once again underground and into conditions where the health and safety of the woman are almost certainly at risk. Women would also circumvent the ban by traveling to countries where abortion is legal. Either the state would have to take the draconian measure of restricting freedom of movement, or it would have to admit that its law is unworkable in practice and abolish it.

Are we really talking about a "life"? At what point does a life begin? Is terminating a fetus, which can neither feel nor think and is not conscious of its own "existence," really commensurate with the killing of a person? If you affirm that human life is a quality independent of, and prior to, thought and feeling, you leave yourself the awkward task of explaining what truly "human" life is.

CONS

Of course, human rights should be respected, but no one has a right to make a decision with no reference to the rights and wishes of others. In this case, does the father have any rights in regard to the fate of the fetus? More important, though, pro-choice groups actively ignore the most important right—the child's right to life. What is more important than life? All other rights, including the mother's right to choice, surely stem from a prior right to life; if you have no right to any life, then how do you have a right to an autonomous one? A woman may ordinarily have a reasonable right to control her own body, but this does not confer on her the entirely separate (and insupportable) right to decide whether another human lives or dies.

Unborn children cannot articulate their right to life; they are vulnerable and must be protected. Many laws are difficult to implement, but degree of difficulty does not diminish the validity and underlying principle. People will kill other people, regardless of the law, but it does not follow that you shouldn't legislate against murder.

Whether the state should restrain women from traveling for abortions is a separate question, but one that can be answered in the affirmative given what is at stake. Restricting someone's freedom is a small price to pay for protecting an innocent life.

The question of what life is can certainly be answered: It is sacred, inviolable, and absolute. The fetus, at whatever stage of development, will inevitably develop the human abilities to think, feel, and be aware of itself. The unborn child will have every ability and every opportunity that you yourself have, given the chance to be born.

PROS	CONS
In cases where terminating a pregnancy is necessary to save a mother's life, surely abortion is permissible.	While emergencies are tragic, it is by no means obvious that abortion is permissible. The "mother vs. child" dilemma is one that defies solution, and aborting to preserve one of the lives sets a dangerous precedent that killing one person to save another is acceptable. This is a clear, and unpalatable, case of treating a human being as a means to an end.
Not only medical emergencies present compelling grounds for termination. Women who have been raped should not have to suffer the additional torment of being pregnant with the product of that ordeal. To force a woman to produce a living, constant reminder of that act is unfair to both mother and child.	While rape is an appalling crime, is it the fault of the unborn child? The answer is no. Denying someone life because of the circumstances of conception is as unfair as anything else imaginable.
Finally, advances in medical technology have enabled us to determine during pregnancy whether the child will be disabled. In cases of severe disability, in which the child would have a very short, very painful and tragic life, it is surely right to allow parents to choose a termination. This avoids both the suffering of the parents and of the child.	What right does anyone have to deprive another of life on the grounds that he deems that life not worth living? This arrogant and sinister presumption is impossible to justify, given that many people with disabilities lead fulfilling lives. What disabilities would be regarded as the watershed between life and termination? All civilized countries roundly condemn the practice of eugenics.

Sample Motions:

This House would forbid abortion on demand.

This House believes in a woman's right to choose.

Web Links:

- American Civil Liberties Union. <http://www.aclu.org/reproductiverights/index.html> Provides information on the status of reproductive issues and reproductive rights from a pro-choice perspective.
- The National Right to Life Committee. <http://www.nrlc.org/Federal/RU486/index.html> Presents information on abortion methodology and alternatives to abortion from a pro-life stance.
- ReligiousTolerance.org. <http://www.religioustolerance.org/abortion.htm> Offers information on both the pro-life and pro-choice positions.

Further Reading:

Dombrowski, Daniel A., and Robert Deltete. *A Brief, Liberal, Catholic Defense of Abortion*. University of Illinois Press, 2006.

Hendershott, Anne. *The Politics of Abortion*. Encounter Books, 2006.

Jacob, Krista, ed. *Abortion Under Attack: Women on the Challenges Facing Choice*. Seal Press, 2006.

Rose, Molody. *Safe, Legal, and Unavailable? Abortion Politics in the United States*. CQ Press, 2006.

ABORTION, PARENTAL NOTIFICATION/CONSENT

Whether a teenager should have to notify or get the permission of her parents before having an abortion is one of the contentious issues surrounding abortion. Parental notification or consent laws exist in 44 US states, although in nine of those states the laws are enjoined or not enforced. Some of the statutes provide for a court-bypass procedure should a teenager be unable to involve her parents. Most include exceptions for medical emergencies. In 2005 the US Supreme Court agreed to hear a challenge to a New Hampshire law requiring parental notification, but the following year avoided a major decision by returning the case to the lower court because the statute did not allow an exemption from notification if the girl's health was in danger. In 2007 New Hampshire became the first state to repeal a parental notification law.

PROS

Children under 16 need parental consent for medical treatment and surgery: abortion should not be an exception. Children need parental consent for many activities—from participating in extracurricular sports or school trips to marrying. Abortion is at least as important a decision as any of these.

Parents have a right to know what their children are doing. They are legally responsible for their care, and, as parents, they have a proper interest. Good parents would want to help their daughter make her decision.

Parental notification helps ensure that pregnant teenagers get support and guidance from their parents in deciding whether to continue the pregnancy. This decision has a major long-term effect on a woman's psychological and emotional well-being, her ability to continue formal education, and her future financial status. She needs the guidance of adults in helping make this decision.

We appreciate that in some exceptional cases notifying parents may be inappropriate—for example, if a daughter is estranged from them, if she has been abused, or if telling her parents would present a serious foreseeable threat to her safety. In such cases, the courts could allow a waiver. In normal circumstances, however, parents should be informed. That unusual circumstances may arise does not affect the principle that this is a sensible law.

CONS

Parental consent is not legally necessary to have a baby nor should it be. The mother, not the grandparents, should have the ultimate authority over whether to have a baby. To say that someone is old enough to have a baby but not old enough to have an abortion is absurd. In any case, parental consent for surgery is a legal sham because physicians can get a court order to override a parent's refusal. The proposition has not presented a good example.

Children have good reasons for not telling parents of a pregnancy. Parents who are opposed to abortion may force their daughter to continue a pregnancy against her wishes, even at a risk to her health or life. Disclosing that a girl is pregnant confirms that she is sexually active. Some parents may be so opposed to premarital sex that they disown their daughter or physically or mentally abuse her.

This measure is unnecessary for stable and supportive families, in which daughters may well choose to discuss their pregnancy with their parents. It is ineffective and cruel in unstable and troubled families, where telling parents that their daughter is pregnant may make the family situation worse.

Obtaining parental consent necessarily imposes a delay into the abortion process, which increases the likelihood of complications. Judicial waivers introduce even more delays—on average at least 22 days in the U.S. For the sake of the mother's health, it is better not to require parental consent.

PROS	CONS
Requiring parental consent will lead to a fall in the number of abortions. In Minnesota, for example, the number of legal teenage abortions fell by 25% when this measure was introduced. Both pro-choice advocates and abortion opponents agree that lowering the number of abortions is good.	Requiring parental consent does not limit abortions. Teens go to states that do not have such requirements.
When the "quick-fix" of abortion is no longer easily available, attitudes change. Teenagers are less likely to have sex or are more likely to use contraception if they do. Abstention and practicing safe sex have positive effects on health by diminishing the risk of unwanted pregnancies and sexually transmitted diseases.	We should encourage campaigns for sexual abstinence and contraceptive awareness, but we must remember that they are not alternatives to abortion. No sensible person would choose abortion as an alternative to contraception. Abortion is a last resort. If sexual abstinence is not a sensible reaction to making abortion more inaccessible, then making abortion more inaccessible is not a sensible way of increasing sexual abstinence.

Sample Motions:

This House would require parental consent for abortion.
This House would look after its children.
This House believes that parental consent is in the best interest of the teen.

Web Links:

- American Civil Liberties Union. <http://www.aclu.org/reproductiverights/youth/16388res20010401.html> Presents arguments against laws that mandate parental involvement in abortion.
- Center for Reproductive Rights. <http://www.crlp.org/pub_fac_mandconsent.html> Essay on the issue from a pro-choice group.
- ReligiousTolerance.org. <http://www.religioustolerance.org/abo_pare.htm> Summary of pros and cons of parental notification laws.

ADVERTISING, IMAGE OF WOMEN IN

In the fall of 2006 Spain banned too-thin models from the Madrid Fashion Week, reigniting the discussion of how fashion's—and advertising's—unrealistic beauty standards influence women's body image, their actual bodies, their aspirations, and their health. Concerned that advertising has given many women, and particularly young girls, a narrow definition of beauty, several corporations have begun campaigns to widen the view of beauty. For example, Dove, which manufactures personal care products, has developed advertising campaigns portraying the diversity of women's physical attractiveness, including size and shape, across all ages.

PROS	CONS
Consumer advertising projects an unrealistic ideal of the female body shape. The vast majority of advertising uses female models whose key features (e.g., thinness, particular figure, unblemished complexion) do not correspond to most women's bodies. This can create false expectations on the part of women and their partners, as well as society at large. The portrayal of women in advertising is also highly stylized and can significantly distort the connection viewers make between what they see in an advertisement and what women actually look like and experience in daily life.	Advertising allows a form of escapism that many women welcome and, indeed, pursue. As with most artistic media, an implicit understanding exists that what is depicted does not necessarily mirror real life—and to many viewers this is the very attraction of the images. Models reflect how many women want to be, which is why they are used to advertise fashion in the first place. Women welcome such pictures as a way of affirming their own focus on certain elements of aesthetic attractiveness. The glamour of the fashion industry in general and its advertising campaigns in particular is a welcome antidote to the humdrum existence many women lead. Women are grateful for the chance to fantasize about a glamorous, fashionable lifestyle.
Much advertising is filtered through a male lens and, even if targeted at women, can reinforce an unbalanced, male chauvinistic view of women as sex objects. We see this in the fact that most advertising uses young, attractive female models—even for products both men and women use (e.g., cars).	Arguing that advertisers must choose between portraying women either as aesthetically perfect, sexually attractive objects or as thinking human beings is a false choice. Models' beauty in no way undermines their intellectual capacity. The use of female models in consumer advertising actually empowers women. The successful models who attract media attention are role models for many women. Women are important consumers; media focus on portraying them in a certain light because advertisers are trying to cater to their interests.
Advertising featuring beautiful women plays on female insecurities, linking beauty and success with consumption. Through its near-relentless focus on "ideal" body-type models, advertising also pressures women into conforming to a "perfect" body. This increases the likelihood of eating disorders, as well as the pursuit of unnecessary cosmetic surgery, anti-ageing treatments, etc.	The use of female models in advertising aimed at women is the inevitable response to market demand. Women want to see other women in ads. Through their ongoing consumption of and demand for pictures of "perfect" bodies, women effectively signal a tacit acceptance of such images. If enough women objected, advertisers would change their approach rather than alienate their target consumers.
Consumer advertising negatively objectifies women, conforming to a misogynist perception of women as commodifiable sexual objects. Most advertising also uses models with a fairly homogenous set of physical characteristics and styles them so that they are often interchangeable. This approach emphasizes the view of women as objects.	Advertising and the fashion industry vary the kind of images they use to suit different markets. Advertising follows social norms; it does not set them. The fashion industry is innocent of the charge of homogeneity as it draws models from ethnic minorities, thus promoting a more diverse view of beauty. Also, advertisers are beginning to use models with more "natural" bodies; as we saw in fall 2006, a backlash has begun against ultra-thin models.

Sample Motions:

This House believes that thin models are poor role models.

This House abhors the male chauvinistic consumer culture.

This House believes that advertising and fashion must "get real."

Web Links:

- CommonSenseMedia. <http://www.commonsensemedia.org/news/press-releases.php?id=28> Summary of relationship between body image and the fashion industry.
- EDReferral.com. <http://www.edreferral.com/body_image.htm> Links to articles and videos on body image.
- HealthyPlace.com. <http://www.healthyplace.com/communities/eating_Disorders/body_image_advertising.asp> Discussion of eating disorders and advertising.
- USAToday.com. <http://www.usatoday.com/news/health/2006-09-25-thin-models_x.htm> Newspaper article on the debate engendered by Spain's ban on ultra-thin models.

Further Reading:

Bordo, Susan, and Leslie Heyword. *Unbearable Weight: Feminism, Western Culture, and the Body*, 10th ed. University of California Press, 2004.

Wolf, Naomi. *The Beauty Myth: How Images of Beauty Are Used Against Women*. Harper Perennial, 2002.

Wykes, Maggie, and Barrie Gunter. *The Media and Body Image: If Looks Could Kill.* Sage, 2005.

AFFIRMATIVE ACTION

Affirmative action in the United States was born of the civil rights and women's movements of the 1960s and 1970s. It is designed to provide historically disadvantaged groups—minorities and women—special consideration in education, housing, and employment. Those institutions with affirmative action policies generally set goals for increased diversity, although the courts have ruled quotas unconstitutional. By the end of the twentieth century, Supreme Court decisions had limited affirmative action, and a vocal opposition movement was arguing that it was no longer necessary. In June 2003, however, the Supreme Court ruled that universities could use race as one factor in making admission decisions, although the deeply divided Court seemed to put limits on the weight race should receive. The court became more conservative following the appointment of John Roberts and Samuel Alito in 2006, and the following year it ruled unconstitutional the use of race as the primary factor in assigning students to specific elementary or secondary schools.

PROS	CONS
Women and minorities have frequently faced obstacles and difficulties in access to education and employment that white males did not. Affirmative action levels the playing field.	All discrimination is negative. It is always wrong to select on any basis other than merit and ability. Affirmative action leads to able applicants being unfairly passed over.
Affirmative action unlocks the unrealized potential of millions. Minority applicants are just as skilled as those from the majority but their talents are untapped because of lack of opportunity. The country gains enormously by using the talents of all our citizens.	Affirmative action results in less able applicants filling positions. Employers must have the flexibility to employ the best candidates to ensure efficiency and productivity.

PROS	CONS
Successful minority members are role models who will encourage the development of minority youngsters.	Affirmative action undermines the achievements of minority members by creating the impression that success was unearned. Some members of minorities see affirmative action as patronizing and as tokenism on the part of the majority.
Bringing more minority applicants into the workplace will change racist and sexist attitudes because workers will begin to know each other as individuals rather than stereotypes.	Affirmative action causes resentment among those who do not benefit from it and creates a backlash against minorities.
The proportion of minorities in particular jobs should mirror that of the minority in the general population. The underrepresentation of minorities and women in certain fields leads to perceptions of institutional racism and sexism.	Granted, we should aim for improving minority representation in high-profile positions, but we should not sacrifice our emphasis on merit and ability. Instead we should give everyone better access to education so that we can choose on merit and without discrimination.
Getting minority candidates into top jobs will enable them to change the system "from the inside" to make it fairer for all.	Educational institutions are becoming more diverse. This diversity ultimately will lead to increasing minority representation in senior positions in business, education, and government. Although the pace of change is not as fast as it might be, we have seen improvement. Continued implementation of affirmative action could lead to a backlash that stops progress

Sample Motions:

This House believes in affirmative action.
This House believes race does matter.
This House would act affirmatively.

Web Links:

- Affirmative Action and Diversity Project. <http://aad.english.ucsb.edu> Site, maintained by the University of California, Santa Barbara, offering articles and theoretical analysis, public documents, current legislative initiatives, and resources on affirmative action.
- PBS. <http://www.pbs.org/now/shows/434/index.html> Provides a brief description of current events relating to affirmative action and provides links to articles.
- Stanford Encyclopedia of Philosophy. <http://plato.stanford.edu/entries/affirmative-action/> Article tracing the history of affirmative action and providing overview of pro and con arguments.

Further Reading:

Anderson, Terry H. *The Pursuit of Fairness: A History of Affirmative Action*. Oxford University Press, 2004.

Cahn, Steven M., ed. *The Affirmative Action Debates*. Routledge, 2002.

Kellough, J. Edward. *Understanding Affirmative Action: Politics, Discrimination, and the Search for Justice.* Georgetown University Press, 2006.

Kranz, Rachel. *Affirmative Action*. Facts On File, 2002.

AGE DISCRIMINATION

Age discrimination occurs when a decision is made on the basis of a person's age. In the workplace these are most often decisions about recruitment, promotion, and dismissal. Although such discrimination can be seen in a reluctance to hire workers who are perceived to be too young and immature for the job, in practice it refers to a bias against older workers. In societies that celebrate youthfulness above almost all else, it can be very difficult for even highly qualified professionals to find new positions after the age of 50. Nationwide laws against age discrimination are some 30 years old in the United States, 20 years old in Canada, and 10 years old in Australia. The European Employment Directive also prohibits age discrimination. But around the world the issue remains controversial, both in general and in particular concerning the practice of setting mandatory retirement ages.

PROS

Older people are just as capable as younger people. Since age is not necessarily an indication of inferior ability or potential, treating people less favorably purely on the basis of their age is just as unreasonable and unfair as doing so on the basis of race or religion. It is also inconsistent with the principles of equal treatment and nondiscrimination at the heart of the notion of individual rights.

For example, if a particular older worker has less concentration or manual strength than a younger worker, and this objectively and reasonably makes someone less qualified for the particular job, employers can still make their decisions based on a worker's relative lack of suitability for the job—not on age. Age by itself is not a determinant.

CONS

In theory, hiring should be based on ability. In reality, certain abilities are hard to test accurately, so employers use age as a proxy—in the same way that they use sports as an indication of one's ability to be a team player, or extracurricular leadership as an indicator of management potential.

Though not foolproof, age is often an indicator of qualities such as concentration, memory, energy, and so on, which may be important in specific cases. For example, a fashion designer justifiably wants salespersons to have a certain level of energy and vitality, and it is crucial for air traffic controllers and surgeons to have high levels of fitness and concentration.

PROS

Discriminatory practices in recruitment and promotion are detrimental to the economy. Age discrimination reduces productivity by inefficiently matching job and advancement opportunities to workers, thus wasting talent. Higher participation rates among older workers lead to better matching of jobs to people, increased employment rates, and enhanced competition among workers, which stimulates the labor market in the long run.

It is a well-known fallacy that the economy has only a limited number of jobs and that when older workers remain in the labor market they deny job opportunities to younger people or push down wages. In fact, wages are especially unlikely to decline in industries with existing or projected shortages, such as teaching and nursing.

CONS

The result of laws against age discrimination may merely be that old people are working more, and not that more old people are working. Research on age discrimination laws in the US shows that increased employment rates among older workers are due mostly to their remaining in jobs longer, and not due to increased hiring rates among older workers.

Worse, the increased supply of older workers, at least in the short term, generates market pressures for wages to fall, such that all existing older workers suffer.

PROS

Without age discrimination and a mandatory retirement age, employers benefit from lower turnover and thus lower recruitment costs.

By contrast, discrimination discourages potentially talented job seekers from applying. Beginning with the recruitment stage, employers lose by having a smaller pool of workers to draw upon and by failing to make the most of the existing skills potential of the population.

CONS

The argument that antidiscrimination laws are good for employers contradicts economics and common sense. If hiring and promoting older workers were in firms' best interests, the firms would do so without the need for such laws.

Furthermore, at any firm there is always a limited number of senior jobs. If older workers staying on indefinitely occupy these jobs, firms may find it difficult

PROS	CONS
	to recruit, motivate, and retain younger workers looking to replace them, which leads to high turnover among younger staff. Firms may also find that with no mandatory retirement age they have no idea when people will leave, which creates problems of uncertainty in manpower planning and possible bottlenecks.
Ageism is the most prevalent form of discrimination in the workforce today. Legislation helps to change these prejudiced attitudes if it operates in conjunction with other policies to promote equal rights and educate employers and workers about their obligations and rights. By protecting a group in society that is often left out and less advantaged, we are also raising the level of equality in society.	In Australia, Canada, and the US, where antidiscrimination laws have long been in place, there is no clear evidence so far of any significant shift in the attitude of employers and society to older workers. In fact, there is some evidence that employers are less likely to hire older workers, and younger coworkers are more resentful because employers are not allowed to set a mandatory retirement age.

Sample Motions:

This House believes that age discrimination should be illegal in the workplace.
This House believes that old is gold.
This House would honor its elders.

Web Links:

- Age Discrimination: How Old Is Too Old? <http://jobsearch.about.com/cs/careerresources/a/agediscriminat.htm> Summary of problems facing older job seekers.
- US Department of Labor: Age Discrimination. <http://www.dol.gov/dol/topic/discrimination/agedisc.htm> Links to anti-age discrimination legislation and regulation.
- US Equal Opportunities Commission: Facts About Age Discrimination. <http://www.eeoc.gov/facts/age.html> Summary of US Age Discrimination in Employment Act.

Further Reading:

Braine, Mohammad, and Ian Glover. *Ageism in Work and Employment.* Ashgate, 2002.

Gregory, Raymond F. *Age Discrimination in the American Workplace: Old at a Young Age.* Rutgers University Press, 2001.

Macnicol, John. *Age Discrimination: An Historical and Contemporary Analysis.* Cambridge University Press, 2006.

Sargeant, Malcolm. *Age Discrimination in Employment.* Ashgate, 2007.

AIDS DRUGS FOR DEVELOPING COUNTRIES

The vast majority of people infected with HIV/AIDS live in Africa, more specifically, sub-Saharan Africa. These typically poorer and developing countries are confronting the issue of the cost of drugs for treating the disease. Some nations say that they cannot afford the drugs and that drug companies are making an immoral profit; some nations have threatened to ignore the patents of pharmaceutical companies and to manufacture generic forms of HIV/AIDS drugs unless the companies agree to lower their prices for poorer markets. Bending to international pressure, in the opening years of the 21st century, some of the world's largest drug companies announced that they planned to cut the cost of HIV/AIDS drugs in the world's poorest countries.

PROS

Without a doubt many of the world's pharmaceutical companies are making large profits by selling drugs to poor nations that have a great portion of their population infected with HIV/AIDS. This is an immoral exploitation of those AIDS sufferers who can least afford to pay for treatment and who have the least power internationally to negotiate cheaper prices.

The countries with the biggest AIDS problems are a captive market and are forced to pay whatever the drug companies demand for their products. Poor nations are thus justified in using the threat of producing generic drugs to force drug companies to lower prices.

Generic drugs would be far cheaper to produce and would avoid the shipping costs from factories in Europe or America. Generic drugs have no research and development costs to recoup, so they could be sold for a price greatly reduced from current levels. The cost of keeping a person on AZT or other drug cocktails is exorbitant; such cost would be greatly reduced through the use of generic drugs.

Millions of people will continue to suffer while drug companies refuse to make AIDS medication available to poorer nations at a price they can afford. Are they trying to use the millions of HIV sufferers as hostages in their battle to get the prices they want?

Drug companies will not lose money by reducing prices; their market will expand. If prices are reduced, the drugs will become affordable to millions of sufferers, many of whom will be using products like AZT for the rest of their lives.

CONS

Just like any business, the pharmaceutical companies need to recoup significant financial investment in research and development. The development of AIDS drugs is highly technical, and a measurable return on initial financial investment is needed if companies are to continue drug research and development.

Drug companies are as much subject to the forces of the free market as any other business. The threat of illegally producing generic drugs only further serves to discourage drug companies from creating new and more effective medicines because the developing nations have shown them that patent protections will be ignored.

Because most of the drug companies are based in richer, First World nations, they have both the technology to produce effective medicines and the funding to ensure that no corners are cut in the process. Poorer nations would almost certainly cut chemical corners in manufacturing generic drugs should the technology for large-scale manufacture even be available. In addition, by contravening international treaties covering patents, they would not benefit from the next generation of AIDS drugs because companies would be reluctant to supply the newer drugs to a country that steals a drug formula to manufacture generic drugs.

Is it right that those infected with HIV in the Third World get huge discounts while those in the First World pay full price? Developed nations may even have to pay more if the drug companies decide to subsidize their "charity sales" to poor countries. Are not poor countries themselves using sufferers as hostages? Many developing nations could realize significant long-term savings by buying and using preventive medicines to stop mother-to-child transmission, etc.

The majority of Third World countries would be unable to afford the drugs even at a breakeven price. One-off treatments to prevent mother-to-child transmission, for example, would be expensive enough. The cost for complex drug cocktails would still be completely out of reach of developing nations. Drug companies would have to sell their medications at a loss to make them affordable to most developing nations.

PROS	CONS
HIV/AIDS treatments are as cheap as they can be at present. By buying the medicines now, especially for preventive purposes, developing nations can reduce the chance of future HIV infection in their populations and thus not need to buy the next generation of (inevitably more expensive) drugs.	No matter how low the drug companies price HIV/AIDS treatments, they are unlikely to ever be cheap enough: As the number of HIV infected people in Africa grows, the strain on national health budgets will become unbearable. Developing countries are better off pursuing preventative measures and education. Governments will need to use their health care funds carefully—producing generic medicines offers significant savings.

Sample Motions:

This House would insist on cheaper drugs.
This House believes that capitalism lets the sick suffer.
This House wants the First World to help.
This House needs help with AIDS.
This House would fight AIDS.

Web Links:

- Avert. <http://www.avert.org/generic.htm> Provides a history of the conflict over AIDS drug pricing and suggests reform for the future.
- International Press Service. <http://www.aegis.com/news/ips/2000/IP000505.html> Article on the controversy surrounding pharmaceutical company agreements to supply inexpensive HIV/AIDS drugs to poor countries.
- USAID. <http://www.usaid.gov/our_work/global_health/aids/index.html#> Summary of US initiatives to fight AIDS in foreign nations.

Further Reading:

Condon, Bradly J., and Tapen Sinha. *Global Lessons from the AIDS Pandemic: Economic, Financial, Legal and Political Implications.* Springer, 2008.

Epstein, Helen. *The Invisible Cure: Why We Are Losing the Fight Against AIDS in Africa.* Picador, 2008.

World Bank Group. *Intensifying Action Against HIV/AIDS in Africa: Responding to a Development Crisis.* World Bank, 2000.

ALTERNATIVELY FUELED CARS, GOVERNMENT INCENTIVES FOR

The increasing global use of automobiles is causing more airborne pollution, despite agreements by many governments to cut such emissions. For years the auto industry has been researching cars that use alternate fuels, for example, hydrogen, solar power, battery or fuel cells, and so on, and these vehicles are beginning to attract political attention. For example, California has long had mandatory targets for sales of alternatively fueled vehicles, and the federal government has introduced tax breaks for environmentally friendly cars. EU member states must develop methods by which a wide variety of biofuels will account for 5.75% of all transportation fuel sold by 2010.

PROS

Cars that use fuel that is less environmentally damaging than petroleum are good for the protection of the environment. Gasoline and diesel engines produce pollution both locally and globally, contributing to poor health and global warming. They are also a major consumer of nonrenewable energy, depleting global reserves and making us dependent on oil-rich states for our energy security. Therefore, encouraging people to use alternative fuels instead of petroleum will have a positive environmental, economic, and political impact.

An incentive is an effective way to encourage more widespread use of alternatively fueled vehicles. New technologies are expensive to research and are often prohibitively expensive in their early stages, before there is a critical mass of adoption. This vicious cycle means that the dominant fuel, petroleum, has an inbuilt defensive advantage over new, possibly competitive rivals. Incentives negate this disadvantage, even if they are used during the initial phases before the alternatively fueled cars are more widely used.

Operating a centralized transportation policy is appropriate for government. A successful, effective transportation system markedly increases a country's economic success. It also has a widespread and positive social impact. Using incentives to advance a particular form of transportation, for example, alternatively fueled cars, is a perfectly natural fit with such a plan.

Incentives are an effective way to make people act in a certain way. Even if people accept that petroleum-fueled cars are environmentally damaging and thus ultimately less desirable than alternatives, this may be a "soft" preference. Monetary incentives are often a more effective way of actually persuading people to amend their choices.

This is an effective policy even if only on a small scale. Granted petroleum-fueled cars are only one factor contributing to environmental problems, but, adopting a policy such as this one sends out a strong message affirming a positive approach to environmental matters. This could have a "snowball" effect. It can be pursued

CONS

The environmental impact of encouraging alternatively fueled cars is mixed. Conventional engines are much more fuel efficient and much less polluting than they were 20 years ago, and further improvements are likely in the future. Alternative fuels may not be less damaging than petroleum: it may just be that they have not been around long enough for their full consequences to be appreciated. For example, the energy to power up batteries or fuel cells, or to produce hydrogen, is often derived from fossil fuels. Even if there is less local pollution, the environmental impact of powering vehicles is simply transferred somewhere else, rather than removed. Whether this is so or not, such a scheme does not encourage people to use public transportation. Indeed, people may interpret the government's inducement to drive certain kinds of cars as support of the use of private cars.

Government incentives are economically inefficient. They are a form of social engineering, since people express their preferences through the market, and incentives are a way of changing the market conditions so people's views change. This is economically inefficient. It amounts to using public funds to "bribe" people to make the choices that the government thinks they should.

Such a plan uses government power to disadvantage private choices. People should be allowed to choose the most suitable form of transportation based on their individual circumstances. Taxpayer-funded government incentives interfere with private choice.

Alternatively fueled automobiles are not what the car-driving public wants. If drivers thought the benefits of such cars were significant, they would buy them in large enough numbers that subsidies would not be necessary. The fact that they do not is an indication that those drivers are content driving petroleum-fueled cars.

This policy is too small to make any difference. First, petroleum-fueled cars are only one of many factors that contribute to environmental problems. Cars in any one country are an even smaller part of this overall picture, and so this policy is only a drop in the ocean in terms of the net effect. This is especially so as it simply pits

PROS

in tandem with other policies, and so even if it is only a relatively small part of the overall environmental problem, tackling it is worthwhile.

CONS

one country's regulation against other countries' more deregulatory approach and can thus lead to shifting of the problem rather than its actual resolution.

Sample Motions:

This House supports government subsidies for alternatively fueled cars.
This House would introduce tax breaks for environmentally friendly cars.
This House would increase taxes on petroleum-fueled cars.
This House would put its money where its motor is.
This House would adopt quotas for the production of alternatively fueled vehicles.

Web Links:

- Alternative fuels. <http://www.fueleconomy.gov/Feg/current.shtml> US government site reviewing alternative fuels and their advantages and disadvantages.
- A Student's Guide to Alternative Fuel Vehicles. <http://www.energyquest.ca.gov/transportation> California Energy Commission introduction to alternative-fuel vehicles with good links to information on specific fuels.

Further Reading:

Hoffman, Peter. *Tomorrow's Energy: Hydrogen, Fuel Cells, and the Prospects for a Cleaner Planet.* MIT Press, 2002.

Vaitheeswaran, Vijay, and Ian Carson. *ZOOM: The Global Race to Fuel the Car of the Future.* Twelve, 2008.

Vigar, Geoff. *Transport, Environmental Politics & Public Safety.* Routledge, 2001.

ANIMAL RIGHTS

In the nineteenth century reformers began urging the more humane treatment of animals and founded groups like the American Society for the Prevention of Cruelty to Animals to improve the conditions first of working animals and then of domestic and farm animals as well. In the 1970s Australian philosopher Peter Singer became one of the first to argue that animals have rights. While most people agree that humans have an obligation to care for animals and treat them humanely, the idea that they have rights remains contentious.

PROS

Human beings are accorded rights on the basis that they are able to think and to feel pain. Many other animals are also able to think (to some extent) and are certainly able to feel pain. Therefore nonhuman animals should also be accorded rights, e.g., to a free and healthy life.

CONS

Human beings are infinitely more complex than any other living creatures. Their abilities to think and talk, to form social systems with rights and responsibilities, and to feel emotions are developed well beyond any other animals. Trying to prevent the most obvious cases of unnecessary suffering or torture of animals is reasonable, but beyond that, nonhuman animals do not deserve to be given "rights."

PROS	CONS
Ever since the publication of Charles Darwin's *Origin of Species* in 1859 we have known that human beings are related by common ancestry to all other animals. We owe a duty of care to our animal cousins.	That we are (incredibly distantly) related to other animals does not mean that they have "rights." This sort of thinking would lead to absurdities. Should we respect the "right" to life of bacteria? We might wish to reduce unnecessary animal suffering, but not because all creatures to which we are distantly related have rights.
We should err on the side of caution in ascribing rights to human or nonhuman creatures. If we place high standards (such as the ability to think, speak, or even to enter into a social contract) on the ascription of rights, there is a danger that not only animals but also human infants and mentally handicapped adults will be considered to have no rights.	Only human beings who are members of society have rights. Rights are privileges that come with certain social duties and moral responsibilities. Animals are not capable of entering into this sort of "social contract"—they are neither moral nor immoral, they are amoral. They do not respect our "rights," and they are irrational and entirely instinctual. Amoral and irrational creatures have neither rights nor duties—they are more like robots than people. All human beings or potential human beings (e.g., unborn children) can potentially be given rights, but nonhuman animals do not fall into that category.
Cruelty to animals is the sign of an uncivilized society; it encourages violence and barbarism in society more generally. A society that respects animals and restrains base and violent instincts is a more civilized one.	Using animals for our own nutrition and pleasure is completely natural. In the wild animals struggle to survive, are hunted by predators, and compete for food and resources. Human beings have been successful in this struggle for existence and do not need to feel ashamed of exploiting their position as a successful species in the evolutionary process.
That a small number of extremists and criminals have attached themselves to the animal rights movement does not invalidate the cause. Why shouldn't animal rights supporters and activists take medicine? They are morally obligated to take care of themselves in the best way they can until more humane research methods are developed and implemented.	Animal rights activists are hypocrites, extremists, and terrorists who don't care about human life. Organizations like the Animal Liberation Front use terrorist tactics and death threats; People for the Ethical Treatment of Animals is also an extremist organization. These extremists still avail themselves of modern medicine, however, which could not have been developed without experiments and tests on animals. Animal welfare is a reasonable concern, but talking of animal "rights" is a sign of extremism and irrationality.

Sample Motions:

This House believes that animals have rights too.
This House would respect animals' rights.
This House condemns the exploitation of animals.

Web Links:

- Animal Rights FAQ. <http://www.animal-rights.com/arpage.htm> Includes about 100 FAQs that address key arguments in favor of animal rights, biographies of animal rights activists, lists of US and UK organizations, and links to other animal rights groups.
- Ethics Update. <http://ethics.sandiego.edu/Applied/Animals/index.asp> Links to surveys and resources addressing current events pertaining to animal rights and discussing the moral status of animals.

- People for the Ethical Treatment of Animals. <http://www.peta-online.org> Home page for animal rights organization includes news stories on animals and animal rights.

Further Reading:

Scully, Matthew. *Dominion: The Power of Man, the Suffering of Animals, and the Call to Mercy.* St. Martin's Griffin, 2003.

Singer, Peter. *Animal Liberation.* Reprint. Harper Perennial, 2001.

Wise, Steven M., and Jane Goodall. *Rattling the Cage: Toward Legal Rights for Animals.* Perseus, 2000.

ANTARCTIC EXPLOITATION

It is little more than 100 years since humans first set foot on Antarctica and even today few people have visited the frozen and hostile southern continent. Although nine countries have territorial claims on the continent, several of them overlapping, these political disagreements were suspended in the Antarctic Treaty of 1959. In the Treaty (covering all areas south of 60 degrees south latitude), it was agreed that Antarctica should be used exclusively for peaceful purposes and that military activities would be prohibited. It also guaranteed continued freedom for scientific research and promoted international scientific cooperation. Successive treaties have built on this foundation, providing strong protection for the Antarctic environment and strictly regulating fishing, for example. These have culminated in the 1991 Protocol on Environmental Protection to the Antarctic Treaty (fully implemented in 1998), which designates Antarctica as a "natural reserve, devoted to peace and science" and establishes environmental principles to govern the conduct of all activities. It also prohibits mining, arguments over which caused the failure of a proposed Convention on the Regulation of Antarctic Mineral Resource Activities (CRAMRA) in the late 1980s. CRAMRA would have potentially allowed future exploitation of Antarctic resources, subject to the agreement of all treaty signatories, but it ran into strong opposition from the international environmental movement, which convinced several of the treaty nations to refuse to sign it. This topic considers whether it is right to maintain Antarctica purely as a "natural reserve, devoted to peace and science." Should some exploitation of its resources be allowed, or should the general ban on economic activity be extended to areas such as fishing and tourism?

PROS

Antarctica is a pristine and unspoiled continent of great scientific value. In particular, it has a critical impact on the world's environment and ocean systems. This means that it must be left undisturbed in order to allow further study of such critical international issues as climate change, ozone depletion, long-range weather forecasting, and the operation of marine ecosystems (crucial to sustainable fishing). It is also essential to ensure that we do not pollute Antarctica so that it does not undergo changes (e.g., melting of its ice caps, a breakup of its ice sheets) that have a potentially disastrous global impact.

CONS

Antarctica is huge and almost completely unpopulated. Only the coastal fringes have any animals or plants. Well-regulated economic exploitation of its resources need not ruin it and could provide valuable raw materials and a boost to the world economy.

In any case, by far the greatest impacts on the Antarctic are external, for example, the impact of chlorofluorocarbons on the ozone layer over the South Pole, global warming, and the effects of whaling and pollution on the marine environment. Compared with these global influences, limited exploitation of Antarctic resources under strict environmental regulation will not make a significant difference.

PROS

Antarctica presents an alternative to a world dominated by political disputes, economic exploitation, and environmental destruction. Placing the southern continent in the care of scientists and out of reach of both politicians and multinational corporations has ensured that it can be preserved unchanged for future generations. This provides a model and a precedent for future international cooperation and global efforts to save the planet.

CONS

There is a danger in allowing a scientific elite to set the global agenda without regard to either economic logic or democratic accountability. If the Antarctic can help to provide additional resources for a rapidly growing world population, then we should be able to have an intelligent debate about the costs and benefits involved. In any case, scientific research does leave a footprint in Antarctica—for example, the ice road the Americans are planning to blast and bulldoze through the continent to the bases at the South Pole, or the waste products of the many scientific bases on the continent.

PROS

Oil and gas exploration should not be allowed in the Antarctic for many reasons. First, proven and probable reserves of oil and gas are still rising faster than global consumption, so there is no economic need to exploit any hypothetical Antarctic sources. Second, as the continent is already suffering as a result of global warming, our priority should be to find renewable alternatives to fossil fuels rather than to continue our dependence upon them. At a practical level, the cost of exploration and production would be completely uneconomic, especially given the hostile climate and the serious iceberg threats to offshore rigs, tankers, and pipelines, as well as the very deep continental shelf. There would also be a serious danger of pollution, both from the increased human presence in this fragile environment, and from oil spills.

CONS

Oil and gas exploration should be allowed, both on the Antarctic continent and in the Antarctic Ocean surrounding it. Although current technology would not enable exploitation of any reserves at economical prices, future technological advances and rises in the price of fossil fuels may change this equation. Deepwater extraction from the hostile North Sea or Arctic Oceans once seemed impossible, but now it is taken for granted. Our prosperity depends on cheap energy from fossil fuels, and it would be wrong to risk this by an arbitrary decision to declare the Antarctic off-limits to exploration, especially given the continuing skepticism of many about claims of global warming.

PROS

Antarctica must be protected from mineral exploitation and the 1991 Protocol upheld. There are no known mineral deposits on the continent, so the argument for exploitation is highly speculative, but it is nonetheless dangerous. Even exploration alone would greatly damage the delicate environment. Actual mineral extraction, with its pollution, processing facilities, and transport infrastructure would be hugely destructive. Politically, placing an economic value on Antarctic claims would renew dangers of territorial conflict that have been frozen since the 1961 Treaty and risk the collapse of the whole system of international cooperation.

CONS

The Antarctic Protocol of 1991 should be amended to allow for the possibility of mineral prospecting. The failed CRAMRA in the late 1980s would have allowed for this possibility subject to strict regulation and the agreement of all treaty nations, reasonable conditions that were rejected by environmental purists. Geological analogies with other continents suggest that several very valuable minerals may be present in Antarctica. If multinational companies are prepared to pay high prices to treaty governments for concessions, why should we turn down this source of revenue? Almost all mining activity would be underground, so it would be little affected by the harsh environment and likely to have little adverse impact upon it.

PROS

Fishing is at present allowed under the 1991 Protocol, and has been increasing in recent years as overfishing is exhausting other global fisheries. Although much about the marine ecosystem of the Southern Ocean is still unknown, it is clear that overfishing could quickly damage it and that any recovery could take decades. At present, limits are set according to our current understanding of

CONS

Fishing provides a crucial source of protein, especially for the relatively poor, and the Antarctic oceans are underexploited compared with all other fisheries. Quotas for different species are set very low by scientists sticking to very conservative precautionary principles and could in most cases be greatly expanded without risk of overfishing. Indeed, increased catch limits would remove much

PROS	CONS
fish stocks, but there is a great deal of illegal activity by a variety of nations, so the situation is not under control. Even legal fishing can do great damage. Thousands of seabirds die each year as a result of longline fishing. Instead of relaxing the Antarctic fishing regime, we should tighten it further. The less legal fishing is allowed, the easier it will be to spot unlicensed activity.	of the incentive for illegal fishing and might reduce the pressure on other, less well-protected fisheries elsewhere. If fish stocks are found to be under pressure, then quotas can be reduced once again.
Access to Antarctica should be restricted to those with a serious scientific purpose. Only a very small number of tourists visit the continent, mostly on cruise ships that call at Antarctic sites for just a few days, but this number is rising rapidly, and some visitors are now undertaking adventurous activities such as ski hiking, scuba diving, snowboarding, and mountaineering. Unchecked, this influx of people is greatly increasing the problems of waste management, and their activities are having a negative impact on the coastal environment and its wildlife. Adventurous tourists will also need to be rescued by the authorities, diverting resources from science. The more vessels visiting the continent, the greater the chance of catastrophic oil spills or for rogue operators to neglect proper waste management (both already problems in the Alaskan cruise industry). Overall, tourism will create a precedent for economic exploitation that may make it harder to defend the unique status of the continent in the future.	Tourism should be greatly expanded to allow as many people as possible to visit this unique environment. Antarctica should be for all of humanity, not just for a few elite scientists who seek to deny others access while simultaneously demanding huge sums of money for their research projects. Revenues from tourism could in any case be taxed in order to offset the cost of scientific research. Tourism could also promote environmental aims because it would educate visitors about the importance of Antarctica and so help to influence environmental policy. The International Association of Antarctica Tour Operators operates a strict code of practice to prevent damage to the environment.

Sample Motions:

This House would continue the ban on exploiting Antarctica's resources.
This House would hold the Antarctic sacred.
This House believes Antarctica belongs only to science.
This House believes capitalism stops in the Southern Ocean.
This House would save the ice.
This House would freeze development.

Web Links:

- Australian Antarctic Division. <http://www.aad.gov.au> General site providing overview of scientific research, environmental concerns, and so on.
- US Department of State: Handbook of Antarctic Treaty System. <http://www.state.gov/g/oes/rls/rpts/ant/> Primary international documents—treaties, protocols, and conventions—on Antarctica.

Further Reading:

Berkman, Paul Arthur. *Science into Policy: Global Lessons from Antarctica.* Academic Press, 2001.

ARRANGED MARRIAGES

In the Western world, people usually choose their own marriage partners, but arranged marriages are still common in Middle Eastern and Asian cultures. The practice can cause culture clash when immigrants maintain this tradition in the West. For Westerners, the practice rouses concern about the rights of women and brings up the question of assimilation vs. cultural identity.

PROS

Arranging marriage is an insult to the very nature of marriage, which should be about creating a loving and lasting partnership and family. It reduces marriage to a commercial transaction and, therefore, undermines family values. It becomes even more of an issue when it occurs in a Western society that values freedom of choice.

Parents and the community often put unacceptable pressure on their children to accept an arranged marriage. Moreover, the line between an arranged and a forced marriage is so hazy that it cannot be policed. We must stop the former to prevent the latter.

Arranged marriages are bad both for the individual women concerned and for women generally. Immigrant women often are very vulnerable: they are far from home, do not speak the local language or dialect, and are totally reliant on the husband's house and family. The lack of a support network, the language to appeal for help, or knowledge of their rights makes women in arranged marriages disproportionately likely to suffer abuse. Arranged marriages commodify women, who are bartered between the male heads of houses. This is not acceptable in an egalitarian society that emphasizes individual rights.

Arranged marriage separates immigrant communities and the wider society. It leads to cultural ghettoization and distrust in the wider community, which emphasizes individual rights and freedom of choice.

CONS

Arranged marriages are often very successful; only a very small number end in divorce. Millions of people marry for the "wrong" reasons: financial security, desire for children, parental pressure, and lack of choice among potential partners. To claim that all marriages must be love matches is pure romanticism.

Arranged marriages do involve choice. The difference is merely that whole families are involved in the decision. Many of what we would call arranged marriages are either parents introducing their children to potential partners or engaging in the negotiations necessary for marriage after their children have chosen a partner. Moreover, it is totally illogical for the government to intervene to stop people having the marriages that they and their families have chosen in the name of freedom of choice. We must stop forced marriages, but in a free society, people have the right to choose an arranged marriage.

Arranged marriages in Europe and North America have low levels of abuse and marital violence. Vulnerability of those without language skills is a problem for all immigrants, not just those in arranged marriages. Finally, most marriage organizers are women, who gain prestige and authority through their role. What you are really saying is that Islamic societies are patriarchal and that Muslims have arranged marriages.

Groups practicing arranged marriage are not the only ones set on maintaining cohesive communities; many groups retain a distinct cultural life while fully taking part in the life of this country. Their cultural contributions are one of the most valuable additions to modern multicultural societies. A multicultural society values people with different perspectives and traditions.

PROS	CONS
Arranged marriage is not an inviolate cultural value. Every major religion, including Islam, guarantees freedom of choice in marriage. Further, the custom is a product of a patriarchal culture that oppresses women. Although we cannot intervene in countries with such value systems, we can stop the importation of such systems. True multiculturalism relies on shared commitment to a tolerant and fair society.	Arranged marriage is a cultural tradition confirmed by ethnographic data. There is no conflict between arrangement and a guarantee of free choice; the two are entirely consistent. Western societies cannot dictate what is culturally valid for ethnic minorities. To do so would be ethnocentrism writ large. Furthermore, how can immigrants understand the importance we place on toleration if we deny them cultural freedom?
Arranged marriage provides a cover for illegal immigration. Authorities will challenge marriages of convenience between citizens and aliens but are reluctant to investigate arranged marriages because of the danger of being seen as culturally insensitive.	Most arranged marriages last beyond the time required for citizenship, so they would be legitimate under any circumstances.

Sample Motions:

This House would ban arranged marriages.
This House believes a true marriage is a free marriage.
This House believes marriage should be for love.

Web Links:

- Daily Princetonian. <http://www.dailyprincetonian.com/archives/2004/10/20/news/11161.shtml> Multiple perspectives on arranged marriage by Indian students.
- First Comes Marriage, Then Comes Love. <http://www.geocities.com/Wellesley/3321/win4a.htm> Essay describing how a marriage is arranged.
- NPR. <http://www.npr.org/templates/story/story.php?storyId=1054253> Discussion of the pros and cons of arranged marriage.

Further Reading:

Batabval, Amitrajeet A. *Stochastic Models of Decision Making in Arranged Marriages.* University Press of America, 2006.

Palriwala, Rajni, and Patricia Uberoi. *Marriage, Migration and Gender.* Sage, 2008.

Schwartz, Mary Ann, and Barbara Marliene Scott. *Marriages and Families: Diversity and Change.* 4th ed. Prentice Hall, 2003.

ASSASSINATION OF A DICTATOR

Often considered in the context of Adolf Hitler and Joseph Stalin, the issue regained topicality in the 1990s as leaders such as Saddam Hussein in Iraq and Slobodan Milosevic in Yugoslavia pursued bloody policies that led to war, ethnic cleansing, and genocide.

PROS	CONS
Deaths and much suffering could be prevented if one man is killed. The greater good demands a single evil act, especially if it would avert the immediate and certain danger of much worse evil.	Murder can never be justified. If we assume the role of executioner without the backing of law, we are sinking to the level of the dictators. Any new government founded upon such an arbitrary act will lack moral legitimacy, undermining its popular support and making its failure likely.
Dictatorial systems are highly personal, so removing the driving force behind such a regime will result in its collapse, allowing a more popular and liberal government to replace it.	Killing the individual will achieve nothing. Dictators are part of a wider ruling elite from which someone sharing the same autocratic values will emerge to take the assassinated leader's place. This successor is likely to use the assassination as the excuse for further repression.
Assassination of a dictator may be the only way to effect change in a country where a repressive police state prevents any possibility of internal opposition. Cowed populaces need a signal in order to find the courage to campaign for change.	Assassination is likely to be counterproductive, rallying popular feeling around a repressive regime as external enemies or internal minorities are blamed, rightly or wrongly, for the act. An unsuccessful assassination attempt is even more likely to bring about such a result.
Dictators are a threat to international peace, not just to their own people. They tend to attack other countries to divert attention from their unpopular actions at home, thus assassination is justified as a means of preventing a war that might rapidly become regional or global.	Sometimes dictatorship is preferable to the alternatives, especially for those outside the country itself. Great powers have often supported autocrats who promote such powers' geopolitical interests in a way that a democratic regime would not. Sometimes dictators have successfully held together countries that otherwise might have descended into civil war and ethnic strife.
If scruples over the morality of our actions prevent us from pursuing a greater good, effectively opposing evil will never be possible. Dictators themselves ignore most ethical standards and international conventions, thereby effectively placing themselves beyond the protection of the law.	By assuming the power to take life arbitrarily, even in an apparently good cause, we cheapen the value of life itself. Many terrorists, criminals, and dictators could and have claimed similar legitimacy for their violent actions. Only if we respect human rights absolutely will our promotion of these values seem valid to others.
The alternatives to assassination would all leave a dictator in power for many years. In that time not only will many more people suffer under a repressive system, but also the policies pursued by an out-of-touch and unrepresentative regime are likely to do serious harm to the whole nation and its economy, making eventual rebuilding much more costly in both human and economic terms.	Alternatives such as constructive engagement or economic sanctions are preferable and much more likely to result in eventual liberalization of the regime, albeit slowly. The examples of Eastern Europe in 1989 and Yugoslavia in 2000 show that even in apparently hopeless cases, change can come through popular action, often quickly and without great violence.
Tyranny and oppression are obvious wherever they take place. Tyrants use their power to inflict great suffering, ignoring universally accepted human rights. If leaders guilty of crimes against humanity can be brought to account through the normal democratic process or the courts, fine; if they cannot, their people have the moral right to take up arms against them. Sometimes this will mean assassination.	Who decides who deserves to be assassinated? Politics is not a black-and-white affair, and states viewed as dictatorships by some are seen quite differently by others. For example, Slobodan Milosevic could claim a popular mandate for many of his actions in the former Yugoslavia. General Augusto Pinochet in Chile seized power by force but later gave it up, allowing the emergence of a democratic state. Even if we had the right to make judgments as to which leaders deserve to die, our decisions would be arbitrary and without widespread support.

Sample Motions:

This House would assassinate a dictator.

This House would assassinate . . . (supply name of current dictator).

This House believes that murder isn't always wrong.

Web Links:

- The Future of Freedom Foundation. <http://www.fff.org/comment/com0508o.asp> Discusses past US involvement in the assassination of foreign dictators.
- Time to Kill? State Sponsored Assassination and International Law. <http://world-ice.com/Articles/Assassinations.pdf> Thorough analysis of international law relating to assassination.

Further Reading:

Boesche, Robert. *Theories of Tyranny: From Plato to Arendt.* Pennsylvania State University Press, 1995.

Brooker, Paul. *Non-Democratic Regimes: Theory, Government & Politics.* St. Martin's Press, 2000.

Lee, Stephen. *European Dictatorships, 1918–1945.* Routledge, 2000.

ASSISTED SUICIDE

Assisted suicide is currently being discussed and debated in many countries. The central question is: If a terminally ill person decides that he or she wishes to end his or her life, is it acceptable for others, primarily physicians, to assist them? For many years assisted suicide was illegal in all US states, but in the past decades organizations such as the Compassion and Choices have campaigned for a change in the law. They argue that terminally ill patients should not have to suffer needlessly and should be able to die with dignity. In 1997 Oregon became the first state to legalize physician-assisted suicide. Four years later conservative Attorney General John Ashcroft ordered federal drug agents to punish doctors who used federally controlled drugs to help the terminally ill die. In 2002 a district judge ruled that Ashcroft had overstepped his authority; in 2006 the Supreme Court let the Oregon law stand. In 2001 the Netherlands became the first country to legalize euthanasia and physician-assisted suicide.

PROS

Every human being has a right to life, perhaps the most basic and fundamental of all our rights. However, with every right comes a choice. The right to speech does not remove the option to remain silent; the right to vote brings with it the right to abstain. In the same way, the right to choose to die is implicit in the right to life.

Those in the late stages of a terminal disease have a horrific future: the gradual decline of the body, the failure of organs, and the need for artificial life support. In some cases, the illness will slowly destroy their minds, the essence of themselves. Even when this is not the case, the huge amounts of medication required to "control" pain will often leave them in a delirious and incapable state. Faced with this, it is surely more humane that these individuals be allowed to choose the manner of their own end and die with dignity.

CONS

There is no comparison between the right to life and other rights. When you choose to remain silent, you may change your mind at a later date; when you choose to die, you have no such second chance. Participating in someone's death is to participate in depriving them of all choices they might make in the future and is therefore immoral.

It is always wrong to give up on life. Modern palliative care is immensely flexible and effective, and helps to preserve quality of life as far as possible. Terminally ill patients need never be in pain, even at the very end. Society's role is to help them live their lives as well as they can. Counseling, which helps patients come to terms with their condition, can help.

PROS	CONS
Society recognizes that suicide is unfortunate but acceptable in some circumstances. Those who end their own lives are not seen as evil. The illegality of assisted suicide is therefore particularly cruel for those who are disabled and are unable to die without assistance.	Those who commit suicide are not evil, and those who attempt to take their own lives are not prosecuted. However, if someone is threatening to kill himself or herself, your moral duty is to try to stop them. You would not, for example, simply ignore a man standing on a ledge and threatening to jump simply because it is his choice; and you would definitely not assist in his suicide by pushing him. In the same way, you should try to help a person with a terminal illness, not help him to die.
Suicide is a lonely, desperate act, carried out in secrecy and often is a cry for help. The impact on the family can be catastrophic. By legalizing assisted suicide, the process can be brought out into the open. In some cases, families might have been unaware of the true feelings of their loved one. Being forced to confront the issue of a family member's illness may do great good, perhaps even allowing the family to persuade the patient not to end his life. In other cases, it makes the family part of the process. They can understand the reasons behind a patient's decision without feelings of guilt and recrimination, and the terminally ill patient can speak openly to them about her feelings before her death.	Demanding that family members take part in such a decision can be an unbearable burden. Many may resent a loved one's decision to die and would be either emotionally scarred or estranged by the prospect of being in any way involved with the death. Assisted suicide also introduces a new danger, that the terminally ill may be pressured into ending their lives by others who are not prepared to support them through their illness. Even the most well regulated system would have no way to ensure that this did not happen.
At the moment, doctors are often put into an impossible position. A good doctor will form close bonds with patients and will want to give them the best quality of life possible. However, when a patient has lost or is losing his ability to live with dignity and expresses a strong desire to die, doctors are legally unable to help. To say that modern medicine can totally eradicate pain is a tragic oversimplification of suffering. While physical pain may be alleviated, the emotional pain of a slow and lingering death, of the loss of the ability to live a meaningful life, can be horrific. A doctor's duty is to address his or her patient's suffering, be it physical or emotional. As a result, doctors are already helping their patients to die—although it is not legal, assisted suicide does happen. It would be far better to recognize this and bring the process into the open, where it can be regulated. True abuses of the doctor-patient relationship and incidents of involuntary euthanasia would then be far easier to limit.	A doctor's role must remain clear. The guiding principle of medical ethics is to do no harm: A physician must not be involved in deliberately harming her patient. Without this principle, the medical profession would lose a great deal of trust; admitting that killing is an acceptable part of a doctor's role would likely increase the danger of involuntary euthanasia, not reduce it. Legalizing assisted suicide also places an unreasonable burden on doctors. The daily decisions made to preserve life can be difficult enough. To require them to also carry the immense moral responsibility of deciding who can and cannot die, and the further responsibility of actually killing patients, is unacceptable. This is why the vast majority of medical professionals oppose the legalization of assisted suicide: Ending the life of a patient goes against all they stand for.

Sample Motions:

This House would legalize assisted suicide.
This House would die with dignity.

Web Links:

- End of Life Choices. <http://www.hemlock.org> Right-to-die group provides information on organization services and the progress of legislation legalizing assisted suicide.

- FinalExit.Org. <http://www.finalexit.org> General site containing information on legislation, euthanasia in practice, and individuals prominent in the campaign to legalize assisted suicide.
- Should an Incurably-Ill Patient Be Able to Commit Physician-Assisted Suicide? <http://www.balancedpolitics.org/assisted_suicide.htm> Provides an overview of arguments for and against doctor-assisted suicide.

Further Reading:

Gorsuch, Neil M. *The Future of Assisted Suicide and Euthanasia.* Princeton University Press, 2006.

Humphry, Derek. *Final Exit: The Practicalities of Self-Deliverance and Assisted Suicide for the Dying.* 3rd ed. Random House, 2002.

Terman, Stanley A. *The Best Way to Say Goodbye: A Legal Peaceful Choice At the End of Life.* Life Transition Publications, 2007.

BIODIVERSITY AND ENDANGERED SPECIES

"Biodiversity" refers to the variety of bacteria, plants, and animals that live on our planet and the unique behavioral patterns and activities of each species. Scientists believe that biodiversity is essential to human life on Earth. In recent years environmentalists have become concerned about the decline in the number of species. International agreements such as the Convention on International Trade in Endangered Species of Wild Fauna and Flora (CITES) aim to protect biodiversity. Nevertheless, current research suggests that species are disappearing at an alarming rate and that approximately one-quarter of all species will be extinct within the next few decades. Environmentalists are particularly concerned about endangered species in developing nations, where the economic needs of a poor population may threaten the existence of other life.

PROS

The species Homo sapiens is unprecedented and unique among all life on Earth. Human sentience and intelligence far surpass those of other creatures. These gifts have allowed human beings to populate the Earth, construct civilizations and build industry, and affect the environment in a way that no other species can. This great power comes with great responsibility, and we should avoid abusing our planet, lest we cause irreparable damage—damage like the extinction of species and the consequent reduction in biodiversity caused by deforestation, overfishing, hunting, and the illegal trade in animal products and exotic animals.

Protecting endangered species is an extension of our existing system of ethics. Just as modern civilization protects its weaker and less able members, so humanity should safeguard the welfare of other, less-privileged species. Animals are sentient creatures whose welfare we should protect (even if they may not have the same full "rights" that we accord to human beings).

CONS

The idea that extinctions will lead to ecological disaster is an exaggeration. Fossil evidence shows that mass extinctions have occurred many times throughout the history of life on Earth, one of the most recent being the die-out of the dinosaurs. After every collapse of biodiversity, it has rebounded, with Earth coming to no lasting harm. Extinctions are simply part of the natural evolutionary process.

No species on Earth would put the interest of another species above its own, so why should human beings? Furthermore, since the very beginnings of life, nature has operated by the Darwinian principle of "survival of the fittest." Life forms will always risk extinction unless they adapt to new challenges. Humans have no obligation to save the weaker species; if they cannot match our pace, they deserve to die out and be supplanted by others.

PROS	CONS
The most successful pharmaceuticals have often used nature as a starting point. Antibiotics were first discovered through the study of fungi, and many anti-cancer drugs are derived from the bark of Amazon trees. Every time a species becomes extinct, scientists forever lose an opportunity to make a new discovery.	Modern science has advanced to the point where inspiration from nature is no longer required. Today, medicines derived from natural products are in the minority. In any case, the upcoming era of genetic engineering will allow humankind to rid itself of disease without resorting to medicines.
As occupants of this planet, we must have respect for other life forms, especially since life on Earth may be the only life in the universe. We can show this respect by making every effort to prevent the extinction of existing species, thereby preserving biodiversity.	Even if this respect was justified, its expression comes at a significant cost. Biodiversity policies are costly and spend taxpayers' money that could better be used on health care and social services. It does not make sense for us to concentrate on other species when humanity has not yet sorted out its own welfare.
Maintaining biodiversity is a global problem and demands a global solution. The developed world should apply pressure on the developing world to adopt more environmentally friendly policies.	Environmental protection and the protection of biodiversity are very much a luxury of developed nations (First World). Many of these policies are beyond the financial means of developing nations, and implementing them would stunt economic growth and disenfranchise their citizens. It is hypocritical for developed nations to criticize the lack of environmental protection in the developing world, considering that the First World got to its current position through an Industrial Revolution that paid no heed to biodiversity, pollution, and other such concerns.

Sample Motions:

This House believes in biodiversity.

This House fears the way of the dodo.

Web Links:

- BBC News. <http://news.bbc.co.uk/2/hi/science/nature/7361539.stm> Article linking biodiversity to the development of medicine.
- EELink.Net: Endangered Species. <http://eelink.net/EndSpp> Offers information on endangered and extinct species, laws and policies on endangered species, and organizations involved in supporting biodiversity.
- The Natural History Museum, London: Biodiversity and World Map. <http://www.nhm.ac.uk/science/projects/worldmap/> Contains map of global biodiversity as well as information on biogeography and conservation priorities.

Further Reading:

Eldredge, Niles. *Life in the Balance: Humanity and the Biodiversity Crisis.* Princeton University Press, 2000.

Novacek, Michael J. *The Biodiversity Crisis: Losing What Counts.* New Press, 2001.

Thomas, Craig W. *Bureaucratic Landscapes: Interagency Cooperation and the Preservation of Biodiversity.* Massachusetts Institute of Technology Press, 2003.

BIOFUELS

Biofuels are sources of energy that come from living, renewable sources, such as corn, palm oil, and even animal manure. In recent years biofuels have come to mean fuels such as ethanol and biodiesel, which can be burned in engines to drive vehicles in place of fossil fuels like petroleum and diesel fuel. Biofuels have also been promoted as a way of reducing carbon emissions and thus tackling global climate change. More than 40 countries now offer some sort of subsidy to encourage the production and use of biofuels instead of fossil fuels. This topic looks at whether biofuels really are better than fossil fuels, and whether governments should continue to develop policies to promote biofuel production and use.

PROS

Biofuels are the best way of reducing our emissions of the greenhouse gases that are responsible for global climate change. As with fossil fuels, burning biodiesel or ethanol to drive an engine or generate electricity releases carbon into the atmosphere. Unlike with fossil fuels, however, growing the plants from which biofuels are made takes carbon from the air, making the overall process carbon neutral. This means policies to increase the use of biofuels could greatly reduce overall levels of carbon emissions, and thus make a major contribution to tackling global climate change. They can also help improve local air quality because mixing ethanol with fossil fuels helps meet clean air standards.

Unlike oil, biofuels are renewable and sustainable. At present humankind is using up fossil fuel resources at an alarming rate, and often damaging the environment in order to extract them. If we continue to rely on fossil fuels, they will one day run out, and not only will our descendants no longer have viable energy reserves, but they will also have to cope with the ecological damage that coal, oil, and gas extraction have inflicted on the earth. Making fuel from crops provides a perfect, sustainable solution.

CONS

In theory, biofuels appear to reduce overall carbon emissions, but in practice, they are much less environmentally friendly than their proponents claim. Although growing plants absorb carbon from the atmosphere, growing crops for biofuels uses large amounts of fertilizers, as well as fuel for running farm machinery and transporting the crops. The manufacture of biofuels also requires a lot of energy. All of this produces additional carbon emissions and means that biofuels are often not much better for the atmosphere than the fossil fuels they would replace, especially as more fuel needs to be burned to travel the same distance (because biofuels are less efficient than fossil fuels). Some biofuel crops (e.g., sugar cane) do produce much more energy than is needed to grow them, but making ethanol from corn may actually take 30% more energy than what it generates as fuel—and it is corn-based ethanol that US policy is backing so heavily.

The increased production of biofuels presents a growing environmental threat. If biofuels are to meet a significant part of our energy needs, vast areas will need to be devoted to crops such as oilseed rape, corn, sugar cane, and oil palms. These monocultures are very bad for biodiversity, denying wildlife and native plants places to live. And as the crops will not be grown for human consumption, it is likely that there will be greater use of pesticides, herbicides, and genetically modified crops—all very bad for the natural environment. The greatest environmental threat will be in the developing world, where profits from biofuel production provide strong incentives to cut down the remaining rainforest areas to create sugar cane or palm oil plantations, a process that can already be seen in Brazil and Indonesia.

PROS	CONS
The reliance of America and its Western allies on conventional fossil fuels, chiefly oil, is a major security issue. Much of the world's oil and gas is produced by unstable, unfriendly, or undemocratic regimes, none of whom can be counted on as reliable long-term partners when considering our future energy security. The past actions of OPEC and the recent willingness of Russia to use its supplies of natural gas to threaten European states both point to a need to reduce our dependence on fossil fuels. Some commentators have also argued that the money we pay to conservative Islamic states for oil often ends up funding terrorism and propping up potential enemies. Increasing the use of biofuels can, therefore, contribute to our security by ensuring that more of our energy needs are met from within our own country, reducing our dependence on foreign suppliers.	Attempting complete independence from other countries is impossible and undesirable—the world is now too interconnected and interdependent. Our prosperity rests on being able to trade goods and services widely with people in other countries and attempts to retreat from this free market will impoverish us as well as them. Nor are the US and its Western allies frighteningly dependent on just one source for their fossil fuel needs—new countries such as Angola, Nigeria, and Canada have all become major energy suppliers in the past decade. In any case, America's demand for energy is so great that there is no possibility of achieving energy independence through biofuels. Trying to produce enough ethanol domestically would require replacing food farming with biofuel crops—meaning the US could no longer feed itself, and would thus become heavily dependent on food imports instead.
There is plenty of scope to produce much greater quantities of biofuels without squeezing food production. Many developed countries have been overproducing crops such as wheat in past decades, leading to programs whereby farmers are paid not to grow crops on some of their land. Agricultural productivity continues to rise, especially in the developing world where new techniques and strains of seed, including types that are genetically modified to suit harsh conditions, will have a major impact.	Using agricultural land to grow biofuel crops means that fewer crops are grown for human consumption (or for feeding livestock). This pushes up the price of food for everyone but especially affects the poor, both in developed countries and in the developing world. Already Mexicans have found the price of their staple tortillas has risen sharply, as American corn is diverted to subsidized biofuel plants in the Midwest. The prices of sugar and palm oil have also experienced steep increases recently. If biofuel production is promoted even more, this trend will continue, contributing to increased poverty, malnutrition, and suffering. Given that our energy needs can be met by fossil fuels, it seems immoral to divert our agricultural resources unnecessarily.
The growth of biofuels will be good for farmers. In recent decades farmers in the developed world have produced more food than the market required, resulting in large surpluses and very low prices. A great many farmers have been driven out of business as a result, and few young people wish to try to make a living from the land. Meanwhile, surplus grain from America and the EU has often been dumped on markets in the developing world, harming local farmers who are unable to compete. Both kinds of farmers stand to benefit from increased demand for biofuels, as farm incomes improve and market-distorting surpluses disappear. Taxpayers may also benefit as there will be less need to subsidize more prosperous farmers.	Biofuels will not guarantee a glorious future for farmers. Oil prices have fluctuated widely over the past 20 years, and may well collapse again in the future, especially as high prices have encouraged investment in new production. Thus, more oil is likely to be produced in the next few years. Changes in the international situation could also reduce the "security premium" paid for fossil fuels since 2001. If oil prices sink back even to the (historically high) level of $50 a barrel, then biofuels will look much less economical and farmers will go bust as a result. And agriculture in the developing world is held back by the web of tariffs and subsidies the rich world uses to support its own farmers, not by market failure. Truly freeing the market in commodities such as cotton, grain, and sugar would do much more to bring prosperity to many desperately poor countries than any promise biofuels may seem to offer. After all, if the US or the EU

PROS

CONS

really wanted to promote biofuels, they would reduce their high tariffs on imports of cheap Brazilian sugarcane ethanol rather than pay their own farmers to produce biofuel from much less efficient corn or rapeseed.

Biofuels are now an economic alternative to fossil fuels, and with advances in technology and the scaling up of production, their price per gallon (or liter) will continue to fall. It appears likely that oil will maintain its current high prices well into the future, due to the exhaustion of many existing fields, strong demand from developing economies such as India and China, and security concerns that are unlikely to go away. Given these long-term trends, without investment in biofuel technology we actually run the risk that our economies will be crippled by sky-high fuel costs. Some subsidies to this investment seem highly justified, especially as they can replace existing agricultural support payments, rather than being additional money.

Biofuels are also a sensible bridge to a greener future, allowing us to develop a more sustainable future without unbearable economic or social cost. Unlike alternatives such as hydrogen fuel cells, biofuels do not need a completely different infrastructure to be widely adopted.

Biofuels are only competitive with fossil fuels because they are heavily subsidized, especially in the US, where the farming lobby has promoted ethanol out of pure self-interest. Subsidies on biofuels at the federal or state level cost American taxpayers about $5.5 to $7.5 billion each year. More costs will come if governments force automakers to build engines that can run on higher proportions of biofuel, as these will be passed on to the consumer in the form of more expensive vehicles. All of this subsidy and investment will be useless if the price of oil returns to its long-term average over the past 30 years, which will make biofuels uneconomic and ruin many farmers and industrial investors.

Biofuels already have a great deal to offer today, but prospects for the future are even more exciting and deserve our support. Crops like Jatropha, which are hearty succulents, promise to produce much more energy from a given amount of land. They also flourish without annual replanting or chemical inputs on marginal land. In the longer term, bioengineers are working on producing "cellulosic" biofuels—in which the stems and leaves, not just the fruits or seeds, of plants or trees are used to produce ethanol. Cellulosic biofuels would allow much more fuel to be produced from a given amount of land and could also be made from the waste products of food or timber production, such as straw and woodchips.

Biofuel technology may improve, but this is not guaranteed, and it may require more use of genetic engineering than the public is willing to tolerate. Even if the industry does live up to its proponents' optimistic promises, biofuels are still not the right focus of our energy policy. They may be a little better than fossil fuels, but they will never realistically replace them entirely, and their promotion takes attention away from more worthwhile approaches. Biofuels not only let the auto industry continue with business much as usual, they also provide a cover for the fossil-fuel industry by prolonging the life of the oil economy. A much better approach would be to concentrate on reducing our use of energy more radically. This could be achieved through conservation measures, improved fuel efficiency standards, new types of engine, replacing much private vehicle use with public transport provision, better town planning, and so on.

Sample Motions:

This House believes that biofuels are the future.
This House calls for more government support for biofuels.
This House believes that the government should act to encourage the production and use of biofuels.
This House believes it is easy being green.

Web Links:

- BBC News. <http://news.bbc.co.uk/2/hi/science/nature/6294133.stm> Overview article on biofuels with good Web links.
- Times Topics. <http://topics.nytimes.com/top/reference/timestopics/subjects/e/ethanol/index.html> Collection of *New York Times* articles on ethanol topic.

Further Reading:

Goettemoeller, Jeffrey, and Adrian Goettemoeller. *Sustainable Ethanol: Biofuels, Biorefineries, Cellulosic Biomass, Flex-Fuel Vehicles, and Sustainable Farming for Energy Independence.* Prairie Oak Publishing, 2007.

Mousdale, David M. *Biofuels: Biotechnology, Chemistry, and Sustainable Development.* CRC, 2008.

Pahl, Greg. *Biodiesel: Growing a New Energy Economy.* Chelsea Green, 2005.

CAPITAL PUNISHMENT

Approximately 90 countries have the death penalty, but nowhere is it debated so often as in the United States where, under the Constitution, each state can formulate its own policy. Thirty-six of the 50 states allow death penalties. In 2000, Gov. George Ryan of Illinois imposed a moratorium on executions in response to the high number of death row inmates found to be innocent of the crime for which they were incarcerated, frequently because new scientific techniques proved their innocence. He ordered a review of the death penalty system, asserting that it was so riddled with error that it came close to taking innocent life. Nine other states followed Illinois' lead. Before Ryan left office in early 2003, he pardoned four death row inmates and commuted the death sentences of all other inmates to life in prison without parole. In a speech justifying his action he said that the state's death penalty system was "arbitrary and capricious—and, therefore, immoral."

PROS

The principle of capital punishment is that certain crimes deserve nothing less than death as a just, proportionate, and effective response. The problems associated with the death penalty are concerned with its implementation rather than its principle. Murderers forgo their rights as humans the moment they take away the rights of another human. By wielding such a powerful punishment as the response to murder, society is affirming the value that is placed on the right to life of the innocent person. Many more innocent people have been killed by released, paroled, or escaped murderers than innocent people executed.

CONS

Execution is, in simplest terms, state-sanctioned killing. It devalues the respect we place on human life. How can we say that killing is wrong if we sanction killing criminals? More important is the proven risk of executing innocent people. The Death Penalty Information Center reports that from 1973 to 2008, 130 individuals sentenced to death were exonerated. They had their conviction overturned *and* were acquitted at retrial or all charges were dropped; or they were given an absolute pardon by the governor based on new evidence of innocence. These people could have been wrongly executed.

PROS

Capital punishment is 100% effective as a deterrent to the criminal being executed; that killer cannot commit any more crimes. As a deterrent to others, it depends on how often the death penalty is applied. In the US, where less than 1% of murderers are executed, it is difficult to assess the true effect of deterrence. But a 1985 study (Stephen K. Layson, University of North Carolina) showed that one execution deterred 18 murders.

CONS

High execution rates do not deter crimes. Murder rates have declined in every region of the United States except in the South where executions are most prevalent. According to a September 15 report, the South was the only region where the murder rate rose in 2008. The South consistently has had the highest murder rate among the four regions.

PROS	CONS
If and when discrimination occurs, it should be corrected. Consistent application of the death penalty against murderers of all races would abolish the idea that it can be a racist tool. Make the death penalty mandatory in all capital cases.	Implementation of the death penalty, particularly in the United States, may be negatively influenced by racial and gender bias. Studies consistently show that those who kill white victims are more likely to receive the death penalty than those who murder blacks. Nearly 90% of those executed were convicted of killing whites, despite the fact that non-whites make up more than 50% of all murder victims. There is also overwhelming evidence that the death penalty is used against men and not women.
Opponents of the death penalty prefer to ignore the fact that they themselves are responsible for its high costs by filing a never-ending succession of appeals. Prisons in many countries are overcrowded and underfunded. This problem is made worse by life sentences or delayed death sentences for murderers. Why should the taxpayer bear the cost of supporting a murderer for an entire lifetime?	Capital punishment costs more than life without parole as state studies in the US have shown. For example, a study found that the death penalty costs North Carolina $2.16 million per execution over the costs of a nondeath penalty system imposing a maximum sentence of imprisonment for life. A 2000 study of executions in Florida revealed that, based on 44 executions from 1976 to 2000, each execution cost $24 million because of legal expenses associated with these cases.
Different countries and societies can have different attitudes toward the justifiability of executing mentally incompetent or teenaged murderers. If society opposes such executions, then implementation of the death penalty in these cases is a problem. For opponents to seize on such cases is to cloud the issue; this is not an argument against the principle.	Defendants who are mentally incompetent will often answer "Yes" to questions in the desire to please others. This can lead to false confessions. Over 30 mentally retarded people have been executed in the US since 1976.
Some criminals are beyond rehabilitation. Perhaps capital punishment should be reserved for serial killers, terrorists, murderers of policemen, and so on.	By executing criminals you are ruling out the possibility of rehabilitation. You have to consider that they may repent of their crime, serve a sentence as punishment, and emerge as useful members of society.

Sample Motions:

This House supports the death penalty.
This House would take an eye for an eye, a tooth for a tooth, and a life for a life.

Web Links:

- Amnesty International and the Death Penalty. <http://www.amnesty.org/en/death-penalty> Takes an anti-death-penalty stance and presents facts and figures as well as current developments pertaining to the issue.
- Derechos Human Rights: Death Penalty Links. <http://www.derechos.org/dp/> Links to hundreds of sites on all aspects of the death penalty, both pro and con.
- Pro-Death Penalty.com. <http://www.prodeathpenalty.com> Offers information from a pro-death-penalty point of view; also contains good statistical information.

Further Reading:

Bedaue, Hugo Adam, and Paul G. Cassell. *Debating the Death Penalty: Should America Have Capital Punishment? The Experts on Both Sides Make Their Case.* Oxford University Press, 2005.

Sarat, Austin. *When the State Kills: Capital Punishment and the American Condition.* Princeton University Press, 2002.

Zimring, Franklin E. *The Contradictions of American Capital Punishment.* Oxford University Press, 2004.

CELL PHONES, BANNING OF USE IN CARS

Safety experts have blamed the use of cell phones while driving for causing a considerable number of traffic accidents. As a result, many countries and a number of US states, following the lead of Ireland and New York State, are seriously considering prohibiting drivers from using them. Although polls indicate that Americans overwhelmingly favor banning the use of handheld cell phones in cars, some contend that such prohibition will not solve the problem of distracted drivers.

PROS

Using a cell phone while driving is very dangerous. Physically holding a handset removes one hand from the controls, making accidents more likely, while dialing is even worse, as it also requires users to divert attention from the road. Research shows that drivers speaking on a cell phone have much slower reactions in braking tests than nonusers; such drivers have reaction times that are worse even than the reaction times of drunk drivers.

CONS

Clearly, using a cell phone while driving can be dangerous in some circumstances, but such use is not risky in many situations, for example while the car is at a standstill in gridlocked traffic, while waiting at traffic lights, or while driving on a quiet road with good visibility. Other actions in a car can be at least as distracting—eating, changing tapes, retuning the radio, arguing with passengers about directions, trying to stop children squabbling, etc. We should not introduce a law that victimizes cell phone users under all conditions, while ignoring many other causes of accidents.

Research shows very little difference between using a handheld and a hands-free cell phone, in terms of impaired concentration and slower reaction times in braking tests. For some reason the brain treats a telephone conversation differently from talking to a passenger, perhaps because the passenger is also aware of possible road hazards in a way the telephone caller cannot be and, accordingly, stops talking when the driver needs to concentrate. In any case, voice-activated technology is often unreliable, thus frustrating drivers, who lose concentration as a result. Banning one kind of cell phone while allowing the use of another kind would be inconsistent. In addition, hands-free cell phones cause just as many accidents.

Hands-free cell phone sets, with earpieces and voice-automated dialing, are the answer. These allow drivers to communicate freely without taking their hands off the controls or their eyes off the road. Effectively there is no difference between talking to someone on a hands-free cell phone and holding a conversation with a passenger next to you; in fact, the latter is more dangerous as you may be tempted to turn your head to directly address the passenger.

Existing laws are inadequate; driving without due care and attention is a limited charge that can be very difficult to prove. In any case, every time a driver of a moving vehicle uses a cell phone, a potentially dangerous situation is created. This justifies a specific offense being introduced.

Society has no need for a specific law relating to cell phone use; almost every country has laws against driving without due care and attention. Thus if someone is driving dangerously because of inappropriate use of a cell phone, the laws to prosecute are already on the books. The police should enforce the existing rules more

PROS	CONS
	consistently. Such enforcement could be coupled with energetic advertising campaigns to warn people of a range of potentially dangerous driving habits.
New laws would be enforceable because billing records show when a phone has been in use. Technological improvements in photography may also allow the automatic detection of drivers breaking laws against cell phone use at the wheel. In any case, just because a law is not completely enforceable does not mean that it should be scrapped.	Banning cell phone use by drivers will be unenforceable—often it will just be a policeman's word against a driver's. This is especially true of hands-free phones, where accused motorists could simply claim to be singing along to the radio or talking to themselves. In any case, the widespread introduction of speed cameras in many countries and an increased public fear of violent crime have led to the redeployment of the traffic police who would be needed to enforce such laws.
Using a cell phone in the car is unnecessary—everyone coped without them 10 years ago, and little else about life has changed radically enough to make them indispensable, so no real loss of personal liberty occurs with the banning of cell phone use while driving. Drivers always have the choice of pulling over and calling from a parked vehicle. The ban will also protect drivers from pressure from bosses who call them while on the road, requiring employees to risk their lives for the company.	Using cell phones on the road could improve safety, for example, by allowing delayed employees to call the office rather than drive recklessly in an effort to arrive on time. Drivers now often use cell phones to report accidents to the emergency services and alert the police to others driving dangerously, stray animals, unsafe loads, etc.
The state's authority to control the actions of drivers is already accepted, for example, through speed limits or rules against drunk driving. Dangerous driving meets the classic liberal test by endangering not just the individual but others, including drivers, passengers, and pedestrians, thus society has a right to intervene to protect the innocent. A new law signals social unacceptability and will send a message to drivers; the New York ban has already been highly effective.	The state has no right to interfere so blatantly in our personal liberties. Cell phones don't kill people, bad driving does, and simply banning the use of phones while driving will penalize the many good drivers without removing the dangerous ones.

Sample Motions:

This House would ban drivers from using mobile phones.
This House would do more to promote road safety.
This House would tame technology.

Web Links:

- Cato Institute. <http://www.cato.org/pub_display.php?pub_id=4414> Provides many statistics and analyzes whether a ban on the use of cell phones while driving is needed.
- Driven to Distraction: Cell Phones in Cars. <http://www.edmunds.com/ownership/safety/articles/43812/article.html> Analyzes the use of handheld and wireless cell phones in cars and their effect on safety.
- Insurance Institute for Highway Safety. <http://www.hwysafety.org> Contains information on all aspects of highway safety, including the use of cell phones.

CENSORSHIP OF THE ARTS

While all modern democracies value free expression, freedom of speech is never absolute. The restrictions a nation puts on speech are a product of its experience and culture. The United States views free speech as the cornerstone of American civil liberties and has few restrictions on expression. Nevertheless, conservatives have called for some type of censorship of art that they find morally offensive. Many people are also disturbed by studies that show a correlation between watching violent films and television shows and violent behavior.

PROS

An individual's rights end when they impinge on the safety and rights of others. By enacting laws against incitement to racial hatred and similar hate speech, we acknowledge that freedom of expression should have limits. Art should be subject to the same restrictions as any other form of expression. By making an exception for art, we would be creating a legal loophole for content such as hate speech, which could seek protection on the grounds that it was a form of art.

CONS

Civil rights should not be curtailed in the absence of a clear and present danger to the safety of others. Furthermore, as long as no illegal acts were committed in the creative process, the public should have a choice in deciding whether to view the resulting content. Arguments about child pornography displayed as art are irrelevant because child pornography is illegal.

PRO: Certain types of content (e.g., sexual content) are unsuitable for children despite their artistic merits. We should be able to develop a system of censorship, based on age, that protects our children.

CON: An age-rated system is a very blunt tool. It does not take into account differing levels of education or maturity. Censorship also deprives parents of the right to raise their children as they see fit. Adults have the right to vote, bear arms, and die for their country. Why should they be deprived of the ability to decide what they or their children see? Finally, we have to remember that people are not forced to view art; they don't have to look at something they think is offensive.

PRO: Censorship may actually help artists. The general public is far more likely to support erotic art if it knows that children won't see it!

CON: Censorship is far more likely to hurt the arts. If the government labels art as unsuitable for children, the general public is not going to want to fund it.

PRO: Many forms of modern art push the boundaries of what is acceptable or aim for the lowest level of taste. This type of content is unacceptable, and governments should have the right to ban it.

CON: Content that we consider acceptable today would have been regarded as taboo 50 years ago. If a novel or controversial piece of art is out of touch with society, society will reject it.

PRO: Excessive sex and violence in the media lead to similar behavior in viewers. This alone should justify censorship.

CON: The correlation between watching violence and committing violent crimes is still not established. These studies are not exhaustive, and often are funded by special interest groups. We must also realize that correlation is different from causation. An alternative interpretation is that people with violent tendencies are more likely to be connoisseurs of violent art. Even if we believe that some people are likely to be corrupted, why should all of society be penalized? There are far better ways of reducing the crime rate, with far less cost in civil liberties, than censorship.

PROS	CONS
Even if some individuals manage to circumvent censorship laws, government has sent an important message about what society considers acceptable. The role of the state in setting social standards should not be underestimated, and censorship (be it through bans or minimum age requirements) is an important tool in this process.	Censorship is ultimately not feasible. Try censoring art on the Internet, for example! In addition, censoring art merely sends it underground and might glamorize the prohibited artwork. It is far better to display it so that people can judge for themselves.

Sample Motions:

This House supports censorship of the arts.
This House believes that nude art is lewd art.
This House fears that artistic license is a license to kill.
This House believes that you are what you see.

Web Links:

- American Civil Liberties Union. <http://www.aclu.org/freespeech/gen/11046res20020227.html> Offers a comprehensive overview of the censorship of art and how it relates to freedom of expression.
- PBS. <http://www.pbs.org/wgbh/cultureshock/> A companion site to a PBS series on art, cultural values, and freedom of expression.
- University of Pennsylvania: Banned Books Online. <http://digital.library.upenn.edu/books/banned-books.html> Online exhibit discussing books that have been the objects of censorship and censorship attempts.

Further Reading:

Atkins, Robert, and Svetlana Mintcheva. *Censoring Culture: Contemporary Threats to Free Expression.* New Press, 2006.

Freedman, Leonard. *The Offensive Art: Political Satire and Its Censorship Around the World from Beerbohm to Borat.* Praeger, 2008.

Lane, Frederick S. *The Decency Wars: The Campaign to Cleanse American Culture.* Prometheus, 2006.

CHILD LABOR

In the past, activists have urged consumers to boycott companies that use child labor to produce goods. Is this response enough? Should the international community impose sanctions against governments that permit child labor? Ultimately the issue of using child labor is more a question of solving poverty than a simple moral or emotional issue. Any proposed sanctions would need to address several considerations—both general (Who would impose sanctions? How and to what extent would they be enforced?) and questions particular to this topic (What age is a "child"? Is child labor inherently an issue or is the debate really about minimum labor standards for all employees and employers?).

PROS	CONS
Governments have a duty to uphold human dignity. All people have the right to the benefits gained from education, a good quality of life, and independent income. Child labor destroys the future of the young and must be stopped.	While sanctions are effective for enforcing political and legal standards, they are less effective in dealing with social and economic ones. The world community cannot force an impoverished state to maintain Western standards of education and labor laws, which did not exist when the West industrialized.

PROS	CONS
Sanctions provide the only means of forcing countries to take action. Consumer pressure is too weak to do so. While people say they are willing to pay more for products manufactured in humane conditions, very few put this into daily practice.	Consumer power has proved highly effective in forcing transnational companies to institute ethical practices. Boycotts of one producer have led others to change their practices out of fear of negative publicity and possible boycotts. The market takes care of the problem itself.
Pressure on transnational companies is not enough. Not all child labor is in sweatshops for multinationals in poor countries. Children also work on family farms and as prostitutes. Some countries also force children into their armies.	Imposing sanctions on states is unfair because they are not wholly responsible for the actions of their citizens. Should we impose sanctions on the United States because it has illegal sweatshops?
Ending child labor will allow the young a greater chance to get an education and to develop fully both physically and socially, thus benefiting a nation's human resources and encouraging economic growth. The large number of underemployed adults in most developing countries can replace children. Often these will be the parents of current child workers, so there will be little or no overall effect on family income.	The vision of all former child laborers leaving work for school is utopian. Evidence shows that many either cannot afford to pay school tuition or continue to work while attending school. In fact, many transnational companies have now set up after-work schools within the very factories that activists criticize.
The international community was able to place human rights over the cause of free trade in the cases of South Africa and Burma—so why not here?	Placing sanctions on some companies will merely push child labor underground. Moving poor children who have to work into unregulated and criminal areas of the economy will only worsen the situation.
This is an argument for a targeted and more sophisticated use of sanctions, not against them in any form. Sometimes free market economics is simply an excuse for denying responsibility.	Sanctions harm the poorest in society. Companies will simply move to areas that do not have restrictions on child labor. Past experience has shown that government interference with the market does more harm than good.

Sample Motions:

This House believes that children should be free.
This House believes that education is the best economics.
This House would end child labor.
This House would put sanctions on states using child labor.

Web Links:

- Child Labor Coalition. <http://www.stopchildlabor.org> Information on child labor around the world and campaigns to end it.
- Free the Children. <http://www.freethechildren.com/getinvolved/geteducated/childlabour.htm> Information about child labor around the globe and the work of Free the Children.
- International Labour Organization. <http://www.ilo.org/ipec/lang--en/index.htm> Statistics and information on the International Programme on the Elimination of Child Labour.

Further Reading:

Hobbs, Sandy, Michael Layalette, and James McKechnie. *Child Labour: A World History Companion.* ABC-CLIO Europe, 2000.

Mizen, Phil, ed. *Hidden Hands: International Perspectives on Children's Work and Labour.* Routledge, 2001.

Schlemmer, Bernard, ed. *The Exploited Child.* Zed Books, 2000.

CHILD OFFENDERS, STRICTER PUNISHMENT FOR

Most US states have separate justice codes and justice systems for juvenile offenders. Traditionally the main goal of these systems has been rehabilitation rather than punishment; courts have frequently sentenced delinquents to probation or counseling rather than jail. During the 1980s and early 1990s, the US experienced an unprecedented wave of juvenile crime, and although juvenile crime had dropped by the mid-1990s, a series of high-profile school shootings and murders by children as young as six kept the issue in the news. In response nearly every state passed laws making it easier for minors to be tried and incarcerated as adults. The result was a 208% increase in the number of offenders under 18 in adult jails between 1990 and 2004. In 2007 the Christian Science Monitor *estimated that annually about 200,000 juveniles are prosecuted as adults—the majority of them for nonviolent offenses.*

PROS

The primary purpose of a justice system is the prevention of crime and the protection of the innocent. It is to achieve these purposes that children should not be entitled to lenient punishment. The purposes of punishment are proportional retribution, deterrence, and prevention of crime. Rehabilitation should at best be a secondary aim.

The "just desserts" theory of punishment argues that the retribution society takes against an offender should be proportional to the harm he has caused the victim. For example, a person who kills is more culpable than a person who robs or hurts. Because the harm children cause is the same as that caused by adults committing a similar offense, children should not receive special treatment. The assumption that children are not as morally culpable as adults is false.

Treating children more leniently than adults undermines the deterrent value of punishment. A 1996 survey in Virginia, for example, showed that 41% of youths have at various times either been in a gang or associated with gang activities. Of these, 69% said they joined because friends were involved and 60% joined for "excitement." This clearly shows that young adults do not take crime seriously because they think the justice system will treat them leniently.

The best way to prevent crime in the short run is to lock up the offenders. This stops them from immediately harming society. In the long term, these children will be reluctant to return to crime because of their memory of harsh punishment.

CONS

Child crime is different from adult crime. In most legal systems the offenders are not deemed to be fully functioning as moral agents. Thus, the best way to handle them is through rehabilitation rather than punishment.

Subjective culpability should play as important a part in punishment as the harm principle. That is why murder is punished more severely than negligent manslaughter, even though both cause the same harm. Children are not capable of making the same moral judgments as adults. It is the inability of children to form moral judgments that makes them less culpable and therefore worthy of lighter punishment.

The deterrence theory assumes that all crime is committed as a result of rational evaluation. If, indeed, 8- or 10-year-old children are capable of making rational calculations, then the prospect of spending several years in reform school should be no less a deterrent then spending the time in jail. It is still a curtailment of their liberty, and if they were rational, they would not want their liberty curtailed. The real problem is that most crimes are committed by people who do not make rational decisions.

This is an argument that would justify imprisoning people for life because that is the surest way to prevent them from harming anyone. Because this is plainly ridiculous, it must be accepted that locking a person up is at best a short-term remedy. The long-term answer lies in rehabilitation.

PROS

Rehabilitation (counseling and psychiatric treatment) is too lenient. It will make children believe that they are spending short periods of time at camp. In the US, more than half the boys who were ordered to undergo counseling rather than sentenced to detention committed crimes while in therapy. Rehabilitation programs should take place in a detention facility. Young offenders should be separated from hardened adult criminals, but they should not be given lighter sentences than adults who committed the same crimes.

CONS

The only long-term solution to juvenile crime is reform of the child. Children's characters are less formed and thus they are more amenable to reform. The rate of recidivism for child offenders in counseling in the US is significantly lower than that of adult offenders. Some children who have had counseling do return to crime, but a significant proportion does not. Putting children in prison with hardened adult offenders is likely to increase recidivism because they will be influenced by and learn from the adults.

Sample Motions:

This House would lower the age of criminal responsibility.
This House would punish children as if they were adults.
This House believes that sparing the rod spoils the child.

Web Links:

- Center on Juvenile and Criminal Justice. <http://www.cjcj.org> Information on alternatives to incarceration.
- Coalition for Juvenile Justice. <http://www.juvjustice.org/fp.html> Links to fact sheets and position papers on different aspects of the juvenile justice system.
- National Criminal Justice Reference Service—Juvenile Justice. <http://www.ncjrs.gov/app/topics/topic.aspx?topicid=122> Links to resources on the subject.

Further Reading:

Agnew, Robert. *Juvenile Delinquency: Causes and Control.* Oxford University Press, 2004.

Bartollas, Clemens, and Stuart J. Miller. *Juvenile Justice in America.* 5th ed. Prentice Hall, 2007.

Parry, David L. *Essential Readings in Juvenile Justice.* Prentice Hall, 2004.

CHILDREN, CHOOSING SEX OF

Until recently, would-be parents could only hope and pray for a baby of a particular gender, but with advances in genetic engineering, couples can select the sex of their child. While this technology may help prevent selective abortions and the abandonment of unwanted infants, it raises a series of ethical questions that divide both the lay and medical communities.

PROS

People should have freedom of choice. Their decision doesn't harm anyone else, so why shouldn't would-be parents be able to choose the sex of their child? Article 16 (1) of the Universal Declaration of Human Rights states that: "Men and women of full age . . . have the

CONS

We applaud freedom of choice, but not when it harms others. Apart from the danger that choosing the gender of the child could result in serious gender imbalances, making sexual selection legal and acceptable will rein force and legitimize gender stereotypes. Inevitably the

PROS	CONS
right to marry and to found a family." They, therefore, should have the right to make decisions about how that family is formed.	practice will result in more oppression of women, who in many cultures are already seen as less valuable than men. Nor does the Universal Declaration of Human Rights support sex selection. The Declaration's writers did not imagine recent developments in genetics when they drafted the document. However, they were determined to provide equal rights for women, which permitting gender selection would undermine.
Guaranteeing (or improving the chances of) a child being of the gender the parents want means that the child is more likely to be accepted and loved. Talk of designer babies is scaremongering nonsense. All babies are, to some extent, designed. Individuals do not procreate randomly: they choose their partners and often choose the time of conception based on their age and economic considerations. Parents give so much to children. They invest years of their lives and a large amount of their earnings in their children's upbringing. Isn't it fair that, in return, they get to decide the sex of the child if they want to? This is an extension of reproductive rights.	Children are not toys; they are not meant to be designed to specifications most convenient to the "owner." Choosing the sex of a child is an extension of our consumer society. If we allow parents to choose gender, soon some will want to choose eye or hair color, and we will encourage false ideas of perfection, damning those that don't look or act a certain way. If scientists discover a "gay gene," would parents be permitted to weed out embryos with it using the technology this proposal would condone? We should encourage parents to accept the children nature gives them. Otherwise, people will want to design more and more traits and be increasingly likely to reject their own child when they don't get exactly what they want.
Some cultures place great importance on having at least one child of a particular gender. We can help realize this goal. If a state's population becomes seriously imbalanced, we might have to rethink our position—but currently most families in most countries do not care about the gender of their children. In any case, over time a scarcity of one gender will produce new pressures to rebalance the population, e.g., the practice of paying dowries may end, women will achieve higher status.	This argument veils the likely result of the policy: reinforcement of already unhealthy cultural practices. Selective abortion has resulted in gender imbalances in China and India that are already extremely high—1.3 boys to each girl in some regions. These imbalances are socially harmful because eventually many young men will be unable to find a partner; in China sexual imbalance is already linked to a rise in sexual violence, kidnapping and forced marriage, and prostitution.
Knowing what gender a child will be is tremendously helpful for parents in planning for the future. Why not extend that ability to plan?	Having a child is a process of wonder and awe. These proposals make having children akin to pre-ordering a car. To many people, the moment of conception is the start of life, touched by God and not to be interfered with or abused out of selfish human motives.
Allowing the couple to have another child of the same gender might help relieve the trauma and grief of having lost a child.	Children are not replacements. They are individuals, unique in themselves. How will children feel if they know that their primary purpose is to serve as a fill-in for a dead sibling?
Some parents are carriers of known sex-specific conditions or diseases. Choosing the gender of the child will ensure that the parents do not pass on these conditions.	Ethical costs outweigh the medical benefits. Preimplantation genetic diagnosis involves the development of embryos outside the womb. These embryos are then tested for gender, and one or two of the desired gender are then implanted in the womb. Those that are not of the desired gender or are surplus to requirements

PROS

CONS

are destroyed (typically, more than a dozen embryos are used to select a single one to be implanted). A human life has been created with the express purpose of being destroyed. This is another form of abortion.

In many countries and cultures, gender selection happens already, usually by selective abortion or abandonment of unwanted babies. Everyone can agree that this is a terrible waste of life and potentially very dangerous for the mother. The use of new technologies to allow gender selection at the start of pregnancy will reduce and, hopefully, eventually end the use of selective abortion.

Many believe that new technologies are not morally different from abortion—in all cases a potential life is taken. In any case, the cost of these new methods is so high, and likely to remain so, that the proposition argument is irrelevant. These new technologies are likely to make selective abortion more common because they appear to legitimize throwing away a human life simply because the parents would prefer that their child were of a different sex.

Sample Motions:

This House would allow parents to choose the sex of their children.
This House would not leave it to chance.
This House believes in the parents' right to choose.
This House would choose a boy.

Web Links:

- DevBio. <http://7e.devbio.com/article.php?id=177> Detailed discussion of the ethical issues involved in topic.
- J Med Ethics. <http://www.pubmedcentral.nih.gov/picrender.fcgi?artid=1734079&blobtype=pdf> Analysis of the controversy surrounding genetic engineering and gender selection.
- Washington Post. <http://www.washingtonpost.com/wp-dyn/articles/A62067-2004Dec13.html> Summary of ethical concerns in gender selection.

CIVIL DISOBEDIENCE

Civil disobedience is the deliberate disobeying of a law to advance a moral principle or change government policy. Those who practice civil disobedience are willing to accept the consequences of their lawbreaking as a means of furthering their cause. Henry David Thoreau first articulated the tenets of civil disobedience in an 1849 essay, "On the Duty of Civil Disobedience." He argued that when conscience and law do not coincide, individuals have the obligation to promote justice by disobeying the law. Civil disobedience was a major tactic in the women's suffrage movement, the campaign for the independence of India, the civil rights movement in the United States, and the abolition of apartheid in South Africa.

PROS

Elections do not give the people sufficient opportunity to express their will. In certain circumstances civil disobedience is a powerful method of making the will of the public heard. If a law is oppressive it cannot be opposed in principle by obeying it in practice. It must be broken.

Civil disobedience has a history of overcoming oppression and unpopular policies where all other methods have failed. For example, Mohandas Gandhi's civil disobedience was instrumental in winning liberty for India, and Martin Luther King's tactics won basic rights for African Americans in the United States. In these cases no other avenue was open to express grievances.

In actual fact, the conflict with the authority gives any protest its power and urgency and brings an issue to a wider audience. The women's suffrage movement in Britain and the civil rights movement in the United States are both examples of an eventually successful campaign that won by its confrontation with authority, where more sedate methods would simply not have succeeded.

CONS

The "voice of the people" is heard in many ways. Elections take place regularly, and members of the public can write their local, state, or national representatives expressing their opinion. Legislators are there to represent and serve the people. Because citizens have many ways to express their views, civil disobedience is unnecessary. Protests can be made perfectly well without breaking the law.

Peaceful protest is quite possible in any society—to go further into actual lawbreaking is pointless. Civil disobedience can devolve into lawlessness. Indeed, it can be counterproductive by associating a cause with terror and violence.

Too often this "productive violence" is directed against innocent members of the public or against the police, often causing serious injuries. No cause is worth the sacrifice of innocent lives; protest must be peaceful or not at all.

Sample Motions:

This House supports civil disobedience.
This House believes the ends justify the means.
This House would break the law in a good cause.

Web Links:

- Civil Disobedience—The History Of The Concept. <http://science.jrank.org/pages/8660/Civil-Disobedience-History-Concept.html> Discusses famous advocates of civil disobedience.
- Civil Disobedience Index. <http://www.actupny.org/documents/CDdocuments/CDindex.html> Information on the history, theory, and practice of civil disobedience.
- Research Institute on International Activism. <http://www.international.activism.uts.edu.au/conferences/civildis/fiedler.html> Essay arguing that civil disobedience is a basic right.

Further Reading:

Arendt, Hannah. *Crises of the Republic.* Harvest Books, 1972.

Bedau, Hugo Adam. *Civil Disobedience in Focus.* Taylor & Francis, 2007.

Thoreau, Henry David. *Civil Disobedience and Other Essays.* Dover, 1993.

Tracy, James. *The Civil Disobedience Handbook: A Brief History and Practical Advice for the Politically Disenchanted.* Manic D Press, 2001.

CLIMATE CHANGE: REGULATIONS VS. MARKET MECHANISM IN DEALING WITH

Over the past 15 years most scientists and many politicians have come to believe that humankind is changing the world's climate. This is often called "global warming," and is blamed on the release of carbon gases into the air. This debate compares the two main ways that have been put forward for cutting carbon emissions: regulations and market mechanisms. Regulations would involve bringing in new government rules that companies and families have to follow. For example, regulations could set new standards for vehicle fuel economy or require companies and families to save energy by putting in green technologies, such as pollution filters, solar panels, more efficient heating systems, and low energy light bulbs. The other proposal is to put a price on carbon, so that it becomes expensive to release it into the air. This approach is called a market mechanism. Pricing carbon would give people and companies a strong reason to find ways of reducing their carbon emissions. There are two ways that a price could be put on carbon—a tax or a cap-and-trade system. A carbon tax would allow the government to charge people a sum of money for every ton of carbon they release into the air. A cap-and-trade system would set an overall limit on the amount of carbon that could be emitted each year. Companies would be given permits allowing them to release a certain amount of carbon into the air, and fined very heavily for exceeding their limit. Companies that could not reduce their emissions to the level allowed in their permit would have to buy permits in a carbon market. They would be buying from other companies that had successfully cut their emissions and so had spare permits to sell.

PROS

Market mechanisms put a cost on carbon emissions so that polluting becomes expensive. They will give a strong push to businesses and families to be more careful in their use of energy. Bringing in new technology to cut the amount of carbon their factories, vehicles, and homes put out will save them money. The more they cut emissions, the more they save (and the more profit companies will make).

The market will work better at a global level. Because each country generally sets its own regulations, pollution limits and vehicle fuel standards differ. This makes it difficult and expensive for international business to follow different regulations. And as increased regulation impacts trade and economic growth, individual countries (especially developing countries) may choose to set weak standards. Market methods are more likely to work across borders, linking every country into the same international system, as is already the case in global trade and finance. Developing states are more likely to accept a market system because they can profit from a carbon tax or from selling carbon permits.

CONS

We already have regulations to cut carbon emissions, so we do not need market methods. After all, businesses' greed has led them to pour pollution into our air, so they are unlikely to stop unless the government makes them. There are good examples of successful regulation. California as well as some European governments have set standards for fuel efficiency and exhaust levels, successfully reducing the environmental impacts of vehicle fuels. We should aim to expand and tighten these existing regulations rather than take a gamble on something untested.

Using the market sounds good in theory but it will not work in practice. There are many different types of carbon emissions, and some damage to the climate much more than others. Allowing for these differences in a market system is hard, but regulations can be more flexible, targeting the worst types of emissions with tougher rules. Moreover, significant polluters such as China and India have less open economies than those of most Western countries. Consequently, a market system would not work equally across the world. Unless we put off dealing with climate change until all economies work the same way, regulation is the only means to make an immediate difference.

PROS

Using the market will persuade people to choose greener ways of living. Regulations force people to do things against their will, which can be unfair and could make green ideas unpopular. Market mechanisms change the prices people pay but still allow them choices about how they live. A carbon tax or cap-and-trade system would raise the cost of electricity and gasoline, thus encouraging (rather than forcing) many people to change their lifestyle. They may choose to live closer to where they work or to their children's schools, take the bus or train rather than drive, vacation at home rather than abroad, or update their home heating system to one that uses less energy. Such changes will come quite quickly with market mechanisms, but regulations often take a long time to be implemented and effective. While tough standards generally apply only to new buildings, cars, or products, most people make do with what they already own for many years. This means it might take more than a decade after new rules are adopted for emissions to drop significantly.

Market solutions can take advantage of the fact that the cost of reducing carbon emissions is not the same everywhere. Western cars, homes, and factories are often so efficient that reducing their carbon output by even a tiny amount would cost a huge sum of money. In contrast, the older technology in less developed countries is often much more polluting. Spending a little bit of money to update it would prevent a huge amount of carbon from being pumped out. Putting a price on carbon means that money will be spent where it has the greatest effect. This means we can tackle climate change more quickly and with less damage to the world economy than we can by using regulations. That market mechanisms are likely to move money from the rich world to the poor is a positive side effect of the system.

The European trading system has run into problems, but this is primarily because politicians have interfered to protect industries in their own countries. Such meddling is even more common with government regulations, which often change so quickly that business cannot plan properly for the future. The EU is already improving its carbon trading scheme, and we can learn to design a global system based on their experience. For example, a smaller number of permits can be issued, and auctioned off to the highest bidders rather than given for free to old and inefficient industries. On the other hand, we could choose to implement a carbon tax instead, thus reliably putting a cost on pollution and ensuring that emissions are cut.

CONS

Economists love the idea of market mechanisms but they do not understand ordinary people. Consumers are actually not very sensitive to increased energy prices. Even if energy prices go up, they still have to cook and to light and heat their homes. So they will grumble about it but pay more rather than cutting the amount of energy they use. Similarly, if they need a car to go to work, they will not drive any less if fuel costs more. Instead they will cut back on other things, like vacations, clothes, or entertainment. Poor people with no spare money will end up suffering more than the rich do, whereas regulations will make everyone contribute to reducing emissions. In the long run, it might make sense to spend money making your house energy efficient or buying a more expensive but greener car, but the up-front cost of doing these things is too high for most people, even if they might recoup it in lower costs many years later. Governments will have to change the law if they want to make people to change their behavior.

Regulations are the best way to make every country play its part in tackling climate change. While rich countries are the ones that have pumped the most carbon into the atmosphere, market mechanisms will allow them to avoid their moral duty to make the most changes. A carbon market would allow them to buy a permit from a poorer country rather than change their own ways. In exchange, the developing country would not even have to actually reduce its own carbon output—it can merely promise not to increase it as much as it might have. Given the weak government and corruption in some developing countries, many people wonder how much some of these promises would be worth.

Instituting regulations is more reliable than trying to put a price on carbon emissions. The European carbon trading system has not worked well. The price for permits to release carbon into the air was extremely volatile before declining to such a low level that it is unlikely to have any impact on companies' behavior. Regulations better ensure that change takes place because they clearly specify the actions businesses must take. This allows companies to plan properly and encourages research and development of green technologies.

PROS	CONS
We all have some responsibility for climate change. Our lifestyles result in the release of large amounts of carbon into the air. Unless ordinary people can be convinced to change their behavior, we will never be able to tackle climate change. It is thus fair to use market methods that raise the price of energy to achieve this goal. Ways can be found to ensure that no one suffers under this new system. For example, other taxes can be cut to compensate for a carbon tax. Furthermore, using regulations to deal with emissions raises the cost of energy and fuel. Producers pass the increased costs of regulation on to consumers, and we have to pay more one way or another.	Putting a price on carbon unfairly punishes ordinary families. Making people pay more to heat their homes, cook meals, drive their cars, and so on will push many into poverty. We already pay high taxes, and this is just another way politicians have found to get their hands into our wallets. By contrast, big business makes plenty of profit and can afford to spend some of it on meeting new emissions regulations.
Market systems are easy to understand and run efficiently because everyone acts out of self-interest. Regulation means government control, and that means plenty of bureaucracy and red tape. A huge, complicated, costly system will be created to manage any new emission rules and standards. This not only raises taxes but also hurts the economy as business struggles to cope with the regulations. And because governments are so bad at regulation, the chances are that the system will fail to cut emissions significantly. Companies may cheat on the rules, realizing correctly that they are unlikely to get caught, and even if they are, any fines will probably be smaller than the cost of obeying the regulations.	Regulations are the best way to cut carbon emissions because, unlike market methods, they can be introduced with public support. Opinion polls show that people understand and back regulations like fuel efficiency rules, home energy standards, and so on. By contrast, carbon taxes are very unpopular because people do not trust the politicians who want to introduce them. Because cap-and-trade systems are so difficult to explain to ordinary consumers, the public will not back them. Moreover, running an international cap-and-trade system would require a big bureaucracy to enforce the emissions limits and prevent cheating. But unlike a system of national regulations, a cap-and-trade bureaucracy would be an international body, and thus be seen as a threat to our national independence.

Sample Motions:

This House believes that market methods are better than regulations in cutting carbon emissions.
This House believes the price is right.
This House believes in market solutions to the problem of climate change.
This House would rather put its faith in the market than in bureaucrats.

Web Links:

- BBC News. <http://news.bbc.co.uk/2/hi/business/4919848.stm> Article explaining the carbon trade.
- Climate Ark: The Lincoln Plan. <http://www.climateark.org/lincoln_plan> Accessible review of the issue.
- Friends of the Earth. <http://www.foe.co.uk/resource/factsheets/energy_climate_change.pdf> Overview of the topic from a broadly pro-regulation perspective.

Further Reading:

Bayon, Ricardo, Amanda Hawn, and Katherine Hamilton. *Voluntary Carbon Markets: An International Business Guide to What They Are and How They Work.* Earthscan Publications, 2007.

Houser, Trevor, et al. *Leveling the Carbon Playing Field: International Competition and US Climate Policy Design.* Peterson Institute, 2008.

Labatt, Sonia, and Rod R. White. *Carbon Finance: The Financial Implications of Climate Change.* Wiley, 2007.

COAL, USE OF

Coal is a fossil fuel extracted by underground or surface mining. Coal is used throughout the developed world for electricity generation, industrial power needs, and household heating. Coal is the largest single source of electricity consumed worldwide. In the United States approximately 50% of electricity is produced by coal power plants. Environmentalists around the world are concerned with the burdens imposed on the earth by an increasing population, demands for a higher standard of living, rising pollution, and increased dependence on fossil fuels. There is a finite amount of coal reserves, estimated to be able to supply the world for somewhere between 200 and 300 more years at current rates of consumption (although this is far longer than oil or natural gas reserves are likely to last). This presents a major problem, as populations are increasing, people are becoming more dependent on power-hungry technology, and business, industry, and agriculture are booming. Some argue that the United States is not making a sufficient effort to investigate and utilize alternative sources of energy, while other similarly situated industrialized countries are. For example, since the 1980s the UK has been decreasing its reliance on coal. Coal now supplies only 28% of its electricity production, with natural gas replacing coal as the primary electricity generating fuel. The US nuclear power industry has been required to invest in expensive measures to greatly reduce releases of radioactivity from nuclear fuel and fission products into the environment, but equivalent environmental measures do not currently apply to coal-fired power plants.

PROS

American has abundant domestic reserves of coal. Historically, access to a ready supply of coal has allowed the American economy to grow and has improved the quality of life in the United States. In the future, other sources of energy such as oil and gas will be limited and coal will become an even more important resource.

Increasing our use of coal fuel would allow the US to become more independent from oil-rich countries in the Middle East. As oil and gas become scarce and prices soar, coal will become the fossil fuel of last resort for many countries. As well as being burned for power, coal can also be turned into petroleum products, gas, and so on for use in transport and in the home. Investment now in coal mining, in coal-fueled power plants, and in substitution of coal for oil and gas will make the transition smoother and cheaper.

Since 1970, energy from coal has become increasingly clean, and technologies are currently being developed to make coal energy even cleaner. The US Department of Energy entered into a partnership with the coal industry to improve the efficiency of electricity generation from coal energy, while reducing carbon emissions and other pollutants. The Department of Energy estimates that new clean-coal–based power plants should be ready between 2010 and 2020. The US leads the world in this area of technology, and should continue to pursue it

CONS

Although the current amount of known coal reserves could sustain the world for 200–300 more years, scientists estimate that the amount of coal extracted from the ground could peak in the US as early as 2046. "Peak" defines the time after which no matter what efforts are expended, coal production will begin to decline in quality, quantity, and energy content.

Despite its abundance, coal will eventually run out and be replaced by alternative energy. It makes more sense to move directly to sustainable energy sources such as solar, tidal, and wind power than to invest in coal now, only to have to invest later in alternative energy.

Substances such as fly ash, bottom ash, and flue gas desulfurization are produced from coal waste. These all contain heavy metals such as arsenic, lead, mercury, nickel, copper, zinc, and radium, as well as low levels of uranium, thorium, and other naturally occurring radioactive isotopes. Although these harmful waste products are released only in trace amounts, so much coal is burned in the US that it may lead to radioactive contamination. This actually results in more radioactive waste than that produced by nuclear power plants.

PROS

as advances can be shared with other countries, to the benefit of the global environment. Much of the developing world will depend on burning coal for its future power needs, regardless of its polluting effect, so it will make a big difference if the US pioneers clean technology that the developing world can adopt.

To eliminate carbon dioxide emissions from coal plants, the method of carbon capture and storage has been proposed in the United States, but has yet to be used. Currently, there is no known limit to the amount of carbon dioxide and other greenhouse gas emissions that can be injected into the ground or into the ocean, to prevent their escape into the atmosphere. Modern power plants already utilize a variety of techniques to limit the harmfulness of their waste products and boost the efficiency of coal burning.

Relying on coal fuel is an economically sound policy. Coal ash is rich in minerals such as aluminum and iron. Such products are of great commercial value and can be extracted and further utilized to boost the US economy. Coal-fired plants are also cheaper to construct than nuclear power plants, mainly because of the absence of regulations necessary to prevent catastrophic accidents.

The nuclear fuel potential of the fertile isotopes released from coal combustion is not being utilized. As well as using coal for power generation, isotopes released from the process of coal combustion can be converted in reactors to fissionable elements by breeding. This would yield a virtually unlimited source of nuclear energy that is frequently overlooked as a natural resource.

CONS

Although technology is being developed to burn coal more cleanly and efficiently, these new methods are designed mainly to keep emissions below (generous) federal limits. They do not remove significant environmentally damaging emissions.

Emissions from coal-fired power plants represent the largest source of carbon dioxide emissions, the primary cause of global warming. The combustion of coal also produces chemicals that react with oxygen and water to produce acid rain. Since the carbon content of coal is much higher than oil, burning coal is a more serious threat to global temperatures. Although carbon capture is being proposed, it is largely untried and unproven. Many experts regard it as unlikely to offer much environmental benefit, with carbon dioxide likely to escape from any storage medium over the longer term.

Burning coal is dirty, and the costs for companies to do it cleanly and to comply with government regulations are prohibitively high. Future regulations are likely to become even more burdensome and expensive as environmental concerns become more important to policy makers, so investment in such plants makes little business sense.

Coal combustion raises significant national security concerns. The uranium residue from coal combustion can, over a few years, be accumulated as fissionable material to provide the equivalent of several World War II–type uranium-fueled weapons. Such fissionable material is accessible to any country that buys coal from the US or has its own reserves. Promoting this technology may, therefore, help hostile regimes equip themselves with weapons of mass destruction.

Sample Motions:

This House believes it is in the US's best interest to continue its current level of reliance on coal energy.
This House believes that the US should increase its dependence on coal energy.
This House would invest in coal.

Web Links:

- Australian Coal Association. <http://www.australiancoal.com.au/cleanoview.htm> Explanation of coal technologies from an industry group.
- Coal Combustion: Nuclear Resource or Danger. <http://www.ornl.gov/info/ornlreview/rev26-34/text/colmain.html> Article discussing the presence of trace amounts of radioactive materials in coal used for fuel, and the radiation released from combustion of such fuel.

- Greenpeace. <http://www.greenpeace.org/seasia/en/asia-energy-revolution/dirty-energy/clean-coal-myth/clean-coal-myths-and-facts> Information on the efficacy of clean coal technology from a site opposed to its use.

Further Reading:

Goodell, Jeff. *Big Coal: The Dirty Secret Behind America's Energy Future.* Mariner Books, 2007.

CONDOMS IN SCHOOLS

Should public schools actively promote the use of condoms as a way to prevent pregnancy, the spread of sexually transmitted diseases, and the proliferation of HIV infection? While scientific evidence overwhelmingly supports the contention that condoms, when properly used, reduce the incidence of these problems, numerous critics fear that advocating condom use would encourage children to become sexually active earlier than they otherwise would. In particular, more conservative religious traditions, as well as religious groups that oppose contraception, oppose the distribution of condoms in schools out of fear that such access might undermine basic religious values in their children.

PROS

Providing condoms to students in public schools will reduce the incidence of underage pregnancy and the spread of sexually transmitted diseases.

Providing condoms to students is the pragmatic thing to do. Educators need not endorse sexual activity, but they can encourage students to make wise choices if they decide to have sex. Such an approach is sensible because it accepts the inevitability that some young people, regardless of the strength of an abstinence message, will still have sex.

Providing condoms to students is a wise investment of government funds. World governments spend a fortune annually addressing the public health problems created by risky sexual behavior. The cost of raising the many children created through unintended pregnancies over a lifetime can be astronomical. The cost of treating a patient with HIV can be enormous.

Condom distribution encourages the responsibility of men and increases choices for women. It can also establish condom use as the norm, not something that women continually have to negotiate, often from a position of weakness.

Condoms are one of the most effective and cost-effective means of protecting against sexually transmitted diseases, HIV, and pregnancy.

CONS

Providing students with condoms actually encourages beginning sexual activity earlier.

Presenting condoms to students in public schools is offensive to people from a variety of religions who oppose birth control and sex outside of marriage.

Taxpayers should not have to support programs that they find morally objectionable, even if there seem to be pragmatic justifications for the action. Moreover, if overall sexual activity increases as the result of encouraging "safer sex," the number of people occasionally engaging in risky behavior will increase, and the risk of these problems spreading will increase with it.

Widespread condom distribution will establish sexual activity as the norm among young teens, creating peer pressure to participate in sex. The added temptation to engage in sexual activity that is "protected" will result in more women having sex at a younger age, perhaps contributing to their exploitation.

The effectiveness of condoms is grossly exaggerated. If not used properly, condoms can be highly ineffective. Young people are more likely to use condoms incorrectly,

PROS

CONS

due to lack of experience or because they are drunk. Moreover, the temptation to have sex without a condom may be significant where the supply of condoms is not plentiful.

Sample Motions:

This House would provide free condoms to all high school students.

This House believes abstinence-based sex education is superior to condom distribution in schools.

This House would give students the option of free access to condoms through their schools.

Web Links:

- Advocates for Youth. <http://www.advocatesforyouth.org/publications/factsheet/fsschcon.htm> Fact sheet on condom availability in high schools written from a pro-availability stance.
- Health Psychology. <http://healthpsych.psy.vanderbilt.edu/condomConumdrum.htm> Brief overview of pro and con arguments as well as empirical evidence and links to information on both sides of the argument.
- The Kaiser Family Foundation. <http://www.kaisernetwork.org/daily_reports/print_report.cfm?DR_ID=17970> Report on the effect of condom availability on high schools.

Further Reading:

Irvine, Janice M. *Talk About Sex: The Battles Over Sex Education in the United States.* University of California Press, 2002.

Levine, Judith. *Harmful to Minors: The Perils of Protecting Children From Sex.* University of Minnesota Press, 2002.

McKay, Alexander. *Sexual Ideology and Schooling: Towards Democratic Sexuality.* State University of New York Press, 2000.

CORRUPTION, BENEFITS OF

Public corruption is generally viewed as an obstacle to the development of a country. Many governments, international organizations, and aid agencies as well as donor-states have special agendas to fight the problem. Yet, in the countries with high levels of corruption, arguments have been made that because corruption is pervasive it has to have some benefit. While definitely not something to be proud of, public corruption is seen as an unavoidable side effect of development.

PROS

Corruption reduces bureaucracy and speeds the implementation of administrative practices governing economic forces of the market. Corrupt public officials acquire incentives to create a development-friendly system for the economy. As a result, corruption starts a chain of benefits for all the economic actors, making overregulated, obstructive bureaucracies much more efficient.

CONS

Countries with lower levels of corruption still have efficient bureaucracies and enjoy better economic well-being. Corruption in the public sector is the biggest obstacle to investment, causing misallocation of valuable resources and subversion of public policies. It is also an invisible tax on the poor. GDP levels for corrupted states could be much higher without corruption.

PROS	CONS
Corruption is a Western concept and is not applicable to traditional societies, where corruption does not have such a negative meaning. Many traditional societies with a "gift culture" have a different understanding of civil responsibilities and etiquette. The social structure and political traditions of many countries are based on the beneficial effect of corruption and cannot survive in its absence.	The very idea of corruption is unethical, regardless of one's traditions. Cultural relativism is just an attempt to legitimize corruption by the corrupted. Not enough evidence has been presented to support the suggestion that corruption is required by certain sociocultural practices. Moreover, regarding corruption as an innate quality of human culture undermines the hope for any improvement and is inherently fatalistic, serving as an excuse for creating cultures of corruption and fear.
Corruption is a condition of developing states, and should be seen as a childhood disease. Western countries themselves were once the most corrupted societies of the world. Not only is corruption endemic in underdeveloped nations, it is also an evolutionary level that precedes development and industrialization. Corruption is a side effect of emerging capitalism and a free market. Underdeveloped countries cannot combat corruption without having achieved the level of economic development necessary to fight it.	Corruption is universal, and the fact that a nation is economically developed does not mean that it has less corruption. Some First World countries have high rates of public corruption. Having a low level of corruption, however, gives a unique advantage to any developing nation. Appropriate policies can substitute for any positive effect of corruption.
In many countries corruption is a natural response to shortages. Often in developing countries the demand for a service such as access to the courts, education, health care, or the attention of civil servants and politicians far outstrips the ability of public officials to cope. To prevent the system from grinding to a complete halt, a way of rationing must be found, and corruption provides such a system. In effect, it places a price on a service and enables officials to prioritize and take some steps toward dealing with the demands on their time and resources.	Corruption may be a response to supply and demand, but it is still not beneficial. It ensures that public services are available only to the rich. Where corruption is widespread, the poor always lose out and society becomes ever more divided. Society suffers when corruption provides incentives for bright young people to get jobs as unproductive public officials because of the financial rewards from corruption. The private sector, already struggling from the added costs of corruption, suffers even more because it is unable to recruit the brightest and most ambitious young people. Economic growth suffers as a result.
Corruption is not a problem in its own right, but rather a symptom of wider problems of governance. Misguided socialist principles have left many developing countries (and some developed ones) with complex and burdensome tangles of rules and regulations administered by huge state bureaucracies staffed by poorly paid public officials. These problems make ordinary people highly dependent on the actions of individual officials and give such officials every incentive to exploit their power. Crackdowns on corruption will achieve nothing until these underlying problems are addressed.	Corruption is very bad for democracy because it can lead to special interests capturing the state. In corrupt societies, even free and fair election results count for little. Once in power, politicians are likely to concentrate on enriching themselves, promoting their own interests rather than those of their constituents or the nation. To avoid accountability, corrupt politicians then have an incentive to corrupt elections. This, in turn, creates contempt for democracy and makes dictatorship more attractive to many people. Finally, failure to deal with corruption is economically disastrous because it gives those in power the incentive to create new laws and regulations that they can exploit in order to extract bribes.

Sample Motions:

This House declares that anticorruption efforts do more harm than good.

This House confirms that corruption is unethical.

This House should fight public corruption.

Web Links:

- Global Corruption Report. <http://www.globalcorruptionreport.org> Project of Transparency International provides an extensive report on corruption around the world.
- Transparency International. <http://www.transparency.org> Information on global corruption.
- UN Office of Drugs and Crimes. <http://www.unodc.org/unodc/en/corruption/index.html> Information on UN action to combat corruption and links to corruption fighting agencies.

Further Reading:

Blundo, Giorgio, et al. *Everyday Corruption and the State: Citizens and Public Officials in Africa.* Zed Books, 2006.

Johnston, Michael. *Syndromes of Corruption: Wealth, Power, and Democracy.* Cambridge University Press, 2006.

Lambsdorff, Johann Grad. *The Institutional Economics of Corruption and Reform: Theory, Evidence and Policy.* Cambridge University Press, 2008.

CREATIONISM IN PUBLIC SCHOOLS

In the mid-nineteenth century, Charles Darwin articulated his theory of evolution, which argues that human beings evolved, over the course of millennia, from more primitive animals. This theory conflicts with the account of man's creation in Genesis, wherein Adam is created by God as the first fully formed human, having no predecessors. Although many believers think that evolution is compatible with the Bible, many others feel that the account in Genesis must be taken literally and that teaching evolution is an affront to their religious beliefs. Many states and school districts have tried to ban the teaching of evolution (most famously, the state of Tennessee, which prosecuted John Scopes in 1925 for violating its ban), but the Supreme Court ruled in 1968 that the purpose of such bans is religious and cannot be permitted in public schools. In 1987 the Supreme Court in Edwards v. Aguillard *declared unconstitutional Louisiana's Creationism Act forbidding the teaching of evolution unless the theory of creation science was also taught because the law specifically intended to advance a particular religion. A separate alternative to creationism has been intelligent design (ID), the belief that life is too complex to be explained by natural evolutionary processes and so can be accounted for only by invoking a designer. Over the years, believers in ID, including President George W. Bush, have continued to insist that it should be taught alongside evolution in the classroom. In 2004 a federal judge barred the teaching of intelligent design in public schools, saying it was the teaching of creationism in disguise.*

PROS

The Constitution forbids the establishment of any one religion, but it also guarantees freedom of religion, which means that the government cannot suppress religion. By teaching that evolution is true, schools are violating the religious beliefs of students.

CONS

In practice, there is no question that the supporters of creationism depend upon one religious tradition—the Judeo-Christian—and upon the account of creation in its sacred texts. Teaching creationism establishes, in effect, only that specific religious tradition, to the detriment of other religions and of nonbelievers. Teaching creationism in a publicly funded school is clearly a violation of the Constitution.

PROS	CONS
Evolution has not been proved; it is a theory used to explain observable facts. But those facts can be explained just as well, and in some cases, even better, by intelligent design theory. Moreover, evolutionists do not acknowledge that the evidence essential for proving their ideas—e.g., fossil remains of transitional, evolving beings—simply does not exist. Creationism is a theory that is at least as worthy as evolution and should be taught along with it.	Evolution is a theory that is based on verifiable scientific facts, but creationism is based on the revelations contained in scripture. Creationism cannot be taught as science because it is not consistent with standard scientific procedure.
By teaching intelligent design theory, a school is not doing anything to establish any particular religion. Intelligent design is accepted by Christians, Jews, Muslims, Native Americans, Hindus, and many others. Therefore, it should not be forbidden by the establishment clause of the First Amendment.	All religions offer a creation story, varying from religion to religion and from culture to culture. A public school might examine all of these beliefs in the context of a history of ideas course, rather than in a science course. In practice, however, creationists are not interested in exploring different beliefs; they are, rather, committed to putting one religious belief on equal footing with prevailing scientific thinking in the science classroom.
Creationism is not, as the Supreme Court has ruled, a religious belief. It is a scientific theory, and has been articulated by many philosophers and scientists, for example, Aristotle, in a completely secular context.	Creationism is not a scientific theory and is not accepted by the scientific community. Schools have a mandate to teach what is currently accepted by the country's scientists—that is, they must teach evolution, not material from outside the discipline of biology.
History has shown that scientific theories are often disproved over time; evolution, thus, should not be considered to be an unassailable truth. In the spirit of scientific inquiry and intellectual skepticism, students should be exposed to competing theories.	Science is morally and religiously neutral. It does not aim to uphold religious beliefs; it does not aim to debunk religious beliefs. Evolution is not taught as an attack on religion; it is taught as the best scientific explanation of available facts. Students are free to pursue their own private religious beliefs.

Sample Motions:

This House favors a curriculum free of creationism teachings in public schools.
This House believes that evolution ought to be taught instead of creationism.
This House thinks that teaching creationism in public schools is justified.

Web Links:

- Evolution and Creationism in Public Schools. <http://atheism.about.com/library/decisions/indexes/bldec_CreationismIndex.htm> Index of court cases on the issue.
- Evolution vs. Creationism. <http://physics.syr.edu/courses/modules/ORIGINS/origins.html> Information on both sides of the debate as well as links to articles, newsgroups, books, and FAQs.

Further Reading:

Binder, Amy J. *Contentious Curricula: Afrocentrism and Creationism in American Public Schools.* Princeton University Press, 2002.

Geisler, Norman. *Creation and the Courts: Eighty Years of Conflict in the Classroom and the Courtroom.* (Kindle Edition). Crossway Books, 2007.

Scott, Eugene C., and Glenn Branch. *Not in Our Classrooms: Why Intelligent Design Is Wrong for Our Schools.* Beacon, 2006.

CUBA, DROPPING OF US SANCTIONS ON

Fidel Castro and his communist government came to power in Cuba in 1959, much to the horror of the Eisenhower administration in the United States. Cuba was supported throughout the Cold War by the Soviet Union and became a flashpoint for Cold War tensions, notably during the Cuban Missile Crisis of 1962, when Nikita Khrushchev sparked the most dangerous Cold War confrontation by attempting to place nuclear weapons on the island. America has maintained near total sanctions on Cuba since 1959, but before 1990 they were largely offset by the support, trade, and subsidy offered by the Soviet Union. Since the collapse of the Soviet Union, the withdrawal of these subsidies has caused a 35% drop in Cuba's GDP. The decreased threat of communism has led to a reevaluation of the sanctions by the United States, but so far the wounds of the twentieth century, and the electoral significance of Florida where most Cuban émigrés live, has steeled the resolve of the White House. Sanctions were, in fact, strengthened significantly in the Helms-Burton Act of 1996, although recent measures have made food and medicine a little easier to move from the United States to Cuba. In November 2003 almost 180 UN delegations voted to end the unilateral sanctions. Nevertheless, the Bush administration remained adamantly opposed to lifting the embargo and has tightened restrictions on travel to Cuba. The administration has insisted that sanctions will remain until the Cuban government takes "meaningful steps" toward freedom, human rights, and the rule of law.

PROS

The sanctions cause real and unacceptable harm to the Cuban people. In the 1990s Cuba lost US$70 billion in trade and US$1.2 billion in international loans because of US sanctions. Cuba is too poor a country not to suffer from these losses. The dominance of America in the pharmaceuticals industry, moreover, means that Cubans are unable to gain access to many drugs. America would be the natural market for most Cuban products, and its refusal to accept goods with even the most minor Cuban components from third nations damages Cuba's ability to trade with other countries. Other South American countries have recently relied on the types of loans that Cuba is denied to keep their economies on track.

Sanctions are pointless and counterproductive. They've made no political difference in the last 43 years, why would they now? They result the US being blamed for all the failures of the Cuban economy, and sanctions are also used to justify repressive measures for security. President George W. Bush claims to want to empower civil society in Cuba, but in 1998, while governor of Texas, he argued that the best way to achieve this in China was to trade and spread "American values."

No legitimate reason has been offered for singling out Cuba for sanctions. Cuba has no biological, chemical, or nuclear weapons and does not sponsor terror. Cuba holds fewer prisoners of conscience than China, Vietnam, Iran, or even Egypt. To maintain sanctions to encourage change in the form of government, as the US

CONS

Sanctions didn't cause economic failure in Cuba. The communist political and economic system has been shown to lead inevitably to economic collapse with or without sanctions. Even if sanctions were lifted, lack of private ownership, foreign exchange, and tradable commodities would hold Cuba back. The International Trade Commission found a "minimal effect on the Cuban economy" from sanctions. In fact, the US can best contribute to an economic recovery in Cuba by using sanctions to pressure that nation into economic and political reforms.

Sanctions are a proven policy tool and can be used to pressure an extremely repressive regime into reforms. Aggressive US engagement and pressure contributed to the collapse of the Soviet Union. Sanctions are also, according to Secretary of State Colin Powell, a "moral statement" of America's disapproval for the Castro regime. Blaming America for all economic woes didn't fool ordinary Russians, and it won't fool Cubans. Now is exactly the time that the US should be tightening the screws so that Castro's successor is forced to make real changes.

Cuba is a repressive regime with one-party rule that holds political prisoners and stifles opposition and economic freedom through constant harassment. The Cuban government has refused to aid in the search for Al-Qaeda suspects and is on the US list of sponsors of terror because it provides a safe haven to many American

PROS	CONS
claims it is doing, is totally illegitimate under international law. Cuba has offered to compensate US citizens whose property was nationalized in 1959.	fugitives. Cuba is known to have a developmental biological weapons "effort" and is recorded as breaking international sanctions to export dual-use technologies to Iran. Finally, Cuba has failed to stop illegal drug shipments through its waters, and its government profits directly from resources stolen from US citizens in 1959.
Sanctions on Cuba are illegal and damage America's international standing. They violate the UN Charter, laws on the freedom of navigation, and repeated UN resolutions since 1992 (passed with only the US and Israel in opposition). Furthermore, some parts of the Helms-Burton Act are extraterritorial in their effects on the business of other nations and thus cause significant protest around the world. This makes a mockery of the US claim to be a guardian of international law, not only in its dealings with Cuba but also in the negotiations over the future of Iraq. America could achieve its goals internationally more easily if it were not for its own lack of respect for international law.	America is attempting to protect the rights enshrined in the Universal Declaration of Human Rights for both its own citizens and citizens of Cuba. If the US breaks international law, it is only to more fully realize the true aims of international law. The UN resolutions condemning the sanctions have never passed the Security Council and therefore lack any authority. America's status as a guardian of human rights and an enemy of terror is enhanced by its moral refusal to compromise with a repressive government just off its own shores.
The US will also benefit from the opening of trade with Cuba economically. Midwest Republicans have voted to drop the embargo because of the potential for profits in their farming states. Further, if sanctions end, Americans will be able to stop pretending that they prefer Bolivian cigars!	Cuba will never account for more than a tiny percentage of America's trade, and it is able to source and sell all its products elsewhere. Even if Cuba were a vital market for American goods, it would be worth giving up some economic growth to maintain a commitment to the freedom of the Cuban people. As it is, the total Cuban GDP is a drop in the ocean.
Sanctions are not the will of the American people but of a small minority of embittered Cuban Americans in Florida who are being pandered to. National opinion generally expresses no preference about or opposes the ban. In recent years the House of Representatives has voted by increasing margins to lift the ban on travel to Cuba, but the Bush administration remains opposed. This is electioneering government at its worst.	The people who care most about the Cuban question oppose dropping sanctions. The Midwest Republicans who voted to drop the travel ban are no less blinkered than the Cuban Americans who vote to keep it. Opinion on sanctions wavers; the separation of powers is in place specifically to allow the White House to maintain a stable policy on issues of national security.

Sample Motions:

This House would drop the sanctions on Cuba.
This House would sanction sanctions.
This House believes in Cuba Libre.
This House condemns US foreign policy.

Web Links:

- CubaNet. <http://www.cubanet.org> Provides latest news on Cuban domestic issues and international relations.
- Global Researcher. <http://www.globalresearch.ca/index.php?context=va&aid=7024>. Article written from an anti-sanction stance.
- Washington Post. <http://www.washingtonpost.com/wp-dyn/content/article/2007/12/19/AR2007121902291.html> Argues that sanctions against Cuba are excessive.

Further Reading:

Askari, Hossein G., John Forrer, Hildy Teegen, and Jiawen Yang. *Case Studies of U.S. Economic Sanctions: The Chinese, Cuban, and Iranian Experience.* Praeger, 2003.

Haney, Patrick. *Cuban Embargo: Domestic Politics of American Foreign Policy.* University of Pittsburgh Press, 2005.

Osieja, Helen. *Economic Sanctions as an Instrument of U.S. Foreign Policy: The Case of the U.S. Embargo Against Cuba.* Dissertation.com, 2006.

CULTURAL TREASURES, RETURN OF

Debate has raged for almost two centuries about the ownership and display of cultural treasures that were frequently acquired from the (then) developing world by imperial powers in the eighteenth and nineteenth centuries and displayed in Western museums. This debate most often uses the Elgin, or Parthenon, Marbles, masterpieces of classical Greek sculpture that Lord Elgin removed from the Parthenon in 1801 and sold to the British Museum in 1816. Greece has consistently demanded their return since independence in 1830. The issue of who owns cultural treasures reemerged following World War II, when the victorious Allies, principally the Soviet Union, seized art from the defeated Axis powers. During the last decades of the twentieth century, Native Americans successfully waged a number of campaigns for the return of their sacred relics.

PROS	CONS
Cultural treasures should be displayed in the context in which they originated; only then can they be truly understood. In the case of the Elgin Marbles, this is an architectural context that only proximity to the Parthenon itself can provide.	Art treasures should be accessible to the greatest number of people and to scholars. In practice this means displaying them in the great museums of the world. Returning treasures to their original context is impossible. Too much has changed physically and culturally over the centuries for them to speak more clearly in their country of origin than they do in museums where they can be compared to large assemblies of objects from a wide variety of cultures. In any case, copies could be placed in original locations.
Display of cultural treasures in Western museums is an unfortunate legacy of imperialism. It reflects the unacceptable belief that developing nations are unable to look after their artistic heritage. The display of imperial trophies in institutions such as the British Museum or the Louvre has become offensive.	For whatever reason the treasures were first collected, we should not rewrite history; sending such artifacts back to their country of origin would set a bad precedent that could denude museums around the world. Placing great artifacts in a geographical and cultural ghetto—African sculptures could be viewed only in Africa, Egyptian mummies only in Egypt—would leave the world much poorer and reduce popular understanding of the achievements of such civilizations.

PROS	CONS
Artifacts were often acquired illegally, through looting in war, under the duress of imperial force, or by bribing officials who were supposed to be safeguarding their country's artistic treasures.	Although some art treasures may have been acquired illegally, the evidence for this is often ambiguous. For example, Lord Elgin's bribes were the common way of facilitating any business in the Ottoman Empire and do not undermine Britain's solid legal claim to the Parthenon marbles based upon a written contract made by the internationally recognized authorities in Athens at the time. Much art was freely sold to the imperial powers, indeed some art was specifically produced for the European market.
Some treasures have religious and cultural associations with the area from which they were taken, but none for those who view them in glass cases. Descendants of their creators are offended by seeing aspects of their spirituality displayed for entertainment.	This may be true, but religious artifacts may have been originally purchased or given in good faith, perhaps with the intention of educating a wider public about the beliefs of their creators. Descendants should not be allowed to second-guess their ancestors' intentions. Also, many cultural treasures relate to extinct religions and cultures; no claim for their return can be validly made.
In the past, countries may not have been capable of looking after their heritage, but that has changed. A state-of-the-art museum is planned in Athens to house the surviving marbles, while pollution-control measures have reduced sulfur dioxide in the city to a fifth of its previous level. At the same time the curatorship of institutions such as the British Museum is being called into question, as it becomes apparent that controversial cleaning and restoration practices may have harmed the sculptures they claim to protect.	In the case of the Parthenon marbles, Lord Elgin's action in removing them was an act of rescue because the Ottoman authorities were pillaging them for building stone. They cared nothing for the classical Greek heritage. Furthermore, had they been returned upon Greek independence in 1830, the heavily polluted air of Athens would by now have destroyed them. Similar problems face the return of artifacts to African or Native American museums. Delicate artifacts would be destroyed without proper handling and preservation techniques. These institutions frequently lack the qualified personnel or necessary facilities to preserve these treasures.

Sample Motions:

This House would return cultural treasures to their country of origin.
This House would return the Elgin Marbles.
This House believes a jewel is best in its original setting.
This House would lose its marbles.

Web Link:

- Stolen Property or Finders Keepers. <http://home.att.net/~tisone/problem.htm> General site offering information on the issues concerning many stolen historical artifacts.

Further Reading:

Carman, John. *Against Cultural Property: Archaeology, Heritage and Ownership.* Duckworth, 2005.

Gibbon, Kate Fitz, ed. *Who Owns the Past? Cultural Policy, Cultural Property, and the Law.* Rutgers University Press, 2005.

Hoffman, Barbara, ed. *Art and Cultural Heritage: Law, Policy and Practice.* Cambridge University Press, 2005.

Merryman, John Henry, ed. *Imperialism, Art and Restitution.* Cambridge University Press, 2005.

CURFEW LAWS

More than 300 US towns have passed local curfew laws making it illegal for youths to be out-of-doors between certain publicized times. In most cases cities imposed nighttime curfews, but a 1997 survey indicated that approximately one-quarter had daytime curfews as well. All curfews are aimed at proactively reducing juvenile crime and gang activity. Officials also see curfews as a way of involving parents and keeping young people from being victimized. Opponents say the curfews violate the rights of good kids to prevent the actions of a few bad ones.

PROS	CONS
Youth crime is a major and growing problem, often involving both drugs and violence. Particularly worrying is the rise of youth gangs, which can terrorize urban areas and create a social climate in which criminality becomes the norm. Imposing curfews on minors can help solve these problems. They keep young people off the street and out of trouble. Curfews are easy to enforce compared to other forms of crime prevention and are therefore effective.	Curfews are not an effective solution to the problem of youth crime. Research finds no link between reduction in juvenile crime and curfews. Although some towns with curfews did see a drop in youth crime, this often had more to do with other law-enforcement strategies, such as zero-tolerance policing, or with demographic and economic changes in the youth population. In any case, most juvenile crime takes place between 3 p.m. and 8 p.m., after the end of school and before working parents return home, rather than in the hours covered by curfews.
The use of curfews can help protect vulnerable children. Although responsible parents do not let young children out in the streets after dark, not all parents are responsible. Inevitably their children suffer, both from crime and in accidents, and are likely to fall into bad habits. Society should ensure that such neglected children are returned home safely and that their parents are made to face up to their responsibilities.	Youth curfews infringe upon individual rights and liberties. Children have a right to freedom of movement and assembly, which curfews directly undermine by criminalizing their simple presence in a public space. This reverses the presumption of innocence by assuming all young people are potential lawbreakers. They are also subject to blanket discrimination on the grounds of age, although only a few young people commit crimes. Furthermore, curfews infringe upon the rights of parents to bring up their children as they choose. Just because we dislike the way some parents treat their children does not mean that we should intervene. Should we intervene in families whose religious beliefs mean girls are treated as inferior to boys, or in homes where parents practice corporal punishment?
Children have no good reason to be out alone late at night, so a curfew is not really a restriction on their liberty. They would be better off at home doing schoolwork and participating in family activities.	Children in their mid-teens have legitimate reasons to be out at night without adults. Many have part-time jobs. Others participate in church groups or youth clubs. Requiring adults to take them to and from activities is unreasonable. It will ensure many children do not participate in after-school activities either because adults are unwilling or are unable to accompany them. On a more sinister note, some children are subject to abuse at home and actually feel safer out on the streets.

PROS	CONS
Child curfews are a form of zero-tolerance policing. The idea of zero tolerance comes from the theory that if the police ignore low-level crimes they create a permissive atmosphere in which serious crime can flourish and law and order breaks down entirely. Child curfews can help the police establish a climate of zero tolerance and create a safer community for everyone.	Youth curfews have great potential for abuse, raising civil rights issues. Evidence suggests that police arrest far more black children than white for curfew violations. Curfews tend to be imposed in inner cities with few places for children to amuse themselves safely and legally. Curfews compound the social exclusion that many poor children feel with physical exclusion from public spaces. This problem is made worse by the inevitable deterioration in relations between the police and the young people subject to the curfew.
Child curfews can help change a negative youth culture in which challenging the law is seen as desirable and gang membership an aspiration. Impressionable youngsters would be kept away from gang activity on the streets at night, and a cycle of admiration and recruitment would be broken. By spending more time with their families and in more positive activities such as sports, which curfews make a more attractive option for bored youngsters, children will develop greater self-esteem and discipline.	Imposing curfews on children would actually be counterproductive because it would turn millions of law-abiding young people into criminals. More American children are charged with curfew offenses than with any other crime. Once children acquire a criminal record, they cross a psychological boundary, making it much more likely that they will perceive themselves as criminals and have much less respect for the law. This can lead to more serious offenses. At the same time, a criminal record decreases the chances for employment and so contributes to the social deprivation and desperation that breed crime.
We should try other ways of reducing youth crime, but they will work best in conjunction with curfews. If a troubled area develops a culture of lawlessness, identifying specific youngsters for rehabilitation becomes more difficult. A curfew takes the basically law-abiding majority off the streets, allowing the police to engage with the most difficult element. Curfews are a tool in the struggle to improve lives in rundown areas. They are likely to be used for relatively short periods to bring a situation under control so that other measures can be put in place and given a chance to work.	A number of alternative strategies exist that are likely to do more to reduce youth crime. Rather than a blanket curfew, individual curfews could be imposed upon particular troublemakers. Another successful strategy is working individually with young troublemakers. For example, authorities can require them to meet with victims of crime so that they understand the consequences of their actions. Youths can also be paired with trained mentors. Overall, the government needs to ensure good educational opportunities and employment prospects so that youngsters feel some hope for their futures

Sample Motions:

This House would introduce child curfews.

This House would lock up its daughters.

This House believes children should be neither seen nor heard.

Web Links:

- American Civil Liberties Union. <http://www.aclu.org/search/search_wrap.html?account=436ac9516921&q=curfew+laws> Links to articles on the legal status of curfews.
- Status Report on Youth Curfews in American Cities. <http://www.usmayors.org/uscm/news/publications/curfew.htm> Summary of 1997 survey of 374 cities providing status of curfews and information on their effectiveness.

Further Reading:

Jensen, Gary, and Dean G. Rojek. *Delinquency and Youth Crime.* Waveland Press, 1998.

DEMOCRACY, IMPOSITION OF

The US invasion of Iraq has raised the question of whether imposing democracy by force is permissible—or even possible. Many believe that for democracy to be successful, democratic institutions must develop gradually along with various social and economic structures. Countering this stance is the example of West Germany and Japan, which, following World War II, had democratic regimes imposed by the Allies. Both countries have become stable democracies.

PROS

History has shown that democracy is the best form of government. Countries have not only the right but also the duty to intervene to liberate others so they can enjoy their human rights. Furthermore, because war between two true democracies is rare, the removal of repressive regimes promotes world peace.

Merely pressuring dictators to move toward democracy is insufficient, and internal opposition is often too weak to compel reform. The international community cannot permit countries to shroud themselves in the pretense of free elections in order to gain international funding or to prevent invasion.

During the Cold War, Western powers often supported dictatorial regimes for reasons of realpolitik. This is inexcusable in the 21st century. Past complicity in dictatorships requires us to make amends by aggressively promoting democracy.

Limiting those states that harbor and trade with terrorists would reduce terrorism. Preventive attacks on dictatorships thwart future attacks.

Suggesting that people in various regions of the world will not accept the rule of law or protection for civil rights is fallacious. Democracy comes in enough forms to allow for social and historical variations—remember, illiberal political parties can always stand for election.

When a country is already engaged in conflict or civil war, intervention may help resolve the conflict. To wait, as occurred in Rwanda, will only permit carnage to continue longer.

CONS

Arguing that one nation can successfully impose democracy on another is untenable. Democracy relies on the rule of law (undermined by military imposition), freedom of choice and independence (destroyed by external determination), and accountability (impossible when a foreign power chooses one's rulers).

Encouraging democracy is not the same as imposing it. The desire for and fight for democracy must come from within; otherwise the political system will be unstable.

Turning on a regime that we once maintained is morally reprehensible. The 21st-century world is a dangerous place. Stability may be safer than universal democracy bought with many lives and at the price of massive resentment. The idea of democracy may be degraded in the eyes of many who associate it with invasions undertaken for suspect motives and the imposition of a culturally discordant polity.

The doctrine of prevention depends on analyzing unclear evidence; undertaking potentially unjustified invasions will result in increased support for terrorists. "Security" is merely an excuse for intervening in oil- or resource-rich areas, while those in poorer nations are left to suffer.

To impose democracy is to foist a set of Western values onto populations with different cultural backgrounds. Permitting the election of former dictators can lead to potentially serious problems in the future.

Intervention may escalate the conflict. Democracy may be encouraged after a war has ended; dictatorships can be undermined by economic and cultural sanctions. Neither requires costly (in lives and money) military action.

PROS

To rely on multilateral action is utopian. The UN Charter does not permit intervention in the domestic affairs of independent nations, and, in any case, some members of the Security Council are not democracies. Unilateral or bi-lateral action is the only realistic possibility.

CONS

Unilateral action is dangerously dependent on the political whim of foreign electorates who are often unwilling to commit troops and money to long-term nation building. A bloody invasion and regime change, followed by anarchy when the external power swiftly withdraws, is far worse than a dictatorship. Even when invaders remain to oversee the installation of a new regime, they may choose pliant appointees rather than risk the uncertainty of true democracy.

Sample Motions:

This House would force people to be free.
This House would impose democracy.
This House believes that freedom is worth imposing.

Web Links:

- Eurasianet. <http://www.eurasianet.org/departments/civilsociety/articles/eav022305.shtml> Article discussing the problems of imposing democracy.
- San Francisco Chronicle. <http://www.sfgate.com/cgi-bin/article.cgi?file=/chronicle/archive/2005/01/30/EDG7IB0VH01.DTL> Analyzes US foreign policy and how it relates to the imposition of democracy.
- United Nations Association of the United States of America. <http://www.unausa.org/site/pp.asp?c=fvKRI8MPJpF&b=730613> Policy brief on UN and US ways of nation building.

Further Reading:

Caralev, Demetrios James. *American Hegemony: Preventive War, Iraq, and Imposing Democracy.* Academy of Political Science, 2004.

Dobbins, James, et al. *America's Role in Nation-Building: From Germany to Iraq.* RAND Corporation, 2003.

Mead, Walter Russell. *Power, Terror, Peace, and War: America's Grand Strategy in a World at Risk.* Vintage, 2005.

DEVELOPING WORLD DEBT, CANCELLATION OF

For many years, poor nations in Asia, Latin America, and particularly Africa, have borrowed heavily to reduce poverty and foster development. Over the years external debt payments increased dramatically, often forcing countries to choose between paying their debt and funding social, health, and education programs. By the beginning of the new millennium the situation had reached a crisis in some countries. Sub-Saharan Africa owed lenders approximately US$200 billion, 83% of its GNP. Groups such as the International Monetary Fund (IMF) and the World Bank, with their Heavily Indebted Poor Countries (HIPC) initiative, are working toward a partial reduction or rescheduling of this debt, but demand adherence to strict economic reforms. In 2005 the HIPC initiative was supplemented by the Multilateral Debt Relief Initiative that grants total relief on eligible debts owed to the IMF, the World Bank, and African Development Fund if nations meet certain conditions. Two years later the Inter-American Development Bank developed a similar program for the HIPCs in the Western Hemisphere.

PROS

The burden of debt costs lives. Some of the most heavily indebted poor countries are struggling to pay even the interest on their loans, let alone paying down the principal. This massively distorts their economies and their spending priorities. African nations currently spend four times as much on debt repayments as they do on health. The reforms demanded by the IMF in return for rescheduled debt make this problem even worse. In Zimbabwe, spending on health care has dropped by a third, in Tanzania, school fees have been introduced to raise more money. Progress made in health and education over the past 50 years is actually being reversed in some countries. It is obscene that governments are cutting spending in these vital areas to repay debts. The debts must be cancelled now.

To raise the cash for debt repayments, poor countries have to produce goods that they can sell internationally. Often this means growing cash crops instead of the food needed to support their population. People in fertile countries can find themselves starving because they cannot afford to buy imported food.

Debt repayments often punish those who were not responsible for creating the debt in the first place. In a number of poorer countries, huge debts were amassed by the irresponsible spending of dictators in the past. They have now been overthrown, yet the new government and the people of that country still are required to pay the price for the dictator's actions. This is clearly unfair.

All poor countries need is the chance to help themselves. While their economies are dominated by the need to repay debt, it is impossible for them to truly invest in infrastructure and education. By canceling debt, we would give them a fresh start and the opportunity to build successful economies that would supply the needs of generations to come.

The developed world has a moral duty to the developing world because of the historical background of developing world debt. In the rush to invest in the 1970s, many

CONS

There are many reasons for the current problems in the world's poorest nations. They may often have heavy debt burdens, but the debt is not necessarily the cause of the problems. Many countries spend huge amounts of money on weapons to fight local wars instead of investing in their people. Many are led by dictators or other corrupt governments, whose incompetence or greed is killing their own population. The money to pay for social programs and, at the same time, repay debt may well exist, but it is being wasted in other areas.

Again, there are many potential causes for starvation—famines are caused by war or by freak weather conditions, not by debt. While growing cash crops can seem to be counterintuitive, the money they bring in helps boost the country's economy. The idea that a nation could and should be agriculturally and industrially self-sufficient is outdated.

This thinking has dangerous implications on an international level. Governments are always changing in democracies, but nations are expected to honor their debts. A crucial element in lending money is the promise that the debt will be repaid. If every new government could decide that it was not responsible for its predecessor's debts, then no one would ever lend money to a country. Developing countries in particular still need loans to invest in infrastructure projects. Canceling debt now would make lenders far less likely to provide loans on good terms in the future and would retard economic growth in the long term.

Reform must come first. Corrupt and incompetent governments and economic systems cripple many poor countries. Canceling debt would therefore make no difference, it would be the equivalent of giving a one-time payment to dictators and crooks, who would siphon off the extra money and become rich while the people still suffer. Even worse, dictators might spend more money on weapons and palaces, thus reincurring possibly even greater debt. A country's government must be accountable and its economy stable before debt reduction or cancellation is even considered.

The parallel with bankruptcy cannot work on a national scale. First, when an individual is declared bankrupt, most assets and possessions are seized to pay as much debt as

PROS

banks made hasty loans, pouring money into pointless projects without properly examining whether they would ever make a profit. Because of these bad investments, some of the world's poorest countries are so burdened with debts that they can now no longer realistically expect to pay them off and are instead simply servicing the interest. An important parallel may be made with bankruptcy: If an individual is unable to repay his or her debts, he or she is declared bankrupt and then allowed to make a fresh start. The same system should be used with countries. If they are unable to repay their debts, they should be given the opportunity to start again. A country making contributions to the world economy is far better than a country in debt slavery. At the same time, banks would be discouraged from making bad loans as they did in the 1970s.

CONS

possible. This is why banks find bankruptcy an acceptable option. In national terms, this would mean the total loss of sovereignty. Foreign governments and banks would be able to seize control of the infrastructure or the resources of the "bankrupt" country at will. No government could, or should, ever accept this. Second, the difference in scale is vitally important. Whereas the bankruptcy of a single individual within a country is unlikely to cause major problems for that country's economy, the bankruptcy of a nation would significantly affect the world economy. The economic plans of banks and nations currently include the interest payments on developing world debt; if this substantial revenue stream were suddenly cut off, economic repercussions could be catastrophic. Even if this debt relief would be helpful to the "bankrupt" countries in the short term, a world economy in recession would be in nobody's best interest.

Sample Motions:

This House would end developing world debt.
This House would kill the debt, not the debtors.
This House would break the chains of debt.

Web Links:

- International Monetary Fund. <http://www.imf.org/external/np/exr/facts/hipc.htm> Offers information on IMF debt-relief programs and progress.
- Jubilee Debt Campaign. <http://www.jubileedebtcampaign.org.uk/?lid=98> Research, analysis, news, and data on international debt and finance presented by an advocacy group dedicated to ending developing world debt.
- Worldwatch Institute. <http://www.worldwatch.org/node/1696> Statistics on debt in less developed countries.

Further Reading:

Hertz, Noreena. *The Debt Threat: How Debt Is Destroying the Developing World.* HarperBusiness, 2004.

Jochnick, Chris, and Fraser A. Preston. *Sovereign Debt at the Crossroads: Challenges and Proposals for Resolving the Third World Debt Crisis.* Oxford University Press, 2006.

United Nations Conference on Trade and Development. *Economic Development in Africa: Debt Sustainability: Oasis or Mirage?* United Nations, 2004.

DNA DATABASE FOR CRIMINALS

DNA evidence is playing an increasing role in criminal cases—both in convicting the guilty and clearing the innocent. The federal government and the states are building interlinked computerized databases of DNA samples. Initially these samples were taken from people convicted of sex crimes and a few other violent offenses, but recently the suggestion has been made to gather the DNA of all convicted criminals. Some officials have recommended expanding the database to include all individuals arrested, while others want the database to include DNA from everyone. Many people view extending the database beyond convicted criminals as an invasion of privacy and a violation of civil liberties.

PROS

DNA detection has considerable advantages over conventional fingerprinting. Fingerprints attach only to hard surfaces, can be smeared, or can be avoided by using gloves. Comparison of even a clear print from a crime scene with a print in the national database requires significant scientific expertise. Scientists can build an accurate DNA profile from very small amounts of genetic data, and they can construct it even if it has been contaminated by oil, water, or acid at the crime scene. The accused should appreciate a "fingerprinting" technique that is both objective and accurate.

The use of a DNA fingerprint is not an affront to civil liberties. The procedure for taking a sample of DNA is less invasive than that required for taking a blood sample. The police already possess a vast volume of information; the National Crime Information Center Computer in the United States contains files relating to 32 million Americans. A forensic DNA database should be seen in the context of the personal information that other agencies hold. Insurance companies commonly require an extensive medical history of their clients. Mortgage lenders usually demand a full credit report on applicants. Many employers subject their employees to random drug testing. If we are prepared to place our personal information in the private sector, why can we not trust it to the police? Law enforcement officials will use the DNA sample only in the detection of a crime. In short, the innocent citizen should have nothing to fear.

The creation of a DNA database would not require a disproportionate investment of time or public resources. The requisite computer and laboratory technology is already available. The United States has developed the Combined DNA Index System. The expense of sampling the entire population of most countries would be substantial and is unlikely to be offset by any subsequent saving in police resources, but this is part of the price for justice. Popular support for "law and order" suggests that the public puts a very high premium on protection from crime.

CONS

Although DNA detection might have advantages over fingerprint dusting, the test is nevertheless fallible. Environmental factors at the crime scene such as heat, sunlight, or bacteria can corrupt any genetic data. DNA evidence must be stored in sterile and temperature-controlled conditions. Criminals may contaminate samples by swapping saliva. There is room for human error or fraud in analyzing samples. In 2003, for example, in Houston, Texas, the police department was forced to close down its crime lab because of shoddy scientific practices that led to inaccuracies in DNA testing. Hundreds of cases were involved, including death-penalty cases. Even a complete DNA profile cannot indicate the length of time a suspect was present at a crime scene or the date in question. The creation of a database cannot be a panacea for crime detection.

DNA fingerprinting would have to be mandatory, otherwise those liable to commit crime would simply refuse to provide a sample. Individuals consent to pass personal information to mortgage or insurance agencies. When citizens release information to outside agencies they receive a service in return. In being compelled to give a sample of DNA, the innocent citizen would receive the scant benefit of being eliminated from a police investigation. Moreover, the storage by insurance companies of genetic information remains highly controversial because of the potential abuse of that information. Finally, creation of the database would change the attitude of government toward its citizens. Every citizen, some from the moment of their birth, would be treated as a potential criminal.

The initial and continuing expense of a DNA database would be a gross misapplication of finite public resources. Public confidence in the criminal justice system will neither be improved by requiring individuals to give time and tissue to the police nor by the creation of a bureaucracy dedicated to administering the database. The funds would be better spent on recruiting more police officers and deploying them on foot patrol.

PROS	CONS
Persons who create violent crimes are unlikely to leave conventional fingerprints. However, the National Commission on the Future of DNA Evidence estimates that 30% of crime scenes contain the blood, semen, or saliva of the perpetrator. DNA detection can identify the guilty even when the police have no obvious suspects.	The most serious violent crimes, notably rape and murder, are most commonly committed by individuals known to the victim. When the suspects are obvious, DNA detection is superfluous. Moreover, it is harmful to suggest that crimes can be solved, or criminals deterred, by computer wizardry. Unless the DNA is used to identify a genetic cause for aggression, violent crimes will continue.
A DNA database is not intended to replace conventional criminal investigations. The database would identify potential suspects, each of whom could then be investigated by more conventional means. Criminal trials frequently feature experts presenting scientific evidence. The jury system is actually a bastion against conviction on account of complicated scientific facts. If the genetic data and associated evidence is not conclusive or is not presented with sufficient clarity, the jury is obliged to find the defendant not guilty. O. J. Simpson was acquitted of the murders of Nicole Brown Simpson and Ron Goldman in spite of compelling DNA evidence linking him to the scene of the crime.	There is a serious risk that officials will use genetic evidence to the exclusion of material that might prove the suspect innocent. Moreover, there is the possibility that not only the police, but also the jury, will be blinded by science. It seems unlikely that juries will be able to comprehend or, more importantly, to question the genetic information from the database. The irony is that forensic evidence has cleared many wrongly convicted individuals but might now serve to create miscarriages of its own.
The increased use of DNA evidence will minimize the risk of future wrongful convictions. An FBI study indicates that since 1989 DNA evidence has excluded the initial suspect in 25% of sexual assault cases. Moreover, forensically valuable DNA can be found on evidence that has existed for decades and thus assist in reversing previous miscarriages of justice.	We do not need a database to acquit or exclude non-offenders. When the police have identified a suspect they ought to create a DNA profile and compare it to the crime scene data. Likewise, a DNA sample should be taken if there is concern that an individual was wrongly convicted of a crime.

Sample Motions:

This House would have a criminal DNA database.
This House would give away its DNA.
This House would catch a crook by his genes.

Web Links:

- DNA Tests and Databases in Criminal Justice: Individual Rights and the Common Good. <http://209.85.129.132/search?q=cache:pR9QYffjoLAJ:www.hks.harvard.edu/dnabook/Amitai%2520Etzioni%2520II.doc+dna+database+for+criminals+violation+of+privacy&hl=en&ct=clnk&cd=8&client=safari> Analyzes the conflict between individual rights and the common good presented by the issue.
- Genelex. <http://www.genelex.com/paternitytesting/paternitybook5.html> Detailed discussion of the use of DNA evidence in the courtroom.
- Los Angeles Times. <http://articles.latimes.com/2007/apr/05/opinion/oe-mnookin5> Article examining the injustice of a DNA database that is solely for criminals.

Further Reading:

Corrigan, O. *Genetic Databases: Socio-Ethical Issues in the Collection and Use of DNA.* Routledge, 2004.

Garfinkel, Simon. *Database Nation: The Death of Privacy in the 21st Century.* O'Reilly Media, 2001.

Rudin, Norah, and Keith Inman. *Introduction to Forensic DNA Analysis.* 2nd ed. CRC Press, 2001.

DRILLING IN THE ARCTIC NATIONAL WILDLIFE REFUGE

In 2002, the US Congress rejected a motion that would allow drilling for oil in the Arctic National Wildlife Refuge (ANWR) on the grounds that the area was ecologically sensitive. In 2006, however, as oil prices skyrocketed, the House voted to open the refuge to drilling. The Senate took no action. Oil developers and environmentalist have never engaged in a more highly charged and symbolic debate. Supporters of drilling claim that growing foreign dependence on oil threatens American security and that drilling in ANWR would help reduce that dependence. Opponents maintain that US dependence on foreign oil is inevitable and that drilling in ANWR would not significantly reduce dependence.

PROS

An oil pipeline runs through ANWR, and the same argument (ecology) was used to oppose its construction. However, the pipeline actually increased caribou numbers. Perhaps "keystone" species are not as "key" as has been supposed.

CONS

Drilling would disrupt certain ecologically sensitive areas. Alaska has caribou herds that move north to ANWR seasonally; drilling carries the risk of diverting and potentially reducing the herd. In addition, other key species live on Alaska's shoreline.

PRO: Drilling requires substantial amount of time, in some cases years. If we don't put the exploration and drilling structure in place now, it won't be available in times of crisis.

CON: Drilling would undercut a vital reserve that we may need in the future. The US is without long-term recourse, it is dependent on foreign oil; in times of crisis, however, drilling in ANWR could regulate prices for a limited time. So we should not drill now, we need to hold these reserves for an emergency.

PRO: The U.S. urgently needs to reduce its dependence on foreign oil. At present the United States needs 10 million barrels of imported oil a day, with much of this supply coming from unstable or unfriendly areas. National security depends on ensuring that the economy is never held hostage to foreign oil interests; the government should act to achieve energy independence. An important part of this is the development of untapped U.S. reserves, including the huge ANWR oil fields.

CON: Drilling in the ANWR will do nothing to make America more energy independent. Even the most optimistic estimates suggest that the fields under the refuge contain only 10 billion barrels of oil—equivalent to only two years U.S. consumption. Pumping a million barrels a day from the refuge would not even offset the likely growth in U.S. oil imports over the next 10 years. Achieving true energy independence means getting serious about conserving energy and investing in alternative energy sources, not feeding the U.S. addiction to fossil fuels.

PRO: Consumption is inevitable. Proponents of renewable energy have not made clear how opening ANWR would delay a transition to renewable energy. Opening ANWR could speed the transition by making the U.S. more dependent on foreign oil in the future (once the ANWR reserves were depleted) and thus give more of an incentive to convert.

CON: Oil development is unjustified because it further exacerbates the problems of consumption. The more we rely on fossil fuels, the longer we delay the inevitable: the vital shift to renewable energy. We should take other action to limit fuel consumption such as increasing the use of hybrid cars.

PRO: Drilling in the ANWR is an economic necessity. The high cost of oil over the past few years has meant misery for millions of Americans who cannot afford the high price of gasoline or heating oil. Only by bringing more oil to the market can we drive down prices. Opening the ANWR is also necessary for the Alaskan economy,

CON: Drilling in the ANWR won't reduce the price of oil because the amount of oil it contains is tiny compared to America's need. Global conditions such as the rise in Chinese demand set the price. In any case, we must be prepared to pay the costs of protecting the environment. If ANWR is developed for oil extraction, not only is its

PROS	CONS
bringing investment and safeguarding jobs as well as the way of life on America's last frontier.	status as a national wildlife refuge (NWR) under attack, but all other NWRs are also threatened. Big oil and other extraction companies will look greedily at other protected areas. If NWR status is to mean anything, it must be upheld everywhere and absolutely.
We may need to spread out proposed development, but we can make drilling seasonal to avoid disrupting animal migration. Caribou herds move into ANWR during specific and predictable times, thus we can schedule drilling and reduce the impact on the herds.	Proposed "limited development" will still intrude hundreds of miles into pristine areas. Alaska doesn't have a major reserve under ANWR; rather ANWR contains several reserves. Thus, even with "minimal" development, the damage would cover thousands of acres.

Sample Motions:

This House supports measures permitting oil development in ANWR.
This House believes development should be valued over ecology.
This House maintains that limited development in the ANWR is justified.

Web Links:

- Arctic National Wildlife Refuge. <http://www.anwr.org/> Provides justifications for oil development and gives up-to-date information on the status of prospects for drilling in the Arctic. Offers links to fact sheets and various other information in support of drilling.
- Defenders of Wildlife. <http://www.defenders.org/programs_and_policy/habitat_conservation/federal_lands/national_wildlife_refuges/threats/arctic/index.php> Web site of an antidrilling NGO offers information on impacts, campaigns, and legislation.
- US News. <http://www.usnews.com/articles/news/national/2008/05/23/arctic-drilling-wouldnt-cool-high-oil-prices.html> Article analyzing the impact of arctic drilling on oil prices.

Further Reading:

Bass, Rick. *Caribou Rising: Defending the Porcupine Herd, Gwich-'in Culture, and the Arctic National Wildlife Refuge.* Sierra Club Books, 2004.

Corn, M. Lynne. *Arctic National Wildlife Refuge: Background and Issues.* Nova Science Publishers, 2003.

Lieland, Barbara, ed. *Arctic National Wildlife Refuge (ANWR): Review, Controversies and Legislation.* Nova Science Publishers, 2006.

DRINKING AGE, LOWERING

Teenage drinking has long been a concern of policy makers in the United States. In response to widespread drunk driving fatalities among young people during the 1970s, the United States Congress passed a law in 1984 that effectively increased the legal drinking age from 18 to 21. While individual states are presumably free to maintain a legal drinking age of 18, the law would deny those states important federal funds, and has thus operated as a blanket national policy for nearly twenty-five years. Recently, university leaders have reinitiated a debate over the logic and effectiveness behind the prohibition, and a movement to lower the drinking age to 18 is gaining momentum. Among other arguments, proponents claim that the current law is discriminatory and has actually contributed to an increase in alcohol abuse within the targeted age group. Opponents of the measure insist that the current law has saved countless lives and is part of an effective strategy to combat alcoholism nationwide.

PROS

The current drinking age arbitrarily discriminates between people who are 21 years old and those who are younger, in violation of the US Constitution. Eighteen-year-olds are equally capable of making adult choices. In fact, US law assumes that 18-year-olds can handle serious responsibility in other contexts, including military service, jury service, voting, marriage, and contract formation. The decision to drink is arguably less weighty than these important responsibilities. Therefore, the line drawn is arbitrary and unjustified.

CONS

Although the law does distinguish between age groups, it does not violate the US Constitution. While it is true that government allows 18-year-olds greater freedom in other contexts, the government has a legitimate interest in preventing alcohol abuse by young people. Drinking has demonstrated and disastrous consequences and government has a strong interest in preventing these costs to society. Since the law is rationally related to these legitimate goals, it is valid.

The current age restriction is not an effective deterrent because it can never be fully enforced. Those under the age of 21 often use fake IDs and/or have older friends purchase alcohol for them. The law is even more difficult to enforce on college campuses, where young people from 18 to 22 years old socialize together and older students regularly purchase alcohol that is consumed by younger students.

The current law is effective because it makes alcohol more difficult to obtain. Just because a law cannot be fully enforced does not mean that it should not be upheld. There are criminal penalties for giving alcohol to minors, and these act as an additional deterrent. The dangers resulting from underage alcohol consumption are great, and countless lives have been saved since the law was implemented. Even partial deterrence is better than none at all.

Lowing the drinking age makes youth more responsible about drinking and helps to reduce future alcohol problems, including binge drinking. If American youth are allowed to consume alcohol earlier in their lives, as is practiced throughout Europe, they will avoid more destructive behaviors such as binge drinking. Such a culture also ensures that parents have greater oversight of and input into their children's drinking habits.

Lowering the drinking age does not make young people more responsible about drinking. Studies have shown that students who start drinking at younger ages tend to drink more heavily in college and have more drinking problems generally. Studies have also shown a relationship between younger age drinking and other serious problems such as drug abuse and depression. Finally, the idea that children who are allowed to drink at earlier ages will drink more responsibly is largely a middle-class myth. In England, where young people often drink alcohol from quite a young age, binge drinking is a serious nationwide problem.

Lowering the drinking age encourages young people with drinking problems to come forward and seek help. Since selling/providing alcohol to minors is currently criminalized, people with alcohol problems in this age group are unlikely to come forward for fear of punishment, both their own and their friends'.

A lower drinking age does not help alleviate alcohol problems among youth, but actually makes them worse. More teenage drinkers inevitably results in more teenagers with alcohol problems. Even if alcoholic teens felt less fearful about seeking help, there would be far more young people with alcohol problems.

Individual states should have the right to determine an appropriate drinking age for their residents. The law as it now stands punishes states that lower the drinking age by denying them much-needed federal highway funds. This effectively keeps states from being able to make specific, tailored decisions about what is best for their residents, because they cannot afford to forgo the highway funds. Such a law violates the fundamental principle of federalism.

States are indeed free to lower the drinking age to 18 if they so choose. However, the federal government has the right to withhold federal funds if a state does not comply with certain federal policies. Preventing alcohol-related problems is an important federal goal, and the federal government can withhold funds to encourage state compliance with that aim.

Sample Motions:

This House would lower the drinking age to 18.

This House supports maintaining the legal drinking age of 21.

Web Links:

- Alcohol Policies Project Fact Sheet. <http://www.cspinet.org/booze/mlpafact.htm> A Center for Science in the Public Interest summary of scientific data that support maintaining the drinking age at 21.
- Binge Drinking Costing Billions. <http://news.bbc.co.uk/2/hi/health/3121440.stm> BBC News report exploring the social and economic costs of binge drinking in England.
- Drinking Age Debate Spreading. <http://www.time.com/time/nation/article/0,8599,1835324,00.html?xid=feed-cnn-topics> *Time Magazine* article describing the recent debate, especially among university leaders, about lowering the drinking age.

DRIVING AGE, INCREASING

The controversy around increasing the driving age to 18 has swelled over the past several years. Automobile accidents continue to be the leading cause of death among teenagers, and amount to nearly 40% of all teenage fatalities. People who support the age increase point to the fact that 16-year-olds are simply not mature or responsible enough to engage in such an inherently dangerous activity. Opponents counter that increasing the driving age will merely delay consequences, inadvertently punish poorer households, and prevent young people from exercising adult responsibility.

PROS

Sixteen-year-olds are involved in more automobile accidents than 18-year-olds because they are less mature. Therefore, increasing the driving age will save thousands of lives. In a Canadian study, 16-year-old girls were found to have more driving accidents than 17- and 18-year-old girls with the same amount of driving experience. In New Jersey, which has increased the driving age to 17, it is estimated that hundreds of lives are being saved every year. The only way to substantially reduce the risk of automobile accidents for 16-year-olds is to prevent them from driving until they are mature enough to drive more safely.

Saving lives is more important than avoiding economic harm for a small group of people. Automobile accidents are the leading cause of death among teenagers. The fact that poorer families may be economically impacted is unfortunate, but it is not as important as reducing that risk. Furthermore, it is not clear that poorer families would suffer more. Less wealthy households tend to own fewer vehicles and are more likely to use public transportation. Therefore, it is probable that poorer teenagers share vehicles with household members and therefore drive less than their wealthier peers.

CONS

The problem is not maturity, it is lack of experience. Increasing the driving age will merely delay the consequences, not prevent them. First-time drivers will be just as inexperienced at 17 as they are at 16. In New Jersey, where the driving age is now 17, the accident rate among 17-year-old beginners is nearly identical to that of 16-year-old beginners in other states. The solution is not to increase the age threshold, but to require more driving education and practice before licensing. Some states have successfully lowered their teenage driving casualties by requiring more hours of driving lessons and practice with licensed adults.

Increasing the driving age will unfairly impact economically disadvantaged and/or nontraditional families. Not all heads of households are available to drive teenagers to their obligations. Teenagers can legally work at age 16. Many teens between the ages of 16 and 18 work to support themselves and/or their families and need to drive in order to do so. Often in these situations, other family members also work and are not available to provide transportation. If the driving age is raised, more wealthy and/or traditional families (in which a stay-at-home caretaker is available to escort teenagers and other children) will not be affected, but those families who do not fit that economic/social mold will suffer.

PROS

Driving is a dangerous activity that 16-year-olds are not responsible enough to engage in. The law limits children's power to make decisions and engage in certain activities in many other contexts. For example, society has decided that 16-year-olds are not prepared to serve in the military or to vote, due to the possible consequences of allowing them to do so. Most of Europe, China, Brazil, and Japan also prohibit driving for children under the age of 18. Sixteen-year-olds can still practice responsibility in many other ways, but the risks of teenage driving are just too great.

CONS

Driving is a great way for 16-year-olds to learn responsibility in that it allows them to gain independence from their parents, make autonomous decisions about their behavior and safety, and engage in an important adult activity. Increasing the driving age will limit this opportunity and make it more difficult for young people to transition to adulthood. Furthermore, such a law would be contradictory since our society allows 16-year-olds to work, an activity that often requires far greater responsibility than driving.

Sample Motions:

This House would increase the legal driving age from 16 to 18.
This House would vote to maintain the legal driving age at 18.

Web Links:

- Insurance Institute for Highway Safety: Put Off Driver Licensure to Save Lives. <http://www.iihs.org/news/rss/pr090908.html> The Insurance Institute for Highway Safety (IIHS) is an organization that advocates reducing the number of automobile accidents and fatalities.
- National Highway Traffic Safety Administration (NHTSA). <http://www.nhtsa.gov> The NHTSA homepage contains a link to multiple resources and publications about teenage driving.

DRUGS IN SPORTS

Over the past decade, the sports world has been rocked by revelations that world-class athletes have used performance-enhancing drugs. During 2002, major league baseball players Jose Canseco and Ken Caminiti alleged that a large percentage of players used steroids to enhance their performance; since 2003, Barry Bonds, who holds the record from most home runs in a season, has continually been dogged by allegations of having used steroids and other performance-enhancing drugs. In 2006 Tour de France winner Floyd Landis was fired from his team after testing positive for the steroid testosterone.

The use of steroids has not been confined to professional athletes. Young athletes have died as a result of steroid use, leading to bans on performance-enhancing drugs in high school and college programs. Nonetheless, doubts remain about the effectiveness of these tests and the fairness of some of the resulting bans. Some people argue that the whole approach is deeply flawed.

PROS

Using performance-enhancing drugs is an issue of freedom of choice. If athletes wish to take drugs in search of improved performances, let them do so. They harm nobody but themselves and should be treated as adults

CONS

Once some people choose to use these drugs, they infringe on the freedom of choice of other athletes. Athletes are very driven individuals who go to great lengths to achieve their goals. To some, the chance of a

PROS	CONS
capable of making rational decisions on the basis of widely available information. We should not forbid them performance-enhancing drugs even if such drugs have long-term adverse effects. We haven't outlawed tobacco and boxing, which are proven health risks.	gold medal in two years time may outweigh the risks of serious long-term health problems. We should protect athletes from themselves and not allow anyone to take performance-enhancing drugs.
What is the distinction between natural and unnatural enhancement? Athletes use all sorts of dietary supplements, exercises, equipment, clothing, training regimes, medical treatments, etc., to improve their performance. There is nothing "natural" about taking vitamin pills or wearing whole-body Lycra suits. Diet, medicine, technology, and even coaching already give an artificial advantage to those athletes who can afford the best of all these aids. As there is no clear way to distinguish between legitimate and illegitimate artificial aids to performance, they should all be allowed.	Where to draw the line between legitimate and illegitimate performance enhancement? Difficult though that may be, we should nonetheless continue to draw a line: first, to protect athletes from harmful drugs; second, to preserve the spirit of fair play and unaided competition between human beings at their peak of natural fitness. Eating a balanced diet and using the best equipment are clearly in a different category from taking steroids and growth hormones. We should continue to make this distinction and aim for genuine drug-free athletic competitions.
Legalizing performance-enhancing drugs levels the playing field. Currently, suspicion about drug use surrounds every sport and every successful athlete. Those competitors who don't take performance-enhancing drugs see themselves as (and often are) disadvantaged. There are no tests for some drugs, and, in any case, new medical and chemical advances mean that cheaters will always be ahead of the testers. Legalization would remove this uncertainty and allow everyone to compete openly and fairly.	Legalization is very bad for athletes. The use of performance-enhancing drugs leads to serious health problems, including "steroid rage," the development of male characteristics in female athletes, heart attacks, and greatly reduced life expectancy. Some drugs are also addictive.
Legalizing these drugs will provide better entertainment for spectators. Sport has become a branch of the entertainment business, and the public demands "higher, faster, stronger" from athletes. If drug-use allows athletes to continually break records or makes football players bigger and more exciting to watch, why deny the spectators what they want, especially if the athletes want to give it to them?	Spectators enjoy the competition between athletes rather than individual performances; a close race is better than a no-contest in a world record time. Similarly, they enjoy displays of skill more than simple raw power. In any case, why should we sacrifice the health of athletes for the sake of public enjoyment?
Current rules are very arbitrary and unfair. For example, the Olympics forbids athletes from using cold medicines, even in sports where the stimulants in these medicines would have minimal effects on performance. There is also the possibility that some positive tests are simply the result of using a combination of legal food supplements. Cyclists legally have heart operations to allow increased circulation and thus improve performance, but they would be banned if they were to use performance-enhancing drugs.	What about the children? Even if performance-enhancing drugs were legalized only for adults, how would you control the problem among children? Teenage athletes train alongside adults and share the same coaches. Many would succumb to the temptation and pressure to use drugs if these were widely available and effectively endorsed by legalization. Young athletes are unable to make fully rational, informed choices about drug taking, and the health impact on their growing bodies would be even worse than for adult users. Legalization of performance-enhancing drugs would also send a positive message about drug culture in general, making the use of "recreational drugs" with all their accompanying evils more widespread.

PROS	CONS
In many countries bans on performance-enhancing drugs fail to stand up in court. The legal basis for drug testing and the subsequent barring of transgressors from further participation is open to challenge, both as restraint of trade and invasion of privacy. Sports governing bodies often fight and lose such court cases, wasting vast sums of money.	Legalization discriminates against poor nations. Far from creating a level playing field, legalization would tilt it in favor of those athletes from wealthy countries with advanced medical and pharmaceutical industries. Athletes from poorer nations would no longer be able to compete on talent alone.
If drugs were legal, they could be controlled and monitored by doctors, making them much safer. Athletes on drugs today often take far more than needed for performance enhancement because of ignorance and the need for secrecy. Legalization would facilitate the exchange of information on drugs, and open medical supervision will avoid many of the health problems currently associated with performance-enhancing drugs.	Reform is preferable to surrender. The current testing regime is not perfect, but better research, testing, and funding, plus sanctions against uncooperative countries and sports could greatly improve the fight against drugs in sports.

Sample Motions:

This House would legalize the use of performance-enhancing drugs for athletes.
This House would win at all costs.
This House believes your pharmacist is your best friend.

Web Links:

- Patient UK. <http://www.patient.co.uk/showdoc/40024949/> Comprehensive overview of the use of drugs in sports.
- Performance Enhancing Drugs in Sports. <http://www.thedoctorwillseeyounow.com/articles/bioethics/perfdrugs_10/> Lays out arguments for and against the use of drugs in sports.
- Scientific American. <http://www.sciam.com/article.cfm?id=the-doping-dilemma> Article explaining why athletes resort to drugs and makes policy suggestions as to how doping can be prevented.

Further Reading:

Canseco, Jose. *Juiced: Wild Times, Rampant 'Roids, Smash Hits, and How Baseball Got Big*. Regan Books, 2006.

Jendrick, Nathan. *Dunks, Doubles, Doping: How Steroids Are Killing American Athletics.* Lyons Press, 2006.

Kuhn, Cynthia, Scott Schwartzwelder, and Wilkie Wilson. *Pumped: Straight Facts for Athletes About Drugs, Supplements, and Training*. Norton, 2000.

DRUG TESTING IN SCHOOLS

The right of schools to randomly test students for drugs has been debated in the courts for years. In a landmark 1995 decision Vernonia School District v. Acton, *the US Supreme Court ruled that schools could test student athletes for drug use. Three years later the US Court of Appeals for the Seventh Circuit (covering Illinois, Indiana, and Wisconsin) extended the right to test all participants in extracurricular activities, but in 2000 the Indiana Supreme Court banned such testing where the student concerned was not suspected of taking drugs. In 2002 the US Supreme Court ruled that drug testing was permissible for students involved in "competitive" extracurricular activities. Does society's desire to combat a growing drug problem override the right to privacy?*

PROS

Drug use among teenagers is a clear and present problem. Current measures to tackle drugs at the source (i.e., imprisoning dealers and breaking the supply chain) are not succeeding. It is especially important to protect teenagers at an impressionable age and at the time when their attitude to education greatly affects their entire lives. Some sacrifice of human rights is necessary to tackle the drug problem.

Students who do not take drugs have nothing to fear.

The purpose of random drug testing is not so much to catch offenders but to prevent all students from offending in the first place.

Peer pressure is the primary cause of experimentation with drugs. Discouraging drug use among athletes, model students, etc., sends a powerful message to the entire student body.

Urine, hair, and breath samples can be used to detect use of most common drugs, including marijuana, cocaine, heroin, and methamphetamines.

CONS

Our justice system is based on the principle that a person is innocent until proven guilty. To enforce random drug testing (thereby invading the privacy of students who are not suspected of drug use) is to view them as guilty until proven innocent. Nothing justifies the sacrifice of the human rights of innocent people.

Innocent students do have something to fear—the violation of privacy and loss of dignity caused by a drug test.

Other methods of preventing drug abuse are less invasive. These include encouraging extracurricular activities, fostering better relations with parents, tackling the problems of poverty and safety, and so on.

Teenagers, especially drug-taking teenagers, are attracted by rebellion and the chance of beating the system. Draconian, Big Brother–style tactics of random drug testing will only provoke resentment and encourage students to break the law. Peer pressure increases as they unite against school authorities.

Drug users will only turn to drugs that are more difficult to test, such as "designer" drugs, or use masking agents before being tested.

Sample Motions:

This House supports random drug testing in schools.
This House believes in a student's right to privacy.

Web Links:

- British Journal of General Practice: Random Drug Testing in Schools. <http://www.pubmedcentral.nih.gov/articlerender.fcgi?artid=1472793> Article arguing against random drug testing in school, outlining the effectiveness of testing, methods of testing, and problems with testing.
- Office of National Drug Control Policy. <http://www.whitehousedrugpolicy.gov/publications/drug_testing/> Comprehensive report providing an overview of the issue.
- Substance Abuse Resource Center. <http://www.jointogether.org/plugin.jtml?siteID=AMBIOMED&P=1> General site offering links to current news on drug-related topics as well as resources on issues, laws, and government policy.

Further Reading:

Lineburg, Mark. *Random Student Drug Testing in Virginia Public Schools.* VDM Verlag Dr. Müller, 2008.

ECONOMIC DEVELOPMENT VS. ENVIRONMENT

The issue of economic development versus environmental conservation can also be seen as the First World vs. the Third World. Industrialized nations, ironically those that are most responsible for current environmental problems, fear that unregulated economic development in the Third World will have disastrous long-term environmental effects on the planet. They point out that massive clearing of tropical forests for farmland is threatening biodiversity and may impact world climate, while a reliance on heavy industry to fuel economic growth adds more pollutants to the air, ground, and water. Developing countries counter that they must make industrialization and economic development a priority because they have to support their growing populations. Developing countries must address current problems; they cannot afford to worry about the distant future.

PROS

Taking care of the millions of people who are starving is more important than saving natural resources, most of which are renewable anyway.

The industrialized world's emphasis on protecting the environment shackles developing countries and contributes to and widens the great divide between the First and Third Worlds. By limiting the development of profitable but polluting industries like steel or oil refining, we are sentencing nations to remain economically backward.

Economic development is vital for meeting the basic needs of the growing populations of Third World countries. If we do not permit industrialization, these nations will have to implement measures to limit population growth just to preserve vital resources such as water.

Obviously the world would be better if all nations abided by strict environmental rules. The reality is that for many nations such adherence is not in their larger interests. For example, closing China's massive Capital Iron and Steelworks, which ecologists point to as a major polluter, would cost 40,000 jobs. The uniform application of strict environmental policies would create insurmountable barriers to economic progress.

Rapid industrialization does not have to put more pressure on the environment. Technological advances have made industries much safer for the environment. For example, nuclear generating plants can provide more energy than coal while contributing far less to global warming. We are also exploring alternative, renewable types of fuel.

The "Green Revolution" has doubled the size of grain harvests. Thus, cutting down more forests or endangering fragile ecosystems to provide more space for crops is no longer necessary. We now have the knowledge to feed

CONS

We have wasted and destroyed vast amounts of natural resources, and in so doing have put Earth in jeopardy. We must preserve Earth for future generations.

No one wants to stop economic progress that could give millions better lives. But we must insist on sustainable development that integrates environmental stewardship, social justice, and economic growth. Earth cannot support unrestricted growth.

Unchecked population growth has a deleterious effect on any nation and on the entire planet. Limiting population growth will result in a higher standard of living and will preserve the environment.

Nations are losing more from polluting than they are gaining from industrialization. China is a perfect example. Twenty years of uncontrolled economic development have created serious, chronic air pollution that has increased health problems and resulted in annual agricultural losses of billions of dollars. Thus, uncontrolled growth is not only destructive to the environment, it is also unsound economically.

Technological progress has made people too confident in their abilities to control their environment. In just half a century the world's nuclear industry has had at least three serious accidents: Windscale (UK, 1957), Three Mile Island (US, 1979), and Chernobyl (USSR, 1986). In addition, the nuclear power industry still cannot store its waste safely.

The Green Revolution is threatening the biodiversity of the Third World by replacing native seeds with hybrids. We do not know what the long-term environmental or economic consequences will be. We do know that in

PROS

the world's increasing population without harming the environment.

CONS

the short run, such hybrid crops can indirectly cause environmental problems. The farmer using hybrid seed, which is expensive, must buy new seed each year because the seed cannot be saved to plant the following year's crops. Farmers using hybrid seeds in what once was the richest part of India went bankrupt. As a result, fertile lands lay idle and untilled, resulting in droughts and desertification.

Sample Motions:

This House believes that environmental concerns should always take precedence over economic development in both the First and Third Worlds.

This House believes that economic growth, even at the expense of some environmental degradation, is justified by the need to feed the rising world population.

Web Links:

- Center for International Environmental Law. <http://www.ciel.org> Review of major international environmental agreements as well as information on the impact of globalization and free trade on sustainable development.
- International Institute for Sustainable Development. <http://www.iisd.org> Describes the institute's activities and offers reports and research materials on different aspects of sustainable development.
- United Nations Environment Programme: Division of Technology, Industry, and Economics. <http://www.uneptie.org> Presents information on UN programs associated with sustainable development.

Further Reading:

Cherni, Judith A. *Economic Growth Versus the Environment: The Politics of Wealth, Health and Air Pollution.* Palgrave, 2002.

Cole, Matthew A. *Trade Liberalisation, Economic Growth and the Environment.* Edward Elgar, 2000.

Lomborg, Bjorn. *The Skeptical Environmentalist: Measuring the Real State of the World.* Cambridge University Press, 2001.

ECONOMIC SANCTIONS VS. ENGAGEMENT

Economic sanctions are one of the most controversial ways whereby the international community seeks to influence a nation's internal policy and democratize countries. Sanctions helped end apartheid in South Africa, but the almost 50-year-old US embargo of Cuba has not brought down its communist government. China has a terrible human rights record, nevertheless sanctions have not been imposed on it. The question of whether to use trade to effect change is a subject of continuing debate.

PROS

Free trade brings about democratization in three ways: It permits a flow of information from Western countries; it raises a nation's standard of living; and it facilitates the growth of a middle class. These factors generate internal

CONS

Most dictatorial oligarchies welcome free trade as it usually increases their wealth. The West no longer has any leverage over them once they have been accepted into the free trade arena. Although the international community chose

PROS	CONS
pressure and consequent political change—economic freedom leads to political freedom. Free trade helped bring about the downfall of communism in Eastern Europe and is beginning to increase freedoms in China. When the United States linked most favored nation (MFN) status to improvements in human rights, China made only token gestures to improve its rights record to maintain MFN status. Deep structural changes in human rights in any country come only with unlimited free trade.	not to impose sanctions on China because it is a valuable economic and strategic partner, trade, specifically MFN status, can still be used to force China to improve human rights. Believing that free trade can lead to democratization is naïve. Governments against which sanctions are imposed will not permit the growth of a middle class or let wealth filter down to the people. In reality free trade has worsened Chinese living standards by putting domestic industries out of business and forcing people to work for multinational corporations that pay little.
Sanctions are ineffective. For example, France and Russia currently have openly breached international sanctions against Iraq because of their complete failure. Sanctions against Cuba, Haiti, and Burma have also proved useless because many nations do not recognize them. In addition, once sanctions are in place, the government of the country being sanctioned keeps all available resources, ensuring that sanctions adversely affect only the people. In the case of Iraq, sanctions led to terrible suffering.	Sanctions are effective as a long-term tool. They worked in South Africa and they worked in the former Rhodesia. Granted, they can lead to mass suffering of the very people they are designed to help, as they did to the black population of South Africa. However, Nelson Mandela has said that the suffering was worthwhile because it helped end apartheid.
Sanctions block the flow of outside information into a country, thus permitting dictators to use propaganda to strengthen their own position. People cannot believe such propaganda is false when there are no competing external claims.	Sanctions send a strong message to the people of a country that the Western world will not tolerate an oppressive regime.

Sample Motions:

This House would put trade relations above human rights.
This House believes in free trade.
This House would make money not war.
This House would engage, not estrange, nondemocratic nations.

Web Links:

- Are Economic Sanctions Effective Without the Threat of Military Intervention? <http://www.takingitglobal.org/express/panorama/article.html?ContentID=2454> Examines the effectiveness of economic sanctions.
- Cato Institute Center for Trade Policy Studies. <http://www.freetrade.org> Site, advocating free trade, includes essays on China, the Cuban embargo, and the failure of unilateral US sanctions.
- USA*Engage. <http://usaengage.org> Information on current US sanctions and potential sanctions by a coalition of American businesses, trade associations, and agriculture groups that oppose unilateral US action.

Further Reading:

Askari, Hossein G., John Forrer, Hildy Teegen, and Jiawen Yang. *Case Studies of U.S. Economic Sanctions: The Chinese, Cuban, and Iranian Experience.* Praeger, 2003.

Krustev, Valentin. *Bargaining and Economic Coercion: The Use and Effectiveness of Sanctions.* VDM Verlag, 2008.

Von Sponeck, H.C. *A Different Kind of War: The UN Sanction Regime in Iraq.* Berghahn Books, 2006.

ELECTORAL COLLEGE, ABOLITION OF

The presidential election of 2000 gave new prominence to the Electoral College. Although Al Gore received more popular votes than George W. Bush, Bush won the election because his victory in Florida gave him a majority of electoral votes. To some observers, this outcome demonstrated clearly that the Electoral College should be abolished. They feel it is an anachronism that has outlived its usefulness. To others, however, the result demonstrated that the Electoral College is both good and necessary, and that the system had worked as it was designed to do.

PROS

The president should be the person chosen by the greatest number of Americans, via the popular vote. The Electoral College violates this mandate in principle and sometimes in practice.

The Electoral College was established at a time when the people were not trusted to choose wisely; senators, too, were initially not chosen by popular vote. The system should be changed to trust the wisdom of the American people.

The Electoral College system gives greater weight to votes cast in lightly populated states. The result is that a vote cast for the president by a New Yorker counts less than a vote cast by a North Dakotan; this inequality is inherently unfair.

The lightly populated states that are privileged by the Electoral College system are overwhelmingly white. In effect, the system discounts the worth of votes cast by minorities living in urban areas and exacerbates the racial imbalance of power in the country.

The current winner-take-all system effectively eliminates third-party candidates, as they cannot win enough Electoral College votes to gain office. The result? The electoral process is predisposed to the status quo, and change and progress are discouraged.

Too much latitude is given to electors in the present system; in some states, electors are not required to cast their votes for the candidates who have won the popular vote in their states. Electors should not have the power to disregard the will of the people.

CONS

The Electoral College ensures that the person elected president has broad support throughout the country. Without the college, candidates could win by appealing only to heavily populated urban areas.

The principle behind the Electoral College is similar to the principle that determines the composition of the Senate, wherein every state is deemed equal, no matter its size. The college is an integral part of the system of federalism, which gives the states distinct and important rights.

The Electoral College forces candidates to campaign broadly throughout the country to gain the electoral votes of as many states as possible. If it is eliminated, candidates will spend all their time campaigning in the states with the greatest number of voters and ignore smaller states.

Minority voters could be safely ignored by candidates in a national election that depended only on receiving a popular majority. But because these voters can determine who wins a majority—and the electoral votes—in a given state, their influence is significant in the present system.

Because no candidate can win the presidency without an absolute majority of electoral votes, the Electoral College promotes the strength of the two-party system and that system promotes the political stability of the country.

The Constitution designed the US government to include a series of checks and balances, and the Electoral College is part of that system. The Electoral College is meant to limit the "tyranny of the majority" that is possible in unrestrained democracy.

Sample Motions:

This House supports the abolition of the Electoral College.

This House values the will of the people over the rights of the states.

Web Links:

- Center for Voting and Democracy. <http://www.fairvote.org/op_eds/electoral_college.htm> Web site argues for abolition of the Electoral College and has news items as well as links to other sites.
- The Electoral College. <http://www.archives.gov/federal-register/electoral-college/index.html> US government Web site offering a thorough explanation of how the Electoral College functions.
- In Defense of the Electoral College. <http://www.cato.org/dailys/11-10-00.html> Think-tank Web site argues in favor of retaining the Electoral College.

Further Reading:

Bennett, Robert W. *Taming the Electoral College.* Stanford University Press, 2006.

Gregg, Gary L. *Securing Democracy: Why We Have an Electoral College.* ISI Books, 2001.

Schumaker, Paul D., and Burdett A. Loomis, eds. *Choosing a President: The Electoral College and Beyond.* CQ Press, 2002.

ENVIRONMENTALLY LINKED AID

Many parts of the developing world have begun industrializing without regard to the environmental consequences. In light of growing environmental concerns, some individuals and groups have suggested tying aid to environmental goals including curbing emissions of carbon dioxide and chlorofluorocarbon. The international community would still give emergency aid in response to disasters, but it would tie development aid to environmental standards set by the United Nations Environmental Programme (UNEP). Countries with especially low emissions would receive extra aid.

PROS

The scientific community is almost unanimous in believing that emissions are seriously damaging the world ecosystem. The most serious threat is climate change. The effects of global warming include increasing desertification and rising sea levels. In addition, the El Niño phenomenon occurs more often. Air pollution has also resulted in increased acid rain and a growing hole in the ozone layer.

The industrialization of the small number of developed countries caused virtually all the problems laid out above. If developing countries, which have about five times the population of the developed world, were to industrialize unchecked, the effect could be catastrophic. For example, rising sea levels would flood millions of homes in low-lying areas such as Bangladesh. Increased crop failure would kill many more by starvation. Developed

CONS

Environmental pressure groups seriously overstate the evidence for climate change. Even if climate change is occurring, pollution is not necessarily the cause. It may result from natural variations, which the fossil record indicates have occurred in the past.

This is just a new form of imperialism. Developing countries have the right to develop economically and industrially just as developed countries have. Industrialization will improve the living standards of billions of people throughout the globe. In addition, industrialization will lead to economic stability for the world's poorest countries. This, in turn, will increase democratization in these nations.

PROS

countries might be able to protect themselves from these effects, but developing countries would not. The developing world has not acted to prevent environmental disaster and so the developed world must act to save literally billions of lives.

The UN could design initial standards so that all developing countries could meet the goals and receive aid. If they spend this development aid wisely, developing countries could industrialize in an environmentally clean way. In the long run, the combined approach of extra rewards for successful countries and serious sanctions for unsuccessful countries should ensure success.

Developed countries should be guardians of the planet expressly because they have a terrible history of polluting. They must prevent unhindered industrialization elsewhere.

Even if environmentalists have exaggerated their claims, the threat from environmental pollution is still great enough to require action. The potential benefit of acting to save the planet's ecosystem far outweighs any downside. (We are not conceding that the claims are exaggerated, merely that it does not matter even if they are.)

CONS

Developed countries are hypocritical in trying to restrict emissions from developing countries when they do so little themselves. The United States, which is still the world's biggest polluter, consistently refuses to ratify environmental treaties because its own economic self-interest does not appear to be served by doing so. What right does the developed world have to preach to the developing world about emissions?

Asking the UNEP to set emission standards is unfeasible because both developed and developing countries would try to influence the agency. Developed countries would lobby for very restrictive emission standards to decrease the threat from cheap imports. Developing countries would demand standards so lax that they would have no effect.

This proposal has serious consequences for world stability. First, developed countries would certainly not enforce regulations against China (an important trading partner and the linchpin of regional stability), the world's fastest growing polluter. Second, the developing countries, particularly those that fail to meet the standards, would resent such outside intrusion. In addition, withholding aid could cause economic collapse and the subsequent rise of dictatorships. Rogue nations might form alliances that threatened world stability. In their rush to develop, these states would increase pollution because developed countries would have no influence over them.

Sample Motions:

This House would link aid to emissions reductions.

This House believes that the environment must come first.

Web Links:

- Europa. <http://europa.eu/scadplus/leg/en/lvb/l26106.htm> Summary of EU policy on environmental aid.
- World Bank Development Education Program. <http://www.worldbank.org/html/schools/depweb.htm> Information for teachers and students on sustainable development.

Further Reading:

Farley, Joshua, and Herman E. Daly. *Ecological Economics: Principles and Applications.* Island Press, 2003.

Hassler, B. *Science and Politics of Foreign Aid: Swedish Environmental Support to the Baltic States.* Springer, 2003.

Sziládi-Matkovics, Anna. *Official Development Assistance in the Field of Environmental Protection: General Characteristics, Motivations, Decisive Conferences.* VDM Verlag, 2008.

ETHICAL FOREIGN POLICY

For centuries, the foreign policy of most Western nations was based on realpolitik, doing whatever necessary to forward the self-interest of the nation. In the United States, which traditionally has seen itself as held to a higher standard, tension has always existed between realpolitik and a desire to act out of humanitarian concern or to preserve liberty. During the 1990s, ethnic cleansing in the Balkans and, the continuing genocide in Darfur forced Western nations to confront the question of ethics in foreign policy. Should nations whose self-interests are not threatened intervene in other countries solely for humanitarian reasons?

PROS	CONS
Western governments must pursue an ethical foreign policy. This translates into the philosophy that impels us to act whenever there is a moral imperative to do so.	If "ethical foreign policy" means active intervention whenever there is a "moral imperative," then it is a hopelessly naïve notion. Governments are constrained by practical concerns. For example, selling arms to certain nations might be unethical, but if the government stops such sales, citizens lose jobs—and the weapons are purchased elsewhere.
Lobbyists should not influence foreign policy. It should be above special interests and should focus on doing what is right.	In a representative democracy discounting these groups is impossible. Moreover, the "right thing to do" for the nation may be what special interests demand.
The argument for ethical foreign policy is strongest when the West confronts heinous crimes in foreign lands, such as genocide in Rwanda or ethnic cleansing in the Balkans. In both places, the West had a clear moral imperative for active involvement—our action could save lives and free people from oppression.	We concede the principle but reject the practice. Intervening might make matters worse. We also have to be mindful of broader concerns, like the situation in the foreign country and what action might do to our image in other nations. Taking an active and moralistic stance toward African problems, for example, may make the West look like neo-imperialists.
In many cases, such as that of Kosovo in the 1990s, the humanitarian imperative demands intervention: We must act because if we don't people will suffer and die. Taking the pragmatic approach based on a careful assessment of national interests costs lives.	Intervention before a situation is fully assessed may cost more lives in the long run. Being starkly utilitarian is horrible, but foreign policy must solve problems for the long term; it cannot be based on a knee-jerk reaction to an immediate situation.

Sample Motions:

This House would have an ethical foreign policy.

This House believes politics is the art of the necessary not the possible.

Web Link:

- Reflections on the Theory and Practice of an Ethical Foreign Policy. <http://209.85.129.132/search?q=cache:W45iU_qsHNYJ:www.eucm.leidenuniv.nl/content_docs/gudmundson.doc+ethical+foreign+policy&hl=en&ct=clnk&cd=14&client=safari> Analysis of how ethics relates to foreign policy.

Further Reading:

Chandler, David, and Volker Heins. *Rethinking Ethical Foreign Policy.* Routledge, 2006.

Forsythe, David P. *Human Rights in International Relations.* Cambridge University Press, 2000.

Meyer, William H. *Security, Economics, and Morality in American Foreign Policy: Contemporary Issues in Historical Context.* Prentice Hall, 2003.

EXTRAORDINARY RENDITION

"Extraordinary rendition" is the transferring of a person from one jurisdiction to another, without any form of judicial or administrative process ("rendition" in this case means giving something over to someone else). This makes it different from other rendition methods, such as extradition, which is treaty-based, or deportation, which is based on the expelling country's domestic judicial processes. The term is currently connected to the US government's "war on terror." Ever since President Bill Clinton issued a directive in 1995, the Central Intelligence Agency (CIA) has had the possibility of using extraordinary rendition in the US fight against terrorism. The agency's use of it rose significantly after the 9/11 attacks.

The persons who are "rendered" might be captured outside the US and then, without legal process, transferred to the US. They also might be captured on foreign soil and then transferred to another country. It is the latter case that has attracted the most criticism: according to critics, the US uses this specific form of extraordinary rendition to torture those suspected of terrorism, without having to do the torturing itself. That is why extraordinary rendition is sometimes also referred to as "torture flights." This discussions focuses on these alleged "torture flights."

PROS

The US government uses "extraordinary rendition" as "torture by proxy." It delivers those suspected of terrorism to countries that are known to practice torture, and expects certain results from those countries, in the form of information extracted. US practice violates both the UN Convention Against Torture (CAT), which forbids countries to render persons to states that practice torture, and US domestic law, which also prohibits this.

CONS

In 2006 Secretary of State Condoleezza Rice reaffirmed that the US government does not render persons to countries with the purpose of having them tortured. The US government may render those suspected of terrorism for "harsh interrogation," but harsh interrogation is legal both under CAT and domestic law, which determines torture as "inducing severe pain." In any case, the main reasons for rendering a terrorist suspect to another country for questioning have more to do with that state's role in the investigation than with particular interrogation techniques practiced there. The destination state may be better placed to interrogate the suspect in his own language, and may have detailed background information to inform the questioning process that the US lacks. The

PROS

CONS

suspect may also be accused of plotting atrocities in the state to which he has been rendered, so it has a legitimate interest in interrogating him first.

Finally, in ratifying the Convention Against Torture in 1994, the US did so with the reservation that it can render persons to countries when it believes that it is more likely than not that a person will not be tortured. Thus, under the US interpretation of CAT, the US can render individuals to countries that practice torture, as long as the US has reason to believe that the country will not torture in this specific case.

How does the US government know the difference between "harsh interrogation" and "torture," and on what grounds does it base its belief that it is "more likely than not" that torture will not take place? By its nature, the work of the CIA is secretive. So, even if the CIA does obtain assurances, the general public can never check whether these agreements are being enforced. Since the CIA is being held responsible for fighting terrorism, they might even have an incentive to bend the rules a bit—as long as they can later show results to the public.

The CIA has a policy in practice whereby it obtains "diplomatic assurance" that torture will not be used. Under customary international law, the USA is obliged to act "in good faith." So, when America is given diplomatic assurance by another government, it would be a diplomatic blunder not to trust that guarantee. Also, imagine the consequence if it were one day proved that the CIA rendered a person, knowing they would be tortured: not only would those involved lose their jobs, but also the reputation of the CIA would be severely damaged. That is why the CIA has an incentive to make sure that these assurances are believable.

What if the CIA makes mistakes? Because the victims are held in detention without recourse to any kind of judge, they have no possible way of getting out. Even worse, if someone is released out of this type of detention, the victim has no way of seeking redress since the operation was covert. An example of this is the case of Khalid El-Masri, a German of Lebanese descent, who suddenly disappeared in 2003. After he resurfaced in Albania in 2004, he claimed he was "kidnapped" by the CIA and tortured under the policy of "extraordinary rendition," until the CIA realized its mistake and released him, without excuse, and without compensation of any kind. Since there is no official record, his attempts to make a case against the CIA have failed. Worse still, a US judge dismissed his case, under the argument that pursuing the case would be a severe threat to national security.

To ensure that the CIA does not make any mistakes, it has started researching so-called erroneous renditions. In the case of Khalid El-Masri, the CIA has never admitted kidnapping him. The CIA does suspect, and is trying to apprehend, a German-based terrorist with the name Khalid Al-Masri, and it is possible that this person is using the similarity in names to create a backlash against the CIA. Regardless of the merits of this particular case, it is clearly in the interests of America's enemies to blacken its name and undermine its security forces through accusations of torture. Murky and unsubstantiated stories about rendition should thus not be believed uncritically.

For every example of an "effective" rendition, one has to ask: is it worth it? Because for every terrorist successfully caught and convicted after rendition, there may be many more mistakes. For every Ramzi Youssef, there might be dozens of Khalid El-Masris, Abu Omars, Majid Mahmud Abdu Ahmads, Muhammad Bashmilas, and many more. On top of that: consider the loss of reputation that the practice of extraordinary rendition has caused the US to suffer among its chief allies. In 2007 the EU adopted a

What people should not forget is that extraordinary rendition saves lives. It is used to bring people who are known or believed to be terrorists, to justice. These suspects are often stateless and they hide in places where ordinary processes of law do not work. Extraordinary rendition is then the only possible way of tracking them down, getting the necessary information from them, and bringing them to justice. They carry information that could save thousands of lives. The US would be foolish

PROS

report condemning this particular US policy, and this was followed by a massive public outcry against the practice. Such American tactics simply play into the hands of terrorists who seek to stir hatred against America and divide it from its allies. And finally, does the pretext of a terrorist threat really justify taking away a person's right to due process? The question is even more relevant in that many experts believe torture is an ineffective method of acquiring reliable intelligence in any case.

The people targeted by extraordinary rendition are citizens, not combatants, and more important, they are human beings. If there is a reasonable suspicion that these people are terrorists, the US should follow the normal route of asking the country where the suspect is living to extradite him. The suspect can then be tried by a regular US criminal court, where the public eye will ensure his right to due process. Even if one views this person as a "combatant," he still has the fundamental human right to due process. The US should not violate the fundamental democratic rights it proclaims to defend in this war on terror.

CONS

not to try to extract that from them. An example of this is Ramzi Youssef, who masterminded the 1993 bombing of the World Trade Center and plotted to blow up airlines over the Pacific Ocean. After a rendition to the US, he was convicted and is now serving a life sentence. Without rendition, who knows how many people he would have killed?

We should not forget that the people the US targets for extraordinary renditions should be considered "unlawful combatants" in the war on terror. This term is important, because it identifies the US government as taking part in a war and terrorists as the combatants in that war. The people targeted for extraordinary rendition are "unlawful combatants" since their aim is to kill and terrorize US civilians, not US soldiers. Under international law, that is a very severe war crime, requiring the US to take very severe measures. Moreover, since the US is at war with terrorism, it has the obligation to protect its citizens first—and the obligation to dirty its hands in the process. Mistakes will inevitably be made, but in a time of war, the US cannot afford to risk the lives of its own citizens.

Sample Motions:

This House advocates ending the use of extraordinary rendition.
This House would end rendition flights.
This House believes the current US policy of using extraordinary rendition cannot be justified.
This House would end torture flights.
This House advocates denying the use of our airspace and facilities to extraordinary rendition flights.

Web Links:

- Amnesty International. <http://www.amnesty.org/en/library/info/POL30/003/2006> Q&A on: rendition and secret detention.
- Congressional Research Service (CRS) Report: Renditions: Constraints Imposed by Laws on Torture. <http://www.fas.org/sgp/crs/natsec/RL32890.pdf> Overview of laws restricting rendition for torture.
- Times Online. <http://www.timesonline.co.uk/tol/news/world/us_and_americas/article745995.ece?token=null&offset=0> Condoleezza Rice statement justifying US practice.

Further Reading:

Grey, Stephen. *Ghost Plane: The True Story of the CIA Rendition and Torture Program.* St. Martin's Griffin, 2007.

Paglen, Trevor, and A.C. Thompson. *Torture Taxi: On the Trail of the CIA's Rendition Flights.* Melville House, 2006.

Schulz, William. *Tainted Legacy: 9/11 and the Ruin of Human Rights.* Nation Books, 2003.

FACTORY FARMING, BANNING OF

Factory farming is the large-scale, industrial production of livestock and poultry designed to produce the highest output at the lowest cost. The practice began in the 1920s after the discovery of vitamins A and D and vitamin supplements, which allowed large numbers of animals to be raised indoors without sunlight. Proponents of the practice point to its economic benefits, while opponents say it has led to cruelty and environmental destruction.

PROS	CONS
Factory farming is intrinsically cruel. Modern science permits factory farms to raise large numbers of animals indoors with no concern for their physical and emotional needs.	Factory farming involves very little cruelty or suffering—certainly no more than in traditional forms of farming. Animals have always been herded together, confined, branded, killed, and eaten. Furthermore, government regulatory agencies can more easily monitor large factory farms, so the animals often fare better than they would on traditional farms. Activists have ensured that the few isolated incidents of cruelty or bad practice have received publicity greatly out of proportion to their significance.
Factory farming sees animals as commodities for production and sale just like bricks or bread. But animals are conscious and know pleasure and pain. We should treat them humanely and with dignity. Factory farming does not. Yes, we are capable of higher thought and animals are not, but this means that we must be good stewards and care for them. How terribly we fail in fulfilling that duty.	This is sentimental nonsense. Unless the state is going to impose vegetarianism (and that's not being proposed here), farming will continue to be a business. It should be efficient and make a profit for the producer, while keeping prices low for the consumer. Many animals exist simply as a food source. Animals are not our equals and don't have the capacity for higher thought. We can use them without any moral problem.
Factory farming does not practice healthier, traditional farming methods that were more in tune with nature and that were the backbone of a rural way of life that is now dying. The countryside that we love was created by traditional farming methods, particularly grazing, not vast sheds full of imprisoned animals.	Again, sentimentality is interfering with logic. Farming has always been the imposition of artificial, man-made patterns on nature. As for farmers losing jobs, plenty of people are employed in factory farming. Why is that any less worthy? And many farmers have sold off their land for enormous profits.
Factory farming is unhealthy for the environment. The waste from factory farms has contributed to water pollution; large-scale beef farming has produced vast quantities of methane that damages the ozone layer. Factory farming also erodes topsoil at an alarming rate.	Come on! Are we really supposed to believe that cow-produced methane is in the same league as pollution from big business and industry? The topsoil point is more substantial. But that's an argument for regulations requiring the upkeep and replacement of turf, not for banning a whole industry.

Sample Motions:

This House would ban factory farming.
This House would go free range.
This House prefers low-intensity agriculture.

Web Links:

- End Factory Farming. <http://www.factoryfarming.org.uk/whatis.html> Overview of the topic from an anti–factory-farming group.
- FactoryFarming.com. <http://www.factoryfarming.com> Information on specific aspects of the topic by group opposed to factory farming.
- In Defense of Animals. <http://www.idausa.org/facts/factoryfarmfacts.html> Useful source of information from a group opposed to factory farming.

Further Reading:

Masson, Jeffrey Moussaieff. *The Pig Who Sang to the Moon: The Emotional World of Farm Animals.* Ballantine, 2003.

Scully, Matthew. *Dominion: The Power of Man, the Suffering of Animals, and the Call to Mercy.* St. Martin's Griffin, 2003.

FAILED STATES, US INTERVENTION TO PREVENT COLLAPSE OF

A failed state is usually defined as one in which law and order has collapsed and the government can no longer provide services to the people. In 2005 Foreign Policy reported that up to two billion people live in countries in danger of collapse and so are exposed to varying degrees of violence. In the past, the US and the global community have acted to prevent failure, but with mixed results. This debate focuses on whether and how the United States and the United Nations should act to prevent failure.

PROS	CONS
We must help failing states, because once they collapse, they cannot provide services and security for their people. The United States should work with the UN to resolve conflicts and should engage in peacekeeping missions and nation-building initiatives. (This will require both a greater willingness on the part of the US to commit funds and a commitment to conflict resolution that has been largely lacking in recent US policy.)	The United States National Security Strategy (2002) rightly states that the United States "should be realistic about its ability to help those that are unwilling and unready to help themselves. Where and when people are ready to do their part, we will be ready to move decisively." Past US failures in Haiti and Somalia show the wisdom of this principle. The United States should choose its areas of engagement with care based on their strategic importance and the likelihood of success, rather than spread itself too thin to be effective.
We must rescue failing states in the interests of international stability. Failed states often infect an entire region, a problem known as contagion. Neighboring states back different factions and are themselves destabilized by floods of refugees and weapons from next door. Also, their own rebel groups can easily use the lawless country to regroup and mount fresh attacks.	US willingness to step in to help every fragile state will only exacerbate the problem. Irresponsible governments will assume that the US will bail them out to prevent their people from suffering. This in itself makes future failures much more likely.
Failed states often provide havens for illegal activity such as growing opium. Finally, desperate people in failed states may take refuge in religious or political extremism, which can threaten the world.	The contagion theory is hard to apply beyond a small group of countries in West Africa. Elsewhere failed states do not tend to drag their neighbors down with them. For example, none of the countries bordering Somalia

PROS | CONS

are close to failing. In most cases, having regional groups take responsibility for failing states in their areas is far better than overburdening the United States and UN.

Saving fragile states from failure is in the interest of the United States and its allies. Failed states often become havens for terrorists, as happened in Afghanistan and Somalia. The United States should work with the UN to strengthen governments so that they can more effectively maintain internal order while controlling their borders and tracking resource flows.

We have very limited evidence to support the theory that failed states become havens for terrorists. Yes, there are a few Al-Qaeda sympathizers in Somalia, but these are no greater a threat than similar groups in other countries. Nor is Afghanistan a good example; an established government—the Taliban—invited Osama bin Laden to take refuge there. On the other hand, Iran and Syria are both accused of providing bases for terrorists, but neither is a failed state.

The cost of preventive action is dramatically lower than the cost of military action, and we are paying the price for failing states in any case. The United States already spends many billions of dollars annually in handling the humanitarian, drug, and security problems these states create. These states also cost the world economy in terms of lost opportunities for trade and investment.

The cost of intervention is too high. The UN has neither the money nor the support to undertake speculative missions. Currently, it cannot provide enough troops for peacekeeping missions in countries that request them. The US already contributes nearly a quarter of the UN's peacekeeping budget and cannot afford more at a time when it is already stretched by major commitments in Iraq and Afghanistan.

The US and other international financial institutions must change their rules on aid and market access. At present these programs reward only countries that have good governance (e.g., anticorruption measures, etc.). Sensible though it seems, this policy denies international help to failing states, whose people need this aid. Funding micro-credit plans, education, health, and sanitation programs in the more stable parts of failing states, and providing meaningful trade access could provide long-term benefits for the United States.

The United States should maintain and even extend its current approach to international development. Such conditions provide incentives for developing countries to put constructive policies in place and reward those who fight corruption. As past failures show all too clearly, throwing money at chaotic, lawless, and corrupt regimes is pointless—it never reaches the people anyway. In any case, humanitarian relief is not conditional, and the United States continues to respond with compassion to emergencies anywhere in the world.

Finally, special measures to support states identified as failing could in themselves be economically harmful. Even discussing intervention might scare off investors and help to bring about economic collapse, creating a self-fulfilling prophecy.

The US should work with the UN to prevent state failure. The United Nations has the expertise and is widely respected, whereas the international reputation of the US is now sufficiently damaged that the hostility America generates can undermine the good work it wishes to do. The US can provide resources to enable the UN to secure the future stability of many fragile countries, while UN involvement will show that these operations are altruistic and pose no imperialist threat. Over time, the partnership will change the world's perception of the US—an important aspect of the war on terror.

Intervening in fragile states is simply a new form of imperialism. Neither the United States nor the UN should impose its rule on individual countries. Doing so would deny people the right to chart their own future. A policy of intervention would create more hostility toward the United States, with accusations that it is acting out of self-interest. US troops and civilian personnel could rapidly become targets for attacks. And increasing UN intervention in the domestic affairs of member states could encourage the organization in its ambitions to become a world government.

Sample Motions:

This House believes the United States should work together with the UN to prevent the collapse of third-world states.

This House would save failing states.

This House believes the United States should do more to prevent failed states.

Web Links:

- Foreign Affairs. <http://www.foreignaffairs.org/20020301facomment7967/sebastian-mallaby/the-reluctant-imperialist-terrorism-failed-states-and-the-case-for-american-empire.html> Article supporting US intervention in failed states.
- Global Policy Forum. <http://www.globalpolicy.org/nations/sovereign/failedindex.htm> Links to a variety of articles on failed states.
- US Foreign Assistance and Failed States. <http://www.brook.edu/views/papers/rice/20021125.htm> Brookings Institution paper on the subject.

Further Reading:

Cooper, Robert. *The Breaking of Nations.* Atlantic Books, 2004.

Diamond, Jared. *Collapse: How Societies Choose to Fail or Survive.* Viking, 2005.

Fukuyama, Francis. *State Building: Governance and World Order in the Twenty-First Century.* Profile Books, 2004.

FAIRNESS DOCTRINE, REINTRODUCING

Until twenty years ago US broadcasters had to follow the federal government's Fairness Doctrine. This rule, formally introduced in 1949, required radio and television stations to give "ample play to the free and fair competition of opposing views," so that listeners and viewers received a range of opinions and individual stations were not able to promote particular viewpoints to the exclusion of all others. In 1987, during the Reagan administration, the Federal Communications Commission (FCC) judged that the Fairness Doctrine was an outdated and unnecessary interference in the broadcasting business and it was repealed. Congress made an attempt to reinstate it, but President Ronald Reagan vetoed the measure, and the doctrine has never been reintroduced. Since the Fairness Doctrine was removed in 1987, talk radio has become much more prominent, bringing a brash and lively style of political debate into many American homes (and cars). Conservatives dominate the format, and hosts such as Rush Limbaugh make no attempt to hide their own political opinions or to provide a platform for views that disagree with their own. Such stations are now seen as hugely politically influential, with loyal audiences that they can mobilize to lobby, vote, and protest on key issues. In 2007, with partisanship on radio growing, some Republicans as well as Democrats began to call for talk radio to be reined back, perhaps through the reinstatement of the Fairness Doctrine.

PROS

Since the Fairness Doctrine was lifted in 1987 right-wing talk shows have come to dominate the airwaves. Conservative hosts and commentators present a populist and very one-sided viewpoint, routinely abusing callers and guests who disagree with their opinions. The tone of these programs is intolerant and unpleasant, playing to the prejudices of their listeners and promoting a very narrow set of views. This cheapens the quality of public

CONS

Some people may find right-wing radio distasteful or object to the slant Fox News gives to its coverage of politics and world affairs, but such stations are only part of the whole broadcasting spectrum. In fact, talk radio has less than 5% of the total radio market. Most conservatives believe that the mainstream media, such as National Public Radio and the traditional big three television channels (ABC, NBC, and CBS), are strongly left-leaning, and

PROS

debate, as those who disagree with the values and policies of the broadcasters are labeled as not just wrong, but also stupid, immoral, and unpatriotic. Reinstating the Fairness Doctrine would ensure a more balanced diet of opinion and help to bring back a greater degree of civility to the airwaves.

Unbalanced broadcasting also affects policy making in ways that are bad for our country. Talk-radio hosts can fire up their audiences over particular issues, successfully urging them to place so much pressure on their elected representatives that they are able to impose their agenda at state and federal levels. This attacks the representative principle—that elected officials must use their best judgment to make decisions for the good of all, rather than bending to the uninformed and perhaps temporary will of mass opinion. These campaigns are particularly dangerous on issues such as trade and immigration where the populist argument seems simple, easily summed up in appealing nativist slogans. Often the alternative case is more complex, requiring a greater level of economic and political education and a willingness to study dispassionately a range of evidence. Following the collapse in 2007 of attempts at immigration reform, even Trent Lott, a leading conservative Republican senator, lamented that talk radio is running the country and has power without responsibility.

The Fairness Doctrine should be reinstated because a wide range of views is needed to safeguard democracy. We can trust voters to decide for themselves only if they have been given the tools to do so. An uninformed electorate lacks the tools to exercise free political judgments and is open to being swayed by a diet of propaganda. This means broadcasters must challenge their listeners and viewers with a range of opinions on a wide array of issues, rather than reinforcing what they already think. Only through exposure to a balanced diet of opinion and debate can our citizens understand the choices facing our country.

Reintroducing the Fairness Doctrine would promote free speech rather than act to limit it. The Supreme Court found in 1969 that the Fairness Doctrine did not abridge free speech because requiring access for a range of viewpoints does nothing to restrict the right to present a particular opinion. The rights of citizens as listeners and viewers to hear a broad range of ideas easily outweighs any right the broadcasters might claim to put forth any one viewpoint to the exclusion of all others.

CONS

that talk radio acts to balance this bias. As for complaints about the tone of talk-radio programs, what some people label "intolerant" others may see as fearless. In any case, many liberals are horribly rude about President Bush, or show disrespect for the flag and great American institutions such as the US military.

Broadcasting is a business, not different in character from any other. We need to take a market view and let the public as consumers decide what they want to listen to rather than imposing it upon them. There is nothing to stop anyone from launching a liberal talk-radio station, and indeed, there have been many attempts to do so. But these have proved unpopular failures, because the public does not want to buy what they are peddling. Talk radio is successful because its broadcasters share the values of the American people and are able to express the way they feel about the key issues of the day. One of those issues is the way in which strong public opinion (e.g., over immigration, the North American Free Trade Agreement, or school prayer) has been consistently ignored by politicians over many decades. If talk radio publicizes representatives' voting records and enables voters to hold them to account, then so much the better.

When the Fairness Doctrine was in place, it actually prevented controversial issues from being freely debated because stations, fearful of being charged with bias and losing their licenses avoided discussing these issues. By contrast, the lifting of the Fairness Doctrine in 1987 had a liberating effect on broadcasters, allowing talk radio to flourish and encouraging the debate of a great variety of important issues, from a wide range of perspectives. There can be no doubt that reinstating the doctrine would again have a chilling effect on the public debate that democracy needs to flourish.

A Fairness Doctrine would attack the constitutional right to freedom of speech. The state has no business force feeding citizens with opinions or interfering with the media in the name of "balance." Giving the government some kind of editorial control over what is broadcast amounts to censorship, and we must resist this forcefully. Far from being fair, such a restriction stops broadcasters from expressing their opinions freely, and thus abridges the right to free speech.

PROS	CONS
One problem with the existing situation is that conservatism and liberalism are not simple polar opposites, with some stations expressing one view and others providing a clear alternative. First, talk radio presents a particular type of conservative viewpoint. It is libertarian on some issues (low taxes, guns, opposition to a welfare state) but authoritarian on others (against gay marriage, freedom of choice, and the rights . . . of terrorist suspects). It is in favor of military engagement abroad but protectionist on economic issues. So it does not even offer a range of conservative opinion. Second, liberal broadcasters, by their very nature, value pluralism; conservative ones are convinced that only their way is right. As a result, conservative stations have squeezed out opposing views entirely, while liberal broadcasters are still happy to give airtime to right-wing views alongside those of others.	Talk radio actually covers a wide spectrum of opinion. Its commentators do not have a common line on the key issues of the day. In any case, the audience for talk radio is media savvy. They know that particular hosts and stations have particular viewpoints and take account of this when forming their views. Almost no one listens only to talk radio to learn about current affairs. Citizens expose themselves to a wide range of material, including television, radio, newspapers, and the Internet. Because a broad variety of competing views is available every day, there is no need to require each station to pointlessly reflect all viewpoints in its own broadcasting.
Regulation may be difficult, but broadcasting is so politically important to our democracy that we must make the attempt. Even if regulation is imperfect, we can still establish a new norm and thereby greatly improve broadcasting. In fact, when the Fairness Doctrine was in effect, the FCC used a very light touch in order to ensure balanced content. Far from insisting on equal time for all possible viewpoints, it simply required that some time be given to different opinions. After all, similar requirements for fair access operate in many other countries (e.g., the UK, Australia) without any problems.	It is impossible to regulate broadcasting fairly and it will not be possible to limit future government intervention if a new Fairness Doctrine is implemented. Who is to say what constitutes "balance" or what kinds of views deserve access to the airwaves? Will we need a new bureaucracy to monitor the output of stations and impose quotas for different opinions? Should radical Islamists be guaranteed airtime? The FCC and broadcasting companies will be continually tied down by lawsuits from disgruntled pressure groups seeking a public platform. The FCC is already politicized, with officials often divided along party lines; the right to meddle in programming will make this much worse. And dangers can be seen in other countries, such as Italy, Russia, or Venezuela, where the government's right to interfere in broadcasting is used for narrow party advantage rather than the public good.

Sample Motions:

This House would reintroduce the Fairness Doctrine.

This House calls for "fair and balanced" broadcasting.

This House believes that broadcasters should be required to provide ample play to the free and fair competition of opposing views.

Web Links:

- Fairness and Accuracy in Reporting: The Fairness Doctrine: How We Lost It and Why We Need It Back. <http://www.fair.org/index.php?page=2053> Article in support of reinstating the Fairness Doctrine.
- Museum of Broadcast Communications. <http://www.museum.tv/archives/etv/F/htmlF/fairnessdoct/fairnessdoct.htm> Provides background and bibliography on the issue.
- National Review Online. <http://article.nationalreview.com/?q=NmYzNGU0ZjAxNWFlOWE2NmUzYWFjMmEwNWM1OTgyZjQ=> Overview of the latest attempt to reinstate the Fairness Doctrine.
- NOW: What Happened to Fairness? <http://www.pbs.org/now/politics/fairness.html> History of the Fairness Doctrine.

Further Reading:

Hitchens, Leslie. *Broadcasting Pluralism and Diversity: A Comparative Study of Policy and Regulation.* Hart Publishing, 2006.

Kincaid, Cliff, and Lynn Woolley. *The Death of Talk Radio.* Accuracy in Media, 2007.

FREE SPEECH, RESTRICTIONS ON

Freedom of speech is one of the basic tenets of democracy. A fundamental right enshrined in the US Bill of Rights, the UN Declaration of Human Rights, and the European Convention on Human Rights, freedom of speech is, nevertheless, not an absolute. Most nations have laws against sedition, libel, or speech that threatens public safety. Where a nation draws the line between protected and unprotected speech is a continuing subject for debate.

PROS

Free speech is an inherently ambiguous concept that requires definition and interpretation; it is the job of governments to clarify these ambiguities.

As Justice Oliver Wendell Holmes wrote, "the most stringent protection of free speech would not protect a man in falsely shouting fire in a theater and causing a panic." We accept limitations on free speech when it may threaten public safety. Therefore, freedom of speech is never absolute.

Speech leads to physical acts. Pornography, hate speech, and political polemic are linked to rape, hate crimes, and insurrection.

Government must protect its citizens from foreign and internal enemies. Thus, governments should be permitted to curb speech that might undermine the national interest during war.

Some views are antithetical to religious beliefs. To protect the devout, we should ban this type of offensive speech.

We need to protect children from exposure to obscene, offensive, or potentially damaging materials.

CONS

The limits to free speech are too important to be determined by government. If speech is to be regulated, it should be done by an independent body.

The tyranny of the majority is a good reason to resist government censorship. A healthy democracy recognizes that smaller groups must be heard; to guarantee that they have a public voice, no restrictions should be put on speech.

Society is self-regulating. The link between speech and action is a false one. Yes, people who commit hate crimes are likely to have read hate literature, and people who commit sex crimes are likely to have watched pornography. But viewing pornography or reading hate speech does not necessarily lead to crime. In addition, exposing hate speech and extreme political polemic to societal scrutiny increases the likelihood that it will be discredited and defeated, rather than strengthened through persecution.

Regardless of the situation, the public has the right to a free exchange of ideas and to know what the government is doing.

We must defend the right of the nonreligious to express their views.

We all agree that government must protect children, but that does not mean that government should have the right to censor all material.

Sample Motions:

This House would restrict freedom of speech.
This House would muzzle the press.
This House would censor the Internet.
This House would ban books.

Web Links:

- American Civil Liberties Union. <http://www.aclu.org/freespeech/index.html> Coverage of current event issues relating to free speech in the United States.
- American Library Association. <http://www.ala.org/ala/aboutala/offices/oif/firstamendment/firstamendment.cfm> Links to court cases and other resources related to the First Amendment.
- University of Pennsylvania: Banned Books Online. <http://digital.library.upenn.edu/books/banned-books.html> Online exhibit discussing books that have been the objects of censorship and censorship attempts.

Further Reading:

Curtis, Michael Kent. *Free Speech, "The People's Darling Privilege": Struggles for Freedom of Expression in American History.* Duke University Press, 2000.

Eastland, Terry. *Freedom of Expression in the Supreme Court.* Rowman & Littlefield, 2000.

Hensley, Thomas R., ed. *Boundaries of Freedom of Expression and Order in American History.* Kent State University Press, 2001.

Stone, Geoffrey R. *Perilous Times: Free Speech in Wartime from the Sedition Act of 1798 to the War on Terrorism.* W. W. Norton, 2004.

FREE TRADE AND DEVELOPMENT

Economists and politicians have praised the virtues of free trade for over 200 years. By allowing everyone equal access to all markets, the theory goes, you guarantee the most efficient allocation of resources and the cheapest prices for consumers. Can such a theory work in practice? Specifically, could it help the least-developed countries achieve a better quality of life? Western rhetoric says it can and points to international institutions like as the World Trade Organization (WTO) and the World Bank that foster free trade and help these nations. However, as long as the West continues to protect its own agriculture and industries from the international market, its position is arguably hypocritical.

PROS	CONS
Interlocking trade relationships decrease the likelihood of war. If a nation is engaged in mutually beneficial relationships with other countries, it has no incentive to jeopardize these relationships through aggression. This promotes peace, which is a universal good.	Free trade does not promote peace. Trading countries have gone to war against each other. This argument might apply to a good-natured trading relationship, but not necessarily to one that is just tariff free.
A tariff-free international economy is the only way to maintain maximum global efficiency and the cheapest prices. Efficient allocation of the world's resources means less waste and, therefore, more affordable goods for consumers.	International economics isn't as simple as increasing the efficiency of global resource allocation above all else. Tariff revenue is a perfectly legitimate and useful source of government income. Without tariffs governments cannot protect the jobs of their citizens.

PROS	CONS
Free trade might lead to domestic layoffs, but the universal good of efficiency outweighs this. We should not subsidize uncompetitive industries; we should retrain workers for jobs in other fields. Subsidizing inefficiency is not sound economic practice. Moreover, the jobs we subsidize in the West are more needed in the developing world, to which they would inevitably flow if free trade were observed.	Job security is a legitimate concern of governments. The destruction of jobs is clear testimony against free trade serving a "universal good." Free trade supporters fail to factor in the political ramifications of job losses. A starkly utilitarian understanding of "universal good" may dictate that jobs flock to the developing world, but political considerations may dictate a more localized definition of the "good."
The growth of the developing world is a universal good because improving the quality of life of millions of people is clearly a moral imperative. Free trade helps countries by maximizing their comparative advantage in free trade circumstances.	Defending pure, unadulterated free trade is a pointless exercise. Textbook ideas are always mediated by practical constraints. In reality, the conditions developing countries must meet just to join the "not quite free trade" WTO are stringent and may cost the equivalent of the nation's entire annual humanitarian budget. Poor nations have social and development programs that must take priority over trade issues.
Free trade permits developing countries to gain ready access to capital in liberalized international financial markets. This gives them the opportunity to finance projects for growth and development.	If capital flow were rational, it would be beneficial. In practice, liberalized capital flow can destabilize developing economies, which are prone to speculation based on investor whim rather than economic fundamentals.

Sample Motions:

This House believes free trade serves a universal good.

This House believes free trade is good for the developing world.

Web Links:

- International Monetary Fund (IMF). <http://www.imf.org> General site that provides statistics and background on the IMF, offers information on monetary issues and legal issues involving trade, and presents evaluations of IMF programs.
- The World Bank Group. <http://www.worldbank.org> Broad site linking to development statistics, important documents, and reports as well as World Bank publications.
- World Trade Organization (WTO). <http://www.wto.org> Offers general information on the WTO, international trade and trade agreements, and WTO programs.

Further Reading:

Bhagwati, Jagdish N. *Free Trade Today.* Princeton University Press, 2003.

Irwin, Douglas. *Free Trade Under Fire.* 2nd ed. Princeton University Press, 2005.

Wilkinson, Rorden. *Multilateralism and the World Trade Organisation: The Architecture and Extension of International Trade Regulation.* Routledge, 2001.

GAY ADOPTION

At present, US states are divided on the issue of gay adoption. California, Connecticut, Illinois, Massachusetts, and New York have approved the practice, while Florida has prohibited it. Some states make gay adoption impossible by restricting adoption to married couples; in other states adoption laws are unclear or do not address the issue. In 2000, Mississippi passed a law not only banning gay and lesbian couples from adopting children but also forbidding Mississippi to recognize gay adoptions from other states. Civil rights groups are currently challenging bans on gay adoption in federal courts. In February 2004, a federal appeals court upheld the Florida ban, saying the law did not violate the Constitution and that the legislature, not the courts, was the proper forum for the debate. The following year the US Supreme Court announced that it would not hear a challenge to the ban. In 2008, a Florida circuit court judge ruled that the ban violated the state constitution.

PROS

Society is changing, and the traditional idea of the nuclear family with married mother and father is no longer the only acceptable alternative. Many states are beginning to award legal rights to gay couples because the stability of such relationships is now recognized. Such couples can provide a stable and loving upbringing for children.

CONS

The traditional nuclear family is still the ideal. Where its breakdown is inevitable, a close substitute, with maternal and paternal influences, is the only alternative. Evolution and nature have shown that the natural development of the young is aided by both these influences. Research published in the *University of Illinois Law Review* in 1997 found that children raised in homosexual households are significantly more likely to be gay themselves.

PRO: Nature has shown in many species that, when one or both parents die, an uncle or aunt frequently takes on the child-rearing role.

CON: While exceptions occur, the norm in nature is that both mother and father nurture offspring. To legally allow adoption by gay couples is to encourage what is an unnatural upbringing.

PRO: Some babies (both human and of other species) are born with a predisposition to homosexuality, and their upbringing will not affect their sexuality. Attempting to suppress this genetic predisposition has resulted in great misery for many. We should embrace all gay people fully—which must include celebrating gay role models, especially as responsible parents.

CON: A child's primary role models are his or her parents. Bringing a heterosexual child up in a gay household gives the child a distorted view of a minority sexuality, just as a girl brought up by two men would fail to benefit from a female influence.

PRO: In many cases where one of the partners is the biological parent, gay couples are currently responsibly rearing children. Allowing adoption by the other partner merely confers legal rights on an already successful, if informal, family model.

CON: While the law should not penalize gay relationships, it also exists to encourage the nuclear family as the ideal for child raising. Legal prohibition of gay adoption is a natural step toward this ideal.

PRO: Homophobia is wrong and must be fought wherever encountered. Only through the full inclusion of gays in society and all its institutions can we hope to overcome prejudice.

CON: Homophobic language and behavior is still common in society. Placing a child too young to have an opinion of his own in the care of a gay couple exposes him to this prejudice and subjects him to ridicule or violence. Whatever ideal we might have, the psychological and physical welfare of the child must come first.

Sample Motions:

This House would allow gay couples to adopt children.

This House would explode the nuclear family.

Web Links:

- Central News Network. <http://www.cnn.com/2007/US/06/25/gay.adoption/index.html> Article analyzing the status of gay adoption in the United States.
- USA Today. <http://www.usatoday.com/news/nation/2006-02-20-gay-adoption-foster_x.htm> Article on how gay adoption affects children.
- YouDebate.com. <http://www.youdebate.com/DEBATES/gay_adoption.HTM> Pros and cons of gay adoption.

Further Reading:

Mallon, Gerald P. *Gay Men Choosing Parenthood.* Columbia University Press, 2003.

———. *Lesbian and Gay Foster and Adoptive Parents: Recruiting, Assessing, and Supporting an Untapped Resource for Children and Youth.* Child Welfare League of America Press, 2006.

Savage, Dan. *The Kid: What Happened When My Boyfriend and I Decided to Go Get Pregnant: An Adoption Story.* Plume, 2000.

GAY MARRIAGE

American society increasingly supports equal rights for gays and lesbians in areas such as housing, employment, public accommodations, and so on. Yet many people continue to oppose granting homosexuals the right to marry or to formally register their unions with the state. In 2000, Vermont became the first state to grant gay and lesbian couples marriage-like status; in 2004, Massachusetts became the first state to recognize same-sex marriage. In contrast, 41 states have statutory defense of marriage acts defining marriage as between a man and a woman. Legal recognition of same-sex unions became a major issue in the 2004 presidential election, and in 2006, the Senate Judiciary Committee supported a Federal Marriage Amendment to the US Constitution, which would have prohibited states from recognizing same-sex marriages, but the amendment failed in both the Senate and the House. Amendments banning same-sex marriage passed in seven of eight states in the 2006 midterm elections. Arizona was the only state to defeat the proposal.

PROS

The refusal of governments to permit gays to marry is one of the last areas of discrimination against gays. The state should permit gay couples to marry as a means of professing their love to and for each other. Societal views ought to change with the times.

Permitting gay couples to marry would enable them to take advantage of the various financial benefits accorded to heterosexual married couples.

We must modify religious attitudes to reflect changes in society. Many religious views are no longer justifiable (e.g., the notion that women are inferior to men). Conversely, if religious institutions oppose gay marriage as against their beliefs, they should accept civil marriages.

CONS

While contemporary society should reject discrimination in general, some forms of discrimination can be objectively justified. Society has always viewed marriage as a heterosexual institution, the religious and/or civil union between a man and a woman.

Many of the financial benefits that married couples enjoy are not designed to encourage marriage per se but to promote the conventional family.

Historically marriage has been a religious institution. Because most major world religions frown on homosexuality, they would find gay marriage unacceptable.

PROS	CONS
Marriage is not merely an institution for raising children. Many married couples do not have children. In addition, the number of single-parent families is increasing. In any case, many countries permit gay singles and couples to adopt. Advances in medical science also enable gay couples to have children through artificial insemination and the use of surrogate mothers.	Historically society has viewed child rearing as the major purpose of marriage. Because gay couples are unlikely to have children, they have no need for marriage.
A "registered union" is an alternative to gay marriage. However, this arrangement is unacceptable because gay couples still would not enjoy the same rights as married heterosexual couples. Moreover, registering would imply that gay couples had an inferior status to married heterosexual couples, thus leading to discrimination.	Eight countries, including Denmark, Sweden, and the United Kingdom, permit the registered union of gay couples. Registered couples are entitled to joint insurance coverage and enjoy inheritance and tenants' rights. Registration makes no incursions into the sanctity of the institution of marriage. Consequently, it should prove acceptable to the religious sections of society.

Sample Motions:

This House would allow gay couples to marry.
This House would give homosexuals equal rights.
This House believes that discrimination can never be justified.

Web Links:

- Gay Marriage: The Arguments and the Motives. <http://www.bidstrup.com/marriage.htm> Comprehensively covers the arguments against gay marriage as well as other issues relating to the topic.
- Gay Marriage: Why Would It Affect Me? <http://www.nogaymarriage.com/tenarguments.asp> Presents ten arguments against gay marriage.
- Religious Tolerance. <http://www.religioustolerance.org/hom_marr.htm> Useful statistics and information concerning the status of gay marriage in the United States.

Further Reading:

Myers, David G., and Letha Dawson Scanzoni. *What God Has Joined Together: The Christian Case for Gay Marriage.* HarperSanFrancisco, 2006.

Stanton, Glenn T. *Marriage on Trial: The Case Against Same-Sex Marriage and Parenting.* InterVarsity Press, 2004.

Sullivan, Andrew. *Same-Sex Marriage: Pro and Con.* Vintage, 2004.

GAYS IN THE MILITARY

In 1993, President Bill Clinton attempted to remove the long-standing ban on gays in the US military but was forced to compromise in the face of powerful military and congressional opposition. The Clinton administration reached a compromise known as "Don't Ask, Don't Tell." While the ban remained, the compromise permitted gays to serve if they did not disclose their sexual orientation or engage in homosexual behavior. The military was also prohibited from trying to discover the sexual orientation of its personnel. The United States is the only NATO country to maintain such a ban. The United Kingdom had a ban until January 2000, when it changed its policy after the European

Court of Human Rights declared it illegal. Since the adoption of "Don't Ask, Don't Tell," public attitudes have shifted dramatically, and in 2008, in the opinion of 75% of Americans, openly gay men and women should be allowed to serve in the military.

PROS

No one now can realistically doubt that gay men or women are as hard working, intelligent, or patriotic as heterosexuals. Only sheer bigotry would deny the opportunity to join the military (and suffer its pervasive homophobia) to those who want to do so.

CONS

This debate is about soldiers defending their country while sharing close quarters. Their effectiveness depends on mutual trust and uncomplicated camaraderie. Sexual relations or tension between soldiers, no matter the gender, undermine this bond.

PROS: Much of the argument against the admission of gays is based on homophobia, which is encouraged by continued segregation. Permitting straight soldiers to see how effective gays can be will reduce prejudice.

CONS: Not all gay applicants will have a vocational calling to the military. A disproportionate number of gays, lesbians, and bisexuals may apply because the high concentration of individuals of one gender in military units makes them a fruitful source of sexual partners. Using the military for this purpose will provoke even more homophobia.

PROS: Many other professions require a bond of trust and intense living conditions among employees. Gays are not barred from any of them.

CONS: The military is a special case. Its members work in life-or-death situations where any mental distraction could be fatal. Men and women aren't sent into combat together; why should gays and heterosexuals be?

PROS: If the armed forces accepted gays, they would not have to remain in the closet, thus reducing the risk of blackmail. In any case this risk is diminishing as society increasingly accepts homosexuality.

CONS: Closeted homosexuals run the risk of blackmail, which could have implications for national security.

PROS: Gays and lesbians frequently come to terms with their sexuality in their late teens or early twenties, which might be long after they had enlisted. A ban would require the firing of personnel who had joined in good faith. This is discrimination at its worst.

CONS: The problem is not so much the concept of a ban but the halfhearted enforcement of it. If a ban is well publicized and if people understand that encouraging sexual interest among military personal is inappropriate, then gays are not being misled.

Sample Motions:

This House would not admit gays into the armed forces.

This House believes that the military and sexuality do not mix.

Web Links:

- The Ban on Gays in the Military: Links. <http://www.california.com/~rathbone/links001.htm> Links to the history of the "Don't Ask, Don't Tell" policy as well as many resources relating to the issue.
- PBS. <http://www.pbs.org/newshour/forum/january00/gays_military.html> A 2000 PBS forum on gays in the military.
- Washington Post. <http://www.washingtonpost.com/wp-dyn/content/story/2008/07/18/ST2008071802580.html> Discusses the public perception of gays in the military.

Further Reading:

Belkin, Aaron, and Geoffrey Bateman. *Don't Ask, Don't Tell: Debating the Gay Ban in the Military.* Lynne Reinner, 2003.

Lehring, Gary L. *Officially Gay: The Political Construction of Sexuality by the U.S. Military.* Temple University Press, 2003.

Shilts, Randy. *Conduct Unbecoming: Gays and Lesbians in the U.S. Military.* St. Martin's Griffin, 2005.

GENE PATENTING

The pioneering research of the Human Genome Project has given us the ability to isolate our genes. This has engendered hope that scientists may be able to use genetic research to treat or cure disease. By the end of the twentieth century, the US Patent Office had granted more than 1,500 patents on fragments of human DNA. The patents are not on DNA in its natural state, but on the process of discovering and isolating certain strings of DNA, and on DNA developed in the laboratory. But legal—and ethical—questions arise when commercial companies attempt to patent genetic research. Many people fear that these companies are coming close to patenting the building blocks of life itself.

PROS

Companies engaged in genomic research are legally entitled to patent genes, so why should they be prevented from doing so?

If companies are not allowed to patent the products of their research, other companies will exploit their findings. Without the safeguards that a patent provides, companies will end their research because they see no future profit.

An inventor must be able to protect his or her invention. Private companies will continue genomic research because it promises to be extremely lucrative. Competitors will be willing to pay royalties to the patent holder for use of the material because they, too, can foresee future profit.

Patents are granted for a limited time in the United States, 17 years. Companies need this time to recoup their investments. If another company wishes to pursue a project in a patented area, it can always consult the patent owner.

Profit has proved to be the most practical means of promoting medical advances. It is unrealistic and ill conceived to criticize an incentive that has brought us such benefits.

CONS

Genes are the very basis of human life, and to claim that anyone has the right to be regarded as the "owner" of a particular gene shows a basic disregard for humanity. Patenting treatments based on genetic research is morally acceptable, but patenting genes is not.

Most genetic research is not conducted by private companies. The publicly funded Human Genome Project has contributed, by far, the greater amount of knowledge in this area. Patenting stifles research. We need to ban patenting in order to protect the public investment in genome research.

Facts do not support this contention; the Myriad Company, which holds patents on isolating BRCA 1 & 2, genes connected with breast cancer, prevented the University of Pennsylvania from using a test for these genes that was substantially cheaper than the company's own screening procedure. Companies are putting private profit before public good. Instead of protecting their research investment, companies have a moral duty to facilitate the development of inexpensive treatments and screening procedures.

Patenting discourages research because scientists fear costly lawsuits by patent holders. Medical and biotech patent holders frequently exploit their monopolies, charging what they like for their drugs and treatments. It was only after immense public protest, for example, that companies cut the prices of their AIDS medicines for African countries.

The Human Genome Project makes its research readily available to ensure the free flow of information and stimulate further research. The only barriers to genetic research should be those of conscience.

Sample Motions:

This House would allow the patenting of genes.

This House believes that genes are inventions.

Web Links:

- American Medical Association. <http://www.amaassn.org/ama/pub/category/2314.html> Gives an overview of the issue and explains the implications of patenting genes.
- Human Genome Project Information. <http://www.ornl.gov/sci/techresources/Human_Genome/elsi/patents.shtml> Provides overview of pro and con arguments and links to many articles as well as other useful resources.
- The National Human Genome Research Institute (US). <http://www.genome.gov> Excellent source of information on all aspects of the Human Genome Project.

Further Reading:

Caplan, Arthur L., David Magnus, and Glenn Mc Gee. *Who Owns Life?* Prometheus Books, 2002.

Gibson, Johanna. *Patenting Lives (Intellectual Property, Theory, Culture).* Ashgate, 2008.

Shreeve, James. *The Genome War: How Craig Venter Tried to Capture the Code of Life and Save the World.* Ballantine Books, 2005.

GENETICALLY MODIFIED FOODS

The development of genetically modified (GM) foods has precipitated an ongoing debate among consumers, environmentalists, scientists, and even economists. On the one hand, genetic modification has improved crop characteristics—yield, resistance to disease, pests, or drought, etc.—and has contributed to global health. Recently, scientists announced the development of "golden rice"—rice genetically modified to produce greater levels of vitamin A—which can help prevent a variety of diseases in developing countries. On the other hand, the procedure has raised a number of concerns including the long-term risks to humans and the environment. Economists also point out that because biotechnology companies often patent GM crop varieties, farmers will become increasingly dependent on monopolies for seed.

PROS

Genetic modification is unnatural. There is a fundamental difference between modification via selective breeding and genetic engineering techniques. The former occurs over thousands of years and so the genes are changed much more gradually. With change occurring so rapidly, we now have no time to assess the long-term effects of these products on human health and the environment.

CONS

Genetic modification is entirely natural. The process of crop cultivation by selective breeding, which has been performed by farmers for thousands of years, leads to exactly the same kind of changes in DNA as modern modification techniques do. Current techniques are just faster and more selective. In fact, given two strands of DNA created from the same original strand, one by selective breeding and one by modern modification techniques, it is impossible to tell which is the "natural" strand. The changes resulting from selective breeding have been just as radical as current modifications. Wheat, for example, was cultivated through selective breeding from an almost no-yield rice-type crop into the super-crop it is today.

Introducing the DNA of one species into the genes of another is wrong. This attempt to play God is shortsighted and unnatural.

It is perfectly natural and safe to introduce genes from one organism into another. We must remember that all DNA is made up of the same four fundamental

PROS | CONS

molecules regardless of which organism the DNA came from originally. DNA from all organisms is very similar. Human DNA is 99% the same as chimpanzee DNA and about 50% the same as grass DNA. Consequently, the addition of genes from one organism into the DNA of another is like using LEGOs to create a structure. Indeed such processes occur all the time in nature in sexual reproduction.

Testing GM food is often difficult. Biotechnology companies are often unwilling to submit their results for peer review. Furthermore, in some countries government agencies are often unwilling to stop GM foodstuffs from reaching the shelf because of the clout the companies have with the government.

This debate should be decided on the basis of hard facts, not woolly assertions and environmental sentiment. Until scientific tests show that GM food poses a risk to agriculture or health, it should not be banned. GM foods undergo extensive testing before they are placed on the market. This testing takes two forms: peer review by other scientists and testing by the food standards agencies in the countries in which the product is to be marketed. For example, in the United States all GM food must be tested for nine years before being released onto the market.

GM foods are potentially dangerous. Human health is at risk because, despite extensive testing, scientists cannot anticipate all the problems that might occur when food is modified. This risk will increase as biotechnology companies introduce more modifications. GM foods also present a danger to the environment. The use of these crops has resulted in fewer strains planted. If disease wipes out a few these strains, the result could be catastrophic. In addition, removing certain varieties of crops wipes out the organisms that feed on them. Furthermore, pollen produced from GM crops can accidentally fertilize unmodified crops, polluting the natural gene pool. This cross-pollination, in turn, makes labeling foods impossible. Thus consumers will not be able to choose whether to purchase GM crops.

The fears about GM food are a result of media scares about "frankenfood." Few deaths have been directly attributed to genetic modification, and scientists are taking all reasonable precautions to ensure these products are safe. The need for many different strains is not an argument against GM crops. Scientists and farmers cannot produce and plant many different strains. Furthermore, scientists have no evidence that cross-pollination of GM with non-GM varieties is harmful.

GM food will not help solve hunger in developing countries. The problem in such countries is not one of food production but of distribution (due to wars, for example), the emphasis on cash crops rather than staple crops (to pay off the national debt), and deforestation and desertification. In addition, many GM strains are infertile, forcing farmers to buy seed annually from companies that can charge whatever they want because they have a patent on the strain.

The possible benefits from GM food are enormous. Modifications that render plants less vulnerable to pests lead to less pesticide use, which is better for the environment. Other modifications increase crop yield, which leads to lower food prices. This technology is particularly important for developing countries; it can help farmers grow crops in arid soil. More important, it can help prevent diseases as the introduction of "golden rice" has shown.

Yes, banning GM food would decrease consumer choice. However, governments have the right and obligation to intervene to prevent harm to both the population and the environment. Besides, the number of consumers who actually want GM food is tiny.

Banning GM food results in fewer choices for the consumer. Scientists can prevent crossbreeding between GM and non-GM plants so that foods can be properly labeled.

PROS	CONS
Genetically modifying food is yet another means by which multinational corporations can exercise illegitimate economic power over developing nations. The combination of the patenting of genes and the use of the terminator gene is a recipe for exploiting the developing world and destroying traditional agriculture.	The question of whether crop varieties should be allowed to be patented is separate from the debate on whether GM food is itself good or bad.
Issues of principle should always come before pragmatic concerns about unemployment. People have jobs that are dependent on illegal trade in endangered species and in drugs and arms. Maintaining or providing employment is not an argument for the continuation of these harmful and immoral practices nor is it an argument in favor of GM foods.	Unemployment in the biotechnology industry would increase dramatically if GM foods were banned.

Sample Motions:

This House would ban genetically modified food.

This House believes that genetically modified foods are not in the public interest.

This House would not eat "frankenfood."

Web Links:

- Genetically Modified Food News. <http://www.gmfoodnews.com> Links to articles on genetically modified food.
- GM Organism. <http://www.newscientist.com/channel/opinion/gm-food/> Site, sponsored by NewScientist, presents editorials on genetically modified crops.
- PBS. <http://www.pbs.org/wgbh/harvest/> Offers links to news articles, reports, and other Web sites relating to the controversy surrounding genetically modified foods.

Further Reading:

Federoff, Nina, and Nancy Marie Brown. *Mendel in the Kitchen: A Scientist's View of Genetically Modified Foods.* Joseph Henry Press, 2004.

Lambrecht, Bill. *Dinner at the New Gene Cafe: How Genetic Engineering Is Changing What We Eat, How We Live, and the Global Politics of Food.* St. Martin's Griffin, 2001.

Pinstrup-Andersen, Per, and Ebbe Schiøler. *Seeds of Contention: World Hunger and the Global Controversy over GM Crops.* Johns Hopkins University Press, 2001.

Ruse, Michael, and David Castle. *Genetically Modified Foods: Debating Biotechnology.* Prometheus, 2002.

GENETIC SCREENING

Francis Galton coined the term "eugenics" in 1883 during his work on the genetic basis of intelligence. Literally meaning "good breeding," the term referred to the restructuring of the characteristics of the human race through selective mating (and subsequent reproduction) of the higher echelons of society. Some people, including Theodore

Roosevelt, embraced the idea at the turn of the nineteenth century, but it lost favor as a result of its association with Nazi Germany, which took the idea to its extreme. Today, as a result of advances in biotechnology, we can screen fetuses to determine their predisposition to certain congenital disorders. In 2000, a baby boy, Adam Nash, was born after having been genetically screened as an embryo, from several embryos created by in vitro fertilization by his parents. They chose that embryo because tests showed that it was genetically healthy and the baby would be able to act as a bone marrow donor for his sister, who had a genetic disease. The case sparked heated moral debate.

PROS

Testing embryonic cells can help to identify potentially debilitating illnesses or inherited disorders. It can also determine the sex of a baby, allowing parents who carry a sex-linked genetic disorder to have children without passing on the disorder to their children. It is eminently sensible to use this technology to ensure that children are as healthy as possible.

CONS

Embryonic testing could become a slippery slope for future exploitation of the process. It must not develop into the widespread abuse of screening to create "designer babies" chosen for aesthetic or other qualities considered desirable. This is morally wrong.

PRO: We have a duty to give a child the best possible start in life, and if the technology is available to determine whether a baby will have a genetic disease such as Huntington's we should use it. This is not a case of engineering a child.

CON: Are we not presuming that those born with physical or mental defects or genetic predispositions to certain diseases do not enjoy a quality of life as high and a life as fruitful as those born without? To suggest that they be bred out of society is presumptuous and abhorrent. More to the point, many "defective" genes confer advantages of a different nature, e.g., the sickle cell anemia allele protects somewhat against malaria.

PRO: When a number of embryos are created through in vitro fertilization, the embryos not chosen after screening may be offered up for "adoption." Human life will not be thrown away, and childless couples can benefit.

CON: The proposition holds sinister overtones of treating embryos like commodities. Even more morally dubious is the idea of disposing of those embryos that do not conform to the requirements of health.

Sample Motions:

This House would choose its babies.
This House would genetically engineer its children.
This House calls for more genetic screening.

Web Links:

- BreastCancer.org. <http://www.breastcancer.org/risk/genetic/test_pros_cons.jsp> Outlines the pros and cons of genetic screening in relation to breast cancer.
- DNA Genetic Testing: Screening for Genetic Conditions and Genetic Susceptibility. <http://209.85.129.132/search?q=cache:YGESKVulHcwJ:www.genetics.com.au/pdf/factsheets/fs21.pdf+genetic+screening&hl=en&ct=clnk&cd=7&client=safari> Explains the process of genetic testing and its effectiveness.
- Medline Plus. <http://www.nlm.nih.gov/medlineplus/genetictesting.html> Comprehensive overview of genetic testing.

Further Reading:

Cowan, Ruth Schwartz. *Heredity and Hope: The Case for Genetic Screening.* Harvard University Press, 2008.

Rothman, Barbara Katz. *The Book of Life: A Personal Guide to Race, Normality and the Implications of the Human Genome Project.* Beacon, 2001.

Skene, Loane, and Janna Thompson. *The Sorting Society: The Ethics of Genetic Screening and Therapy.* Cambridge University Press, 2008.

Zallen, Doris Teichler. *To Test or Not To Test: A Guide to Genetic Screening and Risk.* Rutgers University Press, 2008.

GLOBALIZATION AND THE POOR

Globalization is the process that spreads economic, political, social, and cultural activity across national boundaries and increases the integration of internationally dispersed activities. Foreign media often focus on the spread of American culture (characterized as fast food restaurants, Hollywood movies, etc.), but academic debates center around more fundamental economic issues. While globalization may have benefited industrialized nations and transnational corporations (TNCs), has the trend eroded global and national solidarity and increased the poverty and isolation of developing nations?

PROS

Globalization marginalizes the poor. It is a means of exclusion, deepening inequality and reinforcing the division of the world into core and periphery. It is a new form of Western imperialism that dominates and exploits through TNC capital and global governance by institutions such as the World Bank and the International Monetary Fund (IMF).

Globalization has intensified global and national inequality. The economic and social gaps within countries and between countries are widening, with the rich becoming richer and the poor becoming poorer. Globalization is an uneven process causing world fragmentation. Trade has also seen increasing inequality. Because of increasing globalization the value of world trade is 17 times greater than 50 years ago, but Latin America's share has fallen from 11% to 5% and Africa's from 8% to 2%. The terms of trade have increasingly moved against developing nations.

Globalization exploits developing nations and their poor through TNCs. Globalization is a euphemism for transnationalization, the spread of powerful companies to areas that best suit corporate interests.

Increased global integration means that poorer countries become more vulnerable to world financial markets. The East Asian economic crisis of the 1990s, a direct result of globalization, increased and intensified poverty. The crisis shows that even the strongest developing states are at the mercy of global economic forces that serve the

CONS

Globalization is eroding the differences between developed and developing nations, sometimes called the North-South divide. It is a progressive force for creating global prosperity. Through free trade and capital mobility, globalization is creating a global market in which prosperity, wealth, power, and liberal democracy are being diffused around the globe.

Globalization has increased world prosperity, and organizational efforts to stabilize the world economy have shown significant progress. By historical standards global poverty has fallen more in the last 50 years than in the previous 500, and the welfare of people in almost all regions has improved considerably during the past few decades. Globalization will bring about the end of the Third World. The fall in the developing nations' share of world trade is due to internal economic, social, and political conditions in individual countries.

Globalization promotes development by spreading technology and knowledge to poor nations. The poorest nations are those countries bypassed by globalization.

Globalization has brought about huge benefits. The emergence of a single global market, free trade, capital mobility, and global competition has permitted the diffusion of prosperity, wealth, and power. Globalization has opened up new opportunities and is the harbinger of modernization and development. It was the force that

PROS	CONS
interests of the dominant capitalist powers. Globalization also resulted in the speedy transition of the crisis to the other East Asian countries—the "contagion effect"—with devastating human consequences. The benefits of the global market accrue to a relatively small proportion of the world's population. The stronger become stronger and the weak become weaker.	led to the successful development of East Asia and its "economic miracle." Far from making developing nations more vulnerable, increased global integration means that better organizational structures are in place to address world political, economic, and social problems.
Globalization is a form of disempowerment. Outside interference from the World Bank and the IMF has weakened the economies of poor nations and constrained development. International negotiations to reduce and eliminate foreign debt have led to increasing exports of capital and deeper indebtedness in developing nations.	The policies of institutions such as the IMF and the World Bank have reinforced the global market. Outside intervention allows the dissemination of effective economic management strategies to less developed areas.

Sample Motions:

This House believes that globalization marginalizes the poor.

This House believes that globalization will bring about the end of the Third World.

This House believes that globalization is a euphemism for transnationalization.

Web Links:

- Africa Economic Analysis: Globalization Still Hurting the Poor. <http://www.africaeconomicanalysis.org/articles/gen/globalisation_0507.html> Article arguing that globalization hurts less developed countries.
- Forbes. <http://www.forbes.com/forbes/2007/0416/064.html>. Article arguing that globalization is beneficial for the poor.
- Poverty and Globalisation. <http://news.bbc.co.uk/hi/english/static/events/reith_2000/lecture5.stm> Part of the BBC lecture series, *Respect for the Earth*. Lecture emphasizes the impact of globalization on food producers, particularly women.

Further Reading:

Allen, Tim, and Alan Thomas. *Poverty and Development into the 21st Century.* Oxford University Press, 2000.

Driscoll, William, and Julie Clark, eds. *Globalization and the Poor: Exploitation or Equalizer?* International Debate Education Association, 2003.

Isaak, Robert A. *The Globalization Gap: How the Rich Get Richer and the Poor Get Left Further Behind.* Prentice Hall/Financial Times, 2005.

GLOBAL WARMING

Since the 1980s, a growing body of evidence has suggested that industrialization is affecting Earth's climate. As a result, in 1997 the industrialized nations of the world agreed to reduce their carbon dioxide emissions under the Kyoto Protocol. The protocol has come under attack from both sides—many environmentalists feel that it does not really address the threat of global warming, while many in industry feel it is an unnecessary burden. Although the United States signed the agreement, in 2001, President George W. Bush announced that the United States would abandon its commitment to the protocol as it was not in the nation's best economic interests. Global warming is a particularly difficult issue because it demands a worldwide response. Many developing nations are understandably angered that a problem that seems to have been created by the rich, developed nations will have the most impact on the Third World. They fear that efforts to curb global warming will also curb economic development. A global consensus remains far off.

PROS

Over the past 100 years, humankind has been burning increasing quantities of fossil fuels to provide energy. This has released large volumes of gases into the atmosphere, particularly CO_2. At the same time, the world's remaining large forests, which help absorb CO_2, are being rapidly felled. Overall, the levels of carbon dioxide in the atmosphere have increased by 30% during the last century. When in the atmosphere, CO_2 and other gases are thought to cause a "greenhouse effect": They allow sunlight to pass through, but absorb heat emitted by the Earth, trapping it and leading to global warming. Weather records seem to support this theory. Average temperatures have increased by 0.6°C since the nineteenth century; the four hottest years since accurate records have been kept have all been in the 1990s. Unusual weather patterns such as floods and droughts have also been on the increase, with the uncharacteristically strong El Niño events of recent years causing widespread disruption. The Intergovernmental Panel on Climate Change (IPCC), an international body set up to study possible global warming, has concluded that ". . . the balance of evidence suggests that there is a discernible human influence on global climate."

Computer models predict that continued global warming could have catastrophic effects. Changes in temperature could devastate wildlife when local vegetation dies off. Patterns of disease could change. Already isolated cases of malaria have been reported far north of traditional danger zones as warmer weather allows the mosquitoes that carry the disease to spread. Most important, a portion of the polar ice caps might melt and lead to a rise in sea level, which has already increased by between 10 and 25 cm in the last 100 years. Giant cracks have been found in the Larsen ice shelf in Antarctica, which suggest that it is breaking apart; a section 48 miles wide and 22 miles long drifted free and melted as early as 1994. If, as experts believe, temperatures rise a further 3°C over the next century, low-lying areas and even entire countries, such as Bangladesh, could disappear under the waves.

Technology has now reached the point where we can continue to increase standards of living without burning fossil fuels. Renewable sources of energy, such as wind

CONS

Scientists have not yet proved conclusively that humankind is causing global warming. Although average temperatures rose during the twentieth century, temperatures actually dropped slightly between the 1930s and the 1970s. This was not associated with a reduction in fossil fuel consumption; emissions actually increased over this period. If the "greenhouse gases" are responsible for global warming, how do you account for this? Accurate records simply do not cover a long enough period to be useful. The Earth's average temperature varies naturally through time, and we have few good explanations of the Ice Ages. Indeed, there was a "mini–Ice Age" around 400 years ago, during which the River Thames in England repeatedly froze over in winter. This was followed by an intense but natural period of "global warming." We do not have enough information to say that current trends are not simply a natural variation.

Again, our computer models for predicting climate change are far from reliable. Weather is a hugely complex system that we are only beginning to understand. It is affected by many factors, including solar activity, volcanic eruptions, ocean currents, and other cycles that we are gradually discovering. Very slight changes in the computer model result in immense differences in predictions. Some scientists, for example, have suggested that global warming could actually cause a drop in sea level as rainfall patterns and ocean currents shift. Indeed, refinements in the models used by the IPCC have caused it to modify its predictions. In 1990, the IPCC estimated to modify its predictions. In 1990, the IPCC estimated that by 2100 the average temperature would rise by 3°C and the sea would rise by about 65cm; in 1995, it revised its estimates to 2°C and 50 cm. The more research that takes place, the less catastrophic global warming seems to be. The media always report the predictions of doom most widely.

Of course greater energy efficiency is important. However, most alternative fuels are simply not effective. They can also cause their own problems. Nuclear power cre

PROS

or solar power, are ripe for development, but have yet to see the levels of investment needed to make them truly effective. More efficient use of energy is also vital. Encouraging the development of electric cars or promoting better insulation of houses could make a substantial difference in CO_2 levels in the long run.

CONS

ates unacceptable radioactive waste; hydroelectric power projects, such as the Three Gorges Dam in China, lead to the flooding of vast areas and the destruction of the local environment; solar and wind power often require the covering of large areas of natural beauty with solar panels or turbines. Environmentalists often paint an idealistic view of renewable energy that is far from the less romantic reality.

PROS

Global warming is a worldwide catastrophe waiting to happen. The emission of greenhouse gases affects everyone. It is, therefore, vital that the entire world respond now. The targets set by the Kyoto Protocol will barely scratch the surface of the problem. The developed world agreed to only minimal reductions in carbon dioxide emissions, and no agreement was reached involving the developing world, which is producing a greater percentage of greenhouse gas emissions every year. Gases like CO_2 remain in the atmosphere for centuries. If we wait until we can see the results of global warming, it may be too late. The damage will have been done. We must act now, and we must act globally. Developed countries must do all they can to reduce their use of fossil fuels. They must assist developing nations to do the same, by sharing technology or perhaps through "emissions trading," allowing poorer countries to sell their quota of pollution in return for hard cash. International pressure must be exerted against those countries that do not cooperate, even if this slows economic growth. The poorest regions of the world would suffer most from more droughts and floods and rising sea levels. However difficult it may be in the short term, such actions now may save millions of lives in the future.

CONS

The evidence for global warming is not strong enough to merit this kind of response. The changes over the past century may certainly have been purely natural. Environmentalists in the developed world can afford the luxury of demanding government action because reducing pollution will have a minimal impact on their technology-based economies. Those in the developing world are not so lucky. Industrialization is a key part of building successful economies and bringing prosperity to the world's poorest people; heavy industry is often the only area in which developing nations can compete. Global action on greenhouse gas emissions would sustain the inequalities of the status quo. The developing world would have to depend on multinational corporations to provide the technology needed to keep pollution levels low, or else they would have to stop expanding their economies. Having apparently caused the problem through the industrialization that made them powerful, developed countries would be pulling the ladder up behind them, depriving other countries of the chance to grow. This is simply unacceptable. In the modern world, one of our first priorities must be to help the poorest people achieve the prosperity they need to support themselves. The current evidence for global warming does not begin to merit endangering this goal.

Sample Motions:

This House believes that the Kyoto Protocol didn't go far enough.
This House calls for urgent action on global warming.
This House fears a global greenhouse.
This House believes that global warming demands global action.

Web Links:

- Intergovernmental Panel on Climate Change. <http://www.ipcc.ch> Offers reports assessing scientific, technical, and socioeconomic information related to human-induced climate change.
- Kyoto Protocol. <http://www.cnn.com/SPECIALS/1997/global.warming/stories/treaty/> Full text of the Kyoto Protocol.
- National Center for Policy Analysis. <http://www.ncpa.org/bothside/gw.html> Site presenting arguments on both sides of the debate.

Further Reading:

Flannery, Tim. *The Weather Makers: How Man Is Changing the Climate and What It Means for Life on Earth.* Atlantic Monthly Press, 2006.

Gore, Al. *An Inconvenient Truth.* Rodale, 2006.

Lovelock, James. *The Revenge of Gaia: Earth's Climate Crisis and the Fate of Humanity.* Basic Books, 2006.

GOD, EXISTENCE OF

This is the "Big" question, the ultimate metaphysical debate. It has occupied the world's best minds for centuries. Followers of many religions have offered proofs of the existence of God. Below are arguments from within the Judeo-Christian and Islamic traditions.

PROS

The world is so magnificent and wonderful, so full of variety and beauty that it is inconceivable that it could have come about purely by chance. It is so intricate that a conscious hand must have been involved in its creation. Therefore, God exists as the creator of the world.

CONS

You cannot infer from the variety and beauty of the world that God was the creator. The conception of God contains many extra attributes that are not necessary for a world creator. Just because the world is beautiful and varied does not mean it was consciously designed. Why can't beauty happen by accident?

PRO: If you saw a watch lying on the sand, you would think that someone must have made the watch—a watchmaker. Similarly, we human beings are so complicated and amazing that we must conclude that we had a conscious maker.

CON: The difference between a watch and humans is that the watch serves a purpose—to tell time. Therefore, seeing something so perfectly serving a purpose suggests design. What purpose do we serve? We don't, we just exist. And even if we were designed for a purpose, the earlier argument applies: A purposeful designer isn't necessarily God.

PRO: Only human beings are capable of rational thought. That we are here at all is amazing. One infinitesimal change in the world and life would not have evolved. Getting something so amazing, on such long odds, smacks of intention.

CON: The argument from probability does not work. It relies on there being something special about us. What is so special about us? We are rational—so what?

PRO: God must be perfect if he exists. But a thing that exists is more perfect than a thing that doesn't exist. But nothing can be more perfect than God. So God must exist.

CON: This ontological argument can be rebutted by rejecting the idea that existence is perfection. Something either exists or it doesn't. The argument is a disguised conditional. You say "if God exists then he must be perfect, and if he must be perfect he must therefore exist." But all this rests on the initial "if God exists." If God doesn't exist, we don't have the problem and the argument doesn't work.

PROS	CONS
Everything in the universe has a cause. It is inconceivable that time is one long chain of cause and effect without beginning, but it must be because we cannot conceive of something happening uncaused. Therefore, God exists as the uncaused first cause.	The cosmological argument doesn't work. For a start, an uncaused first cause still doesn't necessarily have all the attributes it would need to be called God, e.g., omnipotence, benevolence, and omniscience. More important, an uncaused first cause is just as incomprehensible to us as an endless chain of cause and effect. You are just shifting the incomprehension one stage back.

Sample Motions:

This House believes that God exists.

This House believes that reports of God's death have been greatly exaggerated.

Web Links:

- Counterbalance. <http://www.counterbalance.org> Contains summary of the debate about the existence of God from a cosmological standpoint.
- The Existence of God and the Beginning of the Universe. <http://www.leaderu.com/truth/3truth11.html> An academic paper employing a cosmological argument to help prove the existence of God.
- New Advent. <http://www.newadvent.org/cathen/06608b.htm> Detailed essay on a Roman Catholic Web site outlining the various proofs for the existence of God.

Further Reading:

Boa, Kenneth D., and Robert M. Bowman Jr. *20 Compelling Evidences That God Exists: Discover Why Believing in God Makes so Much Sense.* David C. Cook 2005.

Gardiner, Phillip. *Proof? Does God Exist?* Real2Can, 2007.

Strobel, Lee. *The Case for a Creator: A Journalist Investigates Scientific Evidence That Points Toward God.* Zonderan, 2004.

GREENHOUSE GASES: TRADING QUOTAS

A number of methods have been proposed to reduce the emissions of the so-called greenhouse gases that lead to global warming. The European Union has always favored taxing heavy polluters, while the United States has supported Tradable Pollution Quotas (TPQs). The 1997 Kyoto Protocol laid the foundation for TPQs. Under this agreement developing countries are exempt from the emission standards and cannot take part directly in pollution trading. Each country in the TPQ plan is initially permitted to produce a certain maximum amount of each polluting gas. Countries that want to exceed their quotas can buy the right to do so from other countries that have produced less than their quota. Furthermore, countries can also "sink" carbon (by planting forests to remove carbon dioxide from the atmosphere) to offset some of their pollution quotas. Interestingly, two usually opposing groups are against TPQs. Industries claim that they go too far and that such stringent regulation is unnecessary. Environmentalists maintain that they are too lax.

PROS

The scientific community agrees that something must be done to curb emissions of greenhouse gases that may be the cause of global warming. The possible consequences of global warming include crop failure, mass flooding, and the destruction of entire ecosystems with the possible loss of billions of lives. Other consequences of pollution include acid rain and the enlargement of the hole in the ozone layer.

CONS

The environmental lobby has hugely overestimated the claims for pollution damaging the environment. The fossil record indicates that climate change has occurred frequently in the past, and there is little evidence linking climate change with emissions.

PRO: The TPQ plan is the only practical way to reduce emissions of greenhouse gases globally. It will guarantee that global levels of these gases are kept below strict targets and is more realistic than expecting heavy polluters to cut their emissions overnight.

CON: The TPQ plan ensures more pollution in the long run than if limits were strictly enforced for each country and punitive taxes imposed on those exceeding their quotas. Without TPQs, the environment would benefit further if a country kept well below its emissions quota. Adopting the TPQ plan means that this benefit is lost because the right to this extra pollution is bought by another country.

PRO: Emissions are a global problem. The emission of the main greenhouse gas, carbon dioxide, for example, affects the entire planet regardless of where the gas is produced. This validates the use of TPQs, which act to limit the total amount of each polluting gas globally. TPQs are much more effective than the alternative of taxing emissions, because rich companies or countries will be able to pay the tax and still pollute.

CON: Stating that it does not matter where pollution is produced is simplistic and completely untrue for many gases, which do affect the region in which they are created. Furthermore, to permit developing countries to industrialize, they have been exempted from the protocol. This seriously undermines its efficiency. Furthermore, if taxes on pollution were set high enough, big companies would stop polluting because it would be prohibitively expensive. In addition, the introduction of TPQs will make later reductions in global emissions much harder. Once trading in TPQs has started, countries that have bought extra emission rights would certainly not voluntarily give them up to help reduce global emissions further.

PRO: TPQs are tried and tested. The United States has used them successfully since they were introduced in 1990. Therefore, we have good reason to expect them to succeed on a global scale.

CON: TPQs have had some success in the United States, but they failed in Europe for two reasons. First, the European plans were poorly conceived, as was the Kyoto Protocol. Second, whereas the American solution to pollution was always trading emissions, the main European solution was, and still is, to produce new technology to clean the emissions. Extending the TPQ plan to the entire globe will slow the technological developments needed to reduce greenhouse gases.

PRO: Progress in the field of emission control is remarkably difficult because of the opposition from the industrial lobby, most notably in the United States, which sees such restrictions as harmful to its economy. TPQs are the one method of control acceptable to these lobby groups and, more significant, to the US government. As the world's biggest polluter, the United States must be included in any meaningful treaty. Therefore, TPQs are the only practical way forward.

CON: The Kyoto Protocol lacks a comprehensive enforcement mechanism and is thus ineffective. In addition, assessing the effect that an individual country's carbon "sink" is having on the atmosphere is impossible. This merely creates a loophole that allows a country to abuse the protocol and produce more than its quota of gases.

PROS

TPQs cause less damage to an economy than any other emission control regime. Individual companies and countries can trade TPQs on the free market until they have struck the right balance between the cost of paying to pollute and the cost of cleaning up their industry.

CONS

TPQs will hit employment hard. Even developed countries are not so rich that they can simply buy enough quotas to avoid pollution; neither can they afford to install the expensive cleaning technology. Growth will consequently decline and with that decline will come a drop in living standards in developed countries.

Sample Motions:

This House would buy the right to pollute.
This House supports tradable pollution quotas.
This House believes that the Kyoto Protocol got it right.

Web Links:

- Central News Network. <http://edition.cnn.com/2008/TECH/science/09/01/carbon.trading.pv/index.html?iref=intlOnlyonCNN> Answers FAQs related to the issue.
- Leonardo Academy. <http://www.leonardoacademy.org/Resources/emissiontrading.htm> Introduction to emissions trading.
- Peace and Environment News. <http://www.perc.ca/PEN/2004-07-08/s-boddy.html> Describes the pros and cons of carbon trading.

Further Reading:

Labatt, Sonia, and Rodney R. White. *Carbon Finance: The Financial Implications of Climate Change.* Wiley, 2007.

Lohmann, Larry. *Carbon Trading: A Critical Conversation on Climate Change, Privatisation and Power.* Dag Hammarskjöld Foundation, 2006.

Victor, David G. *The Collapse of the Kyoto Protocol and the Struggle to Slow Global Warming.* Princeton University Press, 2001.

GUN CONTROL

The issue of gun control has divided American society for years. Supporters insist that tighter measures are needed to curb crime and to prevent tragedies such as the recent wave of school massacres where students have used guns to kill other students and teachers. Opponents insist that they have the constitutional right to carry guns, and that people, not guns, cause crime. Long considered a uniquely American problem, gun control has become an issue in many European nations as a result of incidents including the school massacre in Erfurt, Germany, in 2002. The issue of gun control again came to the fore in the United States after the 2007 massacre of 33 students at Virginia Tech by a mentally ill student and the 2008 Supreme Court ruling striking down the District of Columbia's ban on handguns.

PROS

The only function of a gun is to kill. The more instruments of death and injury we remove from our society, the safer we will be.

CONS

Prohibition is not the answer. Banning guns would not make them disappear or make them any less dangerous. Citizens have the right to own weapons to protect themselves, their families, and their property. Many people also need guns for other reasons; farmers, for example, need them to protect their stock and crops.

PROS	CONS
The legal ownership of guns by law-abiding citizens inevitably leads to many unnecessary and tragic deaths. Legally held guns end up in the hands of criminals, who would have greater difficulty in obtaining weapons if they were less prevalent. Guns also end up in the hands of children, leading to tragic accidents and terrible disasters like the Columbine massacre.	Guns don't kill people; people kill people. Restricting gun ownership will do nothing to make society safer. Most crimes involve illegal weapons.
Shooting as a sport desensitizes people to the lethal nature of all firearms, creating a gun culture that glamorizes and legitimizes unnecessary gun ownership. The minority who enjoy blood sports should not be allowed to block the interests of society as a whole in gun control.	Shooting is a major sport enjoyed by many law-abiding people. Sportsmen have the right to continue their chosen leisure activity. Spending on guns and ancillary equipment puts large sums into the economy. Hunters also put food on the table.
Burglary should not be punished by vigilante killings. No amount of property is worth a human life. Keeping firearms in the home for protection leads to accidental deaths. And, perversely, criminals may be more likely to carry weapons if they think they are in danger from homeowners.	Law-abiding citizens deserve the right to protect their families in their own homes. Would-be rapists and armed burglars will think twice before attempting to break into a house where owners may keep firearms.
There is a correlation between the leniency of a country's gun laws and its suicide rate—not because gun owners are depressive, but because the means of quick and effective suicide is at hand. The state should discourage and restrict the ownership of something that wastes so many lives.	A country is more able to defend itself if many of its citizens are proficient with firearms. Some countries require adult citizens to maintain weapons and periodically train in their use. Of course, such widespread ownership of weapons is also a safeguard against domestic tyranny.

Sample Motions:

This House calls for stricter controls on gun ownership.

This House believes there is no right to bear arms.

Web Links:

- Guide to Gun Laws, Gun Control and Gun Rights. <http://www.jurist.law.pitt.edu/gunlaw.htm> Maintained by the Legal Education Network, the site offers resources on all sides of the gun control debate.
- National Rifle Association of America. <http://www.nra.org> America's most powerful pro-gun lobby offers information on campaigns to limit gun control.
- You Debate. <http://www.youdebate.com/DEBATES/guncontrol.HTM> Outlines the pros and cons of gun control.

Further Reading:

Carter, Gregg Lee. *Gun Control in the United States: A Reference Handbook*. ABC-CLIO, 2006.

Lott, John R. *The Bias Against Guns: Why Almost Everything You've Heard About Gun Control Is Wrong*. Regnery Publishing, 2003.

Spitzer, Robert J. *The Politics of Gun Control*. CQ Press, 2003.

HABEAS CORPUS, RESTRICTIONS ON

Habeas corpus is a centuries-old legal mechanism that prevents government from arbitrarily detaining its citizens. It is a petition to a state or federal court, on behalf of a prisoner, requesting that the court review the basis of the person's detention. Habeas corpus is considered to be one of the foundations of constitutional democracy and the principle has been adopted by many countries throughout the world. In the US, habeas corpus is a fundamental piece of the legal system that allows capital defendants to challenge death penalty rulings and immigrant detainees to challenge the legality of their detentions. It is protected by Article I, Section 9 of the Constitution, which states: "The privilege of the writ of habeas corpus shall not be suspended, unless when in cases of rebellion or invasion the public safety may require it." After the attacks of September 11, 2001, the Bush administration began to challenge the applicability of habeas corpus to terror suspect detainees. The legal and political battles around restrictions to habeas corpus have been fierce. Most recently, in Boumediene v. Bush, *the Supreme Court held that terror suspects detained at Guantanamo are protected by habeas corpus.*

PROS

The events of September 11 constituted an unprecedented attack against Americans on American soil. The US government must do everything in its power to ensure that the individuals responsible cannot participate in further terrorist activities. Restricting suspected terrorists' rights to challenge their detentions is necessary to achieve that goal. Terror suspects still have recourse to military tribunals, which contain many of the same safeguards as the federal court system.

Unlawful enemy combatants are not US citizens. The only connection they have to this country is the desire to destroy it. As such, they do not fall within the group of people the Constitution is intended to protect.

Global terrorism calls for aggressive responses. We cannot allow our nation to be besieged by terrorists while we stand aside and do nothing. Constitutional freedoms are extremely important, but the security and continued existence of our nation come first. American must make a stand and demonstrate that terrorism will not be tolerated.

There is a longstanding tradition of suspending habeas corpus protections during times of war and conflict. For example, President Lincoln suspended habeas corpus during the Civil War. Habeas was also suspended briefly during World War II, after the attacks on Pearl Harbor.

CONS

There is no reason why the United States cannot uphold constitutional protections such as habeas corpus and effectively combat terrorism at the same time. The two are not mutually exclusive. In fact, ensuring that suspected terrorists have access to Federal Courts will save much-needed resources and ensure more accurate administration of justice. In the present case, it is unclear which of the Guantanamo detainees actually committed the acts that are used to justify their indefinite detention. Allowing detainees to challenge their detention would bring clarity to this uncertain situation and free up resources in the war against terrorism.

Via legal precedent, habeas corpus protections extend to foreign nationals detained in the US. Furthermore, to focus solely on the immigration status and purported guilt of suspected terrorists ignores the fact that habeas exists to protect us all. Eliminating rights for "bad" people necessarily eliminates them for the innocent, as well.

Restrictions to habeas corpus undermine the war against terror and put our national security further at risk. Habeas corpus legitimizes the war against terror by ensuring that US action against suspected terrorists has some legal basis and is not purely subjective. Furthermore, if the US disregards habeas protections, it sets a dangerous precedent for the rest of the world. If other countries followed suit, US citizens abroad could be indefinitely detained with no legal recourse.

The current war on terror is not comparable to past wars during which habeas was suspended. Both the Civil War and World War II were openly declared wars of limited duration following invasions by hostile forces. The "war on terror" is nebulous and open-ended. In any case,

PROS

The war on terror may not follow the rules of traditional warfare, but it is a war nonetheless. Current restrictions on habeas corpus are merely an extension of policies enacted in the past during similarly challenging times.

CONS

history has harshly judged arbitrary detentions during wartime. Lincoln's Civil War detentions and Roosevelt's Japanese internment camps of the 1940s are embarrassing chapters in our national history. The fact that former presidents improperly suspended habeas corpus is all the more reason to exercise caution now.

Sample Motions

This House would reaffirm habeas corpus protections for suspected terrorists.

This House would suspend habeas corpus during the war against terrorism.

Web Links:

- American Civil Liberties Union. <http://www.aclu.org/safefree/detention/habeastimeline.html> A timeline of habeas corpus history, beginning in thirteenth-century England.
- Brennan Center for Justice. <http://www.brennancenter.org/content/section/category/detention_habeas_corpus> Contains links to publications, legal briefs, and other Web resources about restrictions on habeas corpus post–9/11.

Further Reading:

Hafetz, Jonathan. *Ten Things You Should Know About Habeas Corpus*. Brennan Center for Justice, 2007.

Schwarz, Frederick A.O. Jr., and Aziz Z. Huq. *Unchecked and Unbalanced: Presidential Power in a Time of Terror.* New Press, 2008.

HATE SPEECH ON CAMPUS

Over the past few decades, a number of American colleges have reported incidents of verbal abuse and hate speech directed against minorities and homosexuals on their campuses. In response, many schools have adopted codes prohibiting speech that is racist, sexist, homophobic, or offensive to religious groups.

PROS

The rights we enjoy come with responsibilities. Minorities have a right to be free from verbal abuse and fear. If such rights are not informally respected, the college administration has the right and obligation to adopt codes prohibiting offensive speech.

The constant repetition of hate speech promotes offensive racial stereotypes. If children and youths grow up without hearing such views, they will mature without the bigoted attitudes engendered by constantly hearing hate speech.

CONS

Free speech is one of our basic rights and should be upheld at all costs. College administrations may abuse these speech codes, using them to silence those whom they consider disruptive. Upholding the right to hate speech will protect the free speech of everyone. Colleges should outlaw hate crimes, not hate speech. While we may abhor such views, it would be wrong to censor them.

Stereotyping is a result of the underrepresentation of minorities among students, faculty, and administrators on most campuses. University authorities should recruit more members of these minorities.

PROS	CONS
Adopting a speech code sends a strong message. It shows minorities that the authorities support them and, thus, will help in minority recruitment. It also shows bigots that their views will not be tolerated and helps marginalize and punish them.	Codes can often lead to resentment that can cause a backlash against minorities.
Minority students cannot learn in an environment of fear and hatred. If all students are to achieve their potential, they must be allowed to work without harassment.	Ensuring freedom of speech is especially critical in universities. The needs of education are served best in an environment in which free thought and free expression are actively encouraged.

Sample Motions:

This House would censor hate speech on campus.

This House may not agree with what you say, but will defend to the death your right to say it.

Web Links:

- American Civil Liberties Union (ACLU). <http://www.aclu.org/studentsrights/expression/12808pub19941231.html> Section of the ACLU Web site explaining the organization's stance on hate speech on campus.
- Associated Press. <http://www.freedomforum.org/templates/document.asp?documentID=16143> A brief summary of the controversy surrounding hate speech in schools.
- First Amendment Center. <http://www.firstamendmentcenter.org/speech/pubcollege/topic.aspx?topic=campus_speech_codes> Outlines the history of restrictions on hate speech and analyzes possible reform.

Further Reading:

Bayly, Michael. *Creating Safe Environments for LGBT Students: A Catholic Schools Perspective.* Routledge, 2007.

Downs, Donald Alexander. *Restoring Free Speech and Liberty on Campus.* Cambridge University Press, 2006.

Thomas, Andrew Peyton. *The People v. Harvard Law: How America's Oldest Law School Turned Its Back on Free Speech.* Encounter Books, 2005.

HEALTH CARE, UNIVERSAL

The provision of health care to the citizens of the United States has been a contentious issue for decades. Currently, some people are covered under government health plans through programs such as Medicaid, Medicare, and the State Children's Health Insurance Program. But nearly 45 million people in the United States do not have health insurance and 38 million have inadequate coverage. The health statistics for the uninsured are far worse than the statistics for those with insurance. Almost every industrialized country has a system of universal health care. These systems are single-payer programs: The government is the single payer for health care services. Citizens of those countries pay for their own health insurance, but they do not pay as much as we do in the United States. The cost of insurance is income-sensitive, so you pay more if your income is higher. Some believe that the United States should move to a system of universal health care so all our citizens can have access to quality medical care. Others say there are better ways to fix the system.

PROS

With universal health care, people are able to seek preventive treatment. For example, in a recent study 70% of women with health insurance knew their cholesterol level while only 50% of uninsured women did. Ultimately, people who do not get preventive health care will get care only when their diseases and illnesses are more advanced and their care will cost more.

Health insurance premiums are very high. Even employer-subsidized programs are expensive for many Americans. These plans often have high copayments or deductibles. For those without insurance, a relatively minor illness can be financially ruinous. Incremental plans like the ones currently in existence, which cover only individuals who meet certain age or income criteria, will never provide true universal coverage. Even the State Children's Health Insurance Program, which was intended to extend health insurance benefits to more children, has not been able to meet the needs of our nation's children.

The current system of health maintenance organizations (HMOs) has destroyed the doctor-patient relationship and patient choice of health care providers. Patients find that their doctors are not on their new plan and are forced to leave doctors with whom they have established a trusting relationship. Also, patients must get approval to see specialists and then are permitted to see only selected doctors. Doctors usually can't spend enough time with patients in the HMO-controlled environment. Patients would have many more choices in a universal health care system. The HMOs that put profits before people would become obsolete.

The United States spends $2 trillion on health care. Many studies have shown that a single-payer system would cut costs enough to enable everyone in the United States to have access to health care without the nation spending any more than currently. Medicare, a government-administered health care program, has administrative costs of less than 2% of its total budget.

In the current system the employee and the employee's family often depend on the employer for affordable health insurance. If the employee loses his or her job, the cost to get new health insurance can be high and is often unaffordable. Even with the current federal laws related to transportability of health insurance, the costs to the employee are too high. With a single payer, universal health care system, health insurance would no longer be tied to the employer and employees would not have to consider health insurance as a reason to stay with a given employer.

CONS

Universal health care will cause people to use the health care system more. If they are covered, they will go to the doctor when they do not really need to and will become heavier users of the system. As seen in other countries, this heavier utilization results in delays and ultimately the rationing of care.

Many programs are already available where people can get care. Many employers offer health insurance plans. Health insurance plans can be purchased by individuals with no need to rely on an employer. Low-income individuals qualify for Medicaid and seniors qualify for Medicare. Eligible children benefit from the State Children's Health Insurance Program. Health insurance is a necessity and, like other necessities, people must pay for their fair share and not expect the government to provide for them.

With government control of health care, ceilings on costs will be placed and many doctors will not be rewarded for their long hours and important roles in our lives. The road to becoming a doctor is long and hard; without the monetary rewards in place, good people will not enter the field of medicine. Current doctors may find that they do not want to continue their careers in a government-controlled market. The American Medical Association does not endorse a government-controlled, single-payer universal health care system.

The US government cannot afford to fund universal health care. Other universal social welfare policies like Social Security and Medicare have encountered major problems with funding. We should not add another huge government-funded social program. The nations that provide universal health care coverage spend a substantial amount of their GDP on the service.

The current system of offering group insurance through employers covers many Americans with good quality health insurance. The group plan concept enables insurance companies to insure people who are high risk and low risk by mixing them into the same pool. The issues of transportability of coverage are covered by federal laws that mandate that employers must continue to offer health insurance to qualified employees for at least 18 months after the employee leaves the company. These laws give employees time to find new insurance or to find a new job if they leave or lose their job. These laws

PROS	CONS
	mandate that former employees will not have to pay substantially more for health insurance than employees who continue employment.
Universal health care would reduce the burden on human resources personnel in companies. Currently, they must comply with many federal laws related to provision of health insurance. With a single-payer system, these regulations would not apply and the costs of compliance would be eliminated.	Human resources professionals will still be needed to comply with the many other personnel regulations mandated by the federal government. Instead of employees being able to exercise control over their health care choices and work with people in their company, patients will be forced to deal with the nameless, faceless members of the government bureaucracy.

Sample Motions:

This House would adopt a universal health care system.

This House believes that universal health care is more important than financial concerns.

This House believes that it is immoral that US citizens do not have equal access to health care.

Web Links:

- Kaiser Family Foundation Commission on Medicaid and the Uninsured. <http://www.kff.org> Articles with varied perspectives on the issue of health insurance and the uninsured.
- National Coalition on Health Care. <http://www.nchc.org/facts/coverage.shtml> Fact sheet on insurance coverage.
- New Yorker. <http://www.newyorker.com/fact/content/articles/050829fa_fact> *New Yorker* article on America's failing health care system.
- Progressive Policy Institute. <http://www.ppionline.org/ppi_sub.cfm?knlgAreaID=111&subsecID=137> Links to articles on the issue.

Further Reading:

Patel, Kant, and Mark E. Rushefsky. *Health Care Politics and Policy in America.* M.E. Sharpe, 2006.

Quadagno, Jill. *One Nation, Uninsured: Why the U.S. Has No National Health Insurance.* Oxford University Press, 2005.

Sered, Susan, and Rushika Fernandopulle. *Uninsured in America: Life and Death in the Land of Opportunity.* University of California Press, 2005.

Woodhandler, Steffie, and David Himmelstein, M.D. *Bleeding the Patient: The Consequences of Corporate Healthcare.* Common Courage Press, 2001.

HOMEMAKERS, PAID FOR THEIR WORK?

The ideas of traditional family roles have changed markedly since the entry of women into the workplace. As the notion of "natural" family roles has decreased, the awareness of the vital and sizable quantity of unpaid work that homemakers (still predominantly women) do has increased. This raises questions about how voluntary and unpaid, or contractual and commodified the divisions of labor in family life should be.

PROS

Far from being a series of simple chores, running a house has been and remains one of the bedrocks of a functional society. Without the work of a homemaker, other family members would not be free to work and invest in careers for themselves. This would harm the family structure and the economy. The importance of homemakers' work means that they are entitled to some compensation. If the work had to be provided at market rates the cost would run to hundreds of billions of dollars a year.

CONS

While how essential a position is can sometimes influence the amount of its remuneration, it is by no means the only variable society and the market use. For example, compare the earnings of nurses and doctors with that of sports figures. And the affirmative admits that the work is done and has always been done this way, so it is not as if a failure to pay homemakers will mean a decrease in the amount of work carried out. Thus, there is no threat of economic problems. It is merely a case of entitlement, for which there seems to be little basis.

Society should always try to reward its citizens for vital work, at least to some extent. Under a capitalist system the value of goods and services is recognized in financial terms, so a wage would recognize the important contribution of homemakers. As well as being important, housework is physically taxing, time consuming, and, in terms of balancing the needs of a household, a relatively specialized task. The marketplace highly values these features, and it is a pure accident of history that homemakers have not been included in this regard.

The key fact about homemaking is that even if it is hard work, and demanding, it is voluntary. Charity work can be taxing and specialized, but society recognizes that it does not require payment either. Entering into a marriage or relationship implies a similar voluntary attitude toward the work that must be done to sustain it, just as those who volunteer for charities know that they will not be paid.

No one knows for sure what the future will bring when they enter a marriage or relationship. A family's circumstances can change dramatically over time, so members may end up doing work they never expected. If so, their work may be voluntary in the sense that they are not physically coerced, but it is not a situation to which they previously consented. In business, when people's responsibilities change, they frequently renegotiate their contracts. It is the same with a partner in a relationship.

Even though partners cannot foresee the future, both agree that any changes will be discussed and implemented by mutual consent. This is the fundamental part of the marriage or relationship contract. As long as this happens, then the homemaker has no grounds for complaint, unless there is physical coercion, which is illegal in any event. In these and other cases the option of exiting the relationship is always available.

First, domestic violence is still regrettably common and rarely reported when it exists. Second, power imbalances within families are generally more subtle. It is estimated that men own over 90% of the world's property, and they are almost always still the dominant wage earners in a household, both in amount and likelihood of working. Consequently, women can be left in an unequal bargaining position, making the voluntary aspect of domestic agreements highly questionable. Even if divorce is possible, the more vulnerable partner may want to avoid it at all costs, for cultural reasons, or to prevent harm to children. Thus it does not constitute the element of consent the negative is looking for. As such, it is important that we give homemakers at least the option of recompense.

Even if there are some marginal cases where power imbalances affect agreements within relationships, it is not right or useful for the state to interfere in this private and personal sphere. Families will always know their situation better than the state. In the vast majority of units where the current situation works well, paying for housework risks contractualizing the family, which greatly undermines the principles of shared purpose, love, and agreement that make it unique and valuable in the first place.

The improvements in the rights of women all stem from state "interference" in social matters. Prenuptial agreements, child custody, and property sharing upon divorce

Even if we agree that there should not be overt gender discrimination in the workplace, it is not the state's role to enforce its conceptions of gender roles on the household.

PROS

are all enforceable by law. Equalizing the rights, roles, and access to wealth in the household is an important step toward empowering women and ensuring equal opportunity for future generations by showing that gender does not define household roles.

Conservatives are always publicly enthusiastic in promoting the family and the advantages of mothers being able to stay at home to bring up young children. This proposal would provide positive encouragement for couples to decide that one of them should stay at home to care for their children because it provides an economic incentive for one of them (typically the woman) to do so. At the same time, it ensures that although family income will be the same, homemakers retain their own income, thereby receiving proper recognition for their work. This will serve to maintain their status within the relationship and make it easier for them to return to the workplace in the future if they so choose.

CONS

Many cultural and religious groups base their societies squarely on the traditional family unit, and many women are comfortable with this. To enforce a subjectively "progressive" model both violates their cultural rights and risks causing havoc in these established structures.

In reality this proposal would undermine the traditional family, as it attempts to put an economic value on something that is really a vocation. Many people believe that although men and women are equal, they have different roles in life. Men, seen as more career-oriented, occupy the economic sphere, while women are more nurturing and occupy a more domestic role. Monetarizing the domestic sphere ignores the different roles of the genders and strains family relationships. For example, should a wife have the right to strike if she does not think her husband is paying her enough? From another point of view, this measure is highly discriminatory, as it assumes that all couples are in stable partnerships along the lines of the traditional two-parent family. Many families are headed by one parent who has no option but to go out to work, and they would be both ignored and demeaned by this proposal.

Sample Motions:

This House would pay housewives a wage.

This House believes that the distribution of tasks/resources in a household is a matter of public significance.

This House believes that the state should pay homemakers a minimum wage.

This House would allow homemakers to demand a wage from their working spouse.

Web Links:

- MSN. Money. <http://www.moneycentral.msn.com/content/CollegeandFamily/P46800.asp> Evaluation of pay estimates for homemakers.
- National Review Online. <http://article.nationalreview.com/?q=M2Q3YmMwYzRjN2MzMWMwMTViOTJhNmE4M2UwOWZiNDI=> Commentary on salary.com's valuation.
- Salary.com: What Is a Mom Worth? <http://www.salary.com/aboutus/layoutscripts/abtl_default.asp?tab=abt&cat=cat012&ser=ser041&part=Par481> A 2006 valuation of both a stay-at-home mom's and a working mom's job.

Further Reading:

Cranny-Francis, Anne. *Gender Studies: Terms and Debates.* Palgrave Macmillan, 2003.

Crompton, Rosemary. *Restructuring Gender Relations and Employment: The Decline of the Male Breadwinner.* Oxford University Press, 1999.

Mutari, Ellen, and Deborah M. Figart, eds. *Women and the Economy.* M.E. Sharpe, 2003.

HOMESCHOOLING

Over one million children in the United States currently learn at home. Homeschooling is increasing in popularity, with a growth rate of 7% to 15% annually. Parents choose homeschooling for four reasons: dissatisfaction with the public schools, concern about academic excellence, the wish to build stronger family bonds, and the desire to freely impart religious values. Research has shown that homeschooled children do well on standardized tests and are welcome at even highly competitive colleges. As adults, they have a reputation for being self-directed learners and reliable employees. Yet traditional educators have serious concerns, among them fear that the academic quality of homeschooling may be substandard and that homeschooled children lose the benefits of interacting with their peers.

PROS

Parents are responsible for ensuring that their children receive the best education possible. They do not have to surrender that responsibility to the state; if they think it best, they have the right to educate their children at home. Studies have shown that homeschooling can be as effective as traditional education. If some homeschooling has failed, so has state education. Moreover, this is a debate about who has the greater right to guide a child—the state or the parents. We stand firmly on the side of the parents; given the responsibilities inherent in raising a child, parents should have the freedom to choice.

CONS

This debate should focus on how best to educate our children, not on parental rights. With their resources, experience, and expertise, traditional schools can do this best. High-minded arguments about parental rights are all well and good, but a child's future is at stake. You cannot make up for bad schooling, and no one has developed a reliable method for ensuring the quality of homeschooling. This debate is therefore not about a right and not about a choice—parents have no right to choose to fail their child in her or his education.

Parents are entitled to make judgments about the quality of public schools. If they think these schools are failing, why shouldn't they be allowed to make the considerable sacrifice that becoming a "home teacher" constitutes?

Hundreds of educational researchers and experts with many years of experience labor to ensure that schools employ the best pedagogical methods. How presumptuous of parents to think that they know better. Public schools may not be perfect, but they will only get worse as those who can afford to opt to educate at home.

Saying that homeschooling necessarily will be of poor quality is ridiculous. Many parents will be fantastic teachers. Furthermore, it's not as if learning occurs in a vacuum simply because education occurs in the home. In the United States, a network of homeschool support groups and businesses provides expertise on curriculum subjects and teaching methods. The Internet makes all this possible in a way previously unattainable and allows every home to have better research facilities than any school library had 10 years ago.

It's a pretty good bet that parents won't be as good as a teacher, unless they are a member of that profession. Furthermore, even if parents excel in one area, will they cover all the things a school does? Support groups can't make a parent into a teacher, any more than a book on engineering makes one an engineer.

Homes beat schools on two significant fronts: facilities and an atmosphere that encourages learning. The needs of one or a very small number of students are the focus of the entire educative process. Parents often find that local and woefully ill-equipped public schools cannot address their child's specific needs or adapt to a child's learning style. The home also lacks the many distractions found in schools: peer pressure, social stigma attached to achievement, bullying, show-offs, general rowdiness.

Schools beat homes on the two fronts the affirmative has mentioned. For example, homes are very unlikely to have extensive science laboratories. Also, having a parent ask a young child to switch from "learning mode" to "play mode" in the same environment must be very confusing. For the older child, homeschooling gives ample opportunities for abuse—for pushing activities they enjoy instead of a lesson or manipulating the parent to slack off "just this once." Schools are for learning—that's

PROS	CONS
	their essence, their function. The home is an altogether more complex environment, ill-suited to instruction.
Classroom education often fails the bright and the slow and those with special needs. A teacher must, of necessity, teach to the group rather than to a specific individual. This leaves some unchallenged, some humiliated, and some under- or unserved. Special needs students, in particular, often suffer because large school systems cannot individualize instruction. Home education avoids this pitfall. Indeed, parents willing to take on the enormous task of educating their child at home are relieving the state of the burden of doing so—but continue to pay their taxes to benefit others.	The benefits of education in a wider context more than offset this objection. Of course, the state doesn't just leave high achievers and strugglers to rot! While students may not get individual attention, the experience of growing up alongside less and more able students and those with special needs produces individuals with a greater understanding of their society. Furthermore, students with special needs are those that most need the state's enormous resources.
Homeschooling doesn't just offer a better education; it encourages family bonding. Family bonding is an extremely important element of a child's development, one that's constantly undermined in modern society. Isn't it appropriate to educate a child in an environment that cements family bonds?	Parents and children spending day after day at home are sometimes subject to a phenomenon sociologists call the "hothouse relationship." The closeness between them becomes exclusive, with reaction to outsiders almost aggressive by instinct. Such a relationship makes adaptation to life in a wider community even more difficult when the time comes.
Public schools cannot teach the religious values so important to many parents. Also, public schools teach subjects, such as evolution, that are antithetical to some people's religious beliefs. Parents have the right to teach their child in an environment that caters to their religious needs.	Those who wish their children to be educated in a religious environment have the chance to send them to a religious school, the quality of which can be monitored by the state. Furthermore, what is the guarantee that the moral structure parents might be instilling in their children is beneficial? Exclusivity of belief is extremely unhealthy. Children should engage society as a whole so that they can understand other people's beliefs and points of view. In addition, public schools must teach the dispassionate conclusions of science, regardless of parents' religious beliefs.

Sample Motions:

This House supports homeschooling.
This House believes that the state does not know best.
This House would allow parents to educate their children at home.

Web Links:

- Ezine Articles. <http://ezinearticles.com/?The-Great-Home-Schooling-Debate&id=320187> Outlines the controversy surrounding homeschooling.
- FamilyEducation. <http://school.familyeducation.com/home-schooling/parenting/29861.html> Summary of pros and cons of homeschooling.
- Home Schooling Today. <http://www.home-schooling-today.com> Presents the pros and cons of homeschooling and offers links to articles on the subject.

HUMAN CLONING

The cloning of "Dolly" the sheep in 1997 generated worldwide reaction. The United States imposed a moratorium on human cloning and a ban on federal funding for cloning research, which will be reviewed every five years. Congress has rejected bills making human cloning lawful as well as those demanding its prohibition. As of 2008, 15 states also have laws related to human cloning, prohibiting reproductive cloning (cloning to initiate a pregnancy), therapeutic cloning (cloning for research purposes), or both. The opposition of international organizations to human cloning is clear. The European Parliament, the Council of Europe, UNESCO, and the World Health Organization (WHO) have passed resolutions asserting that human cloning is both morally and legally wrong.

PROS	CONS
The technology is unsafe. The nuclear transfer technique that produced Dolly required 277 embryos, from which only one healthy and viable sheep was produced. The other fetuses were hideously deformed, and either died or were aborted. Moreover, we do not know the long-term consequences of cloning.	Cloning is no different from any other new medical technology. Research is required on embryos to quantify and reduce the risk of the procedures.
Cloning is playing God. It is not merely intervention in the body's natural processes, but the creation of a new and wholly unnatural process of asexual reproduction. Philosophers and clerics of many faiths oppose human cloning. They caution that the failure to produce scientific reasons against the technology does not mean we should deny our strong instinctive revulsion.	This argument assumes that we know God's intentions. Moreover, every time a doctor performs lifesaving surgery or administers drugs he is changing the destiny of the patient and could be seen as usurping the role of God. Furthermore, we should be very wary of banning something without being able to say why it is wrong.
Reproductive cloning injures the family. Single people will be able to produce offspring without a partner. Once born, the child will be denied the love of one parent, most probably the father. Several theologians have recognized that a child is a symbolic expression of the mutual love of its parents and their hope for the future. This sign of love is lost when a child's life begins in a laboratory.	This argument is wholly unsuited to the modern age. Society freely allows single people to reproduce sexually. Existing practices such as sperm donation allow procreation without knowledge of the identity of the father. Surely a mother would prefer to know the genetic heritage of her child rather than accept sperm from an unknown and random donor? It might be better for the child to be born into a happy relationship, but the high rates of single parenthood and divorce suggest that this is not always possible.
Many churches and secular organizations, including WHO, view reproductive cloning as contrary to human dignity.	When people resort to talking in empty abstract terms about "human dignity" you can be sure that they have no evidence or arguments to back up their position. Why is sexual intercourse to be considered any more dignified than a reasoned decision by an adult to use modern science to have a child?
Cloning will lead to eugenics. When people are able to clone themselves they will be able to choose the kind of person to be born. This seems uncomfortably close to the Nazi concept of breeding a race of Aryan superhumans, while eliminating those individuals whose characteristics they considered undesirable.	Eugenics is much more likely to arise with developments in gene therapy and genetic testing and screening than in human cloning. Clones (people with identical genes) would by no means be identical in every respect. You need only to look at identical twins (who share the same genes) to see how wrong that assumption is, and how different the personalities, preferences, and skills of people with identical genes can be.

PROS	CONS
Cloning will lead to a diminished sense of identity and individuality for the resultant child. Instead of being considered as a unique individual, the child will be an exact copy of his parent and will be expected to share the same traits and interests. His life will no longer be his own. This is an unacceptable infringement of the liberty and autonomy that we grant to every human person. The confusion of the offspring is likely to be compounded by the fact that the "parent," from whom he is cloned, will be genetically his twin brother. There is no way of knowing how children will react to having such a confused genetic heritage.	Children produced by reproductive cloning will not be copies of their parents. Different environmental factors will mean that children will not be emotionally or mentally identical to the people from whom they are cloned. You would have to apply the same objection to identical twins. A small proportion of identical twins do, indeed, suffer from psychological problems related to feelings of a lack of individuality. However, cloned children would be in a better position than traditional twins because they will be many years younger than their genetic twins, who are, of course, their parents. Therefore, they will not suffer from comparisons to a physically identical individual.
Cloning will lead to a lack of diversity in the human population. The natural process of evolution will be halted, and humankind will be denied development.	Any reduction in the diversity of the human gene pool will be so limited as to be virtually nonexistent. The expense and time necessary for successful human cloning mean that only a small minority will employ the technology. The pleasure of procreation through sexual intercourse suggests that whole populations will choose what's "natural" rather than reproduce asexually through cloning.
Human reproductive cloning is unnecessary. The development of in vitro fertilization and the practice of sperm donation allow heterosexual couples to reproduce where one partner is sterile. In addition, potential parents might better give their love to existing babies rather than attempt to bring their own offspring into an already crowded world.	The desire to have one's own child and to nurture it is wholly natural. The longing for a genetically related child existed long before modern reproductive technology and biotechnology, but only recently has medicine been able to sometimes satisfy that longing.
Cloning treats children as commodities. Individuals will be able to have a child with desired characteristics as a symbol of status, rather than because they desire to conceive, love, and raise another human being.	The effort required to clone a human suggests that the child will be highly valued by its parent or parents. Furthermore, we should not pretend that every child conceived by sexual procreation is born to wholly well-intentioned parents.

Sample Motions:

This House would ban human cloning.
This House would not make a mini-me.
This House would not reproduce itself.

Web Links:

- American Medical Association. <http://www.amaassn.org/ama/pub/category/4560.html> Explains the procedure and legal status of human cloning.
- Human Cloning Foundation. <http://www.humancloning.org> Offers resources, books, and essays in support of human cloning.
- Religious Tolerance. <http://www.religioustolerance.org/cloning.htm> Provides comprehensive overview of multiple different aspects of the human cloning debate and outlines the history of the human cloning controversy.

Further Reading:

Davies, Eryl. *Human Cloning—Right or Wrong?* Evangelical Press, 2003.

Highfield, Roger, and Ian Wilmut. *After Dolly: The Promise and Perils of Cloning.* W.W. Norton, 2007.

Lauritzen, Paul. *Cloning and the Future of Human Embryo Research.* Oxford University Press, 2001.

HUMAN ORGANS, SALE OF

Advances in surgical and diagnostic techniques have substantially increased the success of organ transplant operations. In 2007, over 28,000 organs were transplanted in the United States. However, during the past decade, the waiting list for organs has grown faster than the number of transplants, and thousands of American die each year waiting for transplants. The sale of human organs can be considered as a possible solution to the crippling shortage; in 1984, however, Congress passed the National Organ Transplantation Act, which prohibits the sale of human organs from either dead or living donors. However, the overseas market trade in human organs is thriving.

PROS

The seriously ill are entitled to spend their money on saving their lives. It is preferable that some individuals receive organs, and survive, than that they die. The wealthy will not be the sole beneficiaries of a policy of organ purchase. For each successful kidney transplant operation, valuable hours on a dialysis machine will open up. The expense of palliative care for individuals requiring a transplant will be eliminated.

Let the poor do what they have to do to survive. Donating an organ is better than starving.

The donor of an organ, or his family, will benefit considerably from the sale. Both a kidney and a piece of liver can be removed without significant harm to the individual. Any assertion that an individual cannot make a reasoned decision to donate or sell these organs is patronizing. The family of a recently deceased individual also ought to be able to save the life of another and simultaneously receive remuneration.

The Chinese maintain that they do not trade in human organs. They say that the relatives of executed prisoners voluntarily approve of the use of the organs. If an individual is concerned about Chinese practices, they can go elsewhere.

CONS

A single kidney has a black market price of $20,000. Consequently, the sale of organs will highlight and support the most egregious discrimination between rich and poor. Those who cannot afford to purchase an organ will have no opportunity to receive one. What family, if prepared to donate the organs of a relative, would decide to decline a payment of tens of thousands of dollars? Donated organs will disappear. The poor will die and only the rich will survive.

Overseas travel for organs is fueling a trade in human organs that exploits the poorest of the poor. We do not want to encourage a system where people want money more than their organs.

The market in organs works in one direction—from the Third World to the First. The relative absence of regulation and the comparative value of the rewards mean that healthy individuals in Asia and Africa fall victim to scavenging organ merchants. The financial rewards make the decision to sell an organ one of compulsion rather than consent. Where colonialists raped the land, the neocolonialist surgeon steals from bodies.

The sale of organs will lead to appalling human rights violations. Chinese judicial officials are reported to have executed prisoners for their body parts. The lawful sale of organs would legitimize human sacrifice.

PROS

The transplant surgeon, the nursing staff, and even the pharmaceutical companies producing the anti-rejection drugs receive payment for each operation performed. Why should the donor of the organs, arguably the most important actor in any transplant, not also receive remuneration? What is remarkable is that a lifesaving treatment should apparently have no financial value.

CONS

Putting a price on the human body invites only exploitation by the unscrupulous.

Sample Motions:

This House would legalize the sale of organs.
This House would have a heart—with a price tag.
This House would buy body parts.

Web Links:

- American Bar Association. <http://www.abanet.org/irr/hr/spring03/livingdonors.html> Analyzes the legal status quo of organ sales in the United States and proposes potential reform for the future.
- Central News Network. <http://archives.cnn.com/2002/HEALTH/10/01/ethics.matters.selling.organs/> Article arguing that the human cost of selling an organ exceeds the price organs fetch.
- New York Times. <http://freakonomics.blogs.nytimes.com/2008/04/29/human-organs-for-sale-legally-in-which-country/> Describes the success of the organ market in Iran (the only country to legalize the sale of organs).

Further Reading:

Cherry, Mark. *Kidney for Sale by Owner: Human Organs, Transplantation, and the Market.* Georgetown University Press, 2005.

Goodwin, Michele. *Black Markets: The Supply and Demand of Body Parts.* Cambridge University Press, 2006.

Taylor, James Stacey. *Stakes and Kidneys: Why Markets in Human Body Parts Are Morally Imperative.* Ashgate Publishing, 2005.

Wilkinson, Stephen. *Bodies for Sale.* Routledge, 2003.

HUMAN RIGHTS: EXISTENCE OF

The concept of human rights is central to modern Western culture. But what does "human rights" mean? Do we have such rights, and if we do, why are they needed? The United Nations adopted the Universal Declaration of Human Rights (UDHR) in 1948 in response to the savage inhumanities of World War II. This document sets out a declaration of fundamental entitlements including the political and civil rights common to Western democracies as well as economic, social, and cultural rights that Western nations have not historically considered fundamental. However, the document includes no enforcement mechanism, and states are obliged only to "move towards" a realization of these rights. Thus, while important steps have been made toward an international understanding of rights, there is a long way to go.

PROS

By their nature and birth, human beings possess certain inalienable rights. As Article I of the UDHR states, "All human beings are born free and equal in dignity and rights."

The simple sharing of a common humanity establishes human rights. We extrapolate from this humanity the norms that secure the basic dignity with which we all want to live.

Desires are not what grounds human rights. What human rights are based on is the universal need for basic security in our bodies, our possessions, and our relationships within society. This security isn't just desirable; it is vital. Human rights are those things that rationally assure these vital requirements. Thomas Hobbes recognized that all people benefit from this security because human beings are equal in their capacity to harm one another.

Our understanding of human rights has evolved over several hundred years. The rights contemporary Western societies consider basic are more extensive than those found in past societies because these Western societies have a higher standard of living. People often must experience the lack of something to appreciate how vital it is—this is true of human rights.

Human rights are not meant to be subject to artificial, academic analysis. They are practical guides to life, standards of how we should be able to live. They are an objective standard that people can use when calling on their governments for justice.

CONS

Do animals have the same inalienable rights by virtue of their nature and birth? Isn't this claim a bit arbitrary? Why should everyone have a "right" just because they are born?

This argument is arbitrary and nebulous. It bases fundamental human rights on extrapolating from "feelings." How accurate can this be? Furthermore, isn't this just a wish list of ways we want to be treated? A desire to be treated in a certain way doesn't give one the right to be so treated.

If human rights are requirements of reason, then why do we see so much ambiguity and confusion over what they are? There is huge debate over what rights we have, and many people cannot agree that we have basic economic or development rights. This seems odd if human rights are rational requirements that are vital to life.

This is a very subversive trail to start down. These "requirements of reason" are both subjective and dependent on specific circumstances. Does that mean that humans really don't have inalienable rights, but instead transform accepted standards of living into actual rights? In that case, two cultures could have radically different but valid interpretations of a specific human right. Can this be a satisfactory basis for concrete and actual rights?

This all suggests that human rights can be extremely useful. However, something can be useful, indeed necessary, without it being your right. None of these arguments establishes that human beings have inherent "rights."

Sample Motions:

This House believes in fundamental human rights.
This House believes rights are right.

Web Links:

- Justice and Gross Violations Guide. <http://www.jgvg.com/gross-violations-of-human-rights/the-existence-of-human-rights.html> Analyzes the moral and legal justifications for the existence of human rights.
- Universal Declaration of Human Rights. <http://www.un.org/Overview/rights.html> Text of the document.
- University of Minnesota Human Rights Library. <http://www1.umn.edu/humanrts/> Site provides links to over 7,000 documents on human rights.

Further Reading:

Donnelly, Jack. *Universal Human Rights in Theory and Practice.* Cornell University Press, 2002.

Hayden, Patrick. *The Philosophy of Human Rights.* Paragon House, 2001.

Ignatieff, Michael. *Human Rights as Politics and Idolatry.* Princeton University Press, 2003.

Ishay, Micheline. *The History of Human Rights: From Ancient Times to the Globalization Era.* University of California Press, 2004.

HUMAN RIGHTS: IMPOSITION BY FORCE?

During the 1990s the international community intervened to end massive human rights violations in the former Yugoslavia. But less dramatic infringements of human rights continue. China regularly cracks down on pro-democracy activists, Tibetans, and Christian groups, while civilians "disappear" in Colombia. How should those concerned about human rights address the issues? Intervention, whether by military force, through peacekeeping forces, or by diplomatic means, might curtail human rights abuses, but it poses practical and moral problems.

PROS	CONS
As good international Samaritans, we must intervene to halt human rights violations. The 1948 Genocide Convention calls on countries to "undertake to prevent and to punish" genocide.	Using force to uphold human rights is hypocritical. Force inevitably involves infringing one right (to life or property) for the sake of another. For example, Indonesian intervention in East Timor involved the imposition of martial law: Amnesty International described this as "complaint and cure" being the same.
Because all people have the same rights, countries with the best human rights records have the authority to impose their standards on other nations. Certainly, when one country perceives a breach of human rights as it understands them, it must use force to uphold these rights.	We cannot assume that Western ideas of human rights extend throughout the world. Buddhism, for example, places more emphasis on "human nature" and on the effects of individuals' actions than upon "rights." In any case, which country has the best human rights record? The United States often takes the initiative in launching intervention, but many nations see its use of the death penalty as a human rights violation.
Careful planning can minimize the military violation of human rights. It is possible to hit military bases, runways, bridges, and so on without killing a single civilian or destroying anyone's personal property.	This is totally impossible. Despite tremendous increases in the accuracy of weapons over the past decade, the US still hit civilians when bombing Iraq. The only safe answer is not to bomb.
Force need not mean "violence." Throughout its history the United Nations has deployed peacekeeping missions to stop violence and protect human rights. Individual nations, too, have carried out successful campaigns. If Britain had not deployed troops in Northern Ireland over the past decades, unchecked sectarian violence would have claimed thousands more lives.	The international community deploys peacekeeping forces only in the aftermath of violence. Even peacekeeping forces have violated individual rights and resorted to violence.

PROS	CONS
The nations that are party to international human rights conventions have a responsibility to see that other countries accept these noble ideals.	Guns and unstable peace are a volatile combination; in these situations even the smallest incident can lead to human rights violations.
"Force" does not necessarily involve the military. Diplomatic pressure, including sanctions, can force oppressive regimes to respect human rights.	Sanctions harm diplomatic relations well before they effect any change. No substantial evidence has been offered on the efficacy of sanctions. International sanctions against Iraq, for example, have not led to improved human rights. Instead, they have increased the suffering of the civilian population.
A nation can overthrow a cruel regime only with international support.	Nations do not need outside intervention to remove an oppressive dictator. In 2000, for example, Vojislav Kostunice won the presidential elections that helped oust Serbian dictator Slobodan Milosevic, in part, because he did not side with Western powers. Had the West intervened more forcefully to oust Milosevic, he might have clung to power longer.
Force is the only way to send a clear message that those who infringe on human rights are in the wrong.	Military intervention never provides a lasting solution to human rights abuses.

Sample Motion:

This House would use force to uphold human rights.

Web Links:

- Carnegie Council. <http://www.cceia.org/resources/ethics_online/5405.html> Article arguing that democracy cannot be imposed by force.
- Human Rights Watch. <http://www.igc.org/hrw> Information on human rights by issue and geographical area.
- "Military Intervention to Protect Human Rights: The Humanitarian Agency Perspective." <http://www.jha.ac/articles/a084.htm> Background paper for the International Council on Human Rights.

Further Reading:

Chandler, David. *From Kosovo to Kabul and Beyond: Human Rights and International Intervention.* Pluto Press, 2006.

Gray, Christine. *International Law and the Use of Force.* Oxford University Press, 2001.

Orford, Anne. *Reading Humanitarian Intervention: Human Rights and the Use of Force in International Law.* Cambridge University Press, 2007.

IMMIGRATION REFORM

Although precise numbers are hard to come by, the PEW Hispanic Research Center, working in conjunction with the US Bureau of Labor and Statistics, estimates that at least 50,000 illegal immigrants gain entry into the United States every year; about one million legally enter the country annually.

Illegal immigration is a particularly contentious issue in modern American politics, particularly given post–9/11 fears about border security and concerns that undocumented aliens are taking American jobs and using government services for which they are not paying taxes. In 2004, President George W. Bush proposed a "guest worker" program that would help register immigrants to the United States who would otherwise be purely illegal under current policy. The plan failed, and the United States is still struggling to adopt a national immigration policy. Absent national action, states have passed numerous laws designed to discourage illegal immigration.

PROS

Illegal immigrants represent a pressing security concern. The United States needs to strengthen its borders and should aggressively patrol them to prevent terrorists from entering the country. Moreover, many immigrants already in the country represent a potential threat to national security—both how many are here and their identities are unknown.

Illegal immigrants drain the American economy. The estimated 11 million illegal immigrants in the United States are not taxpayers, yet derive social benefits paid for by US citizens. These range from police protection and emergency response to public transportation. Moreover, because illegal immigrants are willing to work for low wages, they compete unfairly for jobs. Immigrants send much of the money they earn in the United States to relatives in their home countries (remittances), diminishing the American money supply and lessening investment in American goods.

An influx of illegal immigrants chips away at any notion of American national identity. Illegal immigrants are isolated and do not try to assimilate into American society as other groups do; some statisticians correlate illegal immigration with higher levels of crime. Expelling illegal immigrants—or at least forcing them to register for a guest worker program—would allow the government to perform background checks and track immigrant behavior, thus ensuring overall security and peace of mind for citizens.

CONS

The fear of immigrants is irrational, and politicians exploit it for votes. Focusing on illegal immigration is a red herring that draws attention away from the real threat: terrorists, like the 9/11 hijackers, who use sophisticated methods to infiltrate the United States. Initiatives to curb or expel immigrants who are here for largely economic reasons are an irresponsible and dangerous waste of attention and funds.

The problem of "free-riders," people who derive benefits from a system to which they do not contribute, is not as straightforward as the proposition suggests. Illegal immigrants play a fundamental role in keeping the US economy functioning by taking work that Americans are not willing to do. Moreover, industries such as agriculture and construction depend on illegal workers—without these workers the industries could not function, American workers in these industries would lose their jobs, and Americans in general would not have the services and products they need. Finally, economists believe that impact of remittances on the US GDP is negligible. In fact, an outflow of dollars actually can stabilize and vastly improve the standard of living in other countries, potentially preventing or slowing further illegal immigration.

America has a history of nativism. Many immigrant groups that were once despised and discriminated against eventually become bedrock members of American society. Theories attributing crime and other negative social behaviors to illegal immigrants are an easily disproved pseudo-science that cloaks racism and prejudice. Finally, although guest worker programs might serve to cut down on some exploitation of immigrants, establishing social programs—including Spanish-language immigrant community centers and outreach clinics—would go much further to ensure the safety and peaceful integration of new participants in the American Dream.

Sample Motions:

This House would deny amnesty for illegal immigrants.
This House would expel illegal immigrants.
This House would close the nation's borders.

Web Links:

- The American Immigration Law Foundation. <http://www.ailf.org> Facts on immigration and the impact of immigrants on the US.
- The Brookings Institution Center for Immigration Studies. <http://www.brookings.edu/gs/projects/immigration.htm> Commentary and resources on immigration policy.
- Center for Immigration Studies. <http://www.cis.org> Links to recent developments and historical background.
- National Public Radio (NPR). <http://www.npr.org/templates/story/story.php?storyId=5310549> NPR stories and Q&As on the immigration debate.

Further Reading:

Daniel, Roger. *Guarding the Golden Door: American Immigration Policy and Immigrants Since 1882.* Hill and Wang, 2004.

Ngai, Mae M. *Impossible Subjects: Illegal Aliens and the Making of Modern America.* Princeton University Press, 2005.

Zolberg, Aristide R. A *Nation by Design: Immigration Policy in the Fashioning of America.* Harvard University Press, 2006.

INTERNATIONAL CRIMINAL COURT

In 1998, the Rome Statute established the International Criminal Court (ICC) with jurisdiction over genocide, crimes against humanity, war crimes, and aggression. US President Bill Clinton authorized the signing of the statute in December 2000 but said the treaty was "significantly flawed" and recommended that the US Senate not ratify it. Congress and the Bush Administration have been even more hostile. In November 2001, President George W. Bush signed into law an act prohibiting the use of funds of several federal agencies, including the Departments of State, Commerce, and Justice, for cooperation with the ICC. Congress passed a bill restricting use of Defense Department funds the following month. Despite US opposition, the Tribunal came into force on July 1, 2002.

PROS

The ICC will lead to political prosecution. It will subject American service members and senior military and political strategists to criminal charges for military actions that are legitimate and necessary. Any nation can ask the ICC prosecutor to investigate an issue, and the prosecutor has the power to investigate *ex proprio motu.* The UN Security Council cannot override or veto his actions or decisions. Political prosecution is evident in the preliminary investigation by the International Criminal Tribunal for the Former Yugoslavia (ICTY) into the NATO bombing of Kosovo and the Federal Republic of Yugoslavia. The prosecutor chose to investigate a campaign that had been undertaken with clinical precision, that had received the support of the Security Council (although after the fact), and that had been directed against a military carrying

CONS

The US should have nothing to fear if it behaves lawfully. Moreover, determining if a violation of international law (by the US or any other nation) has taken place should be easy as the ICC prosecutor concerns himself only with the gravest offenses. The US certainly would not approve a strategy of genocide or systematic mass violations of human rights that would come under the jurisdiction of the ICC. The prosecutor's power is also limited by the requirement that he obtain the approval of three judges before issuing an arrest warrant or initiating proceedings. A preliminary investigation could benefit the US because it would end doubts about the justifiability of its actions. The US accepted the jurisdiction of the ICTY prosecutor because it did not expect its forces to commit the crimes they were deployed to prevent.

PROS | CONS

out a brutal policy of genocide. This grim precedent suggests that a prosecutor will not hesitate to investigate other good faith and successful military actions across the globe.

The US holds a unique position in maintaining international peace and security. It might be appropriate for other countries to consent to the jurisdiction of the ICC because they do not have the same responsibilities and risks. US armed forces have responded to many more "situations" during the 1990s than during the whole of the Cold War. More than ever, the world looks to the US to ensure peace and safety. US military dominance increases the likelihood of prosecution. When rogue regimes are incapable of defeating the US militarily, they are likely to challenge the US in the ICC. This will damage US interests far more than any conventional military action and will result in US reluctance to intervene in the future. The indispensable nation must be permitted to dispense with the ICC.

The very preeminence of the US demands that it adhere to the rule of international law. A nation can commit war crimes while conducting a military campaign to protect human rights and save lives. The ICC can demand that the US, or any other state, pursue its lawful ends by lawful means. Moreover, victims of gross human rights violations do not care who the perpetrator is. Other nations with significant military commitments overseas, such as the UK and France, have ratified the Rome Statute without hesitation. These states accept the principle that nations intervening in another state to uphold or establish human rights must respect those same human rights.

The Rome Statute has created the novel crime of "aggression," which increases the likelihood of political prosecution. One state could accuse another of aggression for intervening to protect human rights. Governments carrying out a policy of genocide could request that a nation be prosecuted for preventing genocide. Moreover, by a quirk of the statute, a state that refuses to accept ICC jurisdiction can nevertheless request the prosecution of foreign nationals for crimes allegedly committed in its territory. Thus Yugoslav President Slobodan Milosevic could have demanded the investigation of NATO forces for activities during Operation Allied Force but could have prevented an investigation of the Bosnian Serb army in the same territory.

This objection to the ICC is purely hypothetical because the ICC has not yet defined "aggression." In addition, the "crime" of aggression is not novel. Intervening in the domestic affairs of a sovereign state is contrary to norms of conventional and customary law. The UN Charter prohibits both the unauthorized use of force against another state and intervention in its domestic jurisdiction. The US should ratify the Rome Statute so that its negotiators can play an active role in the Assembly of State Parties, which is currently working on drafting a definition of this crime.

The ICC will not deter war crimes or genocide. The Third Reich accelerated its campaign to exterminate Jews when it became clear that the Allies would be victorious. Similarly, Milosevic and the Bosnian Serb army conducted a campaign of genocide in Kosovo while the ICTY was sitting in The Hague. War criminals do not commit gross human rights violations based on reason. The existence of a court, however well intentioned, will have no effect on those states that would commit such crimes.

You cannot claim that the ICC will not deter atrocities when such an institution has never before existed. Moreover, the offenders must be apprehended, tried, and punished. Retribution and protection of society are objectives not only for domestic criminal justice systems but also for the new international system.

ICC expenses will be crippling. Cautious estimates suggest an operating budget of US$100 million per year. The costs of the ICTY and the international criminal tribunal for Rwanda spiraled out of control, and the latter left a legacy of misadministration and internal corruption.

The ICC's budget might seem excessive, but no price should be put on justice for thousands of victims of heinous crimes.

Sample Motions:

This House believes that the United States should not support the International Criminal Court.

This House believes that the creation of the ICC is a crime.

Web Links:

- The Coalition for an ICC. <http://www.iccnow.org> Country-by-country report on the status of the Rome Statute.
- Crimes of War Project. <http://www.crimesofwar.org> Provides up-to-date information on possible violations of human rights and war crimes as well as the status of humanitarian law and justice.
- ICC Resources at the University of Chicago Library. <http://www.lib.uchicago.edu/~llou/icc.html> Bibliography of Web and print resources on the ICC.

Further Reading:

Broomhall, Bruce. *International Justice and the International Criminal Court: Between Sovereignty and the Rule of Law.* Oxford University Press, 2004.

Driscoll, William, Joseph P. Zompetti, and Suzette Zompetti, eds. *The International Criminal Court: Global Politics and the Quest for Justice.* International Debate Education Association, 2004.

Sands, Phillipe. *From Nuremberg to The Hague: The Future of International Criminal Justice.* Cambridge University Press, 2004.

INTERNET CENSORSHIP

The Internet is the fastest growing and largest tool for mass communication and information distribution in the world. In the past few years concern has increased about the Internet disseminating content that is violent and sexual, that gives bomb-making instructions, abets terrorist activity, and makes available child pornography. In response, some have called for censorship. In 1998, the US Congress passed the Child Online Protection Act, restricting access by minors to material deemed harmful on the Internet. However, the courts have blocked implementation, ruling that the act violates constitutional protection of free speech. But even if censorship of the Internet can be morally and legally justified, practical problems with regulation arise.

PROS

Although democratic nations value freedom of speech, all put some restrictions on the right. Such restrictions usually surround hard-core and child pornography, but some nations restrict hate speech as well. The Internet should be no exception to these basic standards. Truly offensive material is no different because it is published on the Web.

Censorship is tailored to the power of the medium. Accordingly, a higher level of censorship is attached to television, films, and video than to newspapers and books: We recognize that moving pictures and sound are more graphic and powerful than text, photographs, or illustrations. Videos are normally more regulated than films seen in theaters because the viewer of a video has

CONS

Censorship is usually evil. Governments should avoid it wherever possible. Child pornography is an extreme example; sufficient legislation is already in place to handle those who attempt to produce, distribute, or view such material. Other forms of speech may well be offensive, but the only way a society can counter such speech is to be exposed to it and have it out in the open. Without such freedom, these groups are driven underground and can take on the aspect of martyrs.

The distinction between censorship of print and broadcast media is becoming increasingly irrelevant. Print media are comparatively unregulated because they are the primary means of distributing information in society. In the near future, the Internet may become this prime disseminator. Thus the Internet must be allowed the same protections now enjoyed by print media. When

PROS

control of the medium—the power to rewind, view again, and distribute more widely. The Internet, which increasingly uses video and sound, should be regulated accordingly.

The Internet would be hard to control, but we must not use that as an excuse not to try. Preventing the sale of snuff movies or hard-core pornography is extremely difficult, but some governments do so because they deem it important. A more intractable issue is the anonymity that the Internet provides pornographers and criminals. Asian countries have experimented with requiring citizens to provide identification before posting content on the Web. If universally adopted, such a requirement could be a relatively simple way of enforcing laws against truly offensive and harmful content.

In many countries producing libelous material or material that incites racial hatred incurs multiple liability. Where the author or publisher cannot be traced or is insolvent, the printers can often be sued or prosecuted. The relatively small number of Internet service providers (ISPs) should be made liable if they assist in the provision of dangerous or harmful information.

The issues at stake in this debate—protection of children, terrorist activity, crime, racial hatred, etc., are all international problems. If a global solution is required, it can be achieved by international cooperation and treaties. All societies consider censorship justified where harm is caused to others by the speech, words, or art. All the examples cited above are clearly causing harm to various groups in society. By a combination of the initiatives listed above, we could limit that harm.

CONS

English philosopher John Stuart Mill considered freedom of speech and the Founding Fathers of the United States spoke in the Constitution of freedom of the press they were concerned about the primary and most powerful organ of information distribution at that time, the print press. Nowadays they would more likely be concerned with preventing censorship of the broadcast media and the Internet.

Even allowing for the extreme problems surrounding curtailment of freedom of speech, Internet censorship would be more or less impossible. Governments can attempt to regulate what is produced in their own countries but regulating material originating outside national borders would be impossible. What is the point in the US removing all domestic links to hard-core pornography when such material from the UK or Sweden could be readily accessed and downloaded? Individuals could also produce banned material and store it in an overseas domain. True freedom of speech requires anonymity in some cases to protect the author. Governments that have introduced ID requirements for Internet use also deny many basic rights to their citizens. The Internet allows citizens to criticize their government and distribute news and information without reprisal from the state. These freedoms clearly could not survive Internet ID requirements.

Internet service providers are certainly the wrong people to decide what can and cannot be placed on the Internet. Big business already controls far too much of this new technology without also making it judge and jury of all Internet content. In any case, the sheer bulk of information ISPs allow to be published is such that reviewing it all would be impossible. Were ISPs to be held liable for allowing such material to be displayed, they would inevitably err on the side of caution to protect their financial interests. This would result in a much more heavily censored Internet.

Many ISPs have shown themselves to be responsible in immediately removing truly offensive content where they have been alerted to it. What is required is self-regulation by the industry, not the imposition of arbitrary and draconian restrictions on Internet content and use. Parents can install software that will filter out offensive sites and sites inappropriate for children.

Sample Motions:

This House would censor the Internet.
This House calls for Net filters.
This House would limit freedom of speech.

Web Links:

- Center for Democracy and Technology. <http://www.cdt.org> Offers policy briefs, reports, and articles on issues regarding Internet freedom.
- Electronic Frontier Foundation. <http://www.eff.org/blueribbon.html> Offers summaries of issues involving Internet censorship as well as information on fair use and privacy on the Web.
- Internet Censorship FAQ. <http://www.spectacle.org/freespch/faq.html> Responses to frequently asked questions about Internet censorship by authors of a book on the subject.

Further Reading:

Herumin, Wendy. *Censorship on the Internet: From Filters to Freedom of Speech.* Enslow, 2004.

Hick, Steven. *Human Rights and the Internet.* Palgrave Macmillan, 2000.

Ringmar, Eric. *A Blogger's Manifesto: Free Speech and Censorship in the Age of the Internet.* Anthem Press, 2007.

INTERNMENT WITHOUT TRIAL

Internment *can be defined as the indefinite detention of a person by a government and the denial of the normal legal processes that would usually be available to them, such as the right to know the charges and evidence against them, the right to a public trial, the right to appeal to a higher judicial authority, etc. While governments often resort to internment in period of national emergency, such as a war or during a terrorist campaign, the practice raises questions about the balance between security and liberty. Following September 11, the Bush Administration interned hundreds of Al-Qaeda and Taliban suspects in Guantanamo Bay under military authority without appeal to the US legal system. The action generated severe criticism from parts of the international community and prompted a series of legal challenges from civil liberties groups that have resulted in Supreme Court decisions recognizing the government's right to detain illegal combatants but finding illegal the special military commissions established to try such combatants.*

PROS

Governments must have the power to address threats to the nation. Everyone would recognize that laws that apply in peacetime might not be appropriate during war. Captured enemy combatants, for example, should not have the rights of habeas corpus and trial by jury that citizens enjoy. The war on terror is in this respect a war like earlier, more conventional conflicts. Just because our enemies do not wear uniforms or conform to a normal military structure does not make them any less of a threat to our society.

CONS

The war on terror is not like past, conventional conflicts, and the administration cannot assume wartime powers simply on its own declaration. The September 11 attacks were horrific, but they did not threaten the existence of the nation—the economy has rebounded surprisingly quickly, and no one believes that even a successful attack on the White House or the Capitol would have ended American democracy. Nor is the war on terror winnable—there is no likely endpoint at which we will declare victory and so allow detained "enemy combatants" to go home. So these harsh but supposedly temporary wartime measures will become the norm.

PROS	CONS
We must reach an appropriate balance between security and freedom. Everyone recognizes the importance of protecting rights and liberties, but this cannot be done at all and any cost. The first duty of our political leaders is to protect us from harm, and the voters will rightly hold them accountable if they fail.	Giving the government the power to detain suspects without due process will not make society safer. The proposition's arguments rely on the accuracy of secret intelligence, which supposedly identifies individuals planning terrorist acts but which cannot be revealed in open court. Recent history suggests that such intelligence is often deeply flawed. Intelligence failures in the campaign against Al-Qaeda point to the difficulties Western intelligence services have in penetrating and understanding terrorist groups, while intelligence on Iraq's weapons programs was also clearly flawed. So not only will many innocent people be unjustly interned, many dangerous ones will be left at liberty.
At a time when our society is under threat, protecting our intelligence sources is more important than giving suspected terrorists public trials. Charging and trying terror suspects in open court would require governments to reveal their intelligence sources, thus risking the identification of their spies. These revelations might lead to the murder of brave agents and shut off crucial intelligence channels that could warn us of future attacks. Even if courts made special arrangements for presenting intelligence evidence, terrorists could use the trials to learn more about our intelligence capabilities and tactics. In these circumstances, detention without public trial is the only safe option.	Not only is intelligence often badly flawed, internment simply doesn't work as a strategy to combat terrorism. It is counterproductive, making martyrs of the individuals detained. And, as Britain's experience with the Irish Republican Army has shown, internment can radicalize detainees. Moreover, the harsh measures undermine the confidence of ordinary citizens in their government, reducing their support for the war on terror. Indeed, if we compromise aspects of our free and open societies in response to pressure, then the terrorists who hate our values are winning.
Tough measures are aimed only at very few suspects—only a few hundred are interned at Guantanamo Bay. Exceptional circumstances call for special measures, but these are so limited in scope that they do not threaten our democratic values.	Rights protect the few as well as the many. Indefinite detention and lack of a normal public trial undermine the key values of habeas corpus and the presumption of innocence. Try suspects if there is evidence and deport them if they are foreign nationals, but release them if the government cannot make a proper case against them. The British government said that internment in Northern Ireland was aimed only at a tiny minority, but thousands passed through the Long Kesh detention camp in the four years it operated.
Although a normal public trial is not possible for security reasons, detainees' rights are still respected. Safeguards are built into the internment process so that each case can be considered fairly, with the suspect represented before a proper tribunal and given a right to appeal to a higher authority. If a trial is held (often to standards of evidence and procedure higher than in regular courts in many countries around the world) and a sentence properly passed, then this is not internment as it has been practiced in the past.	Regardless of the procedures that authorities use as window dressing to justify their actions, internment is open to abuse because trials are secret, with the executive essentially scrutinizing itself. Trials are held in secret with crucial evidence frequently withheld from the accused and his defense team or given anonymously with no opportunity to examine witnesses properly. Appeals are typically to the executive (which chose to prosecute them), rather than to an independent judicial body. In such circumstances, prejudice and convenience are likely to prevent justice being done.

Sample Motions:

This House believes that internment is sometimes justified.
This House would choose the lesser of two evils.
This House supports Guantanamo Bay.
This House would detain terror suspects.

Web Links:

- The Guardian. <http://www.guardian.co.uk/politics/2004/jan/10/september11.guantanamo> Comment from the *Guardian* newspaper claiming that the US example "legitimizes oppression."
- International Commission of Jurists. <http://www.icj.org/news.php3?id_article=2612&lang=en> Statement in opposition to Bush Administration policy on internment.
- Internment Without Trial; The Lessons from the United States, Northern Ireland & Israel. <http://papers.ssrn.com/sol3/papers.cfm?abstract_id=575481> Paper by Fergie Davis, lecturer at University of Sheffield.

Further Reading:

Berkowitz, Peter. *Terrorism, the Laws of War, and the Constitution: Debating the Enemy Combatant Cases.* Hoover Institution Press, 2005.

Fisher, Louis. *Military Tribunals and Presidential Power: American Revolution to the War on Terrorism.* University Press of Kansas, 2005.

Margulies, Joseph. *Guantanamo and the Abuse of Presidential Power.* Simon & Schuster, 2006.

Rose, David. *Guantanamo: The War on Human Rights.* New Press, 2004.

IRAN'S RIGHT TO POSSESS NUCLEAR WEAPONS

Since the revolution against the US-backed shah in 1979, the Islamic Republic of Iran has maintained a difficult relationship with the West. A major regional military power, Iran wields considerable influence in the Middle East, and its emerging economy has grown alongside complicated social and political tensions that mark its relations with its neighbors. Iran has declared its intentions of restarting its nuclear technology program, and it has begun to develop centrifuges for refining uranium—the first step not only toward nuclear power but also, the West fears, toward developing nuclear weapons. Because EU-led negotiations with Iran have failed, the UN, the United States and its allies, and the world as a whole must now determine how to deal with Iran's nuclear ambitions.

PROS

Iran is a signatory of the Nuclear Non-Proliferation Treaty, which permits the development of nuclear technology for peaceful purposes. Iran maintains that as it is enriching uranium for peaceful purposes only, it is legally entitled to continue its nuclear program. Iran also draws comparisons between itself and three nuclear powers (Israel, India, and Pakistan) who never signed the treaty.

CONS

Nothing prevents Iran from enriching uranium for weapons purposes. Although Iran has permitted inspections of its nuclear facilities in the past, we have no guarantee that it will continue to do so once it has the capacity to create weapons. Iran's track record is poor: it hid its nuclear enrichment program from the world for many years prior to the current crisis. Its ongoing activities to influence politics in other Middle Eastern states and its president's outspoken objection to Israel's existence are all ominous signs that it might pursue developing nuclear weapons if given the chance.

PROS

Iran is a democratic state that has a right to determine its own policies—both about nuclear energy and nuclear weapons. Moreover, religious leaders in Iran have spoken against nuclear armament while still advocating the development of nuclear energy. In August 2005, Iran's supreme political and religious leader, Ayatollah Ali Khamenei, issued a fatwa (a religious edict) declaring that Islam forbids the development, stockpiling, and use of nuclear weapons. He also stated that Iran should never possess nuclear arms. Moreover, Iran has the same right to possess nuclear arms as other countries. As one Iranian soldier said to the BBC, "If America has the right to nuclear weapons after dropping bombs on Hiroshima and Nagasaki, why doesn't Iran have that right?"

Iran, like 116 other developing nations, is a member of the Non-Aligned Movement (NAM). The NAM holds that "all countries have a basic and inalienable right to develop atomic energy for peaceful purposes," and strongly opposes what it sees as a double standard—one for developing nations and another for developed nations. Iran has emerged as a leading member of the NAM, and its fight to develop nuclear technology has become a rallying cry for many NAM states. Many developing nations see the distribution of nuclear arms in the world as reinforcing Western hegemony and promoting the interests of the United States and its allies. By allowing nonaligned states to acquire nuclear arms, the world can help counterbalance US imperialism and give Third World nations more influence in global politics.

CONS

Iran's military and political institutions are unstable and are not accountable to the Iranian public. Real power is in the hands of unelected religious leaders (the ayatollah and the Council of Guardians) who can veto policies and parliamentary candidates by invoking *sharia* (Islamic law). The military also includes Islamic fundamentalists, who, like the clerics, believe that they answer to authorities higher than international law. If these groups are given access to the raw materials of nuclear weapons or to weapons themselves, we have no way of predicting how they might use them.

We must not let nuclear weapons proliferate. Iran has a proven track record of supporting terrorism (including Hezbollah) both in the Middle East and beyond, and the country might provide nuclear arms to such groups. Moreover, just as the rogue Pakistani scientist Abdul Qadeer Khan illegally sold nuclear technology, so Iran might sell such weapons on the black market if given an opportunity. If the world hopes someday to eradicate nuclear weapons, allowing other states, particularly a state like Iran, to acquire them is senseless and dangerous.

Sample Motions:

This House would permit Iran to develop nuclear capabilities as it sees fit.
This House believes that Iran is entitled to possess nuclear weapons.
This House believes that Iran's nuclear program is not a threat to world stability.

Web Links:

- International Atomic Energy Agency. <http://www.iaea.org/NewsCenter/Focus/IaeaIran/index.shtml> Links to documents, reports, and newspaper articles on Iran's nuclear program.
- Iran Daily. <http://www.iran-daily.com/1384/2347/html/index.htm> Ayatollah Khamenei's fatwa forbidding nuclear weapons.
- US Department of State. <http://www.state.gov/t/us/rm/60254.htm> Remarks by the undersecretary for arms control and international security on the Iranian nuclear threat.

Further Reading:

Ansari, Ali. *Confronting Iran: The Failure of American Foreign Policy and the Next Great Crisis in the Middle East.* Perseus, 2006.

Cordesman, Anthony H., and Khalid R. Al-Rodhan. *Iran's Weapons of Mass Destruction: The Real and Potential Threat.* Center for Strategic & International Studies, 2006.

Timmerman, Kenneth R. *Countdown to Crisis: The Coming Nuclear Showdown with Iran.* Crown Forum, 2005.

ISLAM AND DEMOCRACY

The growth of Islamic fundamentalism and the absence of democracy in the Muslim areas of the world have raised the question of whether Islam is compatible with democracy. Some suggest that Islamic doctrine or culture make the development of democracy impossible, while others insist that historical factors, not religion, are responsible for authoritarian tendencies among Islamic nations.

PROS

Islam is an antidemocratic religion as it is incompatible with the pluralism necessary for a democratic state. Muslim societies (such as Saudi Arabia) are authoritarian, the natural consequence of the legal and doctrinal rigidity that makes a political culture of compromise impossible. *Sharia* law is viewed as perfect and divine. Consequently, laws are best made through theocratic interpretation rather than democratic debate.

To talk of an Islamic democracy is to distort the concept of democracy to an unrecognizable extent. The fact that some scholars suggest that Islam can be conceptualized as democratic cannot compensate for the absence of political democracy in Islamic countries.

The basic features of democratic rule are absent from the Muslim world. Most Muslim nations do not guarantee freedom of expression. Elections are rare and dominated by one party. Voters are harassed and election laws violated. Most elections are shams. In Iran, for example, the religious leaders, who really rule the country, can veto any party or candidate on the grounds of incompatibility with Islamic doctrine.

Islamic states lack a civil society that fosters democratic dialogue and debate. This is partly because a conservative religious culture discourages questioning and open exchange of differing views.

Extreme Islamic fundamentalism is growing. Groups of Islamic fundamentalists are motivated by religious zeal rather than by a desire for freedom or democracy. They use Islamic concepts such as jihad (holy war) to justify terrorism, which is absolutely antithetical to democratic values.

CONS

Islam is inherently democratic. Qur'anic notions such as *shura* (consultation) and *ijma'* (consensus) are indicative of an Islamic version of democracy and the importance of democratic values in the teachings of the faith. Some Islamic countries seem capable of reconciling religion and democracy. For example, Turkey is a Muslim nation, yet constitutionally it is a secular democracy. Even the most pious nations make concessions to democracy: for example, the Islamic Republic of Iran holds regular elections.

Islamic democracy may not and need not look like its Western cousin. Some commentators argue that Islam requires a democracy because the Qur'an requires Muslims to engage in mutual consultation in managing their political affairs. Legislative assemblies can exist and elections can take place so long as they are not corrupt and are consistent with Islamic teaching.

Democratic reform is taking place throughout the Muslim world: regular elections have been held in Turkey, Pakistan, Bangladesh, Malaysia, and Indonesia as well as in Egypt, Jordan, Lebanon, and Kuwait. Even Saudi Arabia is beginning to consider limited democratic reforms. Democratic elections show the compatibility of Islam and democracy and bode well for more extensive democratization.

Civil society in the Muslim world is made up of a mixture of professional and student associations and indigenously Islamic organizations. In Kuwait, for example, discussion groups are emerging that create a political space between the state and the individual. Civil society also can include religious associations, which can foster a consultative and open exchange of views.

Muslims are not the only people to take up arms for their cause. For example, in Sri Lanka violence has been based on ethnicity rather than religion. Violence is incompatible with democratic values, but the use of violence by Islamic extremists is not indicator of the character of the faith.

PROS	CONS
The Muslim world cannot be democratic until it reforms its position on women. The Qur'an describes women as complementary to men, but not equal. Consequently, polygyny is allowed, and in many Islamic countries, women do not have the same civil and political rights that men enjoy. Some governments insist that women wear a full face veil or a headscarf (*hijab*).	Women are a particularly significant and obvious example of both the interpretative differences of Islamic doctrine and the balance of Western and Islamic values. Interpretations differ significantly over the role of women. For example some claim that the Qur'anic reference allowing polygyny makes this contingent on the equal treatment of wives, which, being impossible, results in the prohibition of the practice. Conversely, in Muslim Turkey, women are prohibited from wearing the *hijab* because of the state's commitment to secularism. The position of women in Islam is one of the most contentious areas of Islamic thought and, as such, open to interpretation.

Sample Motions:

This House believes that there is a Clash of Civilizations.
This House believes that Islam is at war with democracy.
This House believes in secularism.

Web Links:

- Boston Review. <http://bostonreview.net/BR28.2/abou.html> Detailed article on Muslim understanding of democracy.
- Center for the Study of Islam and Democracy. <http://www.islam-democracy.org> Organization dedicated to studying Islamic and democratic political thought.
- Council on Foreign Relations. <http://www.cfr.org/publication/7708/> Basic Q&A on the relation between Islam and democracy.
- Gallup World Poll. <http://media.gallup.com/MuslimWestFacts/PDF/GALLUPMUSLIMSTUDIESIslamandDemocracy030607rev.pdf> Gallup data from ten countries suggesting that Muslims believe Islam and democracy can coexist.
- National Geographic. <http://news.nationalgeographic.com/news/2003/10/1021_031021_islamicdemocracy.html> Analytical article on the pairing of Islam and democracy.

Further Reading:

Diamond, Larry. *Islam and Democracy in the Middle East.* Johns Hopkins University Press, 2003.

Fadl, Khaled Abou El. *Islam and the Challenge of Democracy: A "Boston Review" Book.* Princeton University Press, 2004.

Mernissi, Fatima. *Islam and Democracy: Fear of the Modern World.* Basic Books, 2002.

ISRAEL AND THE PALESTINIANS, US POLICY TOWARD

Since it was founded in 1948, the state of Israel has been in conflict with the Arab nations that surround it, and with the Arab people living within its own borders—and the United States has been part of that conflict. The United States was one of the first countries to recognize the legitimacy of the Israeli government, and for more than 50 years it has supported Israel militarily, economically, and diplomatically. The United States has also been instrumental in negotiating diplomatic agreements between Israel and the Arab world. The central issue in the conflict today is the creation of a Palestinian state that would give autonomy to the Arabs living under Israeli rule (primarily on the West Bank of the Jordan River). Israel has been reluctant to create this state, which Palestinians regard as their right. Although the United States has voiced support for a Palestinian state, many observers see the Bush administration's failure to denounce Israel's assassination of Hamas leader Abdel Aziz Rantisi and its support for Israel maintaining some settlements in occupied territory as openly siding with Israel.

PROS

US policy in the Middle East has been consistently on the side of Israel. The Bush administration's tilt toward Israel was evident since it came to office. George Bush has refused to meet with Yasser Arafat because he views the Palestinian leader as an obstacle to peace.

American policy in the Middle East has been guided by politics, not principles. On the one hand, presidents have responded to the pressure from Jewish voters to support Israel. On the other hand, policy toward Arab states has been shaped largely by economic needs: The US has been friendly to countries with large oil reserves, e.g., Saudi Arabia, but has ignored poorer Arabs, e.g., the Palestinians.

The US has claimed that it supports Israel because it is the only democracy in the region—but such support of democracy has not been a firmly held principle and not acted on in other parts of the world. The US has knowingly supported corrupt and unjust authoritarian regimes in Arab countries when their oil policies favored America.

The US has been inconsistent in the application of its moral principles. It has routinely condemned Palestinians and other Arabs for terrorist actions, but it granted immediate recognition to the state of Israel, which engaged in a terrorist campaign against the British.

CONS

Do not forget that for most of its history, Israel's neighbors said that Israel had no right to exist and must be destroyed. US support has been critical to Israel's survival.

Throughout the world, the United States is committed to the development of open, democratic societies. Israel is the only functioning democracy in the Middle East and shares many of America's political values. It deserves American support.

The US has always acted as an impartial broker, seeking concessions from both sides. The US has used its influence to have Israel consider Arab demands and to have Arab nations and negotiators consider Israel's demands.

The US has acted in good faith with the Palestinian people, but negotiations have faltered because their leader, Yasser Arafat, is corrupt, duplicitous, and unstable. In 2000, Arafat rejected the best settlement he could have won from Israel.

Sample Motions:

This House supports US sponsorship of a Palestinian state.
This House would value democracy more than votes and oil.

Web Links:

- Brookings Institution. <http://www.brookings.edu/views/papers/fellows/indyk_wittes20060519.htm> 2006 memo from the director of the Saban Center for Middle East Policy.
- Helping Palestinians Build a Better Future. <http://www.state.gov/secretary/rm/2006/73895.htm> 2006 Keynote Address by US Secretary of State at the American Task Force on Palestine Inaugural Gala.
- Palestine Center. <http://www.thejerusalemfund.org/carryover/pubs/20011112ftr.html> Summary of 2006 conference on US Policy and the Palestinians held by pro-Palestinian group.

Further Reading:

Aruri, Nasser. *Dishonest Broker: The Role of the United States in Palestine and Israel.* South End Press, 2003.

Peters, Joan. *From Time Immemorial: The Origins of the Arab-Jewish Conflict over Palestine.* JKAP Publishers, 2001.

Said, Edward W. *The End of the Peace Process: Oslo and After.* Knopf, 2001.

IVORY TRADING

The African elephant population decreased from about 1.2 million in 1979 to approximately 600,000 in 1989, in part as a result of intense poaching to supply the international ivory trade. In 1989 the United Nations Convention on International Trade in Endangered Species (CITES) banned ivory trading. This resulted in population increases in some countries. In 1997 the ban was eased for Botswana, Zimbabwe, and Namibia, giving them a one-time opportunity to sell their stockpiled ivory to Japan, the center of ivory demand. The ivory was sold in 1999; in 2000, African nations agreed to a two-year freeze on sales, but in 2002, South Africa announced that it would apply for permission to sell its stockpiles beginning in 2003. South Africa, Namibia, and Botswana received permission from CITES to sell government ivory stocks beginning in 2004. At the same time, conservation groups were reporting increased activity in the ivory market, with the markets in China, Thailand, Burma, and Nigeria larger than in the early 1990s.

PROS

The elephant populations of southern African states are growing rapidly, placing a strain upon the national parks in which they live. This has necessitated government culls that have resulted in large stockpiles of ivory (also acquired from animals that died naturally) that these nations are currently unable to sell. Relaxing the CITES ban on trading ivory, subject to careful regulation, would bring much-needed cash to the environmental programs of these impoverished countries, helping them to safeguard the long-term survival of African elephants.

A trading ban does not choke off demand for ivory. Instead, it raises the price to exorbitant levels, encouraging poaching. Japan is emerging from the economic problems that depressed demand during the 1990s, and China's growing prosperity is creating a new market. Consequently the illegal trade will generate higher profits in the future. Legitimate, regulated sales would undercut the illegal market and drive the poachers out of business.

Poaching has been effectively eliminated in southern Africa through effective management of game parks. The development of ecotourism also gives local peoples an incentive to protect wildlife as a long-term economic resource. To sustain this approach, parks must generate greater income from their elephant populations. Realistically, states can do this only by selling stockpiled ivory. If other countries have a poaching problem, they should follow the example of South Africa and Botswana rather than seek to harm the successful conservancy programs in these states.

CONS

Elephants are highly intelligent animals; to kill them for their ivory is unethical. Lifting the ban would legitimize the view that humankind can exploit them in any way convenient.

At present demand for ivory is low and shrinking; prices are actually lower than before 1989. Lifting the trading ban would renew interest in ivory artifacts and increase the size of the market, thus raising their price. Higher prices present a long-term threat to elephants and encourage continued poaching. In any case, poverty in Africa is so severe that even a drop in price will not stop the poachers.

Although elephant populations in southern Africa are viable and increasing, this is not the case elsewhere in Africa. Nor is it true of the wild Asian elephant populations of South Asia. Testing cannot reveal where carved ivory originated or the subspecies from which it came. Consequently, lifting the trading ban would enable poachers to sell ivory more easily, thus increasing their profits and their motivation to kill more elephants. The widespread corruption in Africa and parts of Asia allows poachers to mask the illegal origins of their ivory, which they pass off as legally obtained.

PROS	CONS
Ivory is expensive to obtain (through culls or monitoring of very elderly animals) and store. It also degrades over time. Therefore, common sense tells us to allow its sale on a permanent, controlled basis, rather than through one-off schemes such as the sale to Japan.	Storage costs and depreciation are problems only if ivory is stored in the hope of eventual sale. Kenya's game conservancy burns the ivory it obtains from culls or confiscates from poachers, avoiding both of these problems and showing its commitment to ending all possibility of renewed trade.
According to the South African government proposal to lift the ban in 2000, "The experimental export of raw ivory in 1999 from Botswana, Namibia and Zimbabwe (conducted under rigorous CITES supervision) was successful in all respects and took place under intense international scrutiny. It can categorically be stated that no ivory, other than the registered stocks, was exported to Japan."	The relaxation of CITES controls coincided with a fivefold upsurge in poaching in Kenya and a similar increase in India because criminals assumed that the ban would soon be lifted.

Sample Motions:

This House would allow trade in ivory.

This House would save the elephants.

This House believes conservation must justify itself economically.

Web Links:

- Convention on International Trade in Endangered Species of Wild Fauna and Flora (CITES). <http://www.cites.org> Provides information on CITES and CITES programs, the text of the CITES convention, and links to resources on endangered species.
- International Fund for Animal Welfare. <http://www.ifaw.org> Links to information on the status of elephants and projects to save them.
- NPR. <http://www.npr.org/templates/story/story.php?storyId=840268> Story about easing of UN ban on ivory trade; links to more information.

Further Reading:

Pearce, David, ed. *Elephants, Economics and Ivory.* Earthscan, 1991.

Snugg, Ike. *Elephants and Ivory: Lessons from the Trade Ban.* Institute of Economic Affairs, 1994.

JUST WAR

War is always evil, but some thinkers have maintained that under limited circumstances it may be the lesser evil. From Cicero to St. Augustine, Thomas Aquinas to Hugo Grotius, philosophers and theologians have proposed numerous criteria for determining if a war is just. According to contemporary Just War Theory, a war is just only if it meets the six conditions presented in the following debate. The theory has been formulated to prevent war, not justify it. A nation must satisfy all six conditions or the war is not just. The theory is designed to show states the rigorous criteria they must meet to justify the use of violence and prompt them to find other ways of solving conflicts.

PROS

A Just War satisfies six criteria:

1. Wars are just if the cause is just. Nations should be allowed to defend themselves from aggression, just as individuals are permitted to defend themselves against violence.

2. The war must be lawfully declared by a lawful authority. This prevents inappropriate, terrorist-style chaos, and ensures that other rules of war will be observed. For example, when states declare war, they generally follow specific legislative procedures; a guaranteed respect for such procedures is likely to ensure that the nation will respect other rules of war, such as the Geneva Convention.

3. The intentions behind the war must be good. States have the right to use war to restore a just peace, to help the innocent, or to right a wrong. For example, the US and NATO where justified in using force in Bosnia. Waging war was far more ethical than standing by and permitting genocide.

4. War must be a last resort. The state is justified in using war after it has tried all nonviolent alternatives. Sometimes peaceful measures—diplomacy, economic sanctions, international pressure, or condemnation from other nations—simply do not work.

5. The war must have a reasonable chance of success. War always involves a loss of life, but expending life with no possibility of achieving a goal is unacceptable. Thus, if a fighting force cannot achieve its goal, however just, it should not proceed. Charging an enemy's cannons on horseback or throwing troops at a pointless occupation are clearly not just actions.

6. The goal of the war should be proportional to the offense and the benefits proportional to the costs. For example, when an attacker violates a nation's border, a proportionate response might extend to restoring the border, not sacking the attacker's capital. A war must prevent more suffering than it causes.

CONS

The criteria for just war present several problems:

1. Just cause is an elastic concept. Who determines what is "aggression"? Could violating a border or imposing economic sanctions be aggression? And if a state is unable to defend itself, can another state intervene militarily on its behalf? These borderline cases make invoking this criterion very problematic.

2. Many nations wage war without an official declaration. Moreover, who is to decide which entities can and cannot issue calls to arms? Legitimate authorities have sanctioned some of the most horrific wars in history.

3. Reality is a lot murkier than theory. How are we to determine a state's intent? Sometimes good intentions are bound up with bad. And who is to determine if a peace is just or a wrong has been committed? The nation initiating the war will use its own values to justify its intentions, and these values may be at odds with those of other the party in the conflict. Furthermore, the best way to protect innocent lives is by peaceful means, not by endangering them further through armed conflict.

4. Sometimes going to war before all alternatives are exhausted is the most moral action. For example, a nation might decide to go to war if it determines that waiting would enable the enemy to increase its strength and to do much more damage than an early war would have inflicted. Waiting might allow an invading state to entrench itself so that far greater force would be necessary to remove it at a later date.

5. Sometimes it is morally imperative to fight against overwhelming odds, as resistance fighters did in World War II. Also, this condition may give large nations free rein to bully small ones because they could not win a war. It also may cause a country to surrender in a war it might actually win. Weak countries have won wars against powerful ones—look at the American Revolution.

6. We have seen that a proportional response frequently doesn't work. Suicide bombers continue to blow up victims in the Middle East despite the response. Why should a nation tolerate continued aggression for the sake of proportionality? And if a nation knows it is likely to be attacked, why should it wait to disarm the aggressor? Is not preemptive action justified to prevent the loss of innocent life?

Sample Motions:

This House believes that war is sometimes justified.

This House believes swords are as necessary as ploughshares.

This House believes that justifying war is unjustifiable.

Web Links:

- BBC Religion and Ethics. <http://www.bbc.co.uk/religion/ethics/war/index.shtml> Excellent discussion of Just War Theory.
- The Internet Encyclopedia of Philosophy's History of Philosophy. <http://www.iep.utm.edu/j/justwar.htm> Summary of Just War Theory with review of the literature.
- Just War: The Stanford University Online Encyclopedia of Philosophy. <http://plato.stanford.edu/entries/war/> Philosophical analysis of war in general and just war in particular.
- JustWarTheory.com. <http://www.justwartheory.com> Overview of the just war theory with links to other sources for more in-depth treatment.

Further Reading:

Johnson, James Turner. *Morality and Contemporary Warfare*. Yale University Press, 2001.

Temes, Peter S. *The Just War: An American Reflection on the Morality of War in Our Time*. Ivan R. Dee, 2003.

Walzer, Michael. *Just and Unjust Wars: A Moral Argument with Historical Illustrations*. Basic Books, 2006

LANDMINES, US PRODUCTION AND USE OF

The 1997 Ottawa Convention, signed by 135 nations, banned the use and stockpiling of antipersonnel mines. The United States is not a signatory. The Ottawa Convention requires signatories to abandon the use of landmines within 10 years and also requires the destruction of the signatory's stockpile of landmines. The convention's aims became official UN policy in 1998 with the adoption of General Assembly Resolution 53/77. In 2004 the United States announced that it would eliminate persistent landmines from its arsenal and seek a worldwide ban on their sale or export. However, it continued to develop nonpersistent (self-destructing/self-deactivating) landmines that would not pose a humanitarian threat after use in battle.

PROS

Landmines do great harm to people, but so do all weapons of war. Landmines are not uniquely unpleasant, and the debate about them has distorted public perception. In truth, they are little different from a hundred other types of weaponry that remain legal under the Ottawa ban.

CONS

Landmines are a terrible, immoral tool of war. America should neither practice nor condone this kind of warfare. Unlike other weaponry, landmines remain hidden long after conflicts have ended, killing and maiming civilians in some of the world's poorest countries years, even decades later. Just because other weaponry has similar effects, doesn't mean that landmines are acceptable—it means that other weapons are unconscionable, too. But we must start somewhere. We can make a difference by capitalizing on the global movement against landmines and we should.

PRO: Landmines are an excellent way of defending a wide area for very little money and with very few military personnel. This is a legitimate aim in warfare, when military personnel are spread too thinly to protect all civilians, and in peacetime, when poor countries want to invest

CON: The usefulness of landmines is significantly overstated. They are easily removed by quite low-technology military equipment, which means that they are not very dangerous to armed forces, but are incredibly harmful to civilians.

PROS

in infrastructure rather than in defense. In the future, nations may not need landmines, but while armies still depend on conventional weapons, using landmines to defend borders is highly appropriate. Landmines can slow or stop an advance, delaying or even halting conflict; they can deter invasion in the first place. By protecting wide areas from a swift military advance on civilians, they can prevent genocide.

CONS

PROS

The use of landmines is a totally separate issue from removing them. We can do the latter without banning the former. The proposition accepts that those who use landmines must fund clean-up efforts, and the United States is doing this. The attention of the very humanitarian organizations calling for a ban will ensure that this obligation is met.

CONS

Suggesting that the use and removal of landmines are two separate issues is absurd—the two are inextricably interlinked. Most nations that deploy landmines, including those manufactured in the United States, never remove them. As history has shown, relying on goodwill or trust to remove landmines is folly. Simply put, if landmines are deployed, innocent people inevitably die. The United States should not dirty its hands by trading in these wicked weapons.

PROS

Banning landmines disproportionately punishes underdeveloped countries unable to acquire the higher-technology military capacity that has made mines less useful to richer nations. Banning landmines harms precisely the nations most likely to need them for defensive purposes.

CONS

Landmines provide a false sense of security. Nations often use them in lieu of negotiating with their neighbors. Landmines are the symbol of exactly the wrong approach to international affairs. Underdeveloped countries should channel their efforts into improving their economies. The United States should not encourage them or frighten them into to buying US military equipment.

PROS

The ban on landmines has an asymmetric effect: it only stops nations that honor the ban. Nations that want to use landmines will do so regardless of the US position (or that of any other nation)—as demonstrated by the current prolific use of mines despite the large number of signatories to the Ottawa Convention. In addition, if we might one day face an enemy deploying landmines, we must expose our soldiers to their use in training so that they learn how to deal with them.

CONS

Obviously only those nations that stand behind their commitments will honor their commitments. That is a rationale for never entering into international treaties. Certainly some nations will ignore the ban—but as a ban gains acceptance, such nations will eventually succumb to pressure, especially if US diplomatic and moral might is behind it. Even if other nations ignore such ban, doing the right thing in and of itself is very important. Ultimately, this debate is about what kind of global society you want to live in. Do you want to live in a society that tries hard to stop the use of such horrible weapons and occasionally fails, or one that never even bothers to try?

PROS

The ban fails to distinguish between different kinds of mines. The Americans have mines that can deactivate themselves and can self-destruct. America manufactures only nonpersistent "smart mines"; since 1976, the US has tested 32,000 mines with a successful self-destruction rate of 99.996%. The ban also fails to distinguish between responsible and irresponsible users. Under American deployment, only smart mines are used, and they are used responsibly.

CONS

Faith in these so-called smart mines is hugely misplaced. Testing cannot duplicate battlefield conditions, in which areas of deployment are often not properly recorded or marked. Even if smart mines work as claimed, regimes that use them may not want to deactivate them upon a cease-fire, particularly if their dispute still smolders. The equipment required for deactivation may be lost or destroyed. The best way to ensure that these weapons are not left in the soil is never to put them there in the first place. That some users might be responsible is not good enough, since if anyone uses landmines everyone will.

PROS	CONS
Used in peacekeeping initiatives, these mines protect US troops and present little danger to civilians. Stopping their use would endanger the lives of peacekeepers and make the United States less likely to enter into such operations. This is one reason why the United States refused to sign the Ottawa treaty in 1997 and has declined to do so since.	Suggesting that landmines are the prime protector of US forces, or even an important one, is absurd. The principal protection US troops (as opposed to those of other nations) have in peacekeeping is the threat of using overwhelming force if defied. The damage done to relations with the civilian community from using landmines far outweighs any narrow military benefit garnered from landmine deployment.

Sample Motions:

This House believes the US should cease production and export of landmines and sign the Ottawa Convention.
This House would sign the Ottawa Convention.
This House would ban landmines.

Web Links:

- BBC News. <http://news.bbc.co.uk/1/hi/talking_point/2149352.stm> Article and debate on the campaign to ban landmines.
- Global Issues. <http://www.globalissues.org/article/79/landmines> Information about use of landmines throughout the world as well as the US specifically.
- International Campaign to Ban Landmines. <http://www.icbl.org> Information on the impact of landmines and on the campaign to ban them.

Further Reading:

Harpviken, Kristian Berg. *The Future of Humanitarian Mine Action.* Palgrave Macmillan, 2004.

Maslen, Stuart. *Mine Action After Diana: Progress in the Struggle Against Landmines.* Pluto Press, 2004.

Sigal, Leon. *The Landmines Ban in American Politics.* Routledge, 2006.

MANDATORY SENTENCING: THREE STRIKES

Early in the 1980s, national legislators became concerned that the criminal justice system had become inconsistent across the country. Similar crimes were being punished with dramatically different sentences, even though the same laws applied. Accordingly, Congress began to craft rules for mandatory prison sentences in federal cases; these rules were intended to ensure that similar crimes would be punished in similar ways, no matter where these cases were tried. Many state legislatures drafted parallel rules for lower courts. Over time, mandatory sentences in state courts evolved to include "three-strikes" rules: If a newly convicted felon had a criminal record of two prior felony convictions, the judge was obligated to impose the maximum sentence for the third crime. (There are some variations in the laws from state to state.) There has been growing concern, however, that the punishments imposed by three-strikes laws are not simply too severe, but also unconstitutional. In 2003, the US Supreme Court upheld the three-strikes law adopted in California in 1994.

PROS

One of the fundamental principles of criminal justice is that the punishment should fit the crime. That principle is abrogated when a life sentence is automatically imposed for a third felony—whether that felony is serious and violent, or minor and non-violent. Because there is only one sentence possible for many kinds of crimes, it follows that the sentence does not necessarily correspond to the gravity of the offense.

It often happens that the third felony—that is, the one that triggers the automatic sentence—is relatively minor. For example, a life sentence has been imposed on someone for the attempted shoplifting of videotapes. A life sentence for such a crime is "cruel and unusual," and, as such, is forbidden by the Eighth Amendment to the Constitution.

Historically, judges have had discretionary powers when sentencing criminals; this practice recognizes that sentencing should take into account the circumstances of the crime, the character of the criminal, and the amount of harm caused by the crime. Mandatory sentences rob judges of those discretionary powers that are properly theirs. Indeed, mandatory sentences are imposed, in effect, by the legislative branch—thus violating the independence of the judiciary and the separation of powers outlined in the Constitution.

Defenders of the three-strikes laws claim that these laws have a powerful deterrent effect, and reduce the occurrence of crime. Statistics show, however, that recidivism has not been reduced by the presence of such laws, and the general reduction in crime, when and where it has occurred, is due to effective policing, rather than to harsh sentencing.

The three-strikes laws are, in effect, ex post facto laws: that is, criminal sentences can take into account—as first and second strikes—crimes that were committed before the law was passed. Moreover, the imposition of mandatory maximum sentences because of past history constitutes "double jeopardy": Criminals are being punished again for crimes for which they already served time.

CONS

It is a primary obligation of the criminal justice system to establish clear and certain penalties for crime. The three-strikes laws offer such clarity, and their mandatory nature makes punishment certain. These laws prevent inconsistency in the criminal justice system.

Historically, judges have abused the discretion that they have been given by the criminal justice system. Too often, judges have imposed light sentences on criminals, even when those criminals have been repeat offenders. The mandatory sentences imposed by three-strikes laws ensure that recidivists are punished appropriately.

The fundamental purpose of the criminal justice system is to protect the rights and the safety of law-abiding citizens. But these citizens are not protected by "revolving door justice," which allows criminals back on the street after repeat offenses. Three-strikes laws remove repeat offenders from society, and prevent them from committing further crimes.

Since three-strikes laws have been introduced across the nation, crime has dropped dramatically. The reason for this decline is obvious: Convicted recidivists are not free to commit more crimes, and felons with one or two strikes on their records are deterred by the punishment that they know will follow a third offense.

Opponents of three-strikes laws claim that these laws give criminals no chance to rehabilitate and redeem themselves. But studies have shown that rehabilitation is highly unlikely for recidivists. Someone who has committed three felonies is not likely to reform; rather, it is the destiny of the recidivist to keep committing crimes.

Sample Motions:

This House would restore discretion in sentencing to the judiciary.

This House would make the punishment fit the crime.

Web Links:

- CBS. <http://www.cbsnews.com/stories/2002/10/28/60II/main527248.shtml> Report discussing appropriateness of "three strikes" law.
- FACTS: Families to Amend California's Three-Strikes. <http://www.facts1.com> Web site of an advocacy group that focuses specifically on California laws. Includes history and links to key texts and other Web sites.
- The Guardian. <http://www.guardian.co.uk/world/2004/mar/08/usa.danglaister> Article on protest against "three strikes" law.

Further Reading:

Domanick, Joe. *Cruel Justice: Three Strikes and the Politics of Crime in America's Golden State.* University of California Press, 2005.

Walsh, Jennifer E. *Three Strikes Laws.* Greenwood Press, 2007.

Zimring, Franklin E., Gordon Hawkins, and Sam Kamin. *Punishment and Democracy: Three Strikes and You're Out in California.* Oxford University Press, 2003.

MARIJUANA, LEGALIZATION OF

The debate about the legalization of drugs, particularly soft drugs like marijuana, could be characterized as pitting freedom of the individual against a paternalistic state. Advocates of legalization argue that marijuana is not only less harmful than legal substances like alcohol and tobacco, but has been proven to possess certain medicinal properties. Alaska, California, Colorado, Hawaii, Maine, Maryland, Montana, Nevada, New Mexico, Oregon, Rhode Island, Vermont, and Washington permit the medical use of marijuana. However, in 2005 the US Supreme Court in Gonzalez v. Raich *ruled that the Justice Department has the authority to prosecute state-authorized medicinal cannabis patients for violating the federal Controlled Substances Act. Those opposed to legalization argue that it will act as an introduction to harder drugs, lead to addiction, and cause the crime rate to increase.*

PROS

Although marijuana does have some harmful effects, it is no more harmful than legal substances like alcohol and tobacco. Research by the British Medical Association shows that nicotine is far more addictive than marijuana. Furthermore, the consumption of alcohol and cigarette smoking cause more deaths per year than does marijuana. The legalization of marijuana will remove an anomaly in the law whereby substances that are more dangerous than marijuana are legal, while the possession and use of marijuana remains unlawful.

In recent years, scientists and medical researchers have discovered that marijuana possesses certain beneficial medicinal qualities. For instance, marijuana helps to relieve the suffering of patients with multiple sclerosis. The latest research that was conducted by the Complutense University in Madrid indicates that marijuana has the potential to kill some cancerous cells. Governments should acknowledge such findings and legalize marijuana.

CONS

Unlike alcohol and tobacco, marijuana has an inherently dangerous hallucinatory effect on the mind. Furthermore, many individuals addicted to marijuana resort to crime to fund their addiction. The legalization of marijuana will lead to the drug becoming more readily available, which in turn will mean that many more people will gain access to it and become addicted. The crime rate will inevitably rise. Data from the Netherlands show that the decriminalization and eventual legalization of marijuana did lead to an increase in crime.

The US has supported scientific research into the medical benefits of marijuana. Although evidence may show that marijuana may have some medicinal benefits, we should exercise caution about legalizing it because its use also has harmful side effects. More important, the legalization of marijuana will give rise to a host of social problems. The negatives of legalization far outweigh its benefits. We can thus safely say that the present approach represents the most sensible and evenhanded response to the issue at hand.

PROS	CONS
Individuals should be given the freedom to lead their lives as they choose. Of course, such freedom is not absolute, and laws should intervene to limit this freedom, especially when the rights of others are infringed. In the case of the use of marijuana, it is a victimless crime—only the user experiences the effects of the substance. The state should not act paternalistically by legislating against something that harms only the actual user.	The state is justified in introducing legislation to prevent individuals from causing harm to themselves. For instance, many countries have laws requiring the wearing of seatbelts in cars. Moreover, the use of marijuana does lead to medically and socially harmful outcomes that affect other members of society.
Where is the empirical evidence that the use of marijuana will certainly lead users into more dangerous narcotic substances? There is none. Undeniably, a large number of people use the drug despite it being illegal. Rather than turn away from this problem, the government should face reality. The legalization of marijuana will enable the government to regulate its use, thereby protecting its many users from harmful abuse of the substance.	The legalization of marijuana will lead to users moving on to harder drugs like morphine and cocaine. This would ultimately bring about an increase in social ills as well as the need to spend more government funds on rehabilitation programs.
Presently, organized crime sells marijuana. The legalization of marijuana will help facilitate the sale of the drug in establishments like Amsterdam's "coffee houses." This will shift the sale of marijuana away from the criminal underworld. Severing the "criminal link" will ensure that the users no longer need to come into contact with organized crime.	The same criminal elements that now sell marijuana might, when the drug is legalized, diversify and set up "coffee houses" themselves. Legalization will do nothing to separate the sale of marijuana from the criminal underworld. Conversely, it will give criminals a legitimate base from which to continue their activities.

Sample Motions:

This House believes that marijuana should be legalized.

This House supports the legalization of drugs.

This House advocates change in our present drug policy.

Web Links:

- Legalise Cannabis Alliance. <http://www.lca-uk.org> Organization supporting the legalization of marijuana in Great Britain.
- National Organization for the Reform of Marijuana Laws. <http://www.norml.org> Information on marijuana facts, laws, and medical use from the oldest US organization supporting legalization.
- Office of National Drug Control Policy. <http://www.whitehousedrugpolicy.gov> Provides information on US government drug policy, statistics on drug use, news stories and publications from an anti-legalization perspective.

Further Reading:

Earleywine, Mitch. *Understanding Marijuana: A New Look at the Scientific Evidence.* Oxford University Press, 2005.

Gerber, Rudolph. *Legalizing Marijuana: Drug Policy Reform and Prohibition Politics.* Praeger Publishers, 2004.

Rosenthal, Ed, and Steve Kubby, with S. Newhart. *Why Marijuana Should Be Legal.* Thunder's Mouth Press, 2003.

MINORITY SCHOOLS

In 1954, the US Supreme Court ruled that racial segregation in public schools was unconstitutional. In the decades that followed, school systems took steps—often unwillingly—to obey that ruling, sometimes busing students considerable distances to achieve integration. Even so, de facto segregation has remained common, largely because of demographic patterns. In recent years, however, sentiment has grown for a new kind of de jure segregation, one that is deliberate rather than accidental: it has been argued that black males in particular are better served educationally in all-black (and all-male) schools—and that public school systems should provide such an option. Opponents of single-race schools are skeptical about the purported benefits of such institutions, and they reject any system, however well intentioned, that violates the judicial ban on segregation.

PROS

The civil rights movement fought segregation because schools for blacks were inferior to white schools; the real issue was the quality of the education black students received. If studies show that black students will be better educated in all-black schools, then school systems must act to serve these students.

Even though the state requires mandatory education, the Constitution respects the right of free choice and free association. Catholics, for example, are free to attend church schools with all-Catholic populations, and girls can go to private schools that serve only girls. The result is that students are allowed to attend the schools that serve them best. But this should not be a privilege given only to those who can afford private schooling. Public school students, too, deserve options that serve them—and those options should include single-sex, single-race schools. Equality under the law does not mean sameness.

Society benefits from single-race schools. Students who attend such schools perform better academically because the schools give them a proud sense of their cultural identity and a disciplined sense of responsibility. These qualities will make them better citizens after they leave the school system.

Integration does not necessarily represent the blending of disparate cultures into a unified whole; often, it means the dominance of one culture. African-American students learn in distinctive ways, and they should not be forced into schools that promote white culture and white learning styles.

CONS

Constitutional principles are fundamental and not open to negotiation. Segregation in public institutions is unconstitutional and permitting it in schools, for whatever reason, will justify other kinds of segregation that are less well intentioned.

The Constitution respects the right of free association in the private sector, but the public sector is distinctly different. Citizens are guaranteed access to public services, irrespective of race, sex, or creed. The state cannot create schools that, by design, exclude any part of the population.

The logic behind single-sex, single-race schools is patronizing and self-defeating. It assumes that African-American males cannot learn when there are white students present or when there are girls present. Would anyone suggest that white students are incapable of learning when blacks are present? The assumption that blacks are incapable breeds a feeling of inferiority, not pride.

Society must respect the cultural identity and cultural heritage of all of the people who make up America. This may require some reforms in the way schools currently operate. Nevertheless, we must aspire to common understandings and common ways of doing things. A fragmented, atomized country cannot function or prosper. We must not endorse schools that promote a sense of separation rather than a sense of unity.

PROS

After graduation, either in college or in the workforce, African Americans will have to function as members of a minority. It is important for them, while still in school, to have a "majority experience"—that is, to be part of a community in which they are regarded as the norm rather than the exception.

CONS

The working world is not segregated; indeed, one of the most dominant characteristics of American society is its diversity—ethnic, racial, and religious. One of the primary purposes of schooling is to prepare students for the working world; preparing them with a faulty model makes no sense. If the world at large is not segregated, the school should not be either.

Sample Motions:

This House supports the creation of single-race public schools.

This House would serve public school students in the best ways possible.

This House believes in separate but equal.

Web Links:

- The Gateway. <http://www.thegatewayonline.ca/are-afrocentric-schools-segregation-or-advancement-20080204-1800.html> Point-counterpoint style article from University of Alberta's student newspaper.
- Toronto Star. <http://www.thestar.com/article/298714> Article on Toronto school board's decision to allow all-black school.
- Torontoist.com. <http://torontoist.com/2007/11/torontoist_vs_t_14.php> Debate on whether all-black schools are good.

Further Reading:

Ginwright, Shawn A. *Black in School: Afrocentric Reform, Urban Youth & the Promise of Hip-Hop Culture.* Teachers College Press, 2004.

Murrell, Peter C., Jr. *African-Centered Pedagogy: Developing Schools of Achievement for African American Children.* State University of New York Press, 2002.

MULTICULTURALISM VS. INTEGRATION

One of the biggest questions facing societies today, particularly in light of the rise of fundamentalist Islam, is how to deal with a culturally diverse citizenry. Different religions and traditions exist side by side in many cities. Historically, the United States has had a continuing debate about how completely immigrants should adopt the dominant language and culture. Facing growing immigrant communities determined to retain their identity, Europe has had to address the issue. On one side are those who want to enforce a certain degree of integration—a basic knowledge of the national language, the national history, and civil customs. On the other are those who believe that a multicultural society is strong enough to accommodate numerous cultures within it and that it might even gain from the diversity this entails.

PROS

Multiculturalism is clearly better; how can you expect people to give up their heritage? Immigrants do not leave a country to leave their cultural identity behind.

CONS

If you decide that you want to live in a country, you have to respect its traditions. Expecting new citizens or residents to conform to certain national norms is not unreasonable.

PROS

If a society claims to be tolerant of personal choice, it must respect the choice of immigrants to retain their heritage. Anything less smacks of social engineering.

Clinging to an idea of monolithic, national identity is anachronistic. The nation-state model for society is crumbling and is being outstripped by transnational models, such as the European Union. As a result, there is less emphasis on national identity. Such exclusive nationalism is destructive, and history shows it to be so.

Perpetuating a national identity inevitably leads to the alienation of those who for religious or other reasons choose not to conform. If the national identity does not include the wearing of a turban, headdress, or robe, then those who do wear these garments are excluded from the mainstream. Such exclusion gives rise to the notion of the "other" and leaves those perceived as the "other" open to physical assault.

We should embrace the fact that people can support both their old and new nations. It shows that we have moved beyond the divisive national stereotyping that causes conflict. The more tolerance of difference and embrace of other cultures we can achieve, the less conflict there will be.

CONS

What some people call social engineering, integrationists call ensuring that society is as harmonious and conflict-free as possible. If difference breeds contempt, then the least difference the better.

We totally reject the notion of the demise of the nation-state. It is still the primary mode of national identity. As US history has shown, a nation can absorb millions of immigrants and yet maintained a unique identity.

There is a middle point between denying anyone the right to practice their religion openly and denying any sort of national identity or conformity. A shared sense of belonging and purpose is vital for national coherence and serves the nation and the nation's peoples well in times of war. In addition, we want everyone to cheer their favorite ball team.

This is naïve and presumes, arrogantly, that we have moved beyond the point where we are at risk from enemies. As the rise in extremism and its support from some of our own citizens show, we have been too liberal. We have forgotten why nationhood is important and why we all need to feel a communal belonging and affinity with the basic values of our society.

Sample Motions:

This House would be multicultural.
This House believes in multiculturalism.
This House believes that the nation-state is dead.

Web Links:

- Australian Department of Immigration and Citizenship. <http://www.immi.gov.au/media/publications/multicultural/issues97/macpape3.htm> The benefits of multiculturalism in Australia and the policies to control it.
- Diversity & Multiculturalism: The New Racism. <http://www.aynrand.org/site/PageServer?pagename=objectivism_diversity/> Critique of multiculturalism by the Ayn Rand Institute.
- UNESCO. <http://portal.unesco.org/shs/en/ev.php-URL_ID=2552&URL_DO=DO_TOPIC&URL_SECTION=-465.html> Several articles about multiculturalism and integration in modern nation-states.

Further Reading:

Barry, Brian M. *Culture and Equality: An Egalitarian Critique of Multiculturalism.* Harvard University Press, 2002.

Kymlicka, Will. *Politics in the Vernacular: Nationalism, Multiculturalism, and Citizenship.* Oxford University Press, 2001.

Kymlicka, Will, and Wayne Norman, eds. *Citizenship in Diverse Societies.* Oxford University Press, 2000.

Miller, David. *Citizenship and National Identity.* Polity Press, 2000.

NATIONAL TESTING

Responding to mounting concerns that the US educational system was failing its students, Congress passed the No Child Left Behind Act (2001), which mandates that states develop annual assessments (tests) of learning and skills mastered. The scores on these state tests are then compared with those from a sampling of state students who have taken the National Assessment of Educational Progress (NAEP). The intent is to use the results of these tests to chart national academic progress and provide extra help for schools and students who are falling behind. Education in the United States has historically been the responsibility of states and localities; this measure vastly expands federal involvement in education. Many advocates believe this approach to improving the nation's schools is wrong and will not accomplish its objective. Others argue that the only way to know how schools and students are performing is to measure them against other schools and other students in other states.

PROS

A national curriculum for most core subjects already exists without school boards and local communities even realizing it. Most high school students are preparing for standardized college entrance exams and therefore study what is needed to do well on these tests. Also, only a few textbook companies produce texts for high school students. When localities select one of these textbooks, they are, in effect, agreeing to what amounts to a national curriculum. Besides, students across the country should learn the same skills.

As long as school boards and localities follow the national curriculum, student success on the test will follow. Drilling and "teaching to the test" occur only when schools make a decision to test without altering their curriculums. Students undeniably need to have certain basic skills and subject mastery when they graduate. The National Assessment of Educational Progress and the state-developed assessments will test those; the school day affords plenty of time for students to learn the basics and still participate in additional activities and attend classes that go beyond the basics.

The entire reason that public education in America was founded was to develop a more productive workforce. Although education by itself is a worthy goal, ultimately what we want for our children is for them to be successful individuals who are able to earn a living when they graduate from high school or college. Focusing on word choices that may also be used in the business world is just a distracter, used by opponents of national testing to shift the debate away from what really needs to happen in our nation's schools.

CONS

The mandate for a national test makes every locality teach the same curriculum. Each state and locality should be able to determine its own curriculum as schools across the country are very different and should be able to make decisions at the local level on what will be taught within their classrooms. Requiring national testing removes the traditional rights of localities to adapt to community standards and desires when making curriculum decisions.

Mandating a national test will result in teachers "teaching to the tests." Students will face days of learning how to take tests at the expense of learning skills and knowledge that will help them become good citizens and contribute in meaningful ways to society. They will become good test takers but will miss out on the joy of learning for learning's sake. Subjects like art and music that are not covered on the standardized tests could be cut. Our children's education would become narrowly focused on a yearly test.

Using a national test to determine if schools and students are working oversimplifies education. Advocates of national testing use terms that are more specific to business, as if children are simply widgets coming out at the end of an assembly line. Proponents of national testing use terms like "setting objectives," "getting results," and "the bottom line" when talking about our nation's children. We cannot let the unethical, corrupt, and profit-driven world of business encroach into our nation's classrooms.

PROS	CONS
In a society where education is so important to success, we must make sure our schools are performing for our nation's children. The primary reason for national standards and assessment is to make schools and teachers accountable for what goes on in the classroom. If schools and teachers are doing a good job, they have nothing to fear as we move to a national system of accountability through assessment.	Using a national test to determine if students are mastering material is unfair and will drive good teachers out of our classrooms, making existing problems worse. A better alternative is a broad-based assessment, which looks at multiple measures of what a student has learned. Instead of testing a student on one day, a multiple-measure assessment uses teacher evaluations, teacher-created tests, and student demonstrations that occur over the entire school year. This would especially benefit students who are not good test takers.
Developing acceptable national standards is not easy, but other countries have demonstrated that creating good standard tests that motivate students and teachers is possible. Excellence is created by bringing together the right people, examining textbooks, and looking at standards already put in place by many national teachers associations. In the United States, the quality of education that students receive depends on what state, county, and town they live in and even in what part of town they reside. This violates the principle of equality that is fundamental to the values of our country. If all teachers are expected to achieve the same standards, the quality of education for all children can go up.	The idea of national standards may seem like a good one until you start to actually try to create the standards that teachers must teach to. Agreeing what must be taught is difficult enough in a local setting; nationally such agreement is probably not achievable. Which historic figures should all students learn about? What parts of history are most important? Also, good standards are difficult to craft. Standards are either too vague so the test makers and teachers do not know what material to focus on, or they are too detailed so that teachers and students are overwhelmed by the sheer number of subjects that must be mastered.

Sample Motions:

This House would ban national testing.

This House believes that national standards are more valuable than locally developed curriculums.

This House believes that national standards will have a detrimental effect on education.

This House believes that national standards promote equality in education.

Web Links:

- National Education Association (NEA). <http://www.nea.org/accountability> Site, maintained by the major organization opposing national standards, currently focuses on the implementation of the initiative.
- PBS. <http://www.pbs.org/wgbh/pages/frontline/shows/schools> This companion Web site to the PBS show *Frontline* presents a balanced overview of the issue of national testing.
- University of Bristol. <http://www.bristol.ac.uk/news/2008/5910.html> Press release on impact of national testing on teaching of science.

Further Reading:

Jones, M. Gail, Brett D. Jones, and Tracy Hargrove. *The Unintended Consequences of High-Stakes Testing.* Rowman & Littlefield, 2003.

Meier, Deborah, et al., eds. *Many Children Left Behind: How the No Child Left Behind Act Is Damaging Our Children and Our Schools.* Beacon, 2004.

Orfield, Gary, and Mindy Kornhaber, eds. *Raising Standards or Raising Barriers: Inequality and High Stakes Testing in Public Education.* Century Foundation Press, 2001.

Sunderman, Gail L., James S. Kim, and Garry Orfield. *NCLB Meets School Realities: Lessons from the Field.* Corwin Press, 2005.

NUCLEAR VS. RENEWABLE ENERGY

Since the mid-1980s, nuclear power has been a major source of electricity in the United States, second only to coal. Yet the future of nuclear power in the US and the rest of the world is uncertain. Although the US has the most nuclear capacity of any nation, the U.S. Department of Energy predicts that the use of nuclear fuel will have dropped dramatically by 2020, by which time more than 40% of capacity will have been retired. The Bush Administration has supported nuclear expansion, emphasizing its importance in maintaining a diverse energy supply, but currently the US has no plans to build additional reactors on its soil. Many fear nuclear energy, fueled by accidents such as those at Chernobyl and Three Mile Island and concern about disposal of nuclear fuel. But are there viable alternatives?

PROS

Currently, the majority of the world's electricity is generated using fossil fuels. Although estimates vary greatly about the world's supply of fossil fuels, some estimates suggest that oil could be exhausted within 50 years and coal within 25 years. Thus we must find a new source of energy. We must start to convert to nuclear energy now so there is not a major crisis when fossil fuels do run out.

Nuclear energy is clean. It does not produce gaseous emissions that harm the environment. Granted, it does produce radioactive waste, but because this is a solid it can be handled easily and stored away from population centers. Burning fossil fuels causes far more environmental damage than using nuclear reactors, even if we factor in the Chernobyl catastrophe. Consequently, nuclear energy is preferable to fossil fuels. Furthermore, as new technologies, such as fast breeder reactors, become available, they will produce less nuclear waste. With more investment, science can solve the problems associated with nuclear energy, making it even more desirable.

Unfortunately, the nuclear industry has a bad reputation for safety that is not entirely deserved. The overwhelming majority of nuclear reactors have functioned safely and effectively. The two major nuclear accidents, Three Mile Island and Chernobyl, were both in old style reactors, exacerbated in the latter case by lax Soviet safety standards. We are advocating new reactors, built to the highest safety standards. Such reactors have an impeccable safety record. Perhaps the best guarantee of safety in the nuclear industry is the increasing transparency within the industry. Many of the early problems were caused by excessive control due to the origin of nuclear energy from military applications. As a civilian nuclear industry develops, it becomes more accountable.

CONS

Estimates of how long fossil fuel resources will last have remained unchanged for the last few decades. Predicting when these fuels will be depleted is virtually impossible because new deposits may be discovered and because the rate of use cannot be predicted accurately. In addition some experts estimate that the world has 350 years of natural gas. We have no current need to search for a new power source. Money spent on such exploration would be better spent on creating technology to clean the output from power stations.

Even apart from the safety issues, nuclear power presents a number of problems. First, it is expensive and relatively inefficient. The cost of building reactors is enormous and the price of subsequently decommissioning them is also huge. Then there is the problem of waste. Nuclear waste can remain radioactive for thousands of years. It must be stored for this time away from water (into which it can dissolve) and far from any tectonic activity. Such storage is virtually impossible and serious concerns have arisen over the state of waste discarded even a few decades ago.

The nuclear industry has a shameful safety record. At Three Mile Island we were minutes away from a meltdown, and at Chernobyl the unthinkable actually happened. The effects on the local people and the environment were devastating. The fallout from Chernobyl can still be detected in our atmosphere. True, modern nuclear reactors are safer, but they are not perfectly safe. Disaster is always possible. Nuclear power stations have had a number of "minor" accidents. The industry has told us that these problems will not happen again, but time and time again they recur. We have to conclude that the industry is too dominated by the profit motive to really care about safety and too shrouded in secrecy to be accountable. In addition, the nuclear industry has had a terrible impact on those living around power plants. The rate of occurrence of certain types of cancer, such

PROS

CONS

as leukemia, is much higher in the population around nuclear plants.

We must examine the alternatives to nuclear energy. For the reasons explained above, we can rule out fossil fuels immediately. We also see enormous problems with other forms of energy. The most efficient source of renewable energy has been hydroelectric power. However, this usually creates more problems than it solves. Building a large dam necessarily floods an enormous region behind the dam, displacing tens of thousands of people. Dams also cause enormous damage to the ecology and incur enormous social and cultural costs. Solar energy has never lived up to expectations because it is hugely inefficient. Wind energy is only marginally better, with an unsightly wind farm the size of Texas needed to provide the energy for Texas alone. The great irony is that not only are most renewable sources inefficient but many are also ecologically unsound! The opposition to building wind farms in certain areas has been just as strong as the opposition to nuclear power because wind farms destroy the scenery.

Although alternative energy is not efficient enough to serve the energy needs of the world's population today, it could, with investment in all these methods, be made efficient enough to serve humankind. We are not advocating a blanket solution to every problem. Many dam projects could have been replaced by solar power had the technology been available. In addition, most countries usually have at least one renewable resource that they can use: tides for islands, the sun for equatorial countries, hot rocks for volcanic regions, etc. Consequently, any country can, in principle, become energy self-sufficient with renewable energy. The global distribution of uranium is hugely uneven (much more so than for fossil fuels); accordingly, the use of nuclear power gives countries with uranium deposits disproportionate economic power. Uranium could conceivably become subject to the same kind of monopoly that the Organization of Petroleum Exporting Countries has for oil. This prevents countries from achieving self-sufficiency in energy production.

The nuclear industry is a major employer. It creates numerous jobs and, with investment, will create even more.

Suggesting that nuclear power is the only employment provider is completely fatuous. Energy production will always provide roughly the same number of jobs. If spending on the nuclear industry were redirected to renewable energy, then jobs would simply move from the one to the other.

Sample Motions:

This House would look to the atom.

This House would go nuclear.

Web Links:

- Greenpeace Nuclear Campaign. <http://www.greenpeace.org/~nuclear/> Information on the organization's campaigns against nuclear fuels and weapons.
- University of Michigan. <http://www.umich.edu/~gs265/society/nuclear.htm> Overview of several issues surrounding nuclear energy, including waste, weapons, and environment.
- World Nuclear Association. <http://www.world-nuclear.org/why/biosphere.html?ekmensel=c580fa7b_8_0_32_1> Information on the need for nuclear power, by an organization seeking to promote the global use of peaceful nuclear energy.

Further Reading:

Caldicott, Helen. *Nuclear Power Is Not the Answer.* New Press, 2006.

Hopley, George W., and Alan M. Herbst. *Nuclear Energy Now: Why the Time Has Come for the World's Most Misunderstood Energy Source.* Wiley, 2007.

Sweet, William. *Kicking the Carbon Habit: Global Warming and the Case for Renewable and Nuclear Energy.* Columbia University Press, 2006.

NUCLEAR WEAPONS, ABOLITION OF

The nuclear bombs dropped on Hiroshima and Nagasaki, Japan, in 1945 forever changed the face of war, and the half century of Cold War that followed was dominated, above all, by the threat of nuclear destruction. The Soviet Union and the United States raced to produce increasingly powerful arsenals, eventually resulting in their ability to destroy the world several times over. This nuclear arms race led to the concept of "Mutually Assured Destruction," a stalemate in which both sides knew that the use of their weapons would totally annihilate each other and potentially the whole world. The end of the Cold War changed the global situation substantially. The fear of nuclear war between superpowers disappeared and in the early 21st century was replaced by the fear of nuclear proliferation, particularly by rogue states and terrorist groups. The fear escalated in 2006 following North Korea's testing of a nuclear weapon.

PROS

Nuclear weapons are morally repugnant. Over the past 50 years, we have seen a movement toward limited warfare and precision weapons that minimize the impact on civilians. Nuclear weapons have massive, indiscriminate destructive power. They can kill millions and cause catastrophic harm to the world environment.

The idea of a so-called nuclear deterrent no longer applies. During the Cold War, peace was maintained only by a balance of power; neither superpower had an advantage large enough to be confident of victory. However, a balance of power no longer exists. With the proliferation of nuclear weapons, some rogue states may develop the ability to strike at nations that have no nuclear weapons. Would the major nuclear powers then strike back at the aggressor? The answer is unknown. In addition, most of the emerging nuclear threats would not come from legitimate governments but from dictators and terrorist groups. Would killing thousands of civilians ever be acceptable in retaliation for the actions of extremists?

By maintaining a strategic deterrent, the current nuclear powers encourage the proliferation of weapons of mass destruction. Countries believe that being a member of the "nuclear club" increases their international status. Also, nations at odds with a country with nuclear capability feel that they must develop their own capability to protect themselves. Therefore, nuclear powers must take the lead in disarmament as an example for the rest of the world.

Nuclear weapons can fall into the hands of rogue states and terrorists. In 2004, Dr. Abdul Quader Khan, who led Pakistan's nuclear program, admitted that he had provided Iran, Libya, and North Korea with nuclear materials and technology to aid in weapons development. Only destroying the weapons will end the danger of someone stealing a weapon or extremists taking over a nuclear base.

CONS

The use of nuclear weapons would indeed be a great tragedy; but so, to a greater or lesser extent, is any war. The reason for maintaining an effective nuclear arsenal is to prevent war. The catastrophic results of using nuclear weapons discourage conflict. The Cold War was one of the most peaceful times in history, largely because of the nuclear deterrents of the two superpowers.

The deterrent principle still stands. During the Persian Gulf War, for example, the fear of US nuclear retaliation was one of the factors that prevented Iraq from using chemical weapons against Israel. A similar fear may prevent rogue states from using nuclear weapons. Moreover, although the citizens of the current nuclear powers may oppose the use of force against civilians, their opinions would rapidly change if they found weapons of mass destruction used against them.

The nuclear genie is out of the bottle and cannot be put back in. The ideal of global nuclear disarmament is fine in theory but it will not work in practice. Nations will not disarm if they fear a rogue state has secret nuclear capability. Without the threat of a retaliatory strike, a rogue nuclear state could attack others at will.

We do not have to abolish nuclear weapons to prevent nuclear terrorism. Through global cooperation, we can ensure that all nuclear material is secure and accounted for. If we can control access to nuclear material, we can ensure that terrorists and rogue states cannot make a bomb. Simply put: no material, no bomb.

Sample Motions:

This House would abolish nuclear weapons.

This House would ban the bomb.

Web Links:

- Abolition 2000. <http://www.abolition2000.org> Links to sites offering general information in support of global elimination of nuclear weapons.
- Federation of American Scientists: Nuclear Forces Guide. <http://www.fas.org/nuke/guide/index.html> Maintained by an organization of scientists advocating elimination of nuclear weapons, the site offers in-depth information on the status of nuclear proliferation, terrorism, and weapons of mass destruction.
- The Heritage Foundation. <http://www.heritage.org/Research/NationalSecurity/wm721.cfm> Information on the evolving role of nuclear weapons.

Further Reading:

Allison, Graham. *Nuclear Terrorism: The Ultimate Preventable Catastrophe*. Owl Books, 2005.

Campbell, Kurt M., Robert J. Einhorn, and Mitchell B. Reiss, eds. *The Nuclear Tipping Point: Why States Reconsider Their Nuclear Choices*. Brookings Institution Press, 2004.

Ferguson, Charles D. *The Four Faces of Nuclear Terrorism*. Routledge, 2005.

Sagan, Scott D., and Kenneth N. Waltz. *The Spread of Nuclear Weapons: A Debate Renewed*. 2nd ed. W. W. Norton, 2002.

OFFSHORE DRILLING

Offshore drilling is an extremely contentious topic in the national discourse. Due to concerns over the environmental impact of offshore oil extraction, a moratorium on offshore drilling was passed in 1981 and Congress has renewed it every year since. Rising gas prices and increasing political pressure, especially from Republicans, have generated intense debate about lifting the moratorium. Proponents generally contend that offshore drilling is necessary to the economic health and national security of the US and can be accomplished with little environmental impact. Opponents argue that offshore drilling ignores the more fundamental problem of unsustainable American energy consumption, will not contribute to lower gas prices or energy independence, and is not worth the environmental risk.

PROS	CONS
Offshore drilling will lower gas prices. The Energy Information Administration (EIA) estimates that offshore drilling could generate 18 billion barrels of crude oil. Greater availability of domestic oil will result in lower gas prices for American consumers. The current ban has prevented the US from taking advantage of this known resource. The ban must be lifted immediately so that its benefits may be felt as soon as possible.	The impact of drilling on oil prices will be minimal and will take years to be felt by US consumers. Oil prices are based largely on worldwide supply. The amount of oil generated from offshore drilling in the US will not impact world oil markets in any significant way. Additionally, scientists do not know with any certainty how much oil can actually be extracted. Furthermore, oil exploration and oil rig construction take many years to complete. According to the EIA, offshore drilling would not produce any measurable change in oil prices until 2030.
Drilling will decrease US dependency on foreign oil and will make America safer. Currently, the US must buy most of its oil from hostile governments such as Venezuela, Saudi Arabia, and Iran. The oil estimated in offshore	Offshore drilling will not make the US safer or more energy independent. While America only has 3% of the world's oil reserves, it consumes 25% of the global oil supply. Even if the EIA estimates are correct, offshore reserves

PROS	CONS
reserves could supply US energy needs for two years. This could help distance America from antidemocratic regimes.	will have little impact and the US will have to continue buying oil from unfriendly nations for years to come. The only path to true energy independence and greater national security is to decrease American energy consumption and to invest in homegrown renewable energy.
Offshore drilling is a necessary part of a larger energy strategy, including renewable energy sources. Obviously, renewable energy sources must be developed and the way Americans consume energy must be addressed, but that is no reason to ignore an effective solution. The cost of oil is placing a serious strain on the US economy and every available strategy should be used to combat the problem.	Offshore drilling is a Band-Aid solution to a more fundamental problem. Oil is a finite resource. The reality is that the United States consumes energy at rates far greater than any other nation and far greater than the growth in supply. Such consumption is not sustainable and must be addressed. Offshore drilling only addresses the problem of supply, while ignoring the more fundamental problem of US demand. Opening America's coastal waters to offshore drilling will only reinforce this misconception and will never address the real problem—that Americans must consume less and invest in green energy sources.
Offshore drilling can be accomplished with minimal damage to the environment. Technology has improved greatly over the past ten years, leading to safer means of construction and production. While environmental disasters do occur, they are few and far between. In fact, the EIA considers offshore drilling to be 99.99% safe. Additionally, state and federal regulations are in place to monitor and penalize any environmental pollution. Finally, retired rigs can serve as ecosystems for marine life, which even environmental groups have promoted.	The environmental consequences of offshore drilling are not worth the potential financial gain. Oil rigs release chemicals into surrounding water; transporting oil from these rigs has resulted in serious environmental disasters; seismic waves disorient sea animals; and installing rigs erodes the ocean floor, which makes the impact of hurricanes and tropical storms even worse. Safety estimates are largely overstated, as they do not reflect the magnitude of individual catastrophes, such as the Valdez oil spill, which has yet to be completely cleaned up. Furthermore, dismantling retired rigs is hugely expensive.

Sample Motions:

This House would urge Congress to lift the ban on offshore drilling.

This House opposes offshore drilling and supports the development of alternative energy sources.

Web Links:

- Impacts of Increased Access to Oil and Natural Gas Resources in the Lower 48 Federal Outer Continental Shelf. <http://www.eia.doe.gov/oiaf/aeo/otheranalysis/ongr.html> Site managed by the US government, offering official statistics regarding US energy sources.
- Zachary Coile, Offshore Drilling Debate to Begin in Congress. <http://www.dallasnews.com/sharedcontent/dws/news/nation/stories/DN-drilling_16nat.ART.State.Edition1.26a17ee.html> Article offering background and analysis of the current offshore drilling debate.

OLYMPIC GAMES, HOSTING OF

For 17 days every four years the Summer Olympics attract the world's attention and the host city receives immense media coverage. Yet many argue that the huge cost of hosting the Olympic Games means that cities are left with crippling bills and unused infrastructure. Montreal, the host in 1976, is still paying off the cost of staging the games, and the 2004 Olympics ran billions of euros over the original budget—at Greece's expense. The scandal surrounding the bidding process for the Salt Lake City 2002 Winter Games revealed that 13 of the 124 International Olympic Committee (IOC) members who were tasked with deciding who should be awarded the games were "bought" with gifts and bribes. The IOC has since tightened its regulations, but rumors of corruption among some members remain. While proponents of the Games generally accept that they will inevitably cost significant amounts of money, they argue that their "feel good factor" and long-term benefits justify this outlay.

PROS

Hosting the Olympics stimulates redevelopment of the host city. The IOC is enthusiastic about bids that will leave a lasting impact and has looked favorably on cities that locate their Olympic Villages and stadia in deprived areas in need of redevelopment. For example, Barcelona completely overhauled its port and coast for the 1992 Olympics, creating a cultural area that has become a lasting tourist attraction. In addition to cleaning up blighted areas and adding new stadia, Olympic Villages also include between 5,000 and 20,000 new homes, which governments can choose to designate as low-income housing (as is proposed for London 2012). While these projects could be completed without the Olympics, the need to provide an overall package (e.g., transportation, housing, infrastructure, etc.) for a set deadline means that there is greater incentive to complete the projects. An example of this in London is the plan for a new $26 billion underground rail system called "Crossrail," first proposed over 20 years ago but only now being developed for the London 2012 games.

Hosting creates an unquantifiable "feel good" factor. It is difficult to put a price on the buzz that surrounds international sporting events. Some recent examples of this national euphoria are Paris during the World Cup in 1998 and Sydney during the 2002 Olympics. Governments are aware of the huge potential for boosting national pride and unity, and it is partly because of this feel good factor that so many people want their city to host the Olympics.

CONS

Hosting the Olympics is very expensive. In recent times host cities have never made a direct profit. The bidding process alone for 2012 cost each bidding city around $35 million and London is expected to spend over $8 billion on the games. The cost of security has also increased dramatically. Athens spent $1.5 billion on security out of a total of $12 billion on the 2004 games. The burden of these costs falls on government. Residents in Los Angeles have only just stopped paying for the over-budget 1984 Olympics through their local taxes. If cities need to redevelop, they should spend money directly on those projects rather than through subsidizing a sporting event.

There is no guarantee that a city will experience a "feel good" factor. Athens saw many empty seats, as the Greek team failed to do well enough to capture the local imagination. Where tournaments and games have successfully created a "buzz," it has been because the host nation has done well. The fact that this feel good factor can be felt from the other side of the globe means that there is no need to host the Olympics in order to generate it.

In any case, any Olympic excitement will be short-lived compared to the years of disruption and congestion that a host city will suffer in the run-up to the games.

PROS	CONS
Hosting creates an economic boost. While none of the Olympics of recent times have made an immediate profit, the benefits of redevelopment and improved infrastructure mean that this is not a big problem as long as the losses are not huge. The Olympics showcases the host nation to the world, and most hosts have seen a boost in tourism in the years following the Olympics. For example, Australia estimates it gained over $3 billion in tourism revenue in the four years after the 2000 Olympics. An estimated 60,000 to 135,000 jobs are created during the games, which provides skills and training to local people.	Hosting the Olympics does not create long-term benefits for the host city. The demands of the Olympics are very particular (e.g., pools, horse tracks, sand volleyball courts), and much of this infrastructure will never be used again. In Australia, underused stadia in Sydney cost taxpayers $32 million a year in maintenance. In the long term, the money spent on the Olympics would have been better spent on affordable housing and transportation infrastructure for local residents rather than with the intention of impressing IOC members. As for tourism revenues, Greece may have lost out economically in 2002–3 as potential visitors stayed away, frightened off by stories of disruptive building works, security threats, and fears of overcrowding.
The bidding process is now open and trustworthy. While the 1998 Salt Lake City scandal did reveal huge levels of endemic corruption, IOC president Jacques Rogge has taken significant steps to stamp it out. Cities can now be confident that the selection process is fair and that the best bid will win.	The bidding process itself is heavily political, and so it is very possible that a city will spend over $35 million on a bid only to lose to a weaker candidate. Each IOC member decides for which city he or she wishes to vote, which means that personal relationships and international politics can outweigh the quality of the bid. For example, American foreign policy is rumored to have disadvantaged New York in the 2012 bidding process. Also, given that the Olympics are rotated among continents, a city is only truly eligible every 12 years.
Hosting the Olympics promotes sports and its benefits throughout the host nation. The Olympics involves hundreds of events and sports, thus providing an opportunity for the whole nation to feel that they have taken part. Training camps are often located outside the host city, as are events such as rowing, sailing, canoeing, and shooting, so that rural areas also benefit. The lasting impact of this will be a generation of young people who are excited about sports. Given rising levels of childhood obesity and declining emphasis on sports in schools, this can only be a good thing.	Hosting affects only one city. In large countries like the United States or China, the benefits of the Olympics are almost entirely focused on the host city. Even in smaller countries, the benefits of a soccer match played outside the host city or a training camp are negligible. Capital cities are often chosen. For example, after failed bids from Birmingham in 1992 and Manchester in 1996 and 2000, the IOC told the United Kingdom that only a bid from London was likely to win. Favoring capital cities only concentrates growth and development where it is least needed.
Hosting the Olympics can be a way of making a strong political point because of the intense media scrutiny that accompanies the games. During the Cold War, the Soviet Union used Moscow 1980 and the US used Los Angeles 1984 to show their economic strength. Seoul in 1988 used the games to demonstrate South Korea's economic and political maturity. The Beijing Olympics in 2008 are seen by many as evidence of China's acceptance into the global community and a way for it to showcase its economic growth and acceptance of the West.	The Olympic host-city bidding process takes too long. Bidding officially takes only two years (unless a city fails to make the shortlist), but most cities spend nearly a decade working on their bids. The bidding process also ties up development of the land needed for Olympic infrastructure until the bid outcome is known, and diverts government funds away from other sporting events and activities.

Sample Motions:

This House would bid for future Olympic games.
This House believes that hosting the Olympics is a good investment.
This House opposes a bid to host the Olympic games.
This House would make a bid.

Web Links:

- China Economic Net: A Post-Olympic Hurdle for Greece: The Whopping Bill. <http://en.ce.cn/subject/beijing08/po/200807/08/t20080708_16089982.shtml> Assessment of the impact of the 2004 games.
- Haynes, Jill. Socioeconomic Impact of the Sydney 2000 Olympic Games. <http://olympicstudies.uab.es/pdf/wp094_eng.pdf> Assessment of the 2000 games.
- London 2012 Olympic Games. <http://www.london.gov.uk/ mayor/olympics/index.jsp> The mayor of London assesses the benefits of the Olympics.

Further Reading:

Lenskyj, Helen. *The Best Olympics Ever? Social Impacts of Sydney 2000*. State University of New York Press, 2002.

OVERPOPULATION AND CONTRACEPTION

Despite scientific advances, no amount of technological innovation will solve the problem that Earth has only finite resources. Attention has therefore turned to the question of population growth; preserving the environment would be far easier if natural resources were shared among fewer people. Environmental degradation will accelerate if the rate of global population increase is not slowed. Over the years, much debate has been heard about whether widespread use of contraception is the solution to the population explosion in the developing world.

PROS

Population is a major problem today; the world population of 6.6 billion is expected to reach 9.4 billion by 2050. Given the current strain on global resources and the environment, an environmental disaster is clearly waiting to happen as the population time bomb ticks on. While reproduction is a fundamental human right, rights come with responsibilities. We have a responsibility to future generations, and population control is one method of ensuring that natural resources will be available for our descendants.

Contraception is an easy and direct method of slowing population growth. The popularity and success of contraception in the developed world is testament to this.

CONS

Many population forecasts are exaggerated and do not take into account the different phases of population growth. A nation's population may grow rapidly in the early stages of development, but with industrialization and rising levels of education, the population tends to stabilize at the replacement rate. Even if the quoted figure of 9.4 billion by 2050 is true, this is likely to remain steady thereafter, as the developing nations of today achieve maturity. Developed nations can use alternative methods to solve the environmental and social problems arising from overpopulation. All available options should be exhausted before making the drastic decision to curb reproductive rights.

Implementing widespread contraception presents technical difficulties. The cost can be prohibitive, especially when considered on a national scale. Large numbers of trained workers are required to educate the public on the correct use of contraceptives. Even with an investment in training, birth control methods may be used incorrectly, especially by the illiterate and uneducated.

PROS	CONS
Contraception can reduce family size. With smaller families, a greater proportion of resources can be allocated to each child, improving his or her opportunities for education, health care, and nutrition.	Many agricultural families need to have as many children as possible. Children's farm work can contribute to the family food or be a source of income. In an undeveloped nation without a good social welfare system, children are the only security for old age. Furthermore, having a large number of children usually ensures that some reach adulthood; child mortality is very high in the developing world. Until the child mortality rate is reduced, families will not use contraception.
Contraception empowers women by giving them reproductive control. Delaying pregnancy gives opportunities for education, employment, and social and political advancement. Birth control can therefore be a long-term investment in political reform and offers some protection of women's rights.	Women may not have the choice to use contraceptives. In many developing nations, males dominate in sexual relationships and make the decisions about family planning. Religious pressure to have as many children as possible may also be present. Birth control may not even be socially acceptable. Are women's rights advanced by contraception? We don't really know. In reality, contraception typically is one element of a national population control policy. Such policies (e.g., China's one-child policy), when considered as a whole, often violate women's rights.
Contraception can help save the lives of women in the developing world. The lack of obstetric care and the prevalence of disease and malnutrition contribute to a high rate of mortality among pregnant mothers and their newborn children. This risk can be over 100 times that of mothers in developed countries.	While birth control should be a priority of many developing nations, such nations often need to address other, more pressing, issues. Providing basic health care and proper sanitation can improve the health of an entire family, in addition to reducing child mortality (often a major reason for parents wanting to have a large number of children). Spending on such infrastructure and services is a far better long-term investment than providing contraception.
Supporting contraception is an easy way for the developed world to help the developing world cope with the population crisis and the consequent stifling of development. Contraceptives, compared to monetary aid, are less likely to be misdirected into the pockets of corrupt officials.	Contraception is a controversial issue in both developed and developing nations. Some religions prohibit it. This can reduce the success of birth control programs in the developing world and diminish the political appeal of (and thus funding for) pro-contraception policies in the developed world.

Sample Motions:

This House supports contraception in developing nations.
This House would cap population growth in the developing world.
This House believes that there are too many people.
This House believes that there isn't enough room.

Web Links:

- Massachusetts Institute of Technology. <http://ocw.mit.edu/NR/rdonlyres/Writing-and-Humanistic-Studies/21W-732-2Fall-2006/82691041-9DD8-4928-B956-A18BB9AD6A80/0/paper3_overpop.pdf> Paper on international over-population and birth control.
- OverPopulation.com. <http://www.overpopulation.com> Extensive site with information on a wide variety of population issues. Includes a good overview essay on the overpopulation controversy.

- Population Reference Bureau. <http://www.prb.org> Provides a comprehensive directory of population-related resources.
- United Nations Population Information Network. <http://www.un.org/popin/> Offers links to population information on the UN system's Web sites.

Further Reading:

Huggins, Laura E., and Hanna Skandera. *Population Puzzle: Boom or Bust?* Hoover Institution Press, 2005.

Leisinger, Klaus M. *Six Billion and Counting.* International Food Policy Research Institute, 2002.

Maguire, Daniel C. *Sacred Rights: The Case for Contraception and Abortion in World Religions.* Oxford University Press, 2003.

OVERSEAS MANUFACTURING

In the new era of globalization, American companies often locate their manufacturing operations in countries outside the United States. Many countries are eager to attract American industries and the employment they bring; overseas factories usually can be run at substantially lower costs largely because wages for foreign workers are much lower than wages for American workers. The treatment of these foreign employees has engendered many questions and raised many issues. Their working conditions may not be safe; they may be asked to work unreasonable hours; they may be paid less than a living wage. In some parts of the world, many factory workers are school-age children. Increasingly, the public is putting pressure on American corporations to improve the treatment of their foreign workers and to provide the same kind of safeguards that protect American workers.

PROS

Companies build factories overseas for one primary reason: Foreign workers are cheaper. When companies are driven by the profit motive, they have an incentive to pay as little as possible and to skimp on equipment and procedures that would provide comfort and safety to workers. Workers need to be protected from corporations that care more about profits than people.

Some foreign governments are so eager to attract American investment that they favor management over labor. They do not protect their own citizens with strong labor laws, and they do not guarantee workers the right to form unions. Workers are at the mercy of their employers.

American companies located in foreign countries have no incentive for making commitments to the local community. If the workers become too expensive, or if the companies are forced to spend money to improve conditions, they simply pull out and move to another country with cheaper workers and lower standards.

CONS

Manufacturers know that mistreating workers does not pay in the long run. They know that a healthy and a happy workforce is going to be more productive and give their operation long-term stability. Certainly manufacturers care about the bottom line, and it is precisely that concern that motivates them to treat their workers well.

The presence of American companies has a direct benefit on the economies of their host countries. Workers are taught skills and exposed to new technology. Moreover, a strong industrial economy has been proved to be the best way to lift people out of poverty. In time, foreign workers will achieve wages and working conditions comparable to those enjoyed by American workers today.

Wages may be low compared to US standards; however, the cost of living in these countries is also low. It is absurd, therefore, to expect American companies to pay the standard minimum US wage in a country where that wage has 10 times the buying power that it has in America.

PROS	CONS
Because they have no union protections, workers are often asked to work absurdly long hours, with no extra pay for overtime, and in dangerous conditions with hazardous materials. They fear that if they complain, or refuse to work when demanded, they will be fired and replaced by someone who is desperate for a job.	Activists like to say that factory jobs in foreign countries are intolerable and undesirable, but the facts do not support that assertion. People are eager to work in a factory, when their alternative is making less money for a full day of backbreaking agricultural work. To the workers, jobs in American factories represent opportunities to gain a higher standard of living.
Child labor is condoned in many countries where American companies do business, but American companies should refuse to take part in this abuse. There is little hope for the future of countries where a child must provide labor, instead of getting an education.	The American objection to child labor is founded on the idealistic notion that children should be in school. But in many countries where the factories operate, universal schooling is nonexistent, and the child who is thrown out of a factory job goes back on the street. In many cases, the child who does not work in a factory will simply work someplace else; in poor families, it is expected that anyone who is able to work will earn a wage to support the family.

Sample Motions:

This House will not buy materials made in foreign sweatshops.

This House would force American companies to let foreign workers unionize.

Web Links:

- Ending Sweatshops. <http://www.sweatshops.org> This Web site, sponsored by the activist organization Co-op America, discusses "sweatshop" conditions in foreign countries and encourages citizens to take action to eliminate them.
- New York Times Magazine. <http://query.nytimes.com/gst/fullpage.html?res=9D02E6D6163BF937A1575AC0A9669C8B63&sec=&spon=&pagewanted=all> Article defending sweatshops.
- PBS NOW with Bill Moyers. <http://www.pbs.org/now/politics/outsourcedebate.html> Links and information on the outsourcing debate.

Further Reading:

Elliott, Kimberly, and Richard B. Freeman. *Can Labor Standards Improve Under Globalization?* Institute for International Economics, 2003.

Featherstone, Liza, et al. *Students Against Sweatshops: The Making of a Movement.* Verso Books, 2002.

Moran, Theodore H. *Beyond Sweatshops: Foreign Direct Investment and Globalization in Developing Nations.* Brookings Institution Press, 2002.

PACIFISM

Pacifism has a long history in the United States. Although their numbers have been small, pacifists have opposed every American war from the Revolution to the Iraq War. Occasionally their voices have contributed to policy changes, as was the case in the Vietnam War. The debate between nonviolent objection and the use of force to achieve a goal brings up issues like morality vs. practicality: Is violence ever constructive; and, does pacifism in the face of a threat serve to increase or diminish evil. The debate also contrasts the lives lost in war with the liberty that might be lost if war is avoided and thus raises the difficult issue of sacrificing lives to preserve a principle.

PROS

Violence is never justified under any circumstances. Life is sacred, and no cause or belief allows a person to take the life of another.

CONS

We are not arguing that violence is of itself a good thing. We are saying that when others are using violence to endanger principles as fundamental as human rights, people have a duty to stand up against them. Not to do so would merely allow evil to spread unchecked.

PRO: Neither side in a war emerges as a victor. War rarely settles issues. (For example, World War I created the conditions that led to World War II.) War always creates suffering on both sides. Often the innocent suffer, as in the case of the firebombing of Dresden or the dropping of the atomic bomb on Hiroshima in World War II.

CON: Disputes do sometimes persist after wars, but often wars can lead to the resolution of some issues. For example, World War II prevented fascism from taking over Europe, and the Persian Gulf War led to Saddam Hussein's withdrawal from Kuwait. In these cases, the failure to act would have led to the oppression of millions and permitted an aggressor to triumph.

PRO: Pacifists believe that violence begets violence. Pacifists do not have to retreat completely from world and domestic affairs. During World War I, conscientious objectors stood up against the militarism and cynical diplomacy that had led to the conflict. In many countries they were executed for their beliefs.

CON: Pacifism is a luxury that some can practice because others fight. Pacifists claim moral superiority while enjoying the liberty for which others have died. We fought both world wars to combat aggression and injustice. We did our moral duty in resisting tyranny.

PRO: When war is inevitable, pacifists can protest the cruelties of war, such as torture, attacks on civilians, and other contraventions of the Geneva Convention, in an attempt to curb violence's excesses.

CON: This type of protest is not true pacifism, which rejects war outright. By admitting that war is sometimes inevitable, you are acknowledging that sometimes people cannot sit by and do nothing.

PRO: Great religious leaders, such as Jesus and Gandhi, have always advocated pacifism. They believe that "He who lives by the sword dies by the sword." For thousands of years the wisest thinkers have believed that violence does not end suffering, but merely increases it.

CON: In practice, most world religions have adopted violence, in the shape of crusades or holy wars, to serve their ends. And does not the Bible advocate "an eye for an eye"? When an aggressor endangers liberty and freedom, humanity must use violence to combat him.

Sample Motions:

This House would be pacifist.
This House rejects violence.
This House would turn the other cheek.

Web Links:

- Central Committee for Conscientious Objectors. <http://www.objector.org> Group that opposes military action.
- The Good War and Those Who Refused to Fight It. <http://www.pbs.org/itvs/thegoodwar/american_pacifism.html> PBS Web site providing overview of pacifism in American history.
- Pacifism. <http://www.utm.edu/research/iep/p/pacifism.htm> Philosophical discussion of pacifism.

Further Reading:

Gan, Barry L., and Robert L. Holmes. *Nonviolence in Theory and Practice.* Waveland Press, 2004.

Gelderloos, Peter. *How Nonviolence Protects the State.* South End Press, 2007.

Zinn, Howard. *The Power of Nonviolence: Writings by Advocates of Peace.* Beacon Press, 2002.

PARENTAGE, RIGHT TO KNOW

Historically, virtually all adoptions in the United States were "closed," meaning that the birth parents had no contact with their child or the adoptive parents following an adoption. In recent years, many adopted children, as well as children conceived as a result of anonymous sperm donations, have challenged this policy, insisting that they have a right to know who their biological parents are. Some biological parents have contended that forcing them to reveal their identity infringes on their rights.

PROS

The reassurance that comes from knowing one's parentage is a valuable source of psychological security. The child's desires and wishes must take precedence over the wants of anonymous parents.

Biological parents should not have to raise a child if they do not wish to, but children should have the right to learn the identity of their biological parents. Neither the biological nor the adoptive parents should make this choice on the child's behalf.

Children who do not know their biological parents are medically disadvantaged. Knowing parents' medical background and genetic profile is increasingly important in preventing and treating disease.

CONS

The most important factor in raising a child is a secure and loving home environment. Whether biological or adoptive parents provide this is unimportant. If the genetic parents wish to remain anonymous, then they should retain a right to privacy. Removing the right to anonymity from a sperm donor will greatly reduce the number of men willing to become donors—for fear of unwanted contact or even financial responsibility in later life.

Giving adopted children the right to know the identity of their biological parents would simply cause greater emotional distress for all concerned. The child may resent his or her biological parents and even seek revenge. The adoptive parents may see their role undermined as the child tries to connect with his or her biological parents. Adopted children may end up feeling that they do not truly belong anywhere. Similarly, when sperm donation has been used to achieve pregnancy, the child's contact with his or her biological father may undermine role of the mother's partner, who is acting as the father.

Predicting disease through reviewing an individual's genetic heritage is wrong and will likely result in higher insurance premiums and medical discrimination for the child. Gathering and holding medical information on parents who give up their children for adoption will create a genetic underclass whose DNA will be stored for no good reason.

PROS

Parents will not abandon a child to preserve their anonymity. The right to know parentage does not equal the right to contact or depend on biological rather than adoptive families, so parents are unlikely to act in these irresponsible ways.

CONS

Parents who do not wish their identity known would simply abandon a child rather than formally give him or her up for adoption and have their identity recorded. The child may well die of exposure or starvation before it is found. In addition, some expectant mothers may fear identification so much that they do not seek vital medical support when they give birth, but do so alone with all the risks to mother and child that implies.

Sample Motions:

This House believes in the right to know parentage.
This House believes the rights of the child come first.
This House wants to know its parents/children.

Web Links:

- adoption.com <http://www.openadoptions.com/information/pros-cons.html> Pros and cons of open adoptions.
- FindLaw. <http://family.findlaw.com/adoption/adoption-types/open-adoption-comparison.html> Pros and cons of open and closed adoption.
- New York Online Access to Health. <http://www.noah-health.org/en/pregnancy/adoption/types/open.html> Good links to a variety of resources on the advantages and disadvantages of closed/open adoptions.

Further Reading:

Gasper Fitzgerald, Gisela. *Adoption: An Open, Semi-Open or Closed Practice? Reflections by an American Adoptive Mother on Infant Adoption, Birth and Reunion.* PublishAmerica, 2003.

Waters, Jane. *Arms Wide Open: An Insight into Open Adoption.* AuthorHouse, 2005.

PARENTAL RESPONSIBILITY

"Parental responsibility" means different things in different contexts. Most countries have laws making parents or anyone biologically connected to a child responsible for the child's welfare. But in some countries, such the United States and Canada, state and local authorities have gone further. In an effort to stop the rise of juvenile crime, they have taken the more debatable step of holding parents legally responsible for the actions of their children.

PROS

Legal requirements for parental action, particularly those that include sanctions for nonaction, provide an incentive for parents to act responsibly. If parents are liable for their inaction or the inappropriate actions of their children, they are more likely to make sure their children are supervised and well cared for.

CONS

The causes at the core of juvenile delinquency, abusive families and child neglect are not necessarily the kind of problems that can be solved by the leverage of criminal or civil sanctions. In instances where parents are absent or neglectful, deep social problems are often the cause. Problems such as alcoholism, poverty, poor education, poor health and poor health care, and family histories

PROS

CONS

of abuse can lock a family into a negative cycle that continues to perpetuate behaviors that others might view as irresponsible. There is a danger that the proposed sanctions will make families trapped in such problems afraid to seek help from social services for fear of punishment.

Minor children should not be held legally accountable for their actions nor should they be obligated to provide for themselves until they have reached the age of majority. Governments have established laws drawing distinctions between adults and juveniles for a reason. These governments believe that juveniles make mistakes and are not necessarily mature enough to be fully responsible for or completely aware of the consequences of their actions. Parents, and the community at large have a responsibility to raise children to act appropriately in society. If society or more specifically parents fail in the task, it is not reasonable for the children to be charged with sole responsibility for their acts.

While generally true, there are instances where the amount of influence of parents over a child's life is negligible. Some children run away from home or forcibly separate themselves from their parents of their own accord. On occasion, juveniles commit crimes so heinous, and so unexpected, that no reasonable person would think that the parents were ultimately responsible. There are also significant differences between cultures as to what age constitutes "adulthood." The age of majority varies significantly among the nations of the world. While many Western countries consider an 18-year-old an adult, other cultures see the beginnings of adulthood in the early teenage years. Adulthood can also be seen as a phased-in process—a continuum of increasing responsibility, with driving, leaving school, voting, drinking, having sex, getting married without parental permission, joining the armed forces, and standing for public office considered as milestones. Thus, multinational or global accords on parental responsibility or children's rights are potentially problematic.

Laws that enshrine parental responsibility improve family life. As parents are encouraged to take responsibility for their children, and such responsibility becomes a cultural norm, families will develop closer bonds, marriages will become stronger, and the problems of broken families will decrease.

This argument stems from two flawed assumptions: first, that parents who are separated or divorced cannot act responsibly and, second, that doing "the right thing" necessarily equates with positive family values. A parent may play a very active role in the lives of her or his children, yet still have a horrible marriage or mentally or physically abuse the children. A parent who is not married to a child's other parent may still play an active and valuable role in the life of the child, even if the parents do not live in the same home.

Parental responsibility laws help compel parents who are delinquent in their support of a child to become involved—at least on a financial level. This can also discourage irresponsible men from indulging in promiscuous and reckless sexual behavior, and thus possibly fathering a number of children by different mothers.

Decades of legal experience in countries that order child support from separated or divorced parents have demonstrated that parents who want to sever ties (financial or otherwise) can do so, either by defaulting on payments or hiding from the law. These laws may even have a negative effect by fostering resentment toward the child or other parent within the parent compelled to provide support. Child support orders may also harm any subsequent children an estranged parent may have by impoverishing a second family in favor of the first.

PROS	CONS
Children are less likely to engage in acts of delinquency if they feel that their parents are likely to be held legally responsible for their actions.	Children prone to engage in acts of serious juvenile delinquency are rarely interested in the feelings of or effects of their actions on parents. In fact, the worst juvenile delinquents are probably more likely to act out if they believe, first, that the action will result in harm to the parents they seek to rebel against and, second, that their parents will be held responsible in place of them.

Sample Motions:

This House believes parents should be held criminally liable for the illegal activities of their children.
This House believes parents should be held civilly liable for the illegal activities of their children.
This House believes that, on balance, parents are more responsible for the actions of children than the children are themselves.
This House believes an international convention on child welfare should be adopted.

Web Links:

- Family Impact Analysis of Wisconsin Statutes Addressing Parental Responsibility for Juvenile Behavior. <http://www.uwstout.edu/rs/uwsjsr/fmilyimpact_analsis.pdf> Analytical paper by undergraduate at University of Wisconsin-Stout.
- League of Wisconsin Municipalities. <http://www.lwm-info.org/index.asp?Type=B_BASIC&SEC={C856B16B-E3E2-4600-9A0B-62607BC7DF3E}&DE={1F93EBB8-B7FA-43D2-8B59-6F2C39EEB49F}> Sample parental responsibility ordinance.
- University of Florida News. <http://news.ufl.edu/2005/03/14/parental-responsibility/> Article on Americans' reactions to parental responsibility laws.

Further Reading:

Bainham, Andrew, et al. *What Is a Parent? A Socio-Legal Analysis.* International Specialized Book Services, 1999.

van Bueren, Geraldine, ed. *International Documents on Children.* Martinus Nijhoff, 1998.

Wyness, Michael. *Schooling, Welfare, and Parental Responsibility.* RoutledgeFalmer, 1996.

POLITICIANS AND SPECIAL INTERESTS

Political dialogue in America is frequently peppered with accusatory references to "special interests." These special interests are organized groups that play active political roles, either through making contributions to parties and candidates, or through lobbying government officials in an attempt to influence legislation and public policy. Many of these groups have millions of dollars at their disposal. The question is whether this money corrupts the political system—that is, are legislators more concerned with pleasing donors and lobbyists than they are with responding to the will of average citizens? Long a concern, the issue came to the fore during the Administration of George W. Bush as a result of a series of congressional scandals and the revelation of the K Street Project, an effort designed to encourage lobbying firms to hire Republicans and to reward lobbyists loyal to the Republican Party with access to high congressional and Administration officials.

PROS

No person who is financially dependent on someone else is truly free to serve the public good in a disinterested way. When a politician depends on huge sums of money contributed by an organization, his or her vote is inevitably influenced by the wishes of that organization rather than by what is best for the country.

CONS

If a politician were dependent on only one source of funding, undue influence might be a possibility. But so many special interest groups are active in Washington that politicians get contributions from dozens, if not hundreds, of them. The influence of any one group, therefore, is negligible; even a contribution of $10,000 is only a "drop in the bucket" when campaigns cost millions.

PROS: The size of contributions has become so large that donors certainly expect some kind of payback. A manufacturers' association will not give $100,000 away just as a gesture of good will; it expects to see its concerns favorably addressed in legislation.

CONS: Accusations of undue influence are often vague and unsupported by facts. Watchdog organizations like to make statistical correlations between donations and votes, but that is not real evidence that votes have been "bought." Don't forget that actually buying votes is a crime and is vigorously prosecuted.

PROS: For generations, lawmakers have recognized that the power of special interests can lead to corruption; more than 50 years ago, for example, Congress forbade unions from acting to influence federal elections. But the creation of political action committees (PACs) and the proliferation of soft money have allowed special interest groups to violate the spirit of the law while obeying its letter.

CONS: Special interests are condemned for having too much influence, but the causal logic of the accusers is fundamentally flawed. When the National Abortion and Reproductive Rights Action League (NARAL) makes contributions to politicians, it does not buy the votes of legislators who would have voted differently on reproductive issues. Rather, NARAL gives money to candidates who have already indicated their support for policies in line with NARAL's position.

PROS: Money purchases access to politicians, who are more willing to make time for donors than for average citizens. Access leads naturally to influence. The average citizen is shortchanged by the current system, which favors cash-rich organizations.

CONS: People who want to kill special interest groups are usually thinking of groups that support a position they oppose. Special interest groups span the political spectrum and represent many points of view. Indeed, the variety of groups with competing interests is an indication of a healthy and vigorous political system.

PROS: Organizations often spend hundreds of millions of dollars to lobby politicians. They would not spend such sums if they did not think such expenditures were effective in helping them get what they want. Again, money clearly is shaping legislation.

CONS: Individuals should organize themselves into groups to represent themselves more effectively. Congress passes laws that affect the daily lives of teachers, for example; surely, teachers have the right to have their voices heard—through their unions—when those laws are drawn up.

Sample Motions:

This House would change campaign finance laws to allow contributions from individuals only.

This House would lobby Congress to advance its interests.

Web Links:

- Missing the Point on Campaign Finance. <http://www.claremont.org/writings/precepts/20020321ellmers.html> An essay from the Claremont Institute for the Study of Statesmanship and Political Philosophy arguing that the concern about special interest groups is largely unfounded.

- Money and Politics: Who Owns Democracy? <http://www.network-democracy.org/map/bb/nif/contents.shtml> A project of Information Renaissance and National Issues Forums Research, this site discusses the pros and cons of various proposals to change the role of money in politics.
- Public Campaign. <http://www.publicampaign.org> Organization dedicated to reducing the role of special interest money in American politics.

Further Reading:

Continetti, Matthew. *The K Street Gang: The Rise and Fall of the Republican Machine.* Doubleday, 2006.

Grossman, Gene M., and Elhanan Helpman. *Special Interest Politics.* MIT Press, 2002.

Nownes, Anthony. *Total Lobbying: What Lobbyists Want (and How They Try to Get It).* Cambridge University Press, 2006.

POLYGAMY

Polygamy is the state or practice of having two or more mates at the same time. Both the Bible and the Qur'an condone it, but most religions now ban the practice. In most countries, including all Western ones and some Islamic ones, polygamy is illegal, although some Muslim states (e.g., Saudi Arabia) and traditional African societies do allow it. In the United States, polygamy is associated with the Mormon Church, which approved the practice until 1896, when church leaders agreed to abandon it in hopes of winning statehood for Utah. Yet some fundamentalist Mormon splinter groups in Utah, Arizona, and Texas still openly practice polygamy, and in 2006 the practice gained national attention when the FBI placed Warren Jeffs, president of the Fundamentalist Church of Jesus Christ of Latter Day Saints (FLDS), on its most wanted list for felony charges of accomplice rape. He was subsequently tried and convicted on the charges. Two years later, the issue of polygamy again became prominent when Texas Child Protective Services raided the FLDS compound. Although polygamy can involve both the union of one man with more than one woman (polygyny) and the union of one woman with more than one man (polyandry), the focus of contemporary debate is polygyny and its effects on women and children.

PROS

The law should recognize freedom of choice. If I want to marry more than one person, why should the state stop me? If my partner agrees to the addition to the family, then why should the state presume to say it knows better? We have a right to privacy and a right to noninterference in our family life.

The addition of extra parental figures does not necessarily undermine family units. Rather, more providers can make greater contributions to the home. Often there is love, not jealousy, between wives who are happy to have others share their work. Hierarchies exist in monogamous families—between husband and wife, between siblings. That they can exist in polygamous marriages is not a strong argument against such unions, which are capable of producing stable homes. Some marriages are good, some bad—that's true of both monogamy and polygamy.

CONS

These rights are countered by the damage polygamy does to women and families. Polygamy harms children, who are presented with confusing signals about role models and family life. It also reduces a woman's freedom: Women often do not have a say in whether the husband takes another wife.

A polygamous family will develop a hierarchy, with a "head wife" dominating the others. Why encourage and institutionalize the very thing that leads to the breakup of the majority of family units—namely, jealousy and sexual encounters with others? It is true that jealousy exists outside marriages and in monogamous marriages, but why set up a situation in which it is guaranteed?

PROS	CONS
The idea that the individual can love only one person is false, a product of a particular time, place, and culture. Polygamy has been the norm in many societies throughout history. Polygamy is not about freedom to fornicate with anyone; it is about cementing relationships with individuals one wants to spend the rest of one's life with, just as in monogamous marriages.	Marriage is about devotion to another, the giving of oneself wholly to that person, granting love to them to the exclusion of all others. How could one have such a relationship with more than one person? It is not possible to love more than one person. Polygamy, therefore, necessarily involves the exploitation of at least one party and the denigration of the relationship that exists between the others.
Polygamy reduces the desire for adultery by providing alternatives for sexual exploration within the family unit. This reduces the strains on family life and minimizes the likelihood of breakdown and divorce.	Adultery is based on a desire for someone outside the home. Adultery still occurs in polygamous societies. Indeed, polygamy encourages adultery because it dilutes the idea of fidelity to one person, substituting the legitimacy of intercourse with many.
Of course an individual should not belong to another. But this attack displays at best a lack of understanding about the cultures of others and at worst veiled racism. We should not stop people from practicing their faiths in this country. Polygamy is acceptable within the Muslim faith. Why should not the validity of such marriages be recognized?	Legalizing polygamy would legitimize the idea of women as objects belonging to their husbands. This is exactly the thinking we want to discourage. While polygynous marriages are technically possible in the Muslim world, they are very rare because the requirement that all wives be treated fairly (Qur'an 4:3) is almost impossible to meet. It is not possible to love one person as much as another, impossible to give one person as much thought or time as another. The very low rate of polygyny in Islam points to the problems innate in polygamy.
This is a cheap slur. Polygamy does not necessarily create other offenses. You cannot say something should be illegal because there's a theoretical link to other illegal things. Forced marriage is an issue in some monogamous societies. We agree that society needs to decide how it wants to handle that offense, but that question is entirely separate from the issue of allowing polygamy.	Once allowed, polygamy will facilitate forced marriages and increase the potential for incest as men marry close relatives to keep them within the closed community structure polygamy so often creates. Indeed, where polygamy is found, a wealth of other offenses follows. Child abuse, rape, welfare fraud, and incest are all staples of the polygamous communities in the United States. Just as important, polygamy encourages the broader exploitation of women.

Sample Motions:

This House would legalize polygamy.
This House believes monogamy is not the only way.
This House believes that three isn't a crowd.

Web Links:

- Multi-faith Attitudes to Polygamy. <http://www.polygamy.com> Site promoting plural marriage.
- Tapestry of Polygamy. <http://www.polygamy.org> Utah-based organization formed to fight the abuses of polygamy and support former polygamous wives and family members.

Further Reading:

Barash, David P., and Judith Eve Lipton. *Myth of Monogamy: Fidelity and Infidelity in Animals and People.* Owl Books, 2002.

Koktvedgaard Zeitzen, Miriam. *Polygamy: A Cross-Cultural Analysis.* Berg Publishers, 2008.

Llewellyn, John R. *Polygamy Under Attack: From Tom Green to Brian David Mitchell.* Agreka Books, 2004.

PORNOGRAPHY, BANNING OF

Most adult pornography is legal in the United States, where it is protected by the First Amendment guarantee of freedom of speech. Nevertheless, many campaigns to restrict it have been mounted. Initially such suggested restrictions were based on moral grounds, but in recent years women's groups have urged a ban because some studies have shown that pornography contributes to violence against women.

PROS

Pornography debases human interactions by reducing love and all other emotions to the crudely sexual. Sex is an important element in relationships, but it is not the be all and end all of them. Pornography also debases the human body and exploits those lured into it. It also encourages unhealthy, objectifying attitudes toward the opposite sex. Pornography is not a victimless crime. The victim is the very fabric of society itself.

CONS

Freedom of speech is one of our most cherished rights. Censorship might be justified when free speech becomes offensive to others, but this is not the case with pornography. It is filmed legally by consenting adults for consenting adults and thus offends no one. Pornography injures no one and is a legitimate tool to stimulate our feelings and emotions in much the same way as music, art, and literature do.

PROS: Pornography helps to reinforce the side of our sexual identity that sees people as objects and debases both their thoughts and bodies. We have seen evidence of this in the way pictures of seminaked women (hardly ever men) are used in advertising. Society's acceptance of pornography leads to the objectification of women and thus directly to sexual discrimination.

CONS: Pornography is a legitimate exploration of sexual fantasy, one of the most vital parts of human life. Psychologists have confirmed the important, if not driving, role that sexual impulses play in shaping our behavior. Repressing or denying this part of our personalities is both prudish and ignorant. Consequently, pornography should be available for adults to vary their sex lives. Indeed, far from "corroding the fabric of society," pornography can help maintain and strengthen marriages by letting couples fully explore their sexual feelings.

PROS: Society's apparent tolerance of legal pornography encourages illegal forms, such as child pornography. Are we to allow pedophiles the "legitimate sexual exploration" of their feelings? The opposition cannot let human impulses override societal rules that protect children.

CONS: This is not true; no "slippery slope" scenario exists. People interested in child pornography will obtain it regardless of its legal status. Human sexuality is such that mere exposure to adult pornography does not encourage individuals to explore child pornography.

PROS: Many rapists are obsessed with pornography. It encourages them to view women as objects and helps justify their contention that women are willing participants in the act. Indeed, feminists have proposed that pornography is rape because it exploits women's bodies. Pornography serves only to encourage brutal sex crimes.

CONS: Sadly, rape will exist with or without pornography. Rapists may use pornography, but pornography does not create rapists. The claim that pornography is rape is invalid. Our legal system depends on the distinction between thought and act that this claim seeks to blur. Pornography is a legitimate form of expression and enjoyment. Government should not censor it in the interests of sexual repression and prudery.

Sample Motions:

This House believes pornography does more harm than good.
This House would ban pornography.
This House believes that pornography is bad for women.

Web Links:

- BBC News. <http://news.bbc.co.uk/2/hi/uk_news/4195332.stm> Article on proposed ban of violent pornography.
- Council for Secular Humanism. <http://www.secularhumanism.org/library/fi/mcelroy_17_4.html> Several articles on feminism and pornography.
- Pornography and Censorship: The Stanford Encyclopedia of Philosophy. <http://www.science.uva.nl/~seop/entries/pornography-censorship/> Philosophical analysis of the legitimacy of banning pornography.

Further Reading:

Cornell, Drucilla. *Feminism and Pornography.* Oxford University Press, 2000.

Harvey, Philip D. *The Government vs. Erotica: The Siege of Adam & Eve.* Prometheus, 2001.

Strossen, Nadine. *Defending Pornography: Free Speech, Sex, and the Fight for Women's Rights.* New York University Press, 2000.

PREVENTIVE WAR

In 2002 the Bush Administration published The National Security Strategy for the United States, in which it articulated the doctrine of preventive war. In a departure from international law as outlined in the UN Charter, which permits the use of force only in self-defense against an actual or imminent armed attack, the Administration asserted that it would act against "emerging threats before they are fully formed."

PROS

The UN Charter and international law have to catch up with today's reality. Nations and nonstate groups have vastly more sophisticated ways of attacking a country than they did in the 1940s. The development of weapons of mass destruction (WMD) has changed the way we must look at security. The UN Charter should be amended to reflect this. Until it is, states have a right to defend themselves, even if it means engaging in preventive war.

History has shown that the UN and diplomacy in general are often ineffective. When its security is endangered and diplomatic means have been exhausted, a state has to the right to act unilaterally. Article 51 of the UN Charter preserves the "inherent right of individual or collective self-defense if an armed attack occurs against a Member of the United Nations, until the Security Council has taken measures necessary to maintain international peace and security."

The US has the military might and economic power to prevent its enemies from building up the strength to attack. Acting when the threat is still small and manageable is more rational then dealing with it after it has

CONS

The Bush Doctrine of preventive war creates a precedent that seriously threatens the integrity of the international legal order that has been in place since the end of the World War II.

The US doctrine of preventive self-defense contradicts the cardinal principle of the modern international legal order and the primary rationale for the founding of the UN after World War II: the prohibition of the unilateral use of force to settle disputes. The doctrine of preventive war is a recipe for conflict, precipitating wars that might never otherwise have begun.

The Bush Doctrine contributes to global tension. Some states will arm to defend themselves from a preventive war, while others will arm because they want to attack an aggressor who has killed innocent civilians. Some rogue

PROS	CONS
become serious. Preventing the proliferation of WMD is much more efficient than waiting until they have been deployed.	nations will determine that they can avoid a preventive war by acquiring nuclear weapons. Thus, the doctrine of preventive war will stimulate nuclear proliferation. The Bush Doctrine does not achieve the purpose for which it was originally articulated.
The US is a superpower and should act like one when global stability is at stake. As the world's only superpower, the US is responsible for maintaining global stability. It does not have to resort to war if diplomacy proves successful; however, war must be an option if diplomacy fails.	The UN was established with the supreme purpose of taking collective action to remove threats to peace. Moreover, the UN Charter requires that all members settle their international disputes by peaceful means. By initiating a preventive war without the UN's consent, the US has the potential to destabilize the global political situation and put in danger the peace, security, and justice that states have tried to preserve since the UN was established.
The US has the duty to protect its citizens. The world order established by the UN in 1945 could not protect the US from terrorist attacks in 2001. Terrorists are not concerned with international law or morality. The primary responsibility of the US government is to prevent future attacks on its people.	A preventive war lacks any moral justification because it runs counter to the UN Charter, which stipulates that violence is permissible only in response to an imminent threat or open aggression. As we have seen, US deviation from international law in this regard has had serious consequences, creating instability in the Muslim world, isolating the US from its allies, and contributing to the growth of terrorism.

Sample Motions:

This House believes that the US should not engage in preventive war without the consent of the UN.

This House believes that the Bush Doctrine guarantees security from future attacks.

This House believes that states should pursue unilateral military action when acceptable multilateral solutions cannot be found.

Web Links:

- The Defense Strategy Review Page. <http://www.comw.org/qdr/preventivewar.html> Articles supporting and condemning preventive war.
- History News Network. <http://hnn.us/articles/924.html> Article about the immorality of preventive war.
- "Preventive War" and International Law after Iraq. <http://www.globelaw.com/Iraq/Preventive_war_after_iraq.htm#_Toc41379606> Article presenting the legal position for opposing preventive war.

Further Reading:

Caraley, Demetrios James, ed. *American Hegemony: Preventive War, Iraq, and Imposing Democracy.* Academy of Political Science, 2004.

Gray, Colin. *The Implications of Preemptive and Preventive War Doctrines: A Reconsideration.* Juniper Grove, 2008.

Nichols, Thomas N. *Eve of Destruction: The Coming Age of Preventive War.* University of Pennsylvania Press, 2008.

PRIESTLY CELIBACY, ABOLITION OF

One of the requirements set by the Roman Catholic Church for priests is that they remain celibate. Celibacy is the renunciation of sex and marriage for the more perfect observance of chastity. This vow of celibacy has been propelled to the forefront of public discussion by charges, which began arising in 2002, that the church conspired to protect priests accused of child molestation. The vow of celibacy is seen by some as a cause of the pedophilia that seems to be rampant within the Catholic Church in America. The Vatican has not changed its stance on celibacy in the wake of the controversy, but some within the church have called for the elimination of the requirement to be celibate.

PROS

Until 1139, priests in the Western church were permitted to marry. The Bible does not mandate celibacy and, in fact, St. Peter, the first pope, was married. The true history and traditions of the Roman Catholic Church include the option for priests to marry.

The number of priests in America is on the decline, and many parishes are without a priest. The prohibition on marriage pushes some men away from the priesthood. The requirement of celibacy drastically reduces the pool from which the church can select priests and means that the church is not always getting the "best and the brightest."

Protestant clergy successfully balance their work in the church and their families. Were priests permitted to marry and have families, their families could serve as examples to others. In addition, marriage can provide a priest with increased social support and intimacy.

Priestly celibacy is outdated. It sets the priest apart from the world and the experiences of his parishioners.

Celibate priests can never experience the intimate and complicated marital relationship. They lack credibility when conducting marital and family counseling. Married priests can better serve their parishioners because of their marital and family experiences.

CONS

The earliest church fathers, including St. Augustine, supported the celibate priesthood. In the fourth century, church councils enacted legislation forbidding married men who were ordained from having conjugal relations with their wives. We do not know if any of the apostles, other than Peter, were married, but we do know that they gave up everything to follow Jesus. More important, Jesus led a celibate life.

Protestant churches, which do not require celibacy, also are having problems recruiting clergy. Worldwide, the number of new priests is increasing. Only the developed world has seen a decline in priestly vocations. A recent study showed that vocations were on the rise in dioceses in the US that were loyal to the teachings of the church, including priestly celibacy.

A celibate priest can devote all his time to his parishioners. A married priest must spend time with his family. Protestant clergy have balanced their work for the church with their family responsibilities only with difficulty. Many wives and families of Protestant clergy report feeling second to the congregation.

The priest is set apart from the world. He has a unique role: He represents Christ to his parishioners. Just as Jesus led a life of chastity dedicated to God, a priest must offer his life to God's people.

The celibate priest has a unique understanding of the power of self-control and the giving of the self, which are key ideas in marriage. The priest is married to the church and can counsel couples and families using that knowledge.

PROS

The prospect of celibacy draws sexually dysfunctional men to the priesthood. They hope that by totally denying their sexuality, they will not engage in pedophilia, but unfortunately they often cannot overcome their deviant desires. Permitting priests to marry would bring men with healthy sexual desires to the priesthood.

CONS

Celibacy and pedophilia are not connected. Sexual abuse also occurs in religions where clergy are permitted to marry. Studies have shown that sexual abusers account for less than 2% of Roman Catholic clergy, a figure comparable to clergy in other denominations.

Sample Motions:

This House would permit priests to marry.

This House would have the Vatican stop requiring priestly celibacy.

This House believes that a married priest is a better priest.

Web Links:

- Celibacy of the Clergy. <http://www.newadvent.org/cathen/03481a.htm> Detailed article on the history and theology of priestly celibacy.
- How to Refute Arguments Against Priestly Celibacy. <http://www.catholicity.com/commentary/hudson/00199.html> Clear presentation of arguments against celibacy, with refutations.
- Vatican News Agency. <http://www.ewtn.com/library/Liturgy/zlitur97.htm> Questions and answers from ZENIT, a news agency specializing in covering the Vatican.

Further Reading:

Cozzens, Donald. *Freeing Celibacy.* Liturgical Press, 2006.

Schoenherr, Richard A. *Goodbye Father: The Celibate Male Priesthood and the Future of the Catholic Church.* Oxford University Press, 2004.

Sipe, A. W. Richa. *Celibacy in Crisis.* Routledge, 2003.

Stravinska, M. J., ed. *Priestly Celibacy: Its Scriptural, Historical, Spiritual and Psychological Roots.* Newman House Press, 2001.

PRIVACY VS. SECURITY

In the aftermath of the terrorist attacks of September 2001, Congress passed the Patriot Act, which gave new rights and powers to law enforcement agencies. For example, the act gives the FBI greater latitude in wiretapping and in the surveillance of material transmitted over the Internet. Legislators have also proposed national identification cards, facial profiling systems, and tighter restrictions on immigration. All of these measures are aimed at protecting Americans from further terrorist attacks. But this increased security comes at a cost: The government will be able to gather more information about the private actions of individuals. To some observers, this invasion of privacy is unwarranted and represents an attack on fundamental freedoms guaranteed in the Constitution.

PROS

The primary function of government is to "secure the general welfare" of its citizens. Security is a common good that is promised to all Americans, and it must take primacy over individual concerns about privacy.

CONS

The right to privacy underlies the Fourth Amendment to the Constitution, which prohibits unreasonable "search and seizure." When the government collects and shares information about its citizens, it is conducting an electronic version of such prohibited searches.

PROS	CONS
Electronic surveillance—of financial transactions, for example—is an essential tool for tracking the actions of terrorists when they are planning attacks. The government cannot stand by and wait until criminal acts are committed; it must stop attacks before they happen.	Any proposal that increases the power of government agencies should be dismissed. Historically, government agencies (e.g., the IRS) have abused their power over citizens. Increased power means a greater potential for abuse.
Tighter security controls at airports and borders will help prevent damage and loss of life. In addition to their deterrent effect, they will enable officials to stop attacks as they are happening.	Tighter security controls can be used to target specific ethnic and religious groups in a way that is unfair and discriminatory.
Tighter immigration laws and more rigorous identification procedures for foreigners entering the country will reduce the possibility of terrorists entering the country.	Preventive measures affect the innocent as well as the guilty. This is especially true in the case of foreign nationals: Tighter immigration controls may exclude foreigners whose presence in America would be beneficial to the country.
The right to privacy is by no means absolute, and Americans already allow the government to control some of their private actions. (The government can require drivers to wear safety belts, for example.) Any intrusions on privacy for the sake of security would be minimal, and fundamental rights would still be respected.	History has shown that the invocation of national security has often led to the restriction of fundamental rights. For example, Japanese-American citizens were interned during World War II to increase security. We should not allow the government to take even small steps in a direction that can lead to something worse.

Sample Motions:

This House supports the creation of a national identity card.

This House would give the government more power in time of war.

Web Links:

- Privacilla.org. <http://www.privacilla.org> A Web site devoted to gathering information on privacy issues and links to privacy Web sites.
- Privacy vs. Security: A Bogus Debate? <http://www.businessweek.com/technology/content/jun2002/tc2002065_6863.htm> In an interview for *Business Week*, David Brin, author of *The Transparent Society*, argues that the conflict between privacy and security is a false dichotomy.
- Privacy vs. Security? Privacy. <http://www.huffingtonpost.com/marc-rotenberg/privacy-vs-security-pr_b_71806.html> Article supporting respect for privacy over need for security. Contains link to opposing viewpoint.

Further Reading:

Cohen, David B., and John W. Wells, eds. *American National Security and Civil Liberties in an Era of Terrorism.* Palgrave, 2004.

Darmer, M. Katherine, Robert M. Baird, and Stuart E. Rosenbaum, eds. *Civil Liberties vs. National Security in a Post-9/11 World.* Prometheus, 2004.

Dempsey, John X., and David Cole. *Terrorism & The Constitution, Sacrificing Civil Liberties in the Name of National Security.* First Amendment Foundation, 2002.

Leone, Richard C., and Greg Anrig, Jr., eds. *The War on Our Freedoms: Civil Liberties in an Age of Terrorism.* PublicAffairs, 2003.

Sidel, Mark. *More Secure, Less Free? Antiterrorism Policy and Civil Liberties After September 11.* University of Michigan Press, 2004.

PROSTITUTION, LEGALIZATION OF

Prostitution has long been opposed on moral grounds, but recently concerns about sexually transmitted diseases, particularly AIDS, and about the violence that surrounds prostitution have contributed to renewed demands to stop the selling of sex. Criminalizing prostitution has not worked, and some nations have moved to regulate or legalize it to protect prostitutes and monitor the conditions under which they work. In Singapore and Denmark, selling sex is legal; the Dutch city of Amsterdam and the Australian state of New South Wales have no laws for or against prostitution. Nevada has made prostitution lawful in a limited number of licensed brothels. This arrangement also has enjoyed notable success in the Australian state of Victoria.

PROS

Prostitution is an issue of individual liberty. The control of one's own body is a basic human right. We do not impose legal penalties on men and women who choose to be promiscuous. Why should the exchange of money suddenly make consensual sex illegal?

Prostitution has existed in all cultures throughout history. Governments should recognize that they cannot eradicate it. Consequently they should pass legislation that makes prostitution safer, rather than persist with futile and dangerous prohibition.

Prostitutes have performed a valid social function for thousands of years. Prostitution actually helps maintain marriages and relationships. A purely physical, commercial transaction does not jeopardize the emotional stability of a relationship. In Italy, for example, visiting a prostitute does not violate the law against adultery.

Many libertarian feminists believe that prostitution reflects the independence and dominance of modern women. The majority of prostitutes are women. Once the danger of abuse from male clients and pimps is removed, the capacity of women to control men's sexual responses in a financially beneficial relationship is liberating. Furthermore, many campaigners for the rights of prostitutes note that the hours are relatively short and the work well paid. Prostitutes are paid for services other women must provide without charge.

Some studies suggest that prostitution lowers the incidence of sex crimes.

CONS

Prostitutes do not have a genuine choice. They are often encouraged or forced to work in the sex industry before they are old enough to make a reasoned decision. Many have their reasoning impaired by an unhappy family background, previous sexual abuse, or drugs. They may be compelled to enter prostitution by circumstances beyond their control, such as substance addiction or the necessity to provide for a family.

Governments have a duty to protect the moral and physical health of their citizens. Legalizing prostitution would implicitly approve a dangerous and immoral practice. Prostitution is never a legitimate choice for a young girl.

Prostitution harms the fabric of society. Sexual intercourse outside of marriage or a relationship of love shows disregard for the sanctity of the sexual act and for the other partner in a relationship. Emotional commitment is inextricably linked to physical commitment.

Feminists overwhelmingly oppose prostitution. The radical feminist school that emerged in the 1990s supports the idea that prostitution leads to the objectification of women. Men who use women's bodies solely for sexual gratification do not treat them as people. This lack of respect dehumanizes both the prostitute and the client and does not represent a victory for either sex.

How can you prove that some individuals who visit prostitutes would otherwise have committed violent offenses? Psychological therapies that recommended the use of prostitutes have been widely discredited. The number of reported attacks on prostitutes and the considerably greater number of such crimes that go unreported

PROS	CONS
	suggest that prostitutes are the victims of the most serious crimes. In Victoria, where prostitution is legal, two rapes of prostitutes are reported each week.
Legalization would improve the sexual health of prostitutes and, as a result, that of their clients. The sexual transaction would occur in a clean and safe environment rather than on the street. In areas where prostitution is legal, prostitutes have regular health checks as a condition of working in the brothels. Furthermore, the use of contraception is compulsory and condoms are freely available.	More sexual health problems are inevitable. When prostitution is lawful and socially acceptable, a greater number of men will use prostitutes. Medical studies show that the condom is only 99% effective. Moreover, during the period between each health check, a prostitute could contract and transmit a sexually transmitted disease. Consequently, the legalization of prostitution will result in the transmission of more potentially fatal diseases.
Legalizing prostitution would break the link between prostitutes and pimps. Pimps physically abuse prostitutes and often threaten greater violence; they confiscate part, if not all, of their earnings, and often encourage the women to become addicted to drugs. Providing a secure environment in which to work frees men and women of pimps.	The legalization of the Bunny Ranch in Nevada did not prevent the majority of prostitutes from continuing to work outside of the licensed brothel and remain dependent on pimps. Licensed brothels are expensive for prostitutes to work in and for clients to visit. A legal business has to pay for rent, health checks and security; prostitutes working outside the "system" need not worry about such expenses. Some prostitutes use private apartments, while others work on the street. Legalizing prostitution will not remove the street market or the dangers associated with it. The dangerous street environment is a consequence of economics, not legal controls.
Licensed brothels will improve the quality of life for people who live and work in areas currently frequented by prostitutes. Regulations can require brothels to locate in areas away from homes and schools.	Prostitutes will continue to work on the streets and are unlikely to work near the competition offered by the licensed brothels. Furthermore, will local governments want to create "ghettos" of prostitution in certain areas?
Existing legal prohibitions against prostitution do not work. Prostitutes are regularly arrested and fined. To pay the fines, they must prostitute themselves. The laws banning prostitution are counterproductive.	Merely because some individuals break a law does not mean that the law itself is at fault or that it should be abolished. The ease with which prostitutes can return to work suggests that penal sanctions should be more severe rather than removed altogether.
Legalizing prostitution would give governments economic benefits. A tax on the fee charged by a prostitute and the imposition of income tax on the earnings of prostitutes would generate revenue.	An economic benefit cannot offset social harms that result from the legalization of certain prohibited activities. Otherwise we would encourage governments to become involved in other unlawful trades including trafficking in drugs. Moreover, sex workers are unlikely to declare their true earnings from what is a confidential relationship between the worker and client. Thus the amount of revenue generated is likely to be slight.
The problem of a high concentration of "sex tourists" in a small number of destinations will disappear once a larger number of countries legalize prostitution. Supporting this motion, therefore, will reduce the problem of sex tourism.	Legalizing prostitution would render the country in question a destination for sex tourists. Relaxed legal controls on prostitution in Thailand, the Philippines, and in the Netherlands have made these countries attractive to these undesirable individuals.

Sample Motions:

This House would legalize prostitution.
This House would legalize brothels.
This House would decriminalize prostitution.

Web Links:

- International Herald Tribune. <http://www.iht.com/articles/2007/10/05/america/bulgaria.php> Article on Bulgaria's move away from legalizing prostitution.
- Legalized Prostitution: Regulating the World's Oldest Profession. <http://www.liberator.net/articles/prostitution.html> Article in favor of legalizing prostitution.
- UNESCO Courier. <http://www.unesco.org/courier/1998_12/uk/ethique/txt1.htm> Article on whether prostitution should be legal, referencing several countries' policies.
- Vancouver Rape Relief and Women's Shelter. <http://www.rapereliefshelter.bc.ca/issues/prostitution_legalizing.html> Ten reasons for not legalizing prostitution.

Further Reading:

Farley, Melissa. *Prostitution, Trafficking and Traumatic Stress.* Routledge, 2004.

Spector, Jessica. *Prostitution and Pornography: Philosophical Debate About the Sex Industry.* Stanford University Press, 2006.

REBUILDING AFTER DISASTERS, GOVERNMENT ROLE IN

The past several years have seen the United States buffeted by a series of disasters, from 9/11 to hurricanes Katrina and Ike. Traditionally, Americans have looked to government to play a major role in rebuilding efforts, but following allegations of corruption and inefficiency in reconstructing the Gulf Coast after Katrina, citizens are reevaluating the roles of the public and private sectors in recovery.

PROS

The government exists to protect citizens and to help them recover from crises. When disaster strikes, be it a summer of tornados, an earthquake, or a hurricane, the government bears primary responsibility for speeding its citizens' lives back to order. Financing rebuilding efforts is the least the government can do to help individuals recover from incredible personal loss and community tragedy.

CONS

Government intervention in rebuilding is not the answer and only serves to cover up the government's previous failures. Rather than being "acts of God," many disasters happen either because of government laxity (a terrorist attack) or are made worse because of inadequate government preparation (a lack hurricane warning systems or earthquake building codes). Focusing on the role of government in recovery encourages a mentality that excuses earlier government negligence and does not help prevent similar crises in the future.

The government has an obligation to promote the economic redevelopment of regions hit by natural disasters. Helping fund the rebuilding of private homes would be one step. The individuals and families affected by disasters are taxpayers, and if a disaster were to strike another region, their tax money would go to support citizens in

To be sure, the government has a responsibility to fix destroyed infrastructure; however, individuals should rely on their insurance to rebuild their homes. Individuals who cannot afford disaster insurance should not live in high-risk areas such as flood plains. They should not look to government (and the taxpayers) to bail them out.

PROS	CONS
those areas. Citizens must accept this fact if they demand benefits for themselves.	Government subsidies on flood insurance either coddle the rich or allow the poor to take risks without suffering the consequences. We live in an "ownership society"—individuals and private institutions should take responsibility for where they chose to locate.
Because of its huge resources, only the federal government can help regions recover from massive disasters quickly and efficiently. States simply do not have the financial wherewithal to rebuild nor do they have the expertise to coordinate a massive reconstruction campaign. States must rely on federal entities like the Federal Emergency Management Agency (FEMA) that have experience in dealing with overwhelming and continuing crises.	Government-sponsored rebuilding efforts are notoriously inefficient and prone to fraud. In the wake of Katrina, millions of dollars of government assistance were given to "victims," who spent the money on frivolities ranging from exotic dancers to diamond rings. Government rebuilding efforts are by their very nature bureaucratic and politically driven, and do not necessarily respond to cases of greatest need. In contrast, the private sector has a vested financial interest in efficiency and fraud prevention.

Sample Motions:

This House believes that the federal government must rebuild New Orleans.

This House believes that the federal government bears primary responsibility for rebuilding after a disaster.

This House believes that when disaster strikes, government should employ all means necessary to assist affected areas.

Web Links:

- Hoover Digest. <http://www.hooverdigest.org/053/wilson.html> Advice from Pete Wilson (governor of California at the time the state successfully recovered from a major earthquake) on rebuilding New Orleans.
- The Independent Institute. <http://www.independent.org/newsroom/article.asp?id=1589> Public policy institute analysis of public vs. private organization response to Katrina.
- New York Times. <http://www.nytimes.com/2005/10/09/business/09view.html?_r=1&pagewanted=1> Descriptions of several cities' recoveries after disasters.

Further Reading:

Birch, Eugenie, et al. *Rebuilding Urban Places After Disaster: Lessons from Hurricane Katrina.* University of Pennsylvania Press, 2006.

Cooper, Christopher. *Disaster: Hurricane Katrina and the Failure of Homeland Security.* Times Books, 2006.

Posner, Richard. *Catastrophe: Risk and Response.* Oxford University Press, 2004.

RELIGION: SOURCE OF CONFLICT OR PEACE?

Religion has always been one of the most influential forces in the world. It has been a force for peace, but it also has served as a cause, if not a genuine reason, for some of the greatest wars. Today, with the growth of Muslim fundamentalism in Islamic areas, the Western world views religious extremism as the great threat. The events of September 11, 2001, proved that such concerns were justified; however, the war on terror led by the West caused resentment among those for whom Islam was a peaceful source of spiritual stability. So what is religion today? Is it harmful or good? If it can be a source of conflict, can it serve as an instrument of resolution as well?

PROS

Religion is a stronger force than any material incentives. It is far better at directing behavior toward social betterment than either laws or physical force. For example, both Gandhi and Martin Luther King, Jr., conducted nonviolent protests based on religious values.

CONS

Religion is extremely dangerous because it can be used to justify brutal actions. The Inquisition carried out its torture in the name of God. Hitler's followers, among them the so-called German Christians, were also believers in their Führer. Religion should never be involved in politics because it can be used as an instrument of control or to achieve a ruler's aims.

PRO: The very existence of theocratic states, e.g., Iran, proves that religion can be a legitimate source of political power. Governments in theocratic states are much more stable than in secular countries because leaders are viewed as appointed by God. Political stability, in its turn, leads to economic welfare.

CON: Theocratic states become totalitarian regimes because they are based on obedience to a ruler who is seen as God's representative rather than on a democratic constitution.

PRO: Biblical commandments are the basis of Western ethical and legal systems. Religion teaches us tolerance for people of other races and religions. Usually believers are more peaceful and tolerant than nonbelievers.

CON: Religions like Islam justify "holy" wars against the "unfaithful," meaning people of other religions. Religious convictions like these paved the way for the terrorist attacks of September 11.

PRO: In the states where religion develops freely and people have free access to places of worship, churches have always served as a shelter for the poor. Some of the greatest works of art were created in the name of God. Furthermore, Woodrow Wilson suggested that a strong affinity exists between religious commitment and patriotism. Love of country, just like love of God, certainly inspires good deeds.

CON: Religion has led to the creation of great art but it has also led to its destruction. Remember the Taliban's destruction of the great Buddhas in Afghanistan? Still worse, religion can be a source of extreme nationalism. In Islam, Christianity, and Judaism, God is described as "mighty warrior," "just king," or "righteous judge." He punishes the unjust, the unrighteous, and the disobedient. The idea that a nation is the instrument of God's will has led to war and the subjugation of people viewed as ungodly.

PRO: Most wars are not started by religion, although religion often serves to justify them. Most wars are started for economic reasons or for territorial gain.

CON: Whether religion is a genuine reason for war or only its pretext is not important. What is vital is that religion can be and is often used to make people fight in the name of high ideals to further aims of hatred. Thus, religion causes more harm than good.

PRO: Western states grew as a result of religion and religious philosophy. Western European and North American societies are still based on Protestant ideals of diligence, thrift, and moderation.

CON: North American nations emerged only because of economic factors: the existence of famine and overpopulation in Europe on the one hand, and the free markets of the United States on the other. The realities of capitalism, not the tenets of religious faith, prompt people to be diligent and thrifty.

Sample Motions:

This House believes that religion is a positive influence on people.

This House believes that church and state must be kept separate.

Web Links:

- Catholic New Times. <http://findarticles.com/p/articles/mi_m0MKY/is_/ai_n14858518> Remarks on whether faith is a source of conflict or peace.
- Journal of Religion, Conflict and Peace. <http://www.plowsharesproject.org/journal/php/archive/> Archive of a journal that addresses the problems and possible solutions that religion creates.
- United States Institute of Peace. <http://www.usip.org/pubs/specialreports/sr201.html> Report discussing the role of religion as a peacemaker.

Further Reading:

Gopin, Marc. *Holy War, Holy Peace: How Religion Can Bring Peace to the Middle East.* Oxford University Press, 2005.

Kepel, Gilles. *Jihad: The Trail of Political Islam.* Translated by Anthony Roberts. Harvard University Press, 2002.

Smock, David R. *Religious Perspectives on War: Christian, Muslim, and Jewish Attitudes.* Rev. ed. United States Institute of Peace Press, 2002.

RELIGIOUS BELIEF: RATIONAL OR IRRATIONAL?

The majority of the world's population is at least nominally committed to some religion. Despite the perception in some parts of the Western world that religious belief is in terminal decline, or that economic and social development go hand-in-hand with secularization, in many parts of the world religious belief is firmly entrenched, including in the United States, arguably the most "developed" nation on Earth. Religion offers a fascinating topic for debate: the question of the existence of God; the social, moral, and political questions about the effects of religious belief on individuals and communities both now and in the past.

PROS

Religious belief is completely irrational. God exists? Where's the proof? There is none. Reported miracles, healings, etc., are never reliably proved. In any case everyone's religious experiences are different and show the psychological differences between human beings rather than proving any objective divine reality. Belief in God is simply wish fulfillment. A loving all-powerful being watching over us would be nice, but there isn't any.

The world is full of the suffering and pain of the innocent. If God is good and all powerful then why is such suffering permitted? Either God does not exist or he is not worth believing in because he does not care about human suffering.

CONS

Evidence that God is a reality is good. That we live in a beautiful, orderly universe in which human beings exist and have special moral and spiritual awareness points clearly to the existence of a divine creator of the universe. Billions of people have had religious experiences, all of them revealing the existence of divine reality.

Most suffering and pain can be accounted for by the free will that humans exercise. God made us free, and we use that freedom for evil as well as for good. As for illness and disease, it is hard for us to know the mind of God, but it may be that these trials are a necessary part of a world in which free and spiritual human beings can evolve and develop.

PROS	CONS
Modern science has shown religious belief to be wrong. From Galileo to Darwin to the modern day, scientists have continually uncovered the true natural mechanisms behind the beginning and evolution of the universe. These leave no gaps for God to act in; science has revealed a closed natural order governed by natural laws. Science has also proved that there is not a "soul," but that all our mental states are simply caused by brain activity. Accordingly, there is no reason to believe in life after death, one of the main tenets of religious belief.	What an inaccurate caricature of the relationship between science and religion. In fact, most of the great scientists of history have been religious believers. The more we learn about the physical world, the more it seems that an intelligent God designed it to produce human life. The physical side of reality does not, in any case, preclude a spiritual dimension. Nor does the fact that the mind and brain are closely correlated mean that they are the same thing.
Religions through the ages, and still today, have been agents of repression, sexism, elitism, homophobia, conflict, war, and racial hatred. The evils for which religion is responsible in the social and political worlds easily outweigh whatever small psychological comfort religious belief may give.	Religion may have been the occasion for various social and political wrongs, but it is not the cause. You can be sure that if you took away all the world's religions people would still identify themselves with national and political groups and go to war over territory, etc. Equally, elitism and bigotry are, sadly, parts of human nature with or without religion. Serious and sincere religious belief is a force for good in the world, promoting humility, morality, wisdom, equality, and social justice. Social justice is at the heart of the Christian gospel.
Religious traditions and the irrational fervor with which people adhere to them divide humanity. They provide a proliferation of incompatible and contradictory moral codes and values. The only prospect for a global morality is a secular one based on rational consensual views and positions rather than on partisan, local, irrational prejudices. In the interest of global harmony, we should discard religious beliefs.	We need religious traditions to provide us with morals and values in a rapidly secularizing age. Scientists and politicians cannot tell us how to distinguish right from wrong. We need the moral insight of religious traditions, which are repositories of many generations of spiritual wisdom, to guide us in ethical matters.

Sample Motions:

This House rejoices that God is dead.
This House does not believe.
This House believes that religion has done more harm than good.

Web Links:

- Counterbalance. <http://www.counterbalance.org> A "science and religion" site sympathetic to Christianity.
- Theism, Atheism, and Rationality. <http://www.leaderu.com/truth/3truth02.html> Philosophical essay in support of a theistic worldview.
- Wall Street Journal. <http://online.wsj.com/article/SB122178219865054585.html?mod=googlenews_wsj> Article suggesting that there is a correlation between faith and rationality.

RUSSIA: STRONG LEADERSHIP VS. DEMOCRACY

Russia's transition to capitalist democracy following the collapse of communism in 1991 was a difficult one. Vowing to fight corruption, secession, and terrorist threats that had plagued the nation, Vladimir Putin won the presidency in 2000. A former KGB officer, Putin emerged as a quiet yet powerful leader who asserted that Russia must "combine the principles of a market economy and democracy with Russia's realities"—the reality that Russians want a powerful leader and a strong, paternalistic state. Putin won the hearts and minds of the Russian people, who were disillusioned by a decade of economic, social, and political instability, but, his political actions—most recently his assumption of the prime ministership in 2008 when term limits prevented him from being elected president for a third term—and his powerful character risk turning him into more of an authoritarian leader than the president of a democratic country.

PROS

In a period of chaos, stability is more important than democratic reform. After the fall of communism, Russia plunged into a deep economic recession. The introduction of market reforms and privatization led to rising inequality and corruption. The chaos of economic and political reform, coupled with the chaos of the breakup of the former USSR, left the majority of the population disillusioned and distrustful of their government. A strong leader was necessary to set a clear direction and to unify the country.

Putin is the strong leader for whom Russia was waiting. His electoral success and consistently high approval ratings show that the Russian people want a leader who can rid their society of increasing corruption and restore a sense of calm and equality. His ability to maintain a high level of support despite what some have called authoritarian tendencies shows that people are ready to sacrifice a certain degree of freedom for the promise of stability. Enthusiasm for Putin among the young also shows that the desire for stability is not limited to older generations of Russians.

Putin's authoritarian style is not a threat to democracy but rather a requirement for a more successful and speedy transition. Having Putin control the media is probably healthier than having it controlled by a corrupt few who promote their personal interests rather than the interest of the state and thus of the population at large. Democracy is the goal, and Russia is still working toward defining its own version of democracy and finding what works best in its case.

Political corruption is a widespread and potentially dangerous problem in Russia that must be tackled with strong executive power. Increased corruption might prove extremely dangerous—perhaps even more dangerous than the threat of terrorism—since it could create

CONS

Only through democratic reform is a future of freedom and prosperity possible. Transition is chaotic by definition, and reforms are disruptive by nature. While a long transition process can certainly make people distrustful and disillusioned, one must keep in mind that the risk of authoritarian rule is highest precisely at these moments. Polls have repeatedly shown that the Russian people support democracy. We must not let the immediate chaos of reform scare us.

Putin's initial backing was based mainly on his strong promises, his arrest and prosecution of corrupt businessmen, and his tough action on Chechnya. However, Putin's support has eroded as a result of his attempts to control the media and to replace elected governors with his own appointees as well as because of scandals surrounding the disappearance and murder of several important journalists. He has lost the support of the NGO community and the majority of the Russian intelligentsia, and the previously strong backing of the United States.

Putin is not the state, and his ability to control and represent the state and the Russian people is questionable. His authoritarian tendencies have had significant effects. At this point, the state controls most Russian media, decisions continue to be made behind closed doors, Russia has once again become the pariah of the international community.

Putin's "fight against corruption" is a guise for oppression and authoritarian rule. Many corrupt, authoritarian leaders have risen to power through promises of reform. A society living in fear and believing that a powerful leader will solve all its problems can never be truly

PROS

powerful drug, oil, and weapons cartels. Putin has taken important steps toward curbing corruption and he needs consolidated power in order to continue this struggle.

Russia needs strong leadership to recover from the disastrous reforms of the 1990s. Productive state assets were given away to oligarchs in the name of privatization. Government services collapsed, and millions saw their savings and pensions made worthless through inflation. During this period, democracy failed to protect the people, and instead, elected politicians who were beholden to shady businessmen and who promoted their own self-interest. Meanwhile, the economy shrank and billions of dollars of Russian money ended up in foreign bank accounts. In contrast, Putin has not been afraid to stand up to the oligarchs, correcting past injustices and leading the country into a period of increasing economic prosperity and stability.

Historically, Russia has always required strong centralized leadership to achieve progress. This was true both in imperial times under tsars such as Peter the Great (who made Russia a European power and built St. Petersburg) and Alexander II (who freed the serfs), and, since 1917, under Lenin and Stalin. Russia is too big, too diverse, and too thinly populated for Western representative democracy. Culturally, its people are suited to following the decisive lead of a strong ruler who can unite them in the face of great challenges. Without such a ruler, Russia will experience economic stagnation and will be likely to fragment, with local strongmen grabbing power in the regions and religious fundamentalism dominating much of the Caucasus and Central Asia.

CONS

democratic. Even if Putin were above reproach, centralizing power so completely gives his advisers great influence, which makes government corruption more inevitable. Only by building in proper democratic checks and balances, including freedom of the press, can accountability be created and corruption or incompetence tackled.

Many of the reforms of the 1990s were badly handled—often because they did not go far enough—but today's problems have more to do with the bankruptcy of the former Soviet system than with democracy's failings. Putin has done very little to make the lives of ordinary people better and has tackled individual oligarchs and their business empires only if they have posed a political threat. Recent economic progress has been based solely on temporary high oil prices and will not last. Russia has seen no real reforms to secure property rights, reduce bureaucracy, and set free the talents of its people. Instead, Putin's cynical use of power to attack companies such as Yukos has shown how little the rule of law means in Russia today and has put off investment while encouraging capital flight.

History is not destiny, and a highly selective view of Russia's past should not lead us to prefer authoritarian rule. The tsars and their communist successors killed millions of people through brutal rule and failed policies—made possible by the same lack of consultation and accountability that we see in Russia today. Only a vigorous multiparty democracy, fully independent legal system, and free media can ensure that the disasters of the past are not repeated. Nor is there any reason why such a system could not take root in Russia. Russia is no more diverse than many other countries, and modern communications ensure that mere distance is not a problem. Moreover, nothing in their culture or temperament makes Russians uniquely unsuited to democracy.

Sample Motions:

This House favors democracy over authoritarian rule in Russia.

This House prefers a stable Russia under a strong leader to an unstable democratic Russia.

Web Links:

- GlobalSecurity.org. <http://www.globalsecurity.org/wmd/library/news/russia/2008/russia-080208-rferl02.htm> Argument that Medvedev is not a democratic alternative to Putin.
- Taipei Times. <http://www.taipeitimes.com/News/editorials/archives/2005/06/03/2003257769> Article supporting Putin's strong statism.
- Washington Post. <http://www.washingtonpost.com/wp-dyn/content/article/2005/06/06/AR2005060601723.html> Article on Putin's rollback of democracy.

Further Reading:

Baker, Peter, and Susan Glasser. *Kremlin Rising: Vladimir Putin's Russia and the End of Revolution.* Potomac Books, 2007.

Politkovskaya, Anna. *Putin's Russia: Life in a Failing Democracy*. Holt, 2007.

Sakwa, Richard. *Putin: Russia's Choice.* Routledge, 2007.

SCHOOL VOUCHERS

Over the past decades, Americans have been increasingly concerned about the quality of public education, particularly in inner-city neighborhoods, where many public schools are failing. One of the most controversial suggestions for improving education for all children is to establish school voucher programs. Although the specifics of these programs vary with locality, all would distribute monetary vouchers to parents who could then use them to help pay the cost of private, including parochial (religious), schools. Critics fear that vouchers would further damage public schools and argue that they subvert the separation of church and state. Supporters say they will help the children most in need.

PROS

The current public education system is failing countless students, particularly in inner-city neighborhoods. In an era where education is the key to success, these children are not being provided with the chance to develop the skills necessary to compete in the modern world. Vouchers give poor parents the ability to send their children to better schools. These children should not be sacrificed while we wait for public school reform.

The competition for students will force all schools to improve. They will have to use their resources to educate their students rather than squander them on bureaucracies as many do today. Eventually, the unsalvageable schools will close and the others will grow stronger, producing an overall better learning environment. The market will regulate the education produced.

The money would help some families, and that is worth the risks. Not all students in nonperforming schools will be able to attend a private school. However, after the students who can afford such an opportunity leave nonperforming schools, more resources will be available at those nonperforming schools to educate the remaining students. Private schools would have no reason to change admission standards or tuition, nor is there reason to think that a great swell in private school enrollment would result.

CONS

The American public education system has been central to American democracy. It has provided education for all children regardless of their ethnic background, their religion, their academic talents, or their ability to pay. It has helped millions of immigrants assimilate and provided the civic education necessary for future citizens to understand American values. Establishing a voucher system is saying that we are giving up on public education. Instead of giving up, we should put our efforts into reforming the system.

The competition for students would destroy inner-city public schools. Much of their student body would flee to "better" private schools, leaving inner-city schools with little to no funding. Most states' funding of public schools is determined by number of students enrolled. If enrollment lags, then the school is not as well funded as it was the previous year. If enrollment booms, then funding increases. Thus, even if urban schools are motivated to improve they will lack the resources to do so.

The government vouchers are not monetarily substantial enough to give true financial aid to students. They are not large enough to help poor students go to private schools. The vouchers make private education more affordable for people who could already afford it. In addition, private schools may not be willing to accept all students with vouchers. They could always raise tuition or standards for admission, neutralizing any impact vouchers would have.

PROS	CONS
Vouchers will eventually lead to a school system that is liberated from bureaucrats and politicians, enabling educators and parents to determine how best to educate children.	Voucher programs would set up a school system that is not accountable to the public. Investigations of current programs in Milwaukee, Wisconsin, and Cleveland, Ohio, have found unlawful admissions requirements, illegally imposed fees, and even fraud.
No violation of the separation of church and state would occur. No student would be forced to enter a religious school. Only families and students interested in a private or religious education would use the vouchers. Any students who desired a more traditional curriculum would be allowed to study in public schools.	Vouchers involve the indirect giving of public funds to religious schools. This transfer of funds amounts to a violation of the doctrine of separation of church and state.

Sample Motions:

This House believes that the government should cease the use of school vouchers.

This House recommends that educational vouchers be used for private and parochial schools.

This House believes that the issuing of vouchers by the government is justified.

Web Links:

- BalancedPolitics.org. <http://www.balancedpolitics.org/school_vouchers.htm> Discussion of the pros and cons of school vouchers.
- Los Angeles Times Online. <http://www.latimes.com/news/opinion/la-op-dustup13feb13,0,7261921.story> Two experts debate whether or not school vouchers are beneficial.
- School Vouchers: The Wrong Choice for Public Education. <http://www.adl.org/vouchers/vouchers_main.asp> An anti–school-voucher Web site containing a detailed report outlining many reasons why vouchers are a poor policy option.

Further Reading:

Bolick, Clint. *Voucher Wars: Waging the Legal Battle over School Choice.* Cato Institute, 2003.

Kahlenberg, Richard D., ed. *Public School Choice vs. Private School Vouchers.* Century Foundation, 2003.

Kolbert, Kathryn, and Zak Mettger, eds. *Justice Talking: School Vouchers.* New Press, 2002.

Moe, Terry M. *Schools, Vouchers, and the American Public.* Brookings Institution Press, 2002.

SCIENCE: THREAT TO SOCIETY?

In the past few decades, science has extended the boundaries of human knowledge and understanding further than many people are comfortable with. Cutting-edge technologies, such as cloning, and other more established procedures, such as in vitro fertilization, have sparked moral outrage and accusations of "playing God." The development of nuclear weapons is just one illustration of the possible danger introduced by scientific advances.

PROS	CONS
Science gives humans the ability to "play God" and to interfere in areas about which we know nothing. Scientists have already cloned animals, and recently some scientists announced that they will attempt to clone humans. Such irresponsible and potentially dangerous meddling is taking place in the name of scientific advancement.	Talk of "playing God!" Aside from assuming the existence of a deity that many do not believe in, the talk of playing God implies a violation of set boundaries. What boundaries? Set by whom? The proposition is simply afraid of things about which it knows nothing. The assertion that we are meddling in areas we do not understand should be replaced with a call for better regulation of scientific enquiry, not its abolition.
Science has greatly increased the capability of men and women to kill each other. Wars that used to be fought face-to-face on the battlefield, with comparatively few casualties, are now fought from miles away in anonymity. The buildup of nuclear arsenals during the Cold War gave humanity the capability of obliterating the entire world 10 times over. At certain times in history, such as the 1962 Cuban missile crisis, the world has stood on the brink of destruction.	Science does not kill; humans do. We cannot blame science for the flaws in human nature, and we cannot attribute suffering to science any more than to religion or philosophy, both of which have caused wars. The example given illustrates how science brings with it accompanying responsibility. Mutually assured destruction ensured that neither the United States nor the Soviet Union deployed nuclear weapons.
Science has perverted the fundamental basis of human relations. The word "society" itself comes from "socialization"—the idea of interaction and communication. With the Internet, television, and computer games, humans are communing with a lifeless collection of microchips, not each other.	Science has greatly increased the ability of people to communicate. Telephones and e-mail now enable people on opposite sides of the world to stay in touch. The Internet allows people unprecedented access to information, anything from sports scores to debating crib sheets. Any study of preindustrial society will show that computer games appear to have taken the place previously held by recreational violence.
Science is despoiling the natural world. Power grids ruin the countryside, acid rain from coal- and gas-fired power stations kills fish, and animals are cruelly experimented on to further research. Not only does science give us the potential to destroy each other, it also takes a massive toll on our natural surroundings.	Modern medicines have more than doubled our life expectancy and prevented fatal childhood diseases. The world's population could not be fed without fertilizers and pesticides to increase crop yields and machinery to harvest them efficiently. Science and technology are essential to modern existence. We must use them with care and not abuse them. But condemning science as a menace is ludicrous.

Sample Motions:

This House believes science is a threat to humanity.
This House fears science.
This House believes that scientists are dangerous.

Web Links:

- Institute of Science in Society (ISIS). <http://www.i-sis.org.uk> Maintained by ISIS, a nonprofit organization working for social responsibility in science, the site offers information on current issues in science.
- International Center for Technology Assessment. <http://www.icta.org> Site provides information on the organization's initiatives to explore the economic, social, ethical, environmental, and political impacts of technology.
- Scientists for Global Responsibility. <http://www.sgr.org.uk> UK-based organization promoting the ethical use of science provides news on scientific issues and information on its initiatives.

Further Reading:

Grinnell, Richard W. *Science and Society.* Longman, 2006.

Kleinman, Daniel Lee. *Science and Technology in Society: From Biotechnology to the Internet.* Wiley-Blackwell, 2005.

SEX EDUCATION IN SCHOOLS

For years conservatives and liberals in the United States debated whether schools should teach sex education or whether this responsibility is that of the parents. With the rise of teenage pregnancies and sexually transmitted diseases, particularly AIDS, the focus has shifted to what should be taught, rather than where. Should schools advocate sexual abstinence (refraining from sexual activity until the age of consent or marriage), or should society assume that the students will be sexually active and therefore encourage teaching safe sex?

PROS

The primary cause of unwanted pregnancies and the spread of sexually transmitted diseases (STDs) is ignorance about safe sex. The AIDS crisis of the 1980s and 1990s has shown that sex education must be a vital part of the school curriculum and may be supplemented by frank discussion at home.

As the US Guidelines for Comprehensive Sexuality Education (1991) state, "all sexual decisions have effects or consequences" and "all persons have the . . . obligation to make responsible sexual choices." While Hollywood promotes casual, thoughtless sex as the norm, teacher-led discussions can encourage responsible attitudes about sexual relationships.

Abstinence is an outdated approach based on traditional religious teaching. Some young people may choose it, but we cannot expect it to be the norm. Teenagers express their sexuality as part of their development. Having sex is not the problem; having unsafe sex or hurting people through sexual choices is.

CONS

Judging by the number of teenage pregnancies and the continuing spread of STDs, teenagers are not getting the message. Sex education in schools can be counterproductive because teens find it fashionable to ignore what teachers advocate. The most effective channel for sex education is the media, particularly TV, films, and magazines.

This is the wrong approach. Sex education in the classroom encourages young teenagers to have sex before they are ready and adds to peer pressure to become sexually active. In addition, any class discussion may lead to ridicule, thus devaluing the message. Sexual responsibility should be discussed in a one-to-one context, either with older siblings or parents.

Classroom education should promote abstinence. Sex education encourages sexual promiscuity. Advocating both safe sex and restraint is self-contradictory. Children are at risk of severe psychological and physical harm from having sex too young and should be encouraged to abstain.

Sample Motions:

This House believes that sex education should take place at home.
This House would rather not discuss it with its parents.

Web Links:

- MSNBC. <http://www.msnbc.msn.com/id/3071001/> Article discussing sex education debate in United States.

- National Public Radio. <http://www.npr.org/templates/story/story.php?storyId=1622610> Report on sex education in United States.
- Time Online. <http://women.timesonline.co.uk/tol/life_and_style/women/the_way_we_live/article5208865.ece> Article on why England should liberalize sex education programs in state schools.

Further Reading:

Irvine, Janice. *Talk About Sex: The Battles over Sex Education in the United States.* University of California Press, 2004.

Luker, Kristin. *When Sex Goes to School: Warring Views on Sex—And Sex Education—Since the Sixties.* W. W. Norton, 2006.

Moran, Jeffrey P. *Teaching Sex: The Shaping of Adolescence in the 20th Century.* Harvard University Press, 2002.

SEX OFFENDERS: PUBLICLY NAMING

During the 1990s the US Congress passed two laws designed to protect children from dangerous sex offenders released from prison. The first law, the 1994 Jacob Wetterling Act (named after a child abducted at gunpoint), requires states to register individuals who have been convicted of sex crimes against children. The second, Megan's Law (1996), compels states to make information on registered sex offenders available to the public but gives states discretion in establishing the criteria for disclosure. Megan's Law was named after Megan Kanka, a 7-year-old girl who was sexually assaulted and murdered by a paroled sex offender. States vary on how they have implemented this law. Many post the name and address of offenders on Web sites or offer the public this information on CD. Others permit law enforcement officials only to notify neighbors of the offender. Megan's Law has generated heated discussion. Those supporting it maintain that it will protect children; those opposing it say that it is ineffective and will force convicts who had served their sentences to wear a "badge of infamy" for the rest of their lives.

PROS

Sex offenders, even more so than other criminals, are prone to repeat their crimes. Making their names public enables parents to protect their children and reduce the rate of sexual crime by repeat offenders.

CONS

This proposal is a fundamental violation of the principles of our penal system, which are based on serving a set prison term and then being freed. Registration imposes a new punishment for an old crime, and, inevitably, will lead to sex offenders being demonized by their neighbors. Offenders have been forced out of their homes or lost their jobs as a result of notification. Innocent people will also suffer. Families of offenders have been subject to threats, and inaccurate information made public by the police has led to the harassment of innocent people. Such a risk cannot be tolerated; we cannot as a society revert to mob rule in place of justice.

Crimes of a sexual nature are among the most abhorrent and damaging that exist; they can ruin a child's life. Those guilty of such crimes cannot be incarcerated forever, thus extra precautions must be taken on their release to ensure that they pose no threat to the public.

Psychological evaluations can determine accurately whether an offender is still a risk to society or not. Should the offender be found to still be a threat, he should remain in custody. If the tests indicate that the offender is no longer a threat, he should be freed and allowed to live a normal life. Megan's Law eliminates this distinction and stigmatizes those who have genuinely

PROS	CONS
	reformed. Our penal system is based on the principle of reforming offenders. Ignoring the possibility of change is both ludicrous and unfair.
These laws help the police to track down re-offenders more quickly, thus they are also brought to justice more swiftly and surely. These laws and their strong and swift enforcement provide a strong deterrent against repeat offenses.	Registering offenders with the police may help law enforcement, but making public the offender's whereabouts adds no advantage and might be counterproductive. The abuse and harassment that offenders might suffer could drive them underground, making police monitoring more difficult.
We cannot know how many children were saved by these laws, but even one child saved from sexual assault justifies them.	What evidence do we have that these laws have been effective in protecting people and preventing crime? Very little. As a result of the law, many prosecutors are reluctant to charge juveniles as sex offenders because they do not want children stigmatized for life. These offenders are not getting treatment and could pose a future risk to the public.

Web Links:

- BBC News. <http://news.bbc.co.uk/2/hi/uk_news/1706396.stm> Article on Megan's Law.
- Good Housekeeping Online. <http://www.goodhousekeeping.com/family/safety/problem-megans-law-dec05> Article on problems with Megan's Law.
- Revising Megan's Law and Sex Offender Registration: Prevention or Problem. <http://www.appa-net.org/eweb/docs/appa/pubs/RML.pdf> Detailed essay in opposition to Megan's Law.

Further Reading:

La Fond, John Q. *Preventing Sexual Violence: How Society Should Cope with Sex Offenders (The Law and Public Policy: Psychology and the Social Sciences).* American Psychological Association, 2005.

Lovell, Elizabeth. *Megan's Law: Does It Protect Children? A Review of Evidence on the Impact of Community Notification as Legislated for Through Megan's Law in the United States.* National Society for the Prevention of Cruelty to Children, 2001.

Maddan, Sean. *The Labeling of Sex Offenders: The Unintended Consequences of the Best Intentioned Public Policies.* University Press of America, 2008.

SINGLE-SEX SCHOOLS

Studies have shown that boys gain more academically from studying in coeducational schools, but that single-sex schools promote greater achievement in girls. But academic results are not the only criterion on which to judge the success of the education system. In 1996, a long-standing controversy over the Virginia Military Institute's male-only policy resulted in a landmark US Supreme Court ruling that the Institute must admit women. However, the Court left room for private (i.e., not state-run) single-sex institutions and for the establishment of such schools where needed to redress discrimination.

PROS

Women benefit from a single-sex education. Research shows that girls in single-sex schools participate more in class, develop much higher self-esteem, score higher in aptitude tests, are more likely to choose "male" disciplines such as science in college, and are more successful in their careers. In *Who's Who*, graduates of women's colleges outnumber all other women. The United States has only 83 women's colleges.

Children in the formative years, between 7 and 15, gravitate to their own sex. They naturally tend toward behavior appropriate to their gender. Thus implementing an education strategy geared specifically toward one gender makes sense. Certain subjects, such as sex education or gender issues, are best taught in single-sex classrooms.

Boys and girls distract each other from their studies, especially in adolescence as sexual and emotional issues arise. Too much time can be spent attempting to impress or even sexually harass each other. Academic competition between the sexes is unhealthy and only adds to unhappiness and anxiety among weaker students.

Single-sex schools (such as the Virginia Military Institute) are a throwback to the patriarchal society of the past; historically in many cultures, only men were allowed an education of any sort. Such single-sex institutions both remind women of past subservience and continue to bar them from full social inclusion.

Teachers themselves are often discriminated against in single-sex schools; a boys' school will usually have a largely male staff where women may feel uncomfortable or denied opportunity, and vice versa.

CONS

A 1998 survey by the American Association of University Women, a long-time advocate of single-sex education, admitted that girls from such schools did not show academic improvement. That women from single-sex schools are more inclined to study math and science is of questionable importance to society. As the report noted, "Boys and girls both thrive when the elements of good education are there, elements like smaller classes, focused academic curriculum and gender-fair instruction." These conditions can be present in coeducational schools.

The formative years of children are the best time to expose them to the company of the other gender so that they learn each other's behavior and are better prepared for adult life. The number of subjects benefiting from single-sex discussion is so small that this could easily be organized within a coeducational system.

In fact boys and girls are a good influence on each other, engendering good behavior and maturity; particularly as teenage girls usually exhibit greater responsibility than boys of the same age. Academic competition between the sexes is a spur to better performance at school.

Single-sex schools for women are a natural extension of the feminist movement; men have had their own schools, why shouldn't women? If single-sex schools existed only for men, then that would be discriminatory; however, as long as both genders have the choice of attending a single-sex institution (or a coeducational one), you cannot call it discrimination.

Teachers frequently favor their own gender when teaching coeducational classes; for example, male teachers can undermine the progress and confidence of girl students by refusing to call on them to answer questions.

Sample Motion:

This House believes in single-sex education.

Web Links:

- The Guardian: UK News. <http://www.guardian.co.uk/uk/2006/jun/25/schools.gender> Article discussing the lack of benefits for girls from single-sex education.
- The Independent: Education. <http://www.independent.co.uk/news/education/education-news/singlesex-schools-are-the-future-1023105.html> Article discussing the future of single-sex education.
- National Association for Single Sex Public Education. <http://www.singlesexschools.org> Arguments in support of single-sex schools.

Further Reading:

Datnow, Amanda. *Gender in Policy and Practice: Perspectives on Single Sex and Coeducational Schooling.* RoutledgeFalmer, 2002.

Salomone, Rosemary C. *Same, Different, Equal: Rethinking Single-Sex Schooling.* Yale University Press, 2003.

Spielhagen, Frances R. *Debating Single-Sex Education: Separate and Equal?* Rowman & Littlefield Education, 2007.

SMOKING, FURTHER RESTRICTIONS ON

Although most countries put age restrictions on the purchase of tobacco, over a billion adults smoke legally every day. Supplying this demand is big business. By the 1990s major tobacco companies had been forced to admit that their products were addictive and had serious health consequences, both for the user and for those subject to second hand smoke. In the developed world, public opinion shifted against smoking. Many governments substantially increased taxes on tobacco to discourage smoking and to help pay for the costs of smoking-related illness. Yet, while smoking has declined among some groups, it has increased among the young. Meanwhile tobacco companies look to developing nations for new markets.

PROS

Smoking is extremely harmful to the smoker's health. The American Cancer Society estimates that tobacco causes up to 400,000 deaths each year—more than AIDS, alcohol, drug abuse, car crashes, murders, suicides, and fires combined. Worldwide some 3 million people die from smoking each year, one every 10 seconds. Estimates suggest that this figure will rise to 10 million by 2020. Smokers are 22 times more likely to develop lung cancer than nonsmokers, and smoking can lead to a host of other health problems, including emphysema and heart disease. One of the main responsibilities of any government is to ensure the safety of its population; that is why taking hard drugs and breaking the speed limit are illegal. Putting a ban on smoking would therefore be reasonable.

CONS

While a government has a responsibility to protect its population, it also has a responsibility to defend freedom of choice. The law prevents citizens from harming others. It should not stop people from behavior that threatens only themselves. Dangerous sports such as rock climbing and parachuting are legal. No laws have been passed against indulging in other health-threatening activities such as eating fatty foods or drinking too much alcohol Banning smoking would be an unmerited intrusion into personal freedom.

PROS

Of course, personal freedom is important; we should act against the tobacco companies, not individuals. If a company produces food that is poisonous or a car that fails safety tests, the product is immediately taken off the market. All cigarettes and other tobacco products are potentially lethal and should be taken off the market. In short, smoking should be banned.

CONS

Cigarettes are very different from dangerous cars or poisonous foods. Cigarettes are not dangerous because they are defective; they are only potentially harmful. People should still be permitted to smoke them. A better comparison is to unhealthy foods. Fatty foods can contribute to heart disease, obesity, and other conditions, but the government does not punish manufacturers of these products. Both cigarettes and fatty foods are sources of pleasure that, while having serious associated health risks, are fatal only after many decades. They are quite different from poisonous foods or unsafe cars, which pose high, immediate risks.

PROS	CONS
Smoking is not a choice because nicotine is an addictive drug. Evidence suggests that tobacco companies deliberately produce the most addictive cigarettes they can. Up to 90% of smokers begin when they are under age 18, often due to peer pressure. Once addicted, continuing to smoke is no longer an issue of free choice, but of chemical compulsion. The government should ban tobacco just as it does other addictive drugs like heroin and cocaine because it is the only way to force people to quit. Most smokers say that they want to kick the habit, so this legislation would be doing them a favor.	Comparing tobacco to hard drugs is inaccurate. Tobacco is not debilitating in the same way that many illegal narcotics are, it is not comparable to heroin in terms of addictiveness, and it is not a mind-altering substance that leads to irrational, violent, or criminal behavior. It is much less harmful than alcohol. Many other substances and activities can be addictive (e.g., coffee, physical exercise) but this is no reason to make them illegal. People are able to abstain—many give up smoking every year—if they choose to live a healthier life. Nevertheless, many enjoy smoking as part of their everyday life.
Most smokers are law-abiding citizens who would like to stop. They would not resort to criminal or black market activities if cigarettes were no longer legally available; they would just quit. Banning smoking would make them quit and massively lighten the burden on health resources.	Criminalizing an activity of about one-sixth of the world's population would be insane. As America's prohibition of alcohol during the 1920s showed, banning a popular recreational drug leads to crime. In addition, governments would lose the tax revenue from tobacco sales, which they could use to cover the costs of health care.
The effects of smoking are not restricted to smokers. Second hand smoke jeopardizes the health of nonsmokers as well. Research suggests that nonsmoking partners of smokers have a greater chance of developing lung cancer than other nonsmokers. Beyond the health risks, smoke also can be extremely unpleasant in the workplace or in bars and restaurants. Smoking causes discomfort as well as harm to others and should be banned.	The evidence that passive smoking causes health problems is very slim. At most, those who live with heavy smokers for a long time may have a very slightly increased risk of cancer. Smoke-filled environments can be unpleasant for nonsmokers, but reasonable and responsible solutions can be found. Offices or airports could have designated smoking areas, and many restaurants offer patrons the choice of smoking and nonsmoking sections. Allowing people to make their own decisions is surely always the best option. Restricting smoking in public places may sometimes be appropriate; banning it would be lunacy.
At the very least all tobacco advertising should be banned and cigarette packs should have even more prominent and graphic health warnings.	Where is the evidence that either of these measures would affect the rate of tobacco consumption? Cigarette companies claim that advertisements merely persuade people to switch brands, not start smoking. People start smoking because of peer pressure. Indeed, forbidding cigarettes will make them more attractive to adolescents. As for health warnings, if the knowledge that cigarettes have serious health risks deterred people from smoking, then no one would smoke. People start and continue to smoke in the full knowledge of the health risks.

Sample Motions:

This House would ban tobacco.
This House would not smoke.
This House would declare war on the tobacco industry.

Web Links:

- Center for Disease Control and Prevention: Tobacco. <http://www.cdc.gov/tobacco/index.htm> Research, data, and reports relating to tobacco as well as tobacco industry documents and campaigns for tobacco control.
- Phillip Morris. <http://www.philipmorrisusa.com> Major tobacco company site offering government reports on tobacco as well as information on tobacco issues including the marketing of tobacco products.
- Smoking From All Sides. <http://www.cs.brown.edu/~lsh/smoking.html> Links to statistics and hundreds of articles on both sides of the argument.
- The Tobacco Homepage. <http://www.tobacco.org> Provides recent information on tobacco-related issues as well as documents, timelines, and links to all aspects of the tobacco controversy.
- World Health Organization: Tobacco Free Initiative. <http://www.who.int/toh/> Information on WHO's worldwide program to stop smoking, as well as background information on the economic, health, and societal impact of tobacco and smoking.

Further Reading:

Gilmore, Noel. *Clearing the Air: The Battle over the Smoking Ban.* Liberties Press, 2005.

Rabin, Robert L., and Stephen D. Sugarman. *Regulating Tobacco.* Oxford University Press, 2001.

Warner, Kenneth E., Stephen L. Isaacs, and James R. Knickman, eds. *Tobacco Control Policy.* Jossey-Bass, 2006.

SPACE EXPLORATION

The space programs of both the US and the USSR were, perhaps, the most important prestige projects of the Cold War. From the launch of Sputnik—the first artificial satellite—in 1957, through to the first human space flight by Yuri Gagarin in 1961, the first moon landing in 1969, and beyond, both superpowers invested huge amounts of money in outdoing each other in the Space Race. Since the end of the Cold War, however, the future of space exploration has become less clear. Russia no longer has the resources to invest in a substantial space program, and the United States has also cut back. China, however, has spent billions of dollars developing a space program with the goal of establishing a space station by 2020, and eventually will put a man on the moon. European nations, too, have banded together to pursue space exploration.

PROS

Humankind always struggles to expand its horizons. The curiosity that constantly pushes at the boundaries of our understanding is one of our noblest characteristics. The exploration of the universe is a high ideal; space truly is the final frontier. The instinct to explore is fundamentally human; already some of our most amazing achievements have taken place in space. No one can deny the sense of wonder we felt when for the first time a new man-made star rose in the sky, or when Neil Armstrong stepped onto the Moon. Space exploration speaks to that part of us that rises above the everyday.

CONS

High ideals are all well and good, but not when they come at the expense of the present. Our world is marred by war, famine, and poverty, with billions of people struggling simply to live from day to day. Our dreams of exploring space are a luxury we cannot afford. Instead of wasting our time and effort on prestige projects like the space program, we must set ourselves new targets. Once we have addressed the problems we face on Earth, we will have time to explore the universe, but not before then. The money spent on probes to distant planets would be better invested in the people of our own planet. A world free from disease, a world where no one lives in hunger, would be a truly great achievement.

PROS	CONS
The exploration of space has changed our world. Satellites allow us to communicate instantaneously with people on different continents and to broadcast to people all over the world. The Global Positioning System allows us to pinpoint locations anywhere in the world. Weather satellites save lives by giving advance warning of adverse conditions; together with other scientific instruments in orbit they have helped us gain a better understanding of our world. Research into climate change, for example, would be almost impossible without the data provided by satellites.	Satellite technology has benefited humankind. However, launching satellites into Earth orbit differs significantly from exploring space. Missions to other planets and into interstellar space do not contribute to life on our planet. Moreover, most satellites are commercial; they are launched and maintained by private companies. Space exploration requires huge government subsidies and will never be commercially viable. For example, the Voyager missions alone cost almost US$1 billion. This money could be better spent elsewhere.
Space exploration has had many indirect benefits. The space program has brought about great leaps in technology. The need to reduce weight on rockets led to the microchip and the modern computer. The need to produce safe but efficient power sources for the Apollo missions led to the development of practical fuel cells, which are now being explored as possible power sources for cleaner cars. The effects of zero gravity on astronauts have substantially added to our knowledge of the workings of the human body and the aging process. We can never know exactly which benefits will emerge from the space program in the future, but we do know that we will constantly meet new obstacles and in overcoming them will find new solutions to old problems.	These auxiliary advantages could have come from any project. They are a result of giving people huge amounts of money and manpower to solve problems, not a result of a specific program. For example, many of the advances in miniaturization were the result of trying to build better nuclear missiles; this is not a good reason to continue building nuclear weapons. Similar resources would be far better devoted to projects with worthier goals, for example, cancer research or research into renewable energy sources. These, too, could provide many side benefits, but would tackle real problems.
Space exploration is an investment in the future. Our world is rapidly running out of resources. Overpopulation could become a serious worldwide threat. Consequently, ignoring the vast potential of our own solar system—mining resources on asteroids or other planets, or even colonizing other worlds—would be foolish. If we fail to develop the ability to take advantage of these possibilities, we may find it is too late.	Space exploration is a waste of resources. If we want to tackle the problems of overpopulation or of the depletion of resources, we must address them on Earth instead of chasing an elusive dream. We can deal with the problems of our planet in practical ways, and we must tackle them with all the resources and all the political will we have.

Sample Motions:

This House would explore the universe.
This House would explore the Final Frontier.
This House would reach for the stars.

Web Links:

- The Independent: Science. <http://www.independent.co.uk/news/science/the-big-question-is-manned-space-exploration-a-waste-of-time-and-money-406801.html> Pros and cons of space exploration.
- New York Times Blog. <http://freakonomics.blogs.nytimes.com/2008/01/11/is-space-exploration-worth-the-cost-a-freakonomics-quorum/> Several experts discuss whether space exploration is worth the cost.
- The Tech. <http://tech.mit.edu/V123/N66/mattsilver.66c.html> Article in MIT's student newspaper: "In Defense of Space Exploration."

Further Reading:

Schmitt, Harrison H. *Return to the Moon: Exploration, Enterprise, and Energy in the Human Settlement of Space.* Springer, 2006.

STEM CELL RESEARCH AND THERAPEUTIC CLONING

Stem cells are cells that give rise to specialized cells such as heart or brain cells, muscle tissue, or skin in a developing embryo. Researchers believe that these cells hold the promise of future cures for diseases—such as diabetes, Parkinson's disease, and Alzheimer's disease— caused by the disruption of cellular function. Ethical issues surround stem cell use because such cells are "harvested" from embryos created during in vitro fertilization. (Stem cells can also be derived from adults, but they may not be as useful as embryonic cells.) Extracting the cells destroys the embryo and thus ends future human life. In addition, fears have been expressed that humans will clone themselves (therapeutic cloning) to create embryos to mine for stem cells.

PROS

Although therapeutic cloning will involve the creation and destruction of thousands of embryos, the resulting benefits will be so great as to outweigh moral considerations. Once the research goals have been achieved, the use of embryo treatments can be greatly reduced. The likely result of curing people of fatal diseases is worth the cost.

CONS

Merely hoping for a good outcome does not make immoral actions acceptable. Medical research should be governed by moral and ethical concerns. However much sympathy we feel for sufferers of terminal diseases, we cannot tolerate the use of human embryos as means to an end. Stem cell research is inherently contradictory: Lives would be created and then destroyed in order to save other lives.

We already accept the creation and destruction of "spare" embryos for cycles of in vitro fertilization (IVF). IVF facilitates the creation of human life. Stem cell treatments will save existing human lives. The infertile will still survive. The sufferers of Huntington's chorea or Alzheimer's will not. If we accept the morality of IVF, we must accept the morality of stem cell treatment.

The loss of embryos in IVF is a reason to condemn IVF treatment. It is not a reason for allowing another procedure that will sacrifice much more potential life.

The creation, storage, and destruction of embryos can be strictly controlled. There should be no fear of "Frankenstein science."

Media fears of mad scientists free to manipulate and destroy human life may be overstated. However, research projects carry a significant risk of destroying thousands of embryos for little or no scientific gain.

The moral status of the embryo is distinct from that of the fetus. What reason is there to assert that life begins at the stage of embryo creation? The accepted test for clinical death is an absence of brain stem activity. The fetus first acquires a functioning brain six weeks after the embryo has been created. We cannot condone the "wastage" of human embryos. However, we must be wary of regarding the loss of an embryo as the loss of human life.

The embryonic human should have the same moral status as the fetus or the child or the adult. At what physiological point do we declare an embryo "human"? Are we to base a declaration of being human on physical appearance? That the embryo looks different from the fetus and from the adult does not prove that the embryo is not a human being.

PROS	CONS
We cannot equate human embryos with human beings just because they could develop into adults. Between 50% and 70% of embryos are lost naturally through failure to implant in the wall of the uterus. The potential of an embryo to develop does not of itself make the embryo human.	The proper test of humanity should be if the embryo has the potential to organize itself into a "living human whole." Every embryo has this capacity. The fact that embryos are lost naturally does not imply that the destruction of embryos is morally acceptable.
Further research requires the use of the stem cells found in embryos. Research done with adult cells has yielded very little progress because of the difficulty of "reprogramming" an adult cell to develop as the particular neuron or tissue cell required. The greater understanding of human cells that scientists will gain from research with embryo stem cells may increase the utility of adult cells in the future. For the present, resources should be concentrated on research with stem cells harvested from embryos.	Researchers have no need to use embryo stem cells. Research has continued for many years into the use of adult stem cells. These cells are replaceable and could be used for the purposes of treatment and research without the destruction of embryos.

Sample Motions:

This House would allow stem cell research.
This House supports therapeutic cloning.

Web Links:

- International Society for Stem Cell Research. <http://www.isscr.org/public/index.htm> Basics of stem cell science.
- NOVA Online. <http://www.pbs.org/wgbh/nova/miracle/stemcells.html> Article by a member of the National Institutes of Health Human Embryo Research Panel in support of embryonic stem cell research.
- President's Council on Bioethics: Monitoring Stem Cell Research. <http://www.bioethics.gov/reports/stemcell/index.html> Offers introduction and historical background on the topic as well an overview of the ethical arguments on both sides of the debate.

Further Reading:

Bellomo, Michael. *The Stem Cell Divide: The Facts, the Fiction, and the Fear Driving the Greatest Scientific, Political and Religious Debate of Our Time.* AMACOM, 2006.

Caplan, Arthur, and Glenn McGee, eds. *The Human Cloning Debate.* Berkeley Hills, 2006.

Ruse, Michael, and Christopher A. Pynes, eds. *The Stem Cell Controversy: Debating the Issues.* Prometheus, 2003

Waters, Brent, and Ronald Cole-Turner, eds. *God and the Embryo: Religious Voices on Stem Cells and Cloning.* Georgetown University Press, 2003.

TERRORISM, JUSTIFICATION FOR

In the wake of the shocking events of September 11, 2001, terrorism and the "war on terror" became the number one issue for the US government. But terrorism has a far longer, more global history. Political, religious, and national/ethnic groups have resorted to violence to pursue their objectives—whether full recognition of their equal citizen-

ship (in Apartheid South Africa), a separate national state of their own (Israelis in the 1940s, Palestinians from the 1970s onward), or the establishment of a religious/ideological state (Iranian terrorism against the Shah). In some cases former terrorists have made the transition to peaceful politics—for example, Nelson Mandela in South Africa and Gerry Adams in Northern Ireland. Is it possible to justify the use of terrorist tactics if they result in the deaths of innocent civilians in bombings and shootings? This is an issue that calls into question the value we put on our ideals, beliefs, and human life itself.

PROS

In extreme cases, in which peaceful and democratic methods have been exhausted, it is legitimate and justified to resort to terror. In cases of repression and suffering, with an implacably oppressive state and no obvious possibility of international relief, it is sometimes necessary to resort to violence to defend one's people and pursue one's cause.

Terrorism works. In many countries terrorists have succeeded in bringing governments to negotiate with them and make concessions to them. Where governments have not been willing to concede to rational argument and peaceful protest, terrorism can compel recognition of a cause. Nelson Mandela moved from perceived terrorist as head of the African National Congress' armed wing to president of South Africa. In many other countries we see this trend too—in Israel, Northern Ireland, recently in Sri Lanka, and in the Oslo peace process that led to the creation of the Palestinian Authority. Therefore, terrorism is justified by its success in achieving results when peaceful means have failed.

Terrorism can raise the profile of a neglected cause. The hijackings of the 1970s and 1980s publicized the Palestinian cause, helping to bring it to the world's attention. States can use their wealth and media to convey their side of the story; their opponents do not have these resources and perhaps need to resort to terrorism to publicize their cause. In this way, limited and focused use of violence can have a dramatic international impact.

Ideals such as "freedom" and "liberty" are more important than a single human life; they give meaning to the lives of hundreds of thousands of people. Of course, peaceful methods should be tried first, but when all else fails, a nation/ethnic community or other group must be able to fight for its freedom and independence.

CONS

Terrorism is never justified. Peaceful and democratic means must always be used. Even when democratic rights are denied, nonviolent protest is the only moral action. And in the most extreme cases, in which subject populations are weak and vulnerable to reprisals from the attacked state, it is especially important for groups not to resort to terror. Terrorism merely exacerbates a situation, and creates a cycle of violence and suffering.

Terrorism does not work. It antagonizes and angers the community that it targets. It polarizes opinion and makes it more difficult for moderates on both sides to prevail and compromise. A lasting and peaceful settlement can be won only with the freely given consent of both parties to a conflict or disagreement. The bad feeling caused by the slaughter of hundreds, perhaps thousands, of innocent people by terrorists makes such consent desperately difficult to give.

Furthermore, states or institutions created in concession to terror are often corrupt, dominated by men of violence with links to organized crime. Nothing is achieved to improve the lives of the people in whose name terror has been used.

All publicity is definitely not good publicity. Powerful images of suffering and death will permanently mark the terrorists' cause, and cause them to lose the battle for public approval around the world. Furthermore, groups that resort to terrorism play into the hands of their opponents; states being subjected to terrorism can win powerful support from similarly affected nations, such as the US, in combating this threat.

Abstract ideals are insignificant when compared with the value of even a single life. Life is sacred, and to murder anyone in pursuit of an idea—or even the improvement of other people's lives—is shocking, abhorrent, and wrong. No one has the right to say another person's life is worthless, or worth less than the cause that is pursued through terrorism.

PROS	CONS
Actions should be judged by their consequences. In bringing hope, popular recognition, and ultimately relief to the plight of a group, terrorism is aimed at laudable objectives and can achieve sufficient good to outweigh the evil of its methods.	The end does not justify the means. The consequences of any action are by no means clear. The success of terrorism is not guaranteed; it is an immoral gamble to kill people in the hope of achieving something else. And even if the goal were realized, the price paid is literally incalculable. Those who use violence in the pursuit of "higher" aims presume to be able to calculate suffering. But the fear, suffering, and death caused by terrorism damage millions of people. Not just the victims are affected, with their families and fellow citizens, but people in many different countries are also put at risk because terrorists from other countries are inspired by these atrocious acts.
The definition of terrorism depends very much upon one's point of view. The affirmative does not need to defend every atrocity against innocent civilians to argue that terrorism is sometimes justified. A broad definition would say terrorism was the use of violence for political ends by any group that violates the Geneva Conventions (which govern actions between armies in wartime) or ignores generally accepted concepts of human rights. Under such a broad definition, states and their armed forces could be accused of terrorism. So could many resistance groups in wartime or freedom fighters struggling against dictatorships, as well as participants in civil wars—all irregular groups outside the scope of the Geneva Conventions. Effectively, such a definition says that the armies of sovereign states should have a monopoly on violence, and that they can only act in certain ways. Some exceptions to this are surely easy to justify—for example, the actions of the French resistance to German occupation in World War II, or of American patriots against the British in the 1770s. A narrower definition would say that terrorism was the use of violence against innocent civilians to achieve a political end. Such a definition would allow freedom fighters and resistance groups with a legitimate grievance to use force against dictatorship and occupation, providing they targeted only the troops and other agents of oppression. Yet even this tight definition has gray areas—what if the soldiers being targeted are reluctant conscripts? Are civilian settlers in occupied territories not legitimate targets as agents of oppression? What about their children? Does it make a difference if civilians are armed or unarmed? Do civil servants such as teachers and doctors count as agents of an occupying or oppressive state?	States that ignore the Geneva Conventions, for example, by mistreating prisoners or deliberately attacking civilian targets, are guilty of terrorism. Nor are the Conventions applicable only to warfare between sovereign states. Their principles can be clearly applied in other kinds of conflict and used to distinguish between legitimate military struggle and indefensible terrorism. Nor is it reasonable to argue that there are gray areas and that civilians are sometimes legitimate targets. Once such a claim has been made, anything can eventually be "justified" in the name of some cause. All too often the political leaderships of protest movements have decided that "limited physical force" is necessary to advance their cause, only to find the violence spiraling out of control. The "hard men" who are prepared to use force end up in control of the movement, which increasingly attracts criminals and others who love violence for its own sake. This alienates the original base of support for the movement in the wider population and internationally. The authorities against whom the movement is struggling also respond by using increasingly repressive measures of their own, generating a spiral of violence and cruelty.

Sample Motions:

This House can justify terrorism.

This House cannot justify the use of terrorism under any circumstances.

This House believes that extremism in the pursuit of liberty is no vice.

Web Links:

- British American Security Information Council. <http://www.basicint.org/terrorism/US.htm> Information on responses to terrorism by international groups and key nations.
- Israel/Palestine Center for Research and Information. <http://www.ipcri.org/index1.html> Independent think tank analyzing one of the world's most enduring terrorist conflicts.

Further Reading:

Hoffman, Bruce. *Inside Terrorism.* Columbia University Press, 2006.

Lutz, James Michael, and Brenda J. Lutz. *Terrorism: Origins and Evolution.* Palgrave Macmillan, 2005.

Townshend, Charles. *Terrorism: A Very Short Introduction.* Oxford University Press, 2003.

Whittaker, David. *Terrorism Reader.* Routledge, 2003.

TORTURE IN INTERROGATION

One of the most heated controversies of the US war on terror is the use of torture on suspected terrorists. Many policy makers contend that torture is, at times, the most effective method for obtaining critical information that might help maintain national security. Noted jurists such as Alan Dershowitz have argued that regulated torture may be a necessary way to protect Americans. Opponents, however, counter that such interrogation methods violate the basic human rights provisions of the Geneva Conventions and binding UN protocols concerning the laws of waging war (to which the US is a party), as well as the UN Convention Against Torture. Meanwhile, leaks of the so-called White House torture memos, incidents such as the Abu Ghraib prison scandal, and the debate over the use of waterboarding have put the media spotlight on US treatment of detainees.

PROS

Many experienced interrogators have found that aggressive tactics are the best, and sometimes the only, way to obtain information—information that might lead to the arrest or conviction of other terrorists or might protect the US against a future attack. Often such information is needed quickly, so that more subtle means of interrogation are untenable. Moreover, the US has a track record for using aggressive interrogation in a regulated, studied way that does not constitute torture in the conventional sense (defined as methods that will cause permanent damage to vital organs or permanent emotional trauma). The US government has never sanctioned methods that would cause such harm.

CONS

Information obtained by torture is suspect at best. Studies have shown that individuals will say anything to stop the abuse. Moreover, bringing terrorists to justice is important for closure and safety, but evidence obtained from torture may be inadmissible in the courtroom.

PROS	CONS
The US uses aggressive interrogation only against those it has strong reason to believe have engaged in terrorist activities against Americans. Such extralegal activity requires a strong response. These are bad people, trained terrorists who will stop at nothing to kill innocent US civilians. Those who would heavily restrict interrogation methods would have the US lose the war on terror.	Every human being has human rights, no matter how heinous a crime he or she is suspected of committing. Article 5 of the Universal Declaration of Human Rights reads: "No one shall be subjected to torture or to cruel, inhuman, or degrading treatment or punishment." Moreover, the US Constitution prohibits torture.
The Geneva Conventions do not apply to the interrogation of terrorists and suspected terrorists held by the US because they are not prisoners of war. They are illegal enemy combatants, outside the scope of such protection.	Verbal sleight of hand should not obscure the fact that individuals captured in the war on terror are prisoners of war. Moreover, in many cases they are merely suspected of links to criminal activity (and, as past experience has indicated, often wrongly so). Extralegal military tribunals conducted behind closed doors without proper due process leave the US on shaky moral ground.
The US is hardly alone in its use of such interrogation practices and has a good record compared with other nations. Moreover, "torture" is a loaded word that does not accurately differentiate between the studied interrogation practices of US forces and the human rights abuses prevalent in many developing nations.	The United States should set the standard for international human rights, rather than strive only for the average. Furthermore, permitting low-level and undertrained US troops to engage in unsupervised interrogation is a recipe for disaster. Incidents like the abuses at Abu Ghraib prison demonstrate how quickly America's reputation can suffer from such illicit treatment of prisoners.

Sample Motions:

This House believes that the US has the right to use torture to protect national security.

This House believes that torture is sometimes necessary in time of war.

This House believes that the US has the right to use torture against suspected terrorists.

Web Links:

- National Public Radio (NPR): The Drawbacks of Fighting Terror with Torture. <http://www.npr.org/templates/story/story.php?storyId=5519633> Transcript of radio story discussing the problems of using torture to battle terrorism; links to related NPR stories.
- PBS. <http://www.pbs.org/newshour/bb/military/july-dec05/torture_12-02.html> Transcript of *NewsHour* show discussing torture.
- Torture: The Stanford Encyclopedia of Technology. <http://www.science.uva.nl/~seop/entries/torture/> Philosophical discussion of torture.

Further Reading:

Greenberg, Karen J. *The Torture Debate in America.* Cambridge University Press, 2005.

McCoy, Alfred. *A Question of Torture: CIA Interrogation, from the Cold War to the War on Terror.* Metropolitan Books, 2006.

Roth, Kenneth, Minky Worden, and Amy D. Bernstein, eds. *Torture.* New Press, 2005.

TWO-PARTY SYSTEM

Nations such as Australia, the United Kingdom, and the United States have two-party political systems. Other countries have de facto two-party systems: two parties dominate governance, and one or two smaller third parties ensure that one or the other major party maintains power (Germany is a good example). In contrast, nations with multiparty parliamentary systems, Israel, Japan, some Eastern European countries, and some of the Latin American democracies, regularly experience shifting alliances and coalitions among their political parties.

Which system is preferable? Strong voices can be heard on both sides: Advocates of the multiparty system extol its diversity and the fact that it forces coalition building; advocates of the two-party model argue that such governments are more stable and have a larger group of members experienced in governing.

PROS

Two-party systems have emerged either as the result or the reflection of the will of the electorate. Often the two parties represent key ideological divisions in society over the direction of policy, e.g., between left and right, small government and activist government, liberalism and authoritarianism. Most voters have little interest in the minutiae of policy, but they can understand the broad political choices presented to them by the two distinct parties and make their decisions at election time accordingly.

Governments in two-party systems are more able to drive their policies through the legislature because they often have a clear majority of representatives there. Consequently, they can implement important changes quickly and without compromise.

Because two-party systems tend to be less volatile, voters retain their representatives as incumbents longer. Consequently, the legislators are very experienced. This results in better and more consistent policy and more effective scrutiny of the executive branch.

Because parliamentary majorities in multiparty systems can shift suddenly, these systems are far less stable than two-party systems. Multiparty systems are also less fair to the electorate because policies formed after an election are often the result of backroom deals that ignore campaign promises and voter wishes.

Two-party systems better reflect mainstream, centrist views. To remain competitive, parties will tend to moderate their platforms.

CONS

While ideology and the will of the electorate may have been a factor at one stage in the development of a two-party democracy, these are factors that limit political progress today. The Cold War with its divisions of left and right is over and ideological labels are increasingly meaningless. Such historical precedents make the creation of third parties difficult. The dominant parties tend to shape electoral rules to exclude smaller parties, and the more dominant parties tend to be the most successful at fund-raising. Thus a two-party system limits the choice of the electorate.

Multiparty systems tend to produce coalition governments that have to work to balance interests and produce a consensus. Thus, the electorate is likely to accept important changes these governments make and not reverse them at the next election.

Incumbency can mean complacency. The longer people hold office, the more comfortable they become and the less likely they are to take risks and make controversial decisions. They can be highly influenced by lobbyists and lose touch with the people they are supposed to represent. The freer marketplace of ideas in a multiparty system forces politicians to adapt their message and become more responsive to minority voices.

The threat of a no-confidence vote, a collapsing coalition, or the departure of a coalition partner from a governing majority force leaders to make compromises, and compromises make for policies that serve the interests of the majority of the voters. Moreover, most countries have constitutional mechanisms to ensure a relatively smooth transition to a new government.

Moderation is not necessarily in the public's best interest. A multiparty system helps ensure that the views of a variety of different interests are considered in policy making.

Sample Motions:

This House believes rule by a majority party is superior to coalition government.

This House believes a two-party system is superior to a multiparty system.

This House would amend nations' constitutions to increase electoral competition.

Web Links:

- Intellectual Conservative. <http://www.intellectualconservative.com/2007/08/30/the-two-party-system-a-catastrophic-failure/> Article by a conservative writer on why the two-party system has failed.
- LegalJuris.com. <http://www.legaljuris.com/columns/1004/merola1004twopartysystemworks.shtml> Article on why two-party system works best.
- The Vermont Cynic. <http://media.www.vermontcynic.com/media/storage/paper308/news/2006/04/11/Opinion/The-Problem.Of.American.Politics.Is.The.Two.Party.System-1844541.shtml> Opinion piece criticizing US two-party system.

Further Reading:

Bibby, John F. *Two Parties—Or More? The American Party System.* Westview Press, 2002.

Disch, Lisa J. *The Tyranny of the Two-Party System.* Columbia University Press, 2002.

Schoen, Douglas. *Declaring Independence: The Beginning of the End of the Two-Party System.* Random House, 2008.

UNITED NATIONS: A FAILURE?

Over the past few years, support for the United Nations has eroded among the American public. A poll in September 2006 revealed that less than one-third of Americans have a favorable view of the international organization; just two years before that, the public was evenly divided. In 1999, 70% had a favorable opinion of the UN. Declining support has raised the question: Is the United Nations a failure? Debates on the issue tend to degenerate into example swapping. Both sides must avoid this, rather turning their attention to the aims of the United Nations and to establishing criteria for analyzing whether the institution has met or is working toward meeting such goals.

PROS

At its founding, the main objective of the United Nations was to prevent future wars and mass suffering. Because millions have since died in hundreds of conflicts around the world, we must condemn the UN as a failure.

Another key objective of the United Nations was advancing human rights. Yet many regimes violate these rights, often horrifically, as in the genocidal civil wars in the Balkans and Central Africa in the 1990s. Given that voting rights in the UN General Assembly are not linked to a regime's human rights record and that gross human rights abusers such as China sit on the UN Security Council, it is no surprise that the UN has failed in this part of its agenda.

CONS

Despite horrific suffering in many countries, the world has avoided another devastating global conflict in which tens of millions might die—for this the UN can take much credit. It has also resisted aggression in regional conflicts in Korea and the Middle East, thus helping to deter future invasions, and has acted as a peacemaker in many other conflicts, e.g., the Iran-Iraq war. Consider how much more violent the world might have been without the United Nations.

Human rights abuses usually take place within states, often in civil wars. Under its charter, the UN cannot interfere in the internal affairs of a member, so it is unfair to count this a failure. Nonetheless, the UN has placed human rights squarely on the international agenda, raising awareness of human rights around the world and shaming many regimes into improving their policies. Even China makes great efforts to defend its human rights record.

PROS

The UN suffers from a bloated bureaucracy in which responsibility and job title are not linked to ability, resulting in painfully slow decision making and operational failure in such crises as Rwanda and the former Yugoslavia. Some UN organizations, such as UNESCO, have been viewed as so corrupt that countries, including the United States and the United Kingdom, have withdrawn from them; the US Congress has long withheld part of America's dues in protest against corruption and money wasting.

The UN also suffers from institutional problems. A single veto from one of the Permanent 5 (P5) in the Security Council can stymie General Assembly resolutions that have widespread support. The United States and organizations such as NATO have undermined the authority of the UN and its credibility in addressing long-standing issues, for example, the conflict between Israel and the Palestinians, where the United States, among the P5, has strong interests.

Much of the international progress made since 1945 has not involved the UN at all. The Cold War, with its mutually assured destruction, kept the peace between the great powers, while institutions such as the International Monetary Fund, the World Bank, and the World Trade Organization have promoted greater prosperity even as they functioned independently of the UN.

CONS

Errors in strategic decision making are not the fault of the UN Secretariat but of its masters in the Security Council. Abuses have occurred in the past, but these are used as a stick to beat the UN with by those, principally in the United States, who oppose the UN for other reasons. In recent years considerable progress has been made toward improving efficiency and rewarding merit, although these efforts have been hampered by the failure of the US to pay its dues.

UN decision making has improved since the end of the Cold War because key votes in the Security Council are no longer likely to result in deadlock between Eastern and Western blocs. In any case, P5 countries try to avoid using their veto power if at all possible because of the negative image its use creates at home and abroad. Instead, the Security Council acts as a forum in which nations can explain their positions and hammer out compromises, even if action is not collectively authorized. Clearly the workings of the Security Council could be changed to diminish the importance of the P5 and to make taking action easier, but this does not in itself render the unreformed UN a failure.

While other organizations have been important in bringing greater peace and prosperity to the world, none have had the authority of the UN, which derives its authority from the participation of almost every nation in the world. The Security Council is the forum for discussion, deal making, and arbitration in an international crisis. The UN has also made huge contributions to global progress through its agencies, particularly those dealing with refugees, the World Health Organization, and UNICEF. As a result of UN efforts, smallpox has been eliminated, health care improved, and education advanced. We don't often notice these programs, but we should see the UN's responsibility for them as a key part of its success.

Sample Motions:

This House believes the United Nations has failed.
This House would put the UN out of its misery.
This House has no confidence in the UN.

Web Links:

- Heritage Foundation. <http://www.heritage.org/Research/InternationalOrganizations/BG-1700.cfm> Background document by conservative think tank, with recommendations for reform of the UN.
- St. Thomas University School of Law, Diplomatic Monitor. <http://diplomacymonitor.com/stu/dm.nsf/issued?openform&cat=UN_Role> Links to sites on the contemporary role of the UN.

- Washington Post. <http://www.washingtonpost.com/wp-dyn/articles/A36068-2004Dec4.html> Editorial on the failure of the UN to reform itself.

Further Reading:

Gold, Dore. *Tower of Babble: How the United Nations Has Fueled Global Chaos.* Crown Forum, 2004.

Kennedy, Paul. *The Parliament of Man: The Past, Present, and Future of the United Nations.* Random House, 2006.

Weiss, Thomas G., and Sam Daws. *The Oxford Handbook on the United Nations.* Oxford University Press, 2007.

VEGETARIANISM

Very few human societies have forsworn eating meat, fowl, and fish, although in some parts of the world grains constitute almost the whole of the diet, with meat, fowl, or fish rare additions. These diets often have been the result of poverty, not choice. In modern Western societies, however, voluntary vegetarianism is on the increase. Many believe it is immoral for human beings to eat other animals. Some take an even more absolute line, refusing to eat dairy products or eggs as well because of the conditions in which the animals that produce them are raised.

PROS

The main reason to be a vegetarian is to reduce animal suffering. Farm animals are sentient, living beings like humans, and, like us, they can feel pleasure and pain. Farming and killing these animals for food is wrong. The methods of farming and slaughter are often barbaric and cruel, even on "free range" farms. Also, in most countries, animal welfare laws do not cover animals farmed for food.

To suggest that farm factories are "natural" is absurd; they are unnatural and cruel. To eat meat is to perpetuate animal suffering on a huge scale, a larger, crueler, and more systematic scale than anything found in the wild. Humanity's "superiority" over other animals means humans have the reasoning power and moral instinct to stop exploiting other species. If aliens from another planet, much more intelligent and powerful than humans, farmed (and force-fed) human beings in factory farm conditions, we would think it was morally abhorrent. If this would be wrong, then is it not wrong for "superior" humans to farm "lower" species simply because of our ability to do so?

Human beings are omnivores and are rational agents with free will, thus they can choose whether to eat meat, vegetables, or both. It might be "natural" for humans to be violent toward one another but that does not mean that it is right. Some natural traits are immoral

CONS

Eating meat does not need to mean cruelty to animals. A growing number of organic and free range farms can provide meat without cruelty. We can extend animal welfare laws to protect farm animals, but that does not mean that it is wrong in principle to eat meat.

It is natural for human beings to farm, kill, and eat other species. The wild offers only a brutal struggle for existence. That humans have succeeded in that struggle by exploiting our natural advantages means that we have the right to use lower species. In fact, farming animals is much less brutal than the pain and hardship animals inflict on each other in the wild.

Human beings have evolved to eat meat. They have sharp canine teeth for tearing animal flesh and digestive systems adapted to eating meat and fish as well as vegetables. Modern squeamishness about eating animals is an affectation of a decadent society that flies in the face

PROS

and should be restrained. In any case, our closest animal cousins, the apes, eat an all-vegetable diet.

CONS

of our natural instincts and physiology. We were made to eat both meat and vegetables. Cutting out half of this diet will inevitably mean we lose this natural balance.

PROS

Becoming a vegetarian is an environmentally friendly thing to do. Modern farming is one of the main sources of pollution. Beef farming is one of the main causes of deforestation, and as long as people continue to buy fast food, financial incentives will be in place to continue cutting down trees to make room for cattle. Because of our desire to eat fish, our rivers and seas are being emptied and many species face extinction. Meat farmers use up far more energy resources than those growing vegetables and grains. Eating meat, fowl, and fish causes not only cruelty to animals, but also harm to the environment.

CONS

All of these problems would exist without meat farming and fishing. Deforestation has occurred for centuries as human civilizations expand, but planting sustainable forests can now counteract it. Meat farmers contribute little to pollution, and many worse sources of pollution exist. Vegetable and grain farmers also pollute through use of nitrates, pesticides, and fertilizers. Finally, the energy crisis is one of global proportions in which meat farmers play a minute role. Finding alternative sources of energy, not limiting meat farming, will solve this problem.

PROS

"Going veggie" offers significant health benefits. A vegetarian diet contains high quantities of fiber, vitamins, and minerals, and is low in fat. A vegan diet (which eliminates animal products) is even better because eggs and dairy products are high in cholesterol. Eating meat increases the risk of developing many forms of cancer. In 1996 the American Cancer Society recommended that red meat be excluded from the diet entirely. Eating meat also increases the risk of heart disease. A vegetarian diet reduces the risk of serious diseases and, because it is low in fat, also helps to prevent obesity. Plenty of vegetarian sources of protein, such as beans and bean curd, are available.

CONS

The key to good health is a balanced diet, not a meat- and fish-free diet. Meat and fish are good sources of protein, iron, and other vitamins and minerals. Most of the health benefits of a vegetarian diet derive from its being high in fiber and low in fat and cholesterol. We can achieve these benefits by avoiding fatty and fried foods, eating only lean grilled meat and fish, and including a large amount of fruit and vegetables in our diet. A meat- and fish-free diet is unbalanced and can result in protein and iron deficiencies. Also, in the West a vegetarian diet is a more expensive option, a luxury for the middle classes. Fresh fruit and vegetables are extremely expensive compared to processed meats, bacon, burgers, sausages, etc.

PROS

Going vegetarian or vegan reduces the risk of contracting food-borne diseases. The inclusion of animal brains in animal feed led to outbreaks of bovine spongiform encephalitis ("mad cow disease") and its human equivalent, Creutzfeldt-Jakob Disease. Meat and poultry transmit almost all of the potentially fatal forms of food poisoning.

CONS

Of course we should enforce the highest standards of hygiene and food safety. But this does not mean that we should stop eating meat, which, in itself, is a natural and healthy thing to do.

Sample Motions:

This House believes that if you love animals you shouldn't eat them.

This House would go veggie.

Web Links:

- BritishMeat.com. <http://www.britishmeat.com/49.htm> Despite its name, the site offers 49 reasons for becoming a vegetarian categorized by general area—health, economy, environment, ethics.
- Earthsave.org. <http://www.earthsave.org/index.htm> Provides information in opposition to factory farming and in support of a grain-based diet.
- People for the Ethical Treatment of Animals. <http://www.peta.org> Radical animal rights organization offers arguments in favor of vegetarianism and information on how to become a vegetarian.

Further Reading:

Marcus, Erik. *Vegan: The New Ethics of Eating.* Rev. ed. McBooks, 2001.

———. *Meat Market: Animals, Ethics, and Money.* Brio Press, 2005.

Sapontzis, Steve F. *Food for Thought: The Debate over Eating Meat.* Prometheus, 2004.

VOTER IDENTIFICATION LAWS

Voter identification laws are controversial precisely because they touch on one of the most fundamental political rights—voting. Advocates of these laws point to voter fraud as a real and serious threat to democracy and insist that voter identification laws are the most effective way of combating it. Its detractors largely believe that the laws are a Republican strategy to disenfranchise poor and minority voters who tend to vote Democratic. Several challenges to these voter identification laws have been mounted in recent years. Most recently in the Indiana case of Crawford v. Marion County Election Board, *the US Supreme Court held that voter identification requirements are permissible and do not violate the US Constitution.*

PROS

Voter identification laws are necessary to combat the serious danger of voter fraud. There is a long history of voter impersonation throughout the US. Voter fraud not only interferes with individual elections but also undermines voter confidence in representative government generally. Identification requirements are the most direct and effective way of combating election fraud. As such, states have a compelling interest in implementing voter identification laws.

Voter identification laws are not discriminatory because they apply uniformly to all state residents. The laws require everyone to obtain valid, photo identification (ID), and therefore cannot be said to target poor and minority communities. No evidence in states that have enacted such laws reveals any discriminatory intent toward these populations. Furthermore, most of the required IDs can be obtained free of charge. The rationale behind these laws is to increase fairness and confidence in American democracy.

Voting is an important right, but it can be qualified by the government for an important reason. Voting rights are not made totally meaningless by voter ID laws. In most states, voters who lack identification can still cast provisional ballots that can be counted later. The ID

CONS

Voter impersonation fraud is a smokescreen for a growing conservative strategy of disenfranchising poor and minority voters. The extent of voter fraud has been greatly exaggerated. If voter impersonation were such a grave problem, the government would prosecute violators. Although the Department of Justice has poured unprecedented resources into voter fraud prevention under the Bush administration, they have not prosecuted a single offender. This tends to show that the true purpose behind these laws is to resurrect Jim Crow–era barriers to voting for poor and minority communities, who are more likely to vote Democratic.

These laws disproportionately impact poor and minority communities, who are less likely to have the money and/or documents needed to obtain photo ID. Federal passports are not cheap. Although most states do not charge to issue ID, some states do. Furthermore, poor individuals, especially the homeless, are also less likely to have the documents (such as birth certificates, social security cards, etc.) necessary to obtain photo IDs. Since people of color are disproportionately poor, the law disproportionately prevents these populations from voting.

Voting is a fundamental right that should only be infringed by the government for a compelling reason. The interest in preventing voter fraud is not compelling enough to warrant disenfranchising voters. In many states, voter ID laws will completely prevent certain

PROS

requirement is a mere inconvenience, not a complete barrier to voting. And, again, the government's interest in preventing voter fraud greatly outweighs the minor inconvenience suffered by a small group of voters.

CONS

people from voting. It is estimated that roughly 12% of the US population has no photo ID. Although the laws allow voters to vote by provisional ballot, this measure is largely meaningless because voters are then required to travel to the county seat and submit an affidavit in order for their vote to be counted. As previously mentioned, the government's concerns about fraud are exaggerated and largely pretextual. Therefore, the fraud prevention rationale should not trump the right to vote.

Sample Motions:

This House supports overturning voter identification laws.

This House encourages more states to pass voter identification laws.

Web Links:

- American Civil Liberties Union (ACLU) Voting Rights Project. <http://www.aclu.org/votingrights/access/index.html> Site dedicated to ACLU's voting rights initiatives, including links to voting access news.
- The Supreme Court of the United States: Crawford v. Marion County Election Board. <http://www.scotusblog.com/wp/wp-content/uploads/2008/04/07-21.pdf> Case upholding Indiana's voter identification law.

Further Reading:

Fund, John. *Stealing Elections: How Voter Fraud Threatens Our Democracy*. Encounter Books, 2004.

Overton, Spencer. *Stealing Democracy: The New Politics of Voter Suppression*. W.W. Norton, 2006

WAR CRIMES TRIBUNALS

Always controversial and shrouded in the solemn aftermath of terrible crimes, war crimes tribunals are the international community's response to national wrongdoings. They raise serious questions about sovereignty and international law. Whether held after World War II, Rwanda, Bosnia, or Kosovo, they never fail to provoke outrage from one corner and vindictiveness from the other. Would such matters be better left alone? The trial of Slobodan Milosevic in The Hague in the opening years of this century was an example of how complicated issues of international justice and power come to the fore in such tribunals.

PROS

Wrongdoing and wrongdoers must be punished. When a crime has consumed an entire nation, only a foreign trial can supply disinterested due process.

CONS

Of course wrongdoing should be punished. But the trial should be held in the country where the crime was committed. Any outside intervention in matters of sovereign states is high-handed and imperialistic.

PROS	CONS
Countries can explicitly cede jurisdiction for such crimes to international tribunals. These bodies are trying to achieve justice and closure that will benefit the entire nation.	Closure is the last thing tribunals bring. These trials alienate large portions of the nation and turn people against the new government, which is seen as collaborating with foreign imperialists. Such trials increase tension.
The world community must send a clear message that it will act against appalling war crimes. This must be done on an international stage through international courts.	No one can dispute the enormity of such crimes. But these trials damage a nation by reopening old wounds. Spain, for example, did not embark on witch-hunts following the bloody and repressive regime of Francisco Franco. Instead, it turned the page on those years and moved on collectively with no recrimination. Between justice and security there is always a trade-off. Where possible, peace should be secured by reconciliation rather than recrimination.
The issue of sovereignty is increasingly less important in a globalizing world. The pooling of sovereignty occurs with increasing frequency, and any step toward an internationalization of legal systems, such as the use of international tribunals, is welcome.	Whatever the truth about globalization and sovereignty, war crimes tribunals do not standardize justice. They are nothing more than victors' arbitrary justice. This type of justice undermines international law.
We have to uphold the principle that if you commit serious crimes, you will be punished. If we do not take action against war criminals, we will encourage future crimes.	The threat of possible legal action has not stopped countless heinous crimes in the past, so why should it now? These people are not rational and have no respect for international law.

Sample Motions:

This House would have war crimes tribunals.

This House believes war crimes must be punished.

Web Links:

- American University: Research Office for War Crimes Tribunals for the Former Yugoslavia and Rwanda. <http://www.wcl.american.edu/pub/humright/wcrimes/research.html> Detailed site on recent and ongoing tribunals.
- BeyondIntractability.org. <http://www.beyondintractability.org/essay/int_war_crime_tribunals/> Article defining war tribunals and discussing the pros and cons of their use.
- Special International Criminal Tribunals. <http://www.globalpolicy.org/intljustice/tribindx.htm> Provides information on UN war crimes tribunals in Rwanda and Yugoslavia as well as efforts to establish tribunals in East Timor, Cambodia, and Sierra Leone.

Further Reading:

Bass, Gary Jonathan. *Stay the Hand of Vengeance: The Politics of War Crimes Tribunals.* Princeton University Press, 2000.

Fatic, Aleksandar. *Reconciliation Via the War Crimes Tribunal?* Ashgate Publishing, 2000.

Sands, Philippe, ed. *From Nuremberg to The Hague: The Future of International Criminal Justice.* Cambridge University Press, 2003.

WARRANTLESS WIRETAPPING

In December 2005, President George W. Bush acknowledged that he had signed a secret order permitting the National Security Agency (NSA) to wiretap communications between American citizens and terrorists overseas. Several months later, the press revealed that the NSA had amassed the domestic call records of millions of Americans as part of its antiterrorism campaign. Critics say that the NSA's eavesdropping violated the 1978 Foreign Intelligence Surveillance Act (FISA), which makes it a crime to conduct domestic surveillance without a warrant. Asserting an expansive concept of presidential power that many experts reject, the president contended that he had the right to approve the program. In 2008, President Bush signed the FISA Amendments Act, weakening the role of the court in government surveillance. Opponents of the measure are seeking to block its implementation.

PROS

Both the Constitution (Article II) and the 2001 law authorizing the use of "all necessary and appropriate force" against those responsible for the September 11 attacks give the president the legal authority for the no-warrant surveillance. Under the Constitution, the president is commander in chief, and as such he is responsible for defending the nation and should have the right to determine how best to do so.

CONS

Conducting surveillance without FISA authorization is a felony. The Constitution clearly states that the president "shall take Care that the Laws be faithfully executed" and gives Congress the sole right enact or modify laws. Claiming expansive constitutional powers in an effort to justify violating laws is unacceptable—the president cannot choose which laws he will obey. Furthermore, the law that the proposition cites authorized military force against Afghanistan. It was never meant to justify domestic surveillance.

PROS

Communications have changed since the passage of FISA, as has the nature of our enemy. In 1978 the Soviet Union was our foe, and the NSA could easily retrieve telephone satellite communications. Today our enemy is not a superpower but terrorist organizations that can move easily and change cell phones and e-mail addresses at will. To fight terror, US intelligence operatives need to act quickly, with a minimum of red tape, and must gather information in new ways. Also, most of the world's broadband communications pass through the US, making monitoring of potential enemies easy for NSA; however, distinguishing between "foreign" and "domestic" is difficult.

CONS

The United States has faced many threats in its history and has often reacted with policies it later regrets. Consider the mass internment of Japanese Americans during World War II. We have often been tempted to abridge our liberties in times of stress, but this is precisely when we must defend them most vigorously. The United States was founded on certain values—if we ignore or reject these values, we may win the war on terrorism but lose the freedoms that define us.

PROS

As proved by the attacks on September 11, terrorists can do tremendous damage. If we are to protect ourselves in the future, we may have to abridge the privacy of many individuals, however innocent they may ultimately prove to be. Simply put, you can never know who is a terrorist until after his or her privacy has been violated or an attack has occurred; in addition, why should the innocent be afraid if they have nothing to hide?

CONS

The ends do not justify the means. The right to privacy is crucial in a democracy and should not be abridged, particularly as no evidence has been offered that warrantless surveillance is effective in fighting terrorism. Finally, as our own history has shown, we have no guarantee that the government will not violate privacy for its own, less-than-just ends. Look at what happened in the McCarthy era or during Watergate. To date, the government has not articulated the specific criteria it uses to determine which conversations to monitor—itself a reason for worry.

Sample Motions:

This House would impeach the president for violating FISA.
This House believes that in a democracy, the right to privacy should be valued over the need for security.
This House believes that Americans should not give up freedom for security.

Web Links:

- Fox News. <http://www.foxnews.com/story/0,2933,179323,00.html> Summary of arguments on both sides of the issue.
- NPR. <http://www.npr.org/news/specials/nsawiretap/legality.html> Analysis of legal issues involved, with links to more resources.
- Washington Post. <http://www.washingtonpost.com/wp-dyn/content/linkset/2006/02/03/LI2006020301869.html> Summary of events surrounding the controversy, with links to more in-depth information.

Further Reading:

Darmer, M. Katherine, Robert M. Baird, and Stuart E. Rosenbaum, eds. *Civil Liberties vs. National Security in a Post 9/11 World.* Prometheus, 2004.

Keefe, Patrick Radden. *Chatter: Dispatches from the Secret World of Global Eavesdropping.* Random House, 2005.

Leone, Richard. *The War on Our Freedoms: Civil Liberties in an Age of Terrorism.* PublicAffairs, 2003.

WATER PRIVATIZATION

Water is the most common substance on Earth, but 97% of the world's water is in the oceans, and most of what is left is locked in ice caps and glaciers. Only 1% of the world's water is available for human consumption. This water must not only meet household needs, but also those of industry and agriculture.

Because it is vital—and scarce—water has become an issue in both developing and developed nations. Developing countries struggle to find the best way to supply clean water to their populations, while developed countries wrestle with question of how best to allocate water and maintain their water systems. During the 1980s, when countries such as the United States and the United Kingdom moved to limit government, many water systems were privatized and aid to developing countries tied to privatization. The trend continued into the 21st century. This has engendered a firestorm of controversy not only about the economic and political impact of privatization but also on the question of whether water is a right or a commodity.

PROS

Water is a resource subject to the principle of supply and demand, and so should be treated as an economic good. It may fall freely from the skies, but it must be collected, managed, processed, and supplied through an expensive system of reservoirs, channels, processing plants, and pipes. Dirty water and human waste also must be removed and treated in sanitation systems.

Society wastes water when it is not treated as a commodity. On the personal level, people do not conserve water unless they have to pay for it. At a national level, subsidized water for agriculture encourages wasteful practices and the growth of crops in inappropriate regions, often with a damaging impact on the environment. Pricing

CONS

Water, essential for all life, is a natural God-given resource that falls freely from the sky. Therefore, access to clean water is a human right, not something to be traded away or withheld on grounds of cost.

Demand for water increases with population growth, so it does not respond to market forces as do other resources. Rich consumers in the developed world also waste water through extravagant use of luxuries such as garden sprinklers, swimming pools, lush golf courses, etc. We must manage demand to ensure access for all, including the

water according to its true cost would promote more efficient and environmentally friendly practices, e.g., the use of drip-irrigation or dry farming in agriculture.

poor. Letting the market set prices will not achieve this. This is a job for governments, which are accountable to their people, not for private companies.

Addressing the problems of water supply requires huge investments, particularly in the developing world where many people have no access to clean fresh water. Even in the developed world, much water (up to 50% in Canada) is wasted through leaks in pipes and aging infrastructure. The public sector has failed to provide the money for addressing these problems, so private involvement is essential. To encourage private-sector involvement, we must permit water companies to make a profit through charges that reflect the costs of supply. Effective regulation can handle issues of quality, equity, and environmental standards.

The private sector will provide investment only in return for a profit. Because government does not require a profit, the cost of publicly funded development is always lower. Public-sector development also is preferable to privatization because governments can target investment to the most needy, rather than focusing on the most profitable opportunities. Most private companies insist on a monopoly of water sources, so they have no competitive pressures to improve quality and drive down prices.

Even in the developed world, the experience of water privatization is not encouraging: in England, privatization resulted in both higher prices and water rationing. The 2000–2001 power crisis in California has also shown how regulation of private utilities can fail. Australia, however, has successfully improved its water supply system while keeping it in public hands.

Treating water as a commodity is better for the poor. Governments in developing countries often provide water to middle-class areas and wealthy farmers at a fraction of its true cost, while the poor have no supply. Arguing that privatization is bad because it will force the poor to pay for water is misleading. The poor already pay for water, either directly to entrepreneurs who supply it in tubs and cans, or indirectly through the family's labor fetching water of questionable quality from miles away. The poor also pay through ill health caused by unsafe water.

Treating water as a commodity is bad for the poor. Some rich may take advantage of badly targeted subsidies, but these subsidies are essential to the poor. How would farmers in much of India cope without state-funded irrigation water? In South Africa, women chose to fetch dirty river water from a long distance rather than pay even a small amount for clean water. When Cochabamba, Bolivia, contracted with a private company to manage its water supply, the firm doubled water tariffs so that some families paid a third of their income in water bills. Mass protests finally forced the government to cancel the contract.

Charging for water can help the environment. Proper pricing of water would reflect all the costs of providing it, including the costs of environmental protection. Pricing water based on consumption, e.g., through domestic metering, also discourages wasteful use and so reduces the demands on natural water systems such as rivers and underground aquifers.

Private companies are unlikely to care for the environment. Their duties are to their shareholders, not to society at large and nature in general. They will seek to reduce costs and maximize profits, most likely at the expense of high environmental standards.

Sample Motions:

This House would privatize the water supply.
This House believes water should be treated as a commodity.
This House would put a price on water.
This House would make the price of water reflect the cost of supply.

Web Links:

- BBC News. <http://news.bbc.co.uk/1/hi/talking_point/2957550.stm> Q&A on water privatization.
- cbc.ca. <http://www.cbc.ca/news/features/water/> Report on global water privatization.
- Public Citizen. <http://www.citizen.org/cmep/Water/general/> Overview of water privatization and reasons to oppose it.

Further Reading:

Fishbone, Aaron, ed. *The Struggle for Water: Increasing Demands on a Vital Resource.* IDEBATE Press, 2007.

Peter H. Gleick, Gary Wolff, Elizabeth L. Chalecki, and Rachel Reyes, *The New Economy of Water: The Risks and Benefits of Globalization and Privatization of Fresh Water.* Pacific Institute, 2002.

Shiva, Vandana. *Water Wars: Privatization, Pollution, and Profit.* South End Press, 2002.

Ward, Diane Raines. *Water Wars.* Riverhead Trade, 2003.

WATER RESOURCES: A COMMODITY?

With increasing population and growing water usage, water shortages have become a source of potential and ongoing conflicts. One of the main issues is the competing claims of upstream and downstream nations. As downstream nations attempt to win more water rights, upstream nations try to keep control of the water resources in their territories. While current resources are insufficient in many regions, water will become even scarcer in the future, producing tension among nations sharing rivers.

PROS

Water occurs randomly, just like oil and gas, which are treated as commodities that can be bought and sold. If countries can take advantage of their geographic location to sell oil and gas, they are justified in using water resources to support their economies. Failure to view water as a precious, marketable commodity makes it far less valued and leads to unrestricted water use by environmentally unconscious societies.

Control and management of water—the maintenance of dams, reservoirs, and irrigation systems—costs millions of dollars and is a burden on upstream states' budgets. All of these expenses, including the opportunity cost of fertile lands allocated for reservoirs and dams, should be covered by downstream states, which are the primary consumers of water. For example, that an upstream state cannot use the water flowing through it to produce electricity to offset the costs of water management is unfair.

Water resources are distributed unequally. Uneven distribution and wasteful consumption warrant the introduction of the "pay-for-water" approach. Is it fair to prefer to use water to irrigate infertile semi-deserts downstream rather than using water more efficiently upstream?

CONS

Water is the most vital of Earth's randomly occurring resources; it is essential for survival. Consequently, water-rich countries have no moral right to profit from this resource. Every inhabitant of the planet has an equal right to water, and flowing water has no political boundaries.

It is immoral to charge for water beyond the cost of water systems' maintenance. Water is a commodity only up to a certain point. Once water exceeds a reservoir's capacity, it is not a commodity because it will flow free over the dam. Dams may also create dangerous conditions because downstream states may be flooded if a dam breaks.

Faced with scarcity and drought, states may resort to force to gain control of water resources. Therefore, making water a commodity is a potential cause of many conflicts and should be avoided.

Sample Motions:

This House agrees that water flows can be an article of trade.

This House should endorse international commerce in water resources.

This House does not support legislation for trading of water resources.

Web Links:

- The Transboundary Freshwater Dispute Database. <http://www.transboundarywaters.orst.edu> A comprehensive resource on water treaties.
- The Tyee. <http://thetyee.ca/News/2006/03/22/WaterRight/> Article discussing whether water is a commodity or a right.
- World Water Council. <http://www.worldwatercouncil.org> Site maintained by an international organization dedicated to improving world management of water; offers articles and resources on water issues.
- The World's Water. <http://www.worldwater.org> Up-to-date information on global freshwater resources.

Further Reading:

de Villiers, Marq. *Water: The Fate of Our Most Precious Resource.* Mariner, 2001.

Postel, Sandra, and Brian Richter. *Rivers for Life: Managing Water for People and Nature.* Island Press, 2003.

Ward, Diane Raines. *Water Wars.* Riverhead Trade, 2003.

WHALING, LIFTING THE BAN ON

Whaling became an important industry in the nineteenth century because of the increased demand for whale oil used in the lamps of the time. The industry declined in the late nineteenth century when petroleum began to replace whale oil. Nevertheless, whales were still hunted for meat and other products, and modern technology made hunters more efficient. The increasing scarcity of many whale species, together with growing recognition of the intelligence and social nature of whales, led to the creation of the International Whaling Commission (IWC), which instituted a ban on whale hunting effective in 1986. In years since, whale stocks appear to have recovered, although the extent of the recovery is a matter of debate. Some whaling continues for research purposes, mostly by Japan, which has been widely criticized for taking hundreds more whales than can be justified by the needs of scientific inquiry. In 2007 the IWC voted down Japan's bid to lift restrictions on commercial whaling. Pro-whaling countries such as Japan and Norway indicated that they would circumvent the ban by increasing the numbers of whales killed for scientific research programs.

PROS

Whales should be treated in the same way as other animals, as a resource to be used for food and other products. Whales should not be hunted to extinction, but if their numbers are healthy, then hunting them should be permitted. Scientists have conducted studies of intelligence on dolphins, not whales; these studies, however, cannot measure intelligence in any useful way. Although people in some Western nations view whales as special and in need of protection, this view is not widely shared by other countries. To impose it upon others is a form of cultural imperialism.

CONS

Killing whales for human use is morally wrong. Many people believe that no animal should suffer and die for the benefit of humans, but even if you do not hold such views, whales should be treated as a special case. Whales are exceptionally intelligent and social beings, able to communicate fluently with each other. The hunting and the killing of animals that appear to share many social and intellectual abilities with humans are immoral.

PROS	CONS
Whale populations are healthy, particularly those of minke whales, which now number over a million. A resumption of hunting under regulation will not adversely affect their survival. The IWC did not impose the ban on whaling for moral reasons but to prevent extinction. Numbers have now greatly increased. The ban has served its original purpose, and it is time to lift it.	We should adhere to a precautionary principle. Actual whale populations are not truly known, but they appear to be nowhere near as great as pro-whalers suggest. Until the international ban several species were close to extinction. This could easily happen again if the ban were lifted, especially because regulation is difficult. Even if hunting were restricted to the more numerous species of whales, other, less common species may be killed by mistake.
Whale hunting is an important aspect of some cultures. For some groups the hunting of a small number of whales is an important feature in the local subsistence economy, a way of reconnecting themselves with the traditions of their ancestors and affirming their group identity against the onslaught of globalization.	Traditional hunting methods are often cruel; they involve driving whales to beach themselves and then killing them slowly with long knives, or singling out vulnerable nursing mothers with calves. Because only small numbers are taken with relatively primitive equipment, the hunters do not develop enough skill or possess the technology to achieve the clean and quick kills necessary to prevent suffering. Also, what if the whales these groups wish to hunt are from the most endangered species? Should these groups be permitted to kill them because of their "cultural heritage"? In any case, many traditional practices (e.g., slavery, female genital mutilation) have been outlawed as abhorrent in modern society.
Economic factors argue for a resumption of whaling. In both Japan and Norway remote coastal communities depend on whaling for their livelihood. Both countries have an investment in ships, research, processing centers, etc., that would be wasted if the temporary whaling ban were extended indefinitely.	Whale watching now generates a billion dollars a year, more income worldwide than the whaling industry brought in prior to the hunting ban. This industry and the jobs it creates in remote coastal areas would be jeopardized if whale numbers fell or if these intelligent animals became much more wary around human activity.
Modern whaling is humane, especially compared to the factory farming of chickens, cows, and pigs. Most whales die instantly or very quickly, and Japanese researchers have developed new, more powerful harpoons that will make kills even more certain.	Whaling is inherently cruel. Before the whale is harpooned, it is usually exhausted by a long and stressful chase. Because whales are moving targets, a marksman can achieve a direct hit only with great difficulty. The explosive-tipped harpoon wounds many whales, who often survive for some time before finally being killed by rifle shots or by additional harpoons. Even when a direct hit is scored, the explosive often fails to detonate. Japanese whaling ships report that only 70% of whales are killed instantly.
Whales damage the fish stocks on which many people depend for their food and livelihood. Culling whales will reduce the decline in fish stocks.	The decline in fish stocks is caused by overfishing, not whale predation. Many whales eat only plankton. The oceans had plenty of fish before large-scale whaling began. Indeed some whales eat the larger fish that prey on commercially important species. A whale cull might have the perverse effect of further reducing valuable fish stocks.

PROS	CONS
A policy of limited hunting could prevent the potential collapse of the International Whaling Commission. The IWC ban was intended to allow numbers to recover; this temporary measure has served its purpose. If prohibition continues and the IWC becomes more concerned with moral positions than whaling management, Japan and Norway may leave the organization. Nothing in international law prevents them from resuming whaling outside the IWC. Thus, whaling will again be unregulated, with more whales dying and perhaps greater cruelty.	Any system that allows whaling will be open to cheating, given the demand for whale meat in Japan. DNA tests reveal that Japan's "scientific whaling" has resulted in scarce species being taken and consumed. Japan and Norway could leave the IWC but this would provoke an international outcry and possibly sanctions, so it is not in their best interests to do so.

Sample Motions:

This House would allow whaling to resume.
This House would harvest the bounty of the sea.
This House would save the whale.

Web Links:

- Greenpeace. <http://www.greenpeace.org/international/campaigns/oceans/whaling> Information on whaling from an environmentalist organization.
- International Fund for Animal Welfare. <http://www.stopwhaling.org> Web site dedicated to stopping whaling.
- Japan Whaling Association. <http://www.whaling.jp/english/index.html> Information from a pro-whaling group.
- Whale and Dolphin Conservation Society. <http://www.wdcs.org> Provides information on the status of whales, dolphins, and porpoises as well as efforts to protect them.

Further Reading:

Friedheim, Robert L., ed. *Toward a Sustainable Whaling Regime.* University of Washington Press, 2001.

Gillespie, Alexander. *Whaling Diplomacy: Defining Issues in International Environmental Law.* Edward Elgar, 2005.

Heazle, Michael. *Scientific Uncertainty and the Politics of Whaling.* University of Washington Press, 2006.

WIKIPEDIA, FORCE FOR GOOD?

Wikipedia is a free online encyclopedia, produced entirely by the voluntary efforts of hundreds of thousands of people from all over the world. It was founded by Jimmy Wales and Larry Sanger in 2001, after an earlier effort to build a traditional "expert" encyclopedia online became bogged down in the slow complexities of academic review and professional editing. Instead, Wikipedia adopted wiki software, which allows groups of people to cooperate dynamically in writing and editing material online. To many people's surprise, this open-access approach was a rapid success, attracting many high-quality submissions from a wide range of contributors. This was despite (or because of) online warfare between rival volunteers who sought to edit and reedit entries. As of October 2008, the English-language Wikipedia site has over 2.5 million articles; combined with entries from versions in other languages, the total is more than 9.25 million. Wikipedia is one of the most heavily visited sites on the Internet—particularly by school and college students, to the concern of some educators. From the start, Wikipedia has had its critics, and co-founder Larry Sanger left the project early because of disputes over the direction of the site. Past and present editors of Encyclopedia Britannica *have criticized Wikipedia for inaccuracy, arguing that its democratic ethos lacks academic rigor and provides no guarantee that any entry can be relied upon. Others have criticized the agenda of the site, and the way in which its rules for contributors (including the famous "Neutral Point of View" or NPOV) are applied in practice. Despite a number of well-publicized scandals, however, the site has continued to grow, both in size and importance.*

PROS

Wikipedia's goal is to make all human knowledge freely available to everyone with an Internet connection. It already has over 2.5 million articles in English alone. This is more than 25 times those of *Encyclopedia Britannica*, its nearest printed rival. Traditional reference works were incredibly expensive, which meant that knowledge was restricted to the wealthy or those with access to well-funded public libraries. Wikipedia liberates that knowledge.

Wikipedia seeks to achieve its democratic goal by democratic means. As an open-source project, it relies on the collaboration of tens of thousands of people who constantly add, check, and edit articles. This "socialization of expertise" ensures that errors and omissions are rapidly identified and corrected, and that the site is constantly updated. No traditional encyclopedia can match this scrutiny, which has also been used successfully to develop and improve open-source software such as Firefox and Linux.

Wikipedia harnesses the best qualities of humanity—trust and cooperation in pursuit of an unselfish goal. Skeptics essentially take a negative view of society, unable to understand why people would join together to produce something so valuable without any financial incentive. Wikipedia is not naively trusting—the majority of entries are written by a close online community of a few hundred people who value their reputations. Examples of abuse have led Wikipedia to tighten up its rules, so that cyber vandals can easily be detected and editing of controversial topics restricted to the most trusted editors. But overall Wikipedia is a tremendous human success story, which should be celebrated rather than criticized.

Wikipedia emerged very well from the only systematic comparison of its quality against its leading traditional rival, the *Encyclopedia Britannica*. A survey in the leading

CONS

Wikipedia may make articles available for nothing to those with access to the Internet (i.e., still only a minority of people in the world), but many of these articles are not worth reading. Entries are often very badly written and can be very unreliable or misleading. Even on the Internet there is no such thing as a free lunch—the high cost of a traditional encyclopedia pays for articles written, checked, and edited by experts and professionals. And Wikipedia does not simply provide a poor quality alternative. Worse, it will drive traditional, high-quality encyclopedias out of business by destroying their business model.

Knowledge created by consensus or some kind of Darwinian democracy is fatally flawed. A fact is not true simply because lots of people think so. Traditional encyclopedias are written and edited by academics and professional experts, whose reputation is put on the line by the articles they produce. Anyone can write a Wikipedia article, regardless of how much or how little knowledge they have of the subject. Worse, because contributors are effectively anonymous, it is impossible to assess the quality of an article on an unfamiliar topic by assessing the credentials of those who have produced it.

Wikipedia is not immune to the worst qualities of humanity—as is shown by a number of scandals affecting the site. Entries can be deliberately vandalized for comic effect (as happens every April Fool's Day), for commercial gain, or simply to mislead or insult. Some of these deliberate errors are picked up and corrected quickly, but others remain on the site for long periods. Notoriously, a respected journalist, John Siegenthaler, was extensively libeled in an almost solely fictitious article that was not detected for months. Recently, one very senior editor was exposed as a college dropout, rather than the distinguished professor of theology he had claimed to be. Such examples seem to confirm the doubts of Larry Sanger, the original project coordinator for Wikipedia. He has since left and written a number of warning articles about how open to abuse the online encyclopedia is.

The 2005 *Nature* comparison of Wikipedia and *Britannica* clearly found that the online encyclopedia was less reliable. However, the *Nature* study itself was badly

PROS	CONS
journal *Nature* compared 42 pairs of articles on a wide range of subjects. Experts in each topic found that Wikipedia's user-contributed articles had only 30% more errors and omissions than *Britannica*, despite the latter's much vaunted pride in its expert authors and editors. And as Wikipedia is a constant work in progress, these faults were very quickly corrected, whereas a traditional publication will only revise articles at intervals of years, if not decades.	skewed, and *Britannica* disputed nearly half the errors or omissions for which it was criticized. On this basis, Wikipedia is not just 30% less accurate than *Britannica*; it would be two and a half times less reliable. In addition, the *Nature* study did not take the quality of writing into account. All of *Britannica*'s entries are edited carefully to ensure they are readable, clear, and an appropriate length. Much of Wikipedia's material is cobbled together from different contributions and lacks clarity.
Nobody at Wikipedia has ever claimed that it is a definitive account of human knowledge or a replacement for in-depth research. But it is an excellent starting point for an inquiry, giving a quick guide to an unknown subject and pointing the inquirer to more specialist sources. It is used to good effect by students, teachers, journalists, and even judges, among many others—showing that it is a valued reference source. Experienced users can quickly assess the quality of an article by the quality of its writing and the thoroughness of its references. Nothing on the Internet should ever be accepted uncritically, but Wikipedia has earned its reputation and has never tried to oversell itself.	Wikipedia has become a standard source of reference because it is free and easy to access, not because it is good. It is frightening that some US judges are beginning to cite its articles in support of their judgments. Many of its users are students who lack the experience to determine the quality of an article. Overdependence on Wikipedia means that they will never develop proper research skills and thus come to believe that an approximately right answer is good enough. Wikipedia should be banned for student research papers and other serious uses.
Patchiness of coverage has been a recognized shortcoming of Wikipedia, but it is one that the online community of Wikipedians has been debating vigorously, and is being rapidly addressed. Critics often use out-of-date examples to berate the site, failing to recognize that Wikipedia's key strength is that it constantly changes and improves through the contributions of its users. Perhaps those who note that a particular topic is unsatisfactory should sit down and write something to improve it!	One of the major problems with Wikipedia is its very patchy coverage. Traditional reference sources provide consistent coverage over the whole field of knowledge, with priority given to the most important topics in terms of space and thoroughness of treatment. By contrast, Wikipedia has very detailed coverage of topics in which its main contributors are interested, but weak material on other, much more important issues. Thus, just as much space is devoted to the imaginary language of Klingon as to Romany or Welsh—real languages.
It is the nature of any encyclopedia to present facts, and to emphasize these over expressions of opinion. If this is a criticism of Wikipedia, then it is a criticism of any reference work, traditional or collaborative. In any case, the main Wikipedia entry for a controversial topic is not the only material available to the user—discussion pages reveal its editing history, conflicting viewpoints, and rival authorities. These are a rich source of opinion and they complement the main articles.	A notable shortcoming of Wikipedia is its obsession with recording facts and difficulty in presenting rival arguments or hypotheses. For many topics this is not a major problem, but in many more the nature of truth is hotly disputed and any entry that seeks to document the issue should present both (or more) strands of opinion. Yet attempts by contributors to express academic arguments, for example, over different historical interpretations, are often edited out as being insufficiently factual. What remains is then either unhelpfully bland or worryingly one-sided.
Wikipedia is not threatened by variants and rivals that also seek to promote freedom of knowledge. Jimmy Wales, Wikipedia's founder, has consistently said that he is not trying to drive traditional encyclopedias such as *Britannica* out of business, nor to become a monopoly	Wikipedia can also be criticized for its inbuilt bias: its intolerance of dissenting views. Religious conservatives object to the secular liberal approach its editors consistently take and have found that their attempts to add balance to entries are swiftly rejected. This even extends to the

PROS

provider of online information. The key principle is the freedom of information, presented as neutrally as possible. This led to the banning of Wikipedia in China, after Jimmy Wales refused to censor articles to make the site acceptable to the Chinese government.

CONS

censorship of facts that raise questions about the theory of evolution. Some conservatives are so worried about the widespread use of Wikipedia to promote a liberal agenda in education that they have set up Conservapedia as a rival source of information.

Sample Motions:

This House trusts Wikipedia.

This House believes that open-access sources such as Wikipedia are strongly beneficial.

This House believes that Wikipedia is a force for good.

Web Links:

- New Yorker: "Know It All: Can Wikipedia Conquer Expertise? <http://www.newyorker.com/archive/2006/07/31/060731fa_fact> Article on the history and controversy surrounding Wikipedia.
- Wikipedia Watch. <http://www.wikipedia-watch.org> Anti-Wikipedia site.

Further Reading:

Keen, Andrew. *The Cult of the Amateur: How Today's Internet Is Killing Our Culture.* Doubleday Business, 2007.

Lih, Andrew. *The Wikipedia Revolution: How a Bunch of Nobodies Created the World's Greatest Encyclopedia.* Hyperion, 2009.

Sunstein, Cass R. *Infotopia: How Many Minds Produce Knowledge.* Oxford University Press, 2006.

Tabscott, Don, and Anthony D. Williams. *Wikinomics: How Mass Collaboration Changes Everything.* Portfolio, 2006.

WOMEN IN COMBAT

While the roles of woman in the military have expanded, the United States still bars female personnel from ground combat. Feminists have long fought this policy, considering it to be discriminatory, but the Defense Department has refused to lift its ban on women in combat units or in support units that co-locate with combat units. The war in Iraq has raised the issue again. Internal army memos have recommended permitting women in support units in light of troop shortages that make sustaining all-male units difficult. Nevertheless, President Bush has said that he has no intention of sending women into ground combat.

PROS

This position upholds equality between the sexes. As long as an applicant is qualified for a position, gender should not matter. Critics often mention that women cannot meet the performance targets set for their positions. This is rank hypocrisy. The US army regularly calibrates performance targets for age and position. A 40-year-old senior noncommissioned officer faces a much easier set of targets than his 20-year-old subordinate, yet both are deployed in active combat. The

CONS

Women are equal to men in the armed forces, but they are not the same as men. While the vast proportion of jobs in the military is open to both men and women, some are just not physically suitable for women. Some women are able to meet the physical requirements for front-line combat, such as carrying a wounded soldier, throwing grenades, or digging a trench in hard terrain, but most are not. One expert estimate put the number of physically qualified female candidates at 200 a year.

PROS	CONS
20-year-old woman will outperform her NCO in physical tests. Recruiting and deploying women who are in better shape than many men we send into combat is easy. In any case, in modern high-technology battlefields, technical expertise and decision-making skills are more valuable than simple brute strength.	These could be integrated into combat units, but their small number does not make the additional logistical, regulatory, and disciplinary costs associated with integration worthwhile.
Allowing a mixed gender force keeps the military strong. The all-volunteer force is severely troubled by falling retention and recruitment rates. Widening the applicant pool for all jobs guarantees more willing recruits. Not only does it help military readiness, it forestalls the calamity of a military draft. Without the possibility of serving in combat, many patriotic women will not want to enlist because they know they will be regarded as second-class soldiers. Because combat duty is usually required for promotion to the most senior ranks, denying female personnel the possibility of such duty ensures that very few will ever reach the highest ranks and so further entrenches sexism.	Men, especially those likely to enlist, maintain traditional gender roles. On the one hand, they will probably resent the introduction of women into a heavily masculine military subculture. (As we have seen, as more women enter the armed services, abuse incidents rise. At the three US service academies, one in seven women reports being sexually assaulted, and fully half have been sexually harassed.) On the other hand, men are likely to act foolishly to protect women in their combat units. Both attitudes create tensions and affect morale, and so weaken the military in combat situations.
Some studies have shown that women can perform as well as, if not better, than men in combat. The Israelis make frequent use of women as snipers. The Rand Corporation studied increased deployment of women in all three branches of the US military throughout the 1990s. It wholeheartedly endorsed further integration, having found no ill effects from expanding the roles of women in the different services over that period.	Much has been made of integration's effect on morale and readiness. Having women in combat units weakens the will to fight. Combat is a team activity. Soldiers under fire must have confidence in their comrades' abilities, and women don't have the mental and physical toughness to perform combat duties. They cannot contribute equally to the team. Their presence undermines the team's effectiveness.
Of the more than 20 nations that permit women in positions where they might see combat, none has reversed that decision. Regardless of whether women are as well suited to combat as men, they are clearly good enough for many countries to rely on them.	The threat of abuse of women prisoners is also a serious one. Male prisoners also contend with the threat of torture and rape, but misogynistic societies will be more willing to abuse woman prisoners. The threat of female prisoners of war being abused may adversely affect the way in which their captured male comrades react to interrogation. And in a media age, the use of captured female soldiers in propaganda broadcasts may weaken the nation's determination and commitment to the war effort.
This debate is becoming purely academic. We are now fighting in what the military calls "Low Intensity Conflicts" (LICs) in which there is no front line, so the distinction between combat and noncombat positions and units is increasingly moot. Americans have shown broad support for women serving in the armed forces—a 2005 poll revealed that more than 60% favor allowing women to participate in combat.	The fact that the character of war is changing is irrelevant. We should not purposely put women in combat situations. Moreover, the public's support for women in combat is not clear. Another poll taken during the same period as the one the proposition has cited indicates that while American's favor having women serve in support jobs that often put them in or near combat, a majority oppose women serving as ground troops.

PROS	CONS
Women are vitally needed for Low-Intensity Conflicts. LICs require tasks to "win hearts and minds" such as intelligence gathering, medical assistance, policing, and mediation, as well as the ability to kill an opponent in close combat. Cultural differences and demographics enable woman to be vastly more effective in some circumstances than men. For example, conservative populations would be outraged if male soldiers searched women; they would be more accepting of female soldiers performing this task. Allowing women to serve also doubles the talent pool for delicate and sensitive jobs that require interpersonal skills not every soldier has. Having a wider personnel base allows militaries to have the best and most diplomatic soldiers working to end conflict quickly.	Women can perform the tasks the proposition describes without going into combat. As we have seen in Iraq, the army does not teach combat troops the skills needed to win hearts and minds. Obviously, we need more soldiers who can win hearts and minds, but these troops do not need combat skills. And the suggestion that conservative societies may be more willing to accept female soldiers in certain situations is absurd. Conservative Muslim societies do not believe that women should have roles beyond the home, so they are not going to be comfortable with female soldiers under any circumstances.

Sample Motions:

This House believes that women should be allowed to serve in ground combat units.
This House would allow women to serve on the front line.
This House calls for equality in the military.
This House believes female soldiers should not receive special treatment.

Web Links:

- LewRockwell.com. <http://www.lewrockwell.com/orig3/kirkwood3.html> Article opposing women in combat written by a former member of the Presidential Commission on the Assignment of Women in the Armed Forces.
- *Newsweek*. <http://www.newsweek.com/id/61568> Interview with author Kingsley Browne who believes that women are not suited for combat.
- NPR. <http://www.npr.org/templates/story/story.php?storyId=14964676> Five-part radio series on the expanding role of women in the military.

Further Reading:

Browne, Kingsley. *Co-ed Combat: The New Evidence That Women Shouldn't Fight the Nation's Wars*. Sentinel, 2007.

Fenner, Lorry, and Marie deYoung. *Women in Combat: Civic Duty or Military Liability?* Georgetown University Press, 2006.

Gutmann, Stephanie. *The Kinder, Gentler Military: How Political Correctness Affects Our Ability to Win Wars*. Encounter Books, 2001.

ZERO TOLERANCE POLICING

Zero tolerance policing aims at stopping serious crime by clamping down on all types of disorder, including minor misdemeanors such as spray painting graffiti. It mandates set responses by the police to particular crimes, although the courts still maintain discretion in sentencing criminals. Adherents of this policy believe in the "broken windows" theory, which postulates that quality-of-life crimes, like littering or graffiti writing, prompt "respectable" citizens to leave communities, which then fall into decline. They also emphasize that most serious criminals begin their careers with minor crimes. By punishing minor crimes, zero tolerance policing prevents future crimes and, in the process, stops neighborhood decline.

PROS

Zero tolerance policing provides a powerful deterrent to criminals for three reasons. First, it is accompanied by a greater police presence. Research shows a direct link between the perceived chance of detection and crime rates. Second, strict and certain punishment deters criminals. Third, it provides the "short, sharp shock" that stops petty criminals from escalating their criminal behavior. It gives a clear message that crime is not tolerated.

Zero tolerance policing is extremely effective against small-scale drug pushers whose presence in a neighborhood creates an atmosphere in which crime flourishes. Drug use is a major cause of crime because addicts usually steal to support their habit.

Zero tolerance also allows for rehabilitation. A prison sentence, particularly for juveniles, takes them away from the environment that encouraged criminality. Rehabilitation is a central tenet of most penal codes. The large number of police on the streets also increases the supervision of released prisoners, preventing repeat offenses.

Zero tolerance improves the standard of policing. It reduces corruption and racist treatment because individual officers are not given the scope to decide their actions on a case-by-case basis. Their response is set. In addition, zero tolerance policing takes officers out of their cars and puts them into the community where they have contact with individuals. Chases and shootouts actually are less common under zero tolerance.

Zero tolerance is vital for rebuilding inner cities. Zero tolerance reduces the amount of dead ground used for drug dealing and so returns parks and open spaces to the community. By offering protection against petty crime, it encourages small businesses (vital for neighborhood rehabilitation) to return to an area.

CONS

Minor offenders, gang members, and the poor are very unlikely to be aware of the punishments for their crimes, so the threat of punishment has little effect on them. Many crimes are a result of poverty and drugs and can be reduced only by structural changes to the society, not by threatening punishment. The idea of a "short, sharp shock" is unconvincing. Labeling people criminals at an early age causes them to perceive themselves as such. This leads petty criminals to commit more serious offenses.

Arresting small-scale pushers and users targets the victims to stop the crime. As well as being unfair, it is ineffective. As long as there is a demand for drugs, there will be drug dealing. Demand can be stopped only by rehabilitation.

Prison sentences contribute to repeat offenses. Prisons should have a rehabilitative role, but they don't. Juveniles with criminal records have difficulty finding jobs, and so are likely to resort to crime. In prison they meet established criminals who both encourage the lifestyle and teach the skills needed to be a successful criminal. Prison often fosters resentment of the police. The harassment that juveniles associate with zero tolerance also creates an extremely antagonistic relationship with the police.

Zero tolerance gives the police almost limitless power in poor communities. They are able to stop and search and harass individuals constantly. Usually ethnic minorities are targeted. New York City saw a tremendous growth in complaints about police racism and harassment after zero tolerance was instituted.

Rebuilding inner city neighborhoods is one of the most powerful ways of targeting crime, and it occurs independent of zero tolerance. For every city where urban renewal and zero tolerance have together been associated with a falling crime rate (New York City), there is an area where renewal has worked on its own (Hong Kong). Most important for urban renewal is individuals taking pride in their area. This is far more likely to happen when people don't feel persecuted by the police. No police presence is sufficient to defend a business that has not cultivated good relations with the community.

PROS	CONS
We can afford zero tolerance. Protecting businesses and developing a reputation for low crime attracts both people and investment. Deterrence reduces crime and thus the cost of policing; although prisons are expensive, the reduction in recidivism should empty them in time. The most important question is whether we believe spending our tax dollars to guarantee our safety is a good use of that revenue. Most voters say yes.	The enormous expense of zero tolerance in money, manpower, and prisons limits policing. It leaves little money for addressing serious crime. So, although total crime rates may drop, serious crimes may still be a problem.

Sample Motions:

This House believes in zero tolerance policing.
This House would clamp down.
This House believes in strict punishment.

Web Links:

- BBC News. <http://news.bbc.co.uk/2/hi/programmes/politics_show/7385778.stm> Article on London mayor's decision to ban drinking on city transport may be the beginning of zero tolerance policing in London.
- Frontline. <http://www.frontlineonnet.com/fl1901/19011080.htm> Column in India's leading newspaper about whether zero tolerance policing would be effective in India.
- UK Independence Party. <http://www.ukip.org/content/features/250-the-case-for-zero-tolerance> A case for zero tolerance policing.

Further Reading:

Ayers, Rick, et al., eds. *Zero Tolerance, Resisting the Drive for Punishment.* New Press, 2001.

Punch, Maurice. *Zero Tolerance Policing.* Policy Press, 2007.

Topical Index